HISTORIC PHOTOS OF
OMAHA

TEXT AND CAPTIONS BY JEFFREY SPENCER

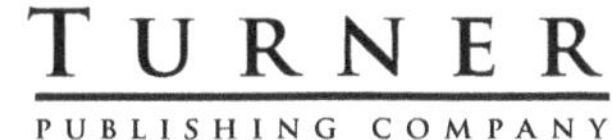

In this view west-northwest from 15th and Farnam streets in 1872, the new Omaha High School sits on the hilltop at upper right. It was completed that year at a total cost of $225,000. The old Douglas County Court House, built in 1857, is visible in the center foreground, and just above it is Redick's Opera House on the northwest corner of 16th and Farnam streets, built by real-estate investor John I. Redick in 1870.

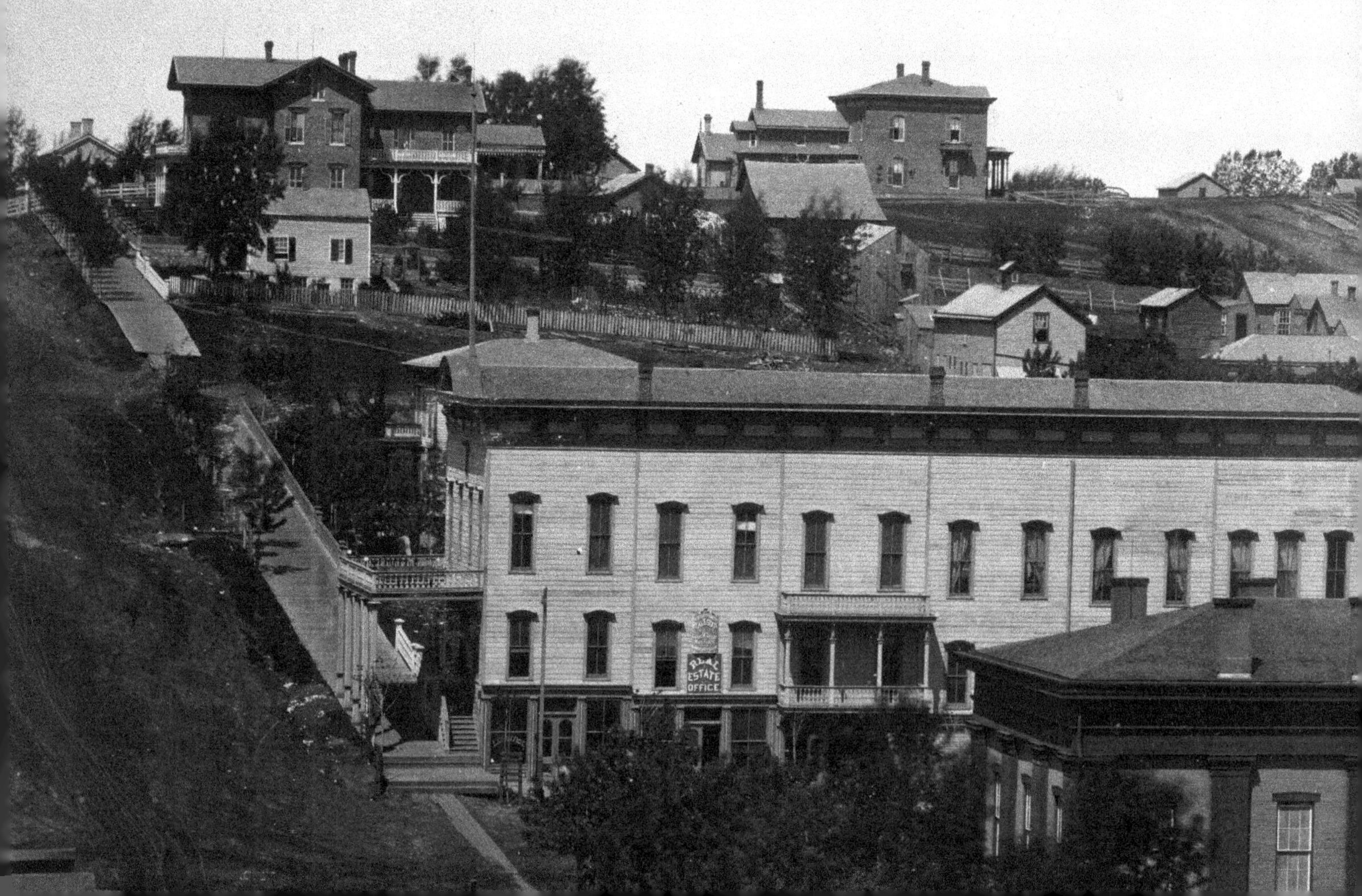

HISTORIC PHOTOS OF
OMAHA

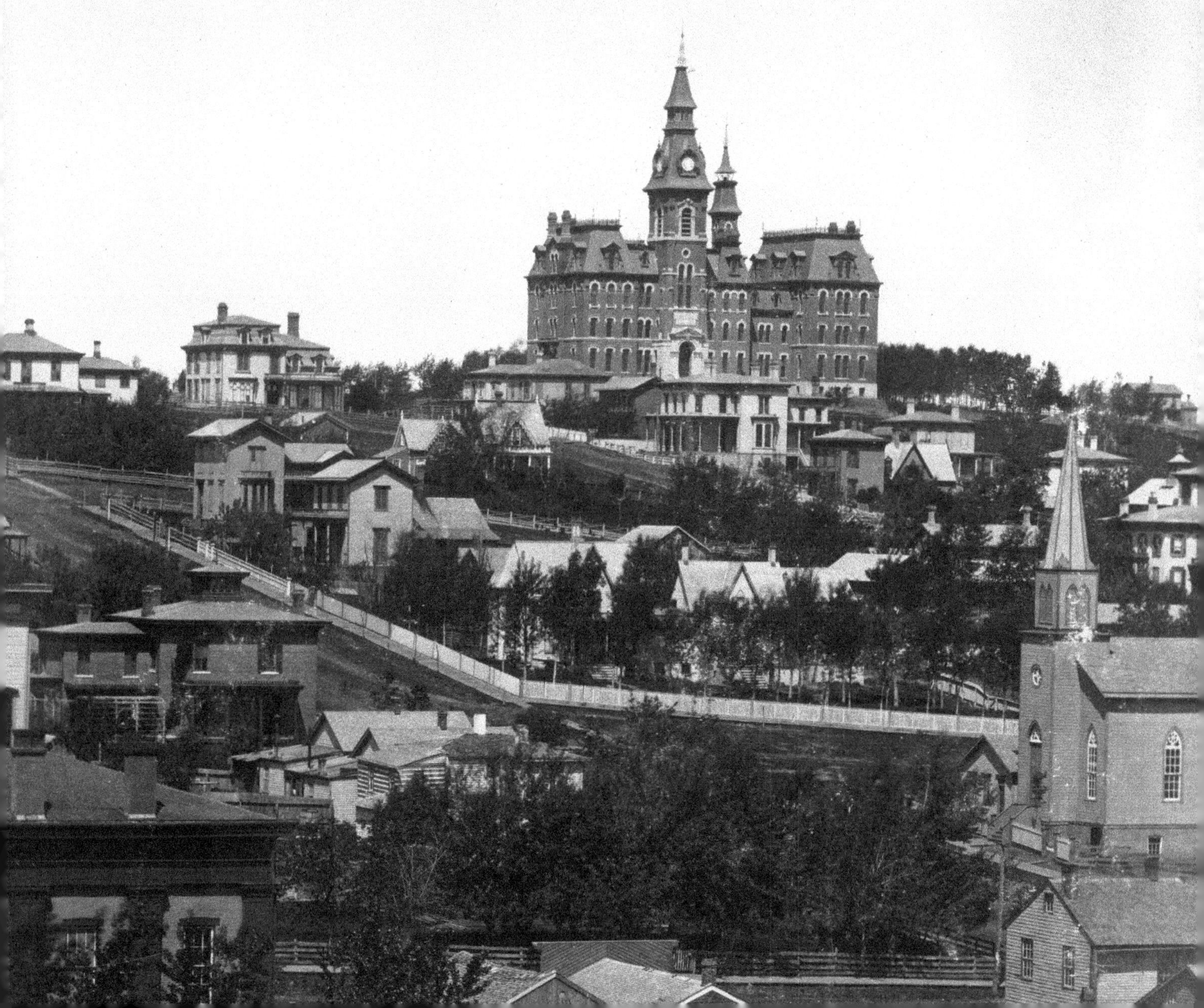

Turner Publishing Company
www.turnerpublishing.com

Historic Photos of Omaha

Library of Congress Control Number: 2007929601

ISBN-13: 978-1-59652-394-4

Printed in the United States of America

ISBN 978-1-68336-975-2 (hc)

Contents

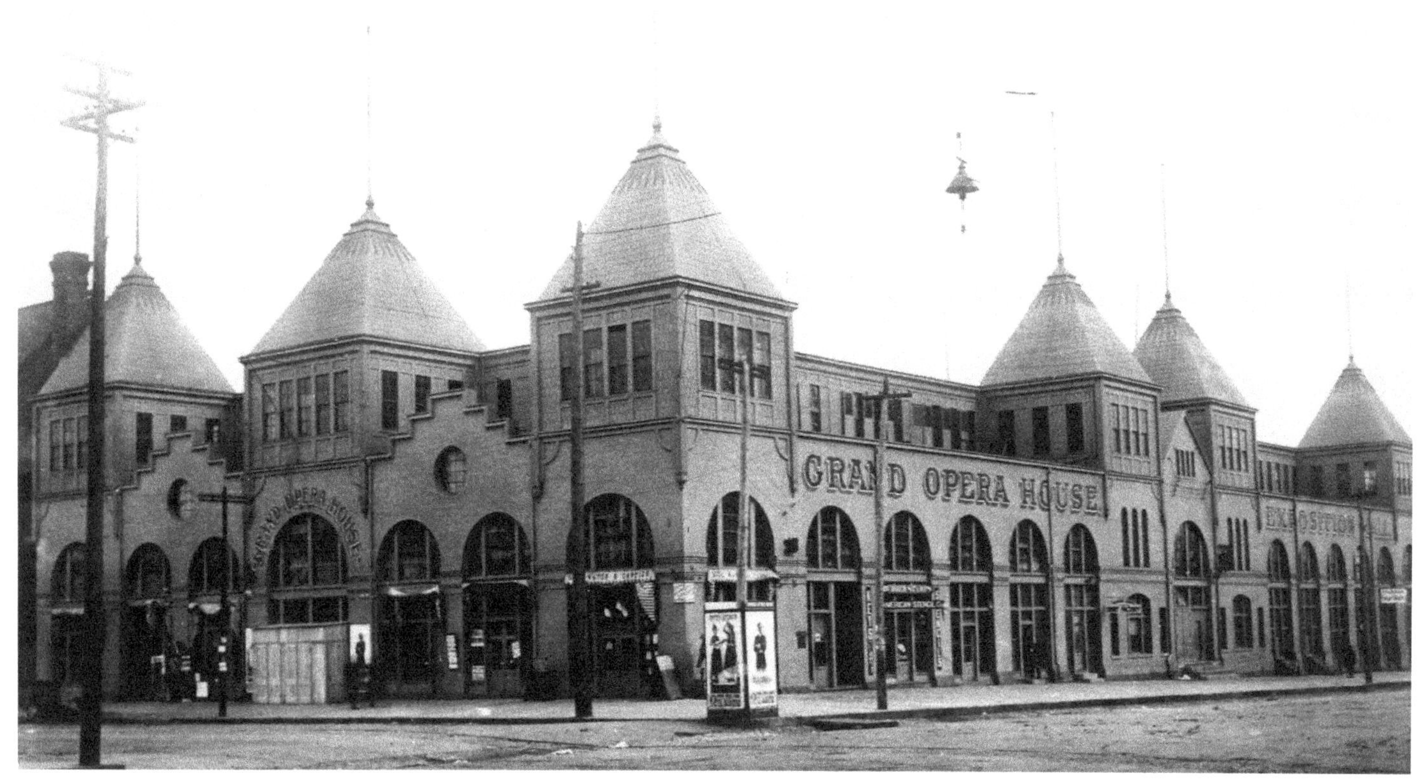

The Exposition Building and Grand Opera House, an enormous brick structure built between 14th and 15th streets on Capitol Avenue in 1886-87. Costing in excess of $50,000 when completed, it could hold more than 5,000 persons. Many large productions were held here, including the traveling company of the New York Metropolitan Opera. The structure was destroyed by fire on December 4, 1894.

ACKNOWLEDGMENTS

This volume, *Historic Photos of Omaha,* is the result of the cooperation and efforts of a number of organizations and individuals.

We would like to thank in particular the
Durham Western Heritage Museum, the Omaha Public Library,
and Joanne Ferguson Cavanaugh, librarian, Omaha Public Library

—Jeffrey Spencer, Author

This project represents countless hours of review and research. The researchers and writer have reviewed thousands of photographs. We greatly appreciate the generous assistance of the archives listed here, without whom this project could not have been completed.

The goal in publishing the work is to provide broader access to a set of extraordinary photographs. The aim is to inspire, provide perspective, and evoke insight that might assist officials and citizens, who together are responsible for determining Omaha's future. In addition, the book seeks to preserve the past with respect and reverence.

With the exception of touching up imperfections caused by the vicissitudes of time and cropping where necessary, no other changes have been made. The focus and clarity of many images is limited to the technology of the day and the skill of the photographer who captured them.

We encourage readers to reflect as they explore Omaha, stroll along its streets, or wander its neighborhoods. It is the publisher's hope that in making use of this work, longtime residents will learn something new and that new residents will gain a perspective on where Omaha has been, so that each can contribute to its future.

—Todd Bottorff, Publisher

Preface

The history of the settlement and subsequent development of Omaha is an extension of the history of the American West, from the explorations of Lewis and Clark to the Manifest Destiny movement of the mid-nineteenth century to the growth of railroads as the frontier pushed ever westward.

By July of 1804, the Corps of Discovery led by Lewis and Clark had reached the area where present-day Omaha is located. By 1820, the United States government had established its first permanent military post in the region, Fort Atkinson. Soon, settlers began moving into the area.

From 1845 until 1848, during the Mormon migration, the Winter Quarters site was established approximately six miles north of the later town site of Omaha. At one time, as many as 15,000 "temporary" residents lived there, resting along their journey to the basin of the Great Salt Lake. Many elected to stay here.

On December 14, 1853, Senator Augustus C. Dodge of Iowa introduced a bill in the United States Senate to organize the Territory of Nebraska. After much discussion and delay, this bill was finally ratified and signed into law by President Franklin Pierce on May 30, 1854. The next month, a treaty was ratified between the United States and the Otoe, Missouri and Omaha Indians, which gave land title in the area to the government and allowed for settlement to commence. On July 4, 1854, the first official gathering took place on what was to be the town site of Omaha, and many people consider this date to be the founding of the city. Immediately, large numbers of people began crossing the Missouri River from the Iowa side, and took up claims in what was then known as Omaha City.

By 1857, the new town boasted 1,700 residents, and the Nebraska Territorial Legislature granted a petition for the incorporation of Omaha as a city. That same year, a great financial panic took hold in the East, which halted the growth of the new town. Almost two-thirds of the residents moved away, and most banks and businesses went bankrupt. The discovery of gold in Colorado in 1859 breathed new life into the community as Omaha became an important supply station for those going west. In 1863, President Abraham Lincoln established the route of the transcontinental railroad through Omaha. From that point forward, the destiny of the community was assured.

Due to its central geographic location, and sitting beside the major inland waterway of the Missouri River, Omaha was poised to become an important trade and transportation center. This became more evident with the completion of the Union Pacific railroad in 1868. The decades of the 1870s and 1880s saw tremendous growth in the area. The temporary, pioneer atmosphere gave way to a community of substance and prosperity. Fine homes, schools and public buildings were constructed.

In 1893, the country was thrown into another serious financial depression. The Midwest was especially affected. After several years of bad weather, crop failures, and a general decline in market demand, the situation had become critical. Business leaders in the community began trying to devise a plan to revitalize the local economy. They decided to host a World's Fair in Omaha, to be held during the summer and fall of 1898. This became the Trans-Mississippi and International Exposition and Indian Congress. For the first time, international attention was focused on Omaha, and the community rose to the occasion. This was by far the most important and significant event which has taken place in Omaha.

By 1900, Omaha was moving forward into the new century with a population well in excess of 100,000. After the decline of the railroad, a new economic force began to emerge with the establishment of the adjacent community of South Omaha (a separate city) and the meatpacking and processing business. The Union Stockyards Company, established in 1883, eventually controlled 22 large packing companies and employed more than 30,000 workers. To fill those jobs, Omaha became a key destination for immigrants coming to America. Although Germans and Irish were the predominant groups, representatives from almost every country in Europe could be found living and working here.

The Omaha of today is moving forward in many significant ways. Commercial development is very active, with many large corporations establishing offices here. Two significant events occurred in 2004: The Lewis and Clark Bicentennial Commemoration and the Omaha 150th Birthday Sesquicentennial Celebration. Now, we are moving ahead into the twenty-first century.

Omaha is fortunate to possess a very extensive visual archive of its history and development. From those priceless resources, we have gathered the historic views presented in this collection. These photographic images open a window through which we can glimpse a view of Omaha as it grew and became the city it is today. We trust that you will enjoy looking at this collection as much as we have enjoyed putting it together and bringing it to you.

—Jeffrey Spencer

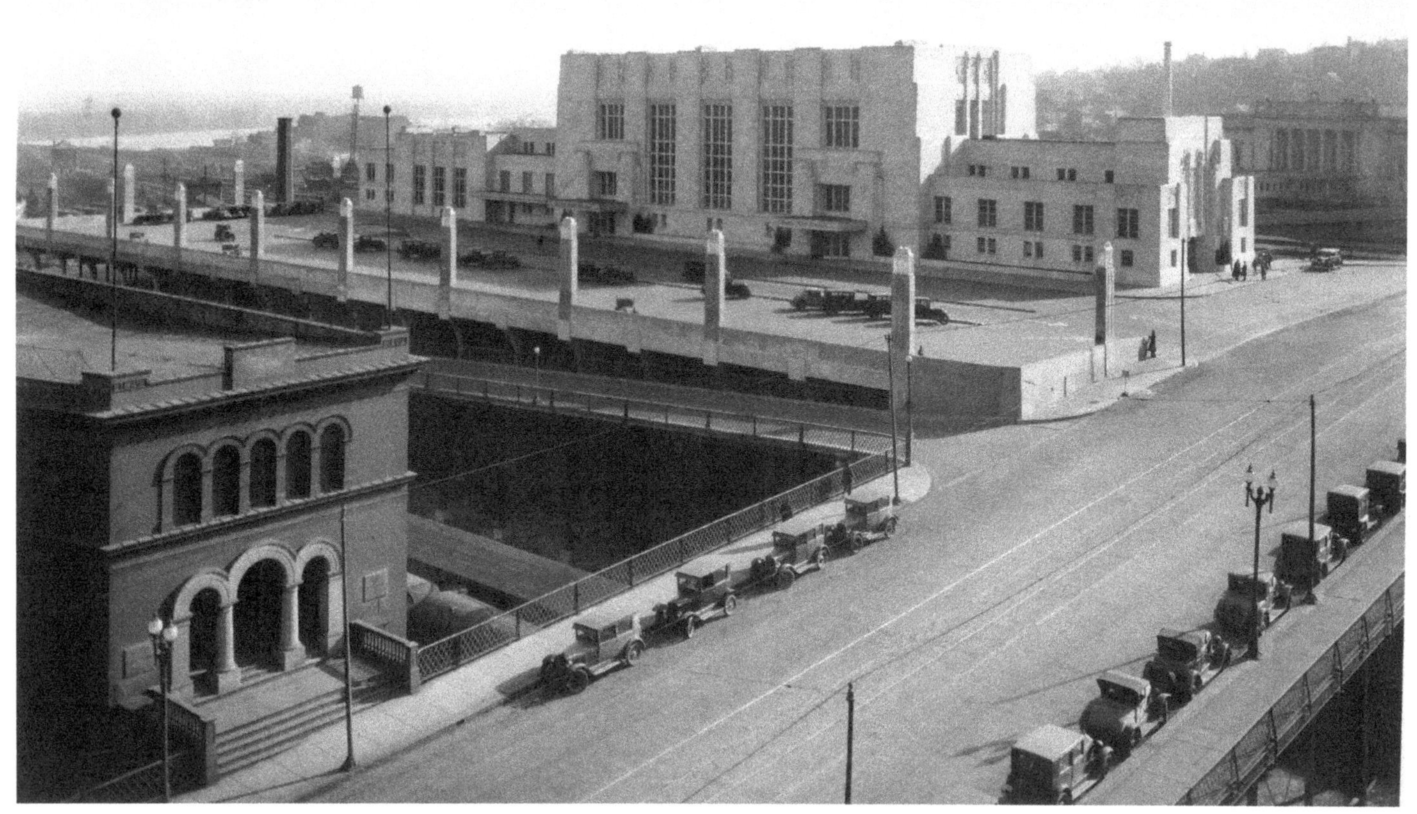

Plans were approved for the construction of a new Union Station at 10th and Mason street in 1929. Noted Los Angeles architect Gilbert Stanley Underwood received the commission. When completed early in 1931 at a cost of $3.5 million, it was considered one of the finest examples of art deco architecture in the country. This is the new depot as it appeared in January 1931.

Frontier on the Missouri

(1860–1890)

"Nebraska; may her gentle zephyrs and rolling prairies invite pioneers from the muddy Missouri River to happy homes, and may her lands ever be dedicated to free soil, free labor and free men." John Gillespie, who would serve as territorial auditor 1865-67 and state auditor 1867-73, offered this toast at the first gathering of settlers on the town site of Omaha, July 4, 1854. This event marked the true beginning of the city.

The site had been surveyed and platted the previous month, and lots were to be offered by the town company for $25 each. The company had also agreed to deed lots to any person who was willing to construct a building at once. Settlement moved quickly after the ratification of the treaty with the Omaha Indians, and within a short time most of the land between the Missouri and Elkhorn rivers had been claimed.

Although there is speculation as to who actually proposed the name of the new community, there is general agreement as to its meaning. The name "Omaha" was derived from the Indian tribe that occupied the town site prior to settlement. The actual meaning of the name was usually defined as "above all others on a stream". The "stream" was, of course, the Missouri River.

In 1857, the Nebraska Territorial Legislature designated "Omaha City" as the new territorial capital. Funds were raised through subscription for the construction of an imposing capitol building on a high point just west of the small settlement. Today, that location is occupied by Omaha Central High School, at 20th and Dodge streets. Omaha remained the seat of government until Nebraska became a state in 1867, when Lincoln was established as the capital.

The first permanent photographer to set up a studio in Omaha was Edric L. Eaton, who arrived in 1857. He worked until 1860, when he left to serve in the Civil War. He returned to the city in 1866. The earliest identified photographic view of the city was made in 1861. In 1868, William Henry Jackson opened a studio in Omaha, in partnership with his brother. This studio operated until 1872, when Jackson left to work in Colorado with the Hayden Expedition, exploring Yellowstone. From those early beginnings, Omaha has been well documented by a significant body of photographic work.

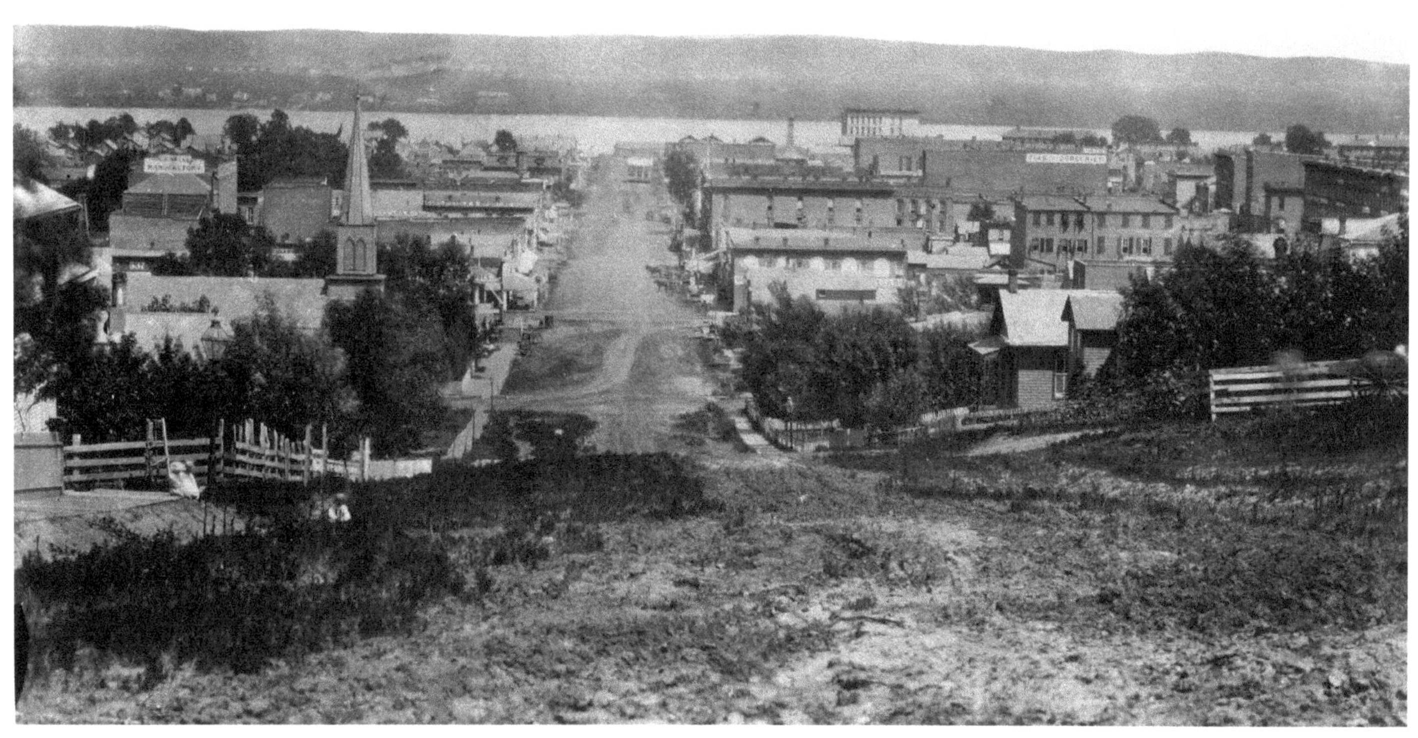

Douglas Street to the east about 1869, from approximately 18th Street. Many of the first wooden pioneer structures have already been replaced by more substantial brick buildings. On the left, is the German Catholic Church at the northwest corner of 16th and Douglas streets. This church was dedicated on Christmas Day 1868. Across the river in the distance is the growing city of Council Bluffs, Iowa.

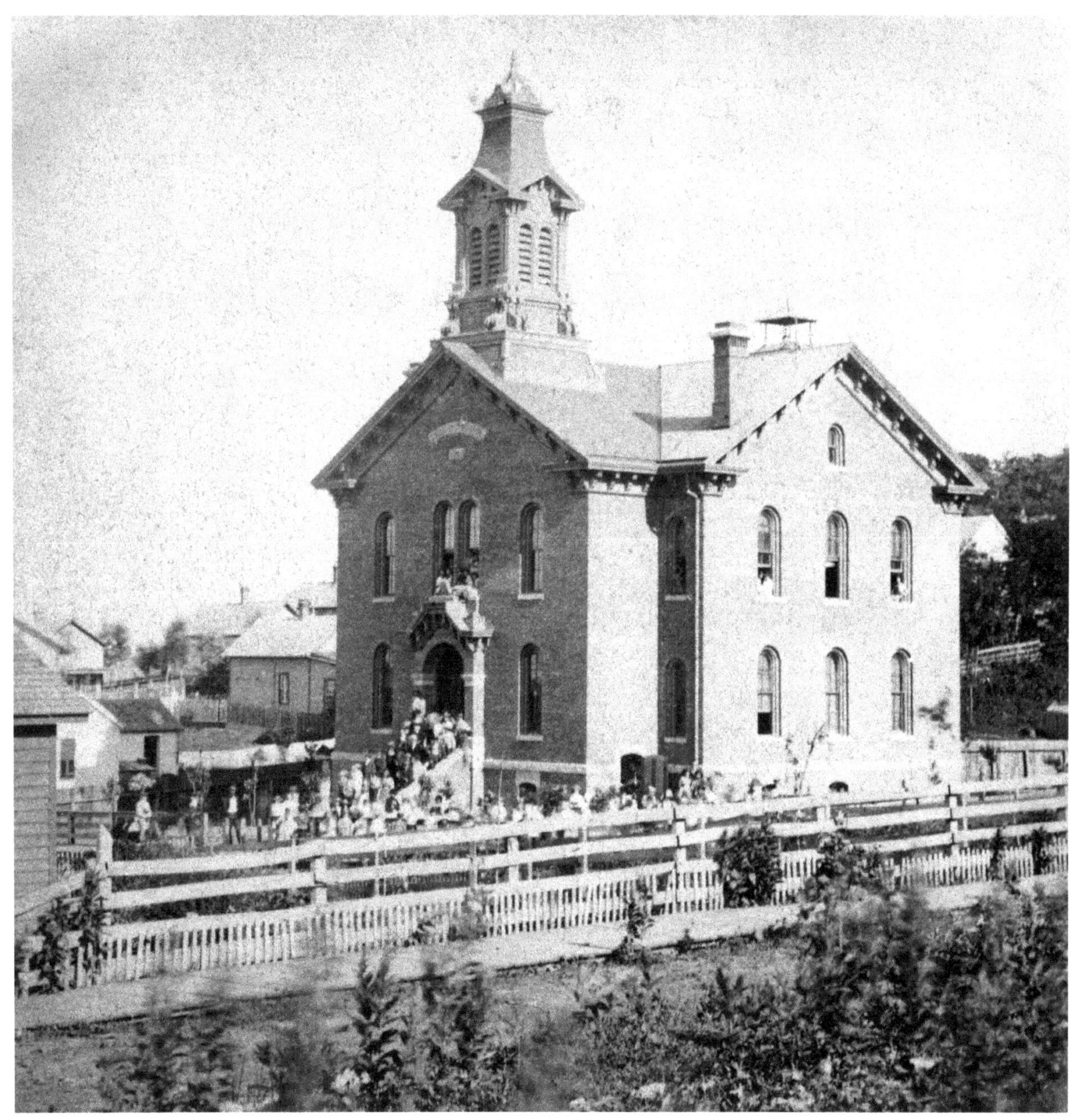

The Pacific Street School was built in 1868 in the vicinity of 11th and Pacific streets at a total cost of $25,000. This photographic view by William Henry Jackson was probably made about 1869. This school was considered the finest elementary school building in the city at that time. The structure was torn down in the mid-1920s.

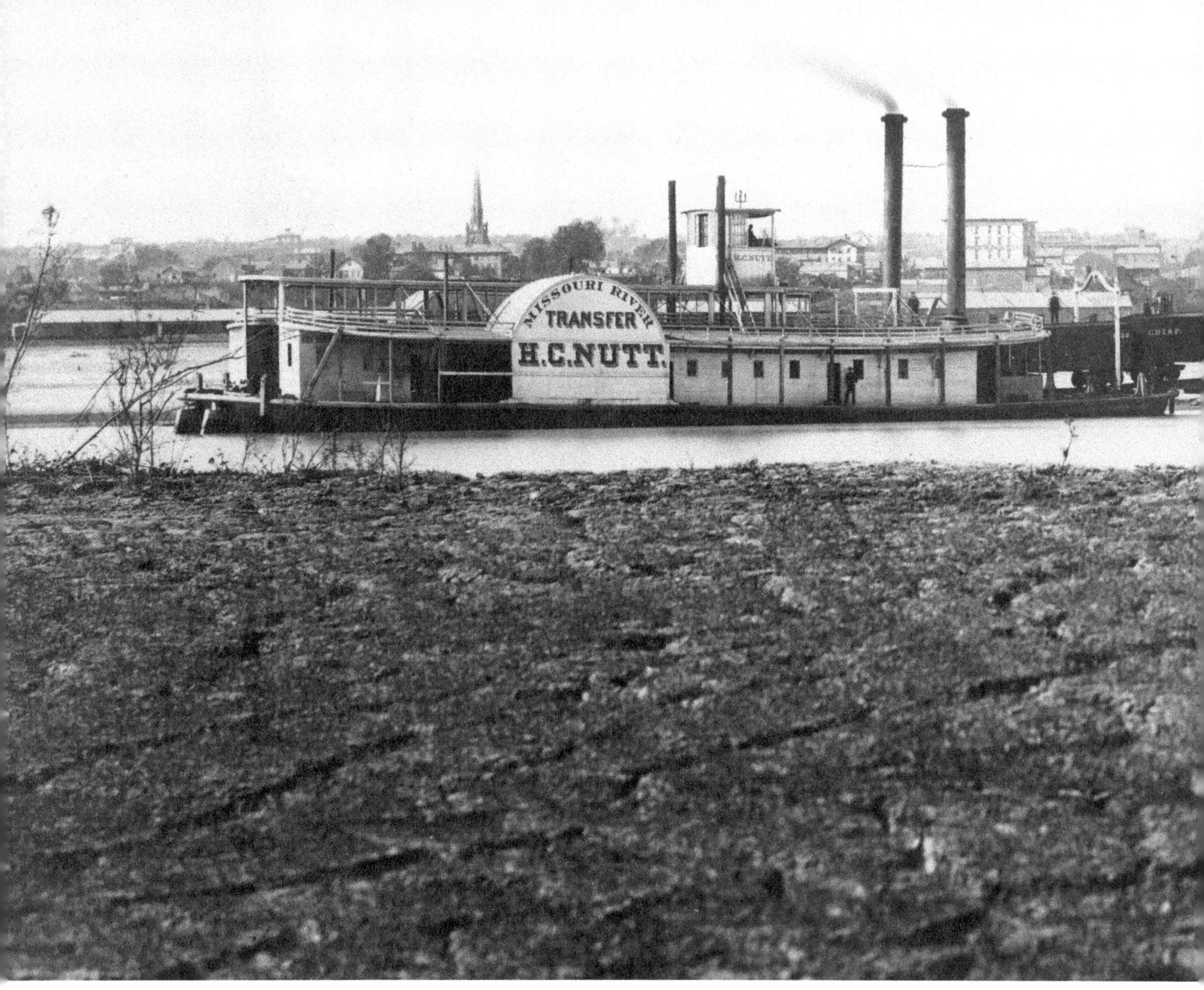

The Missouri River Transfer Company's side-wheel steamboat *H. C. Nutt* in 1866. Prior to the completion of the first railroad bridge in 1872, this boat was moored in the Missouri River and used to ferry railroad cars between Council Bluffs, Iowa, and Omaha. In the winter when the river was frozen, temporary tracks were laid across the ice, so that the trains might cross.

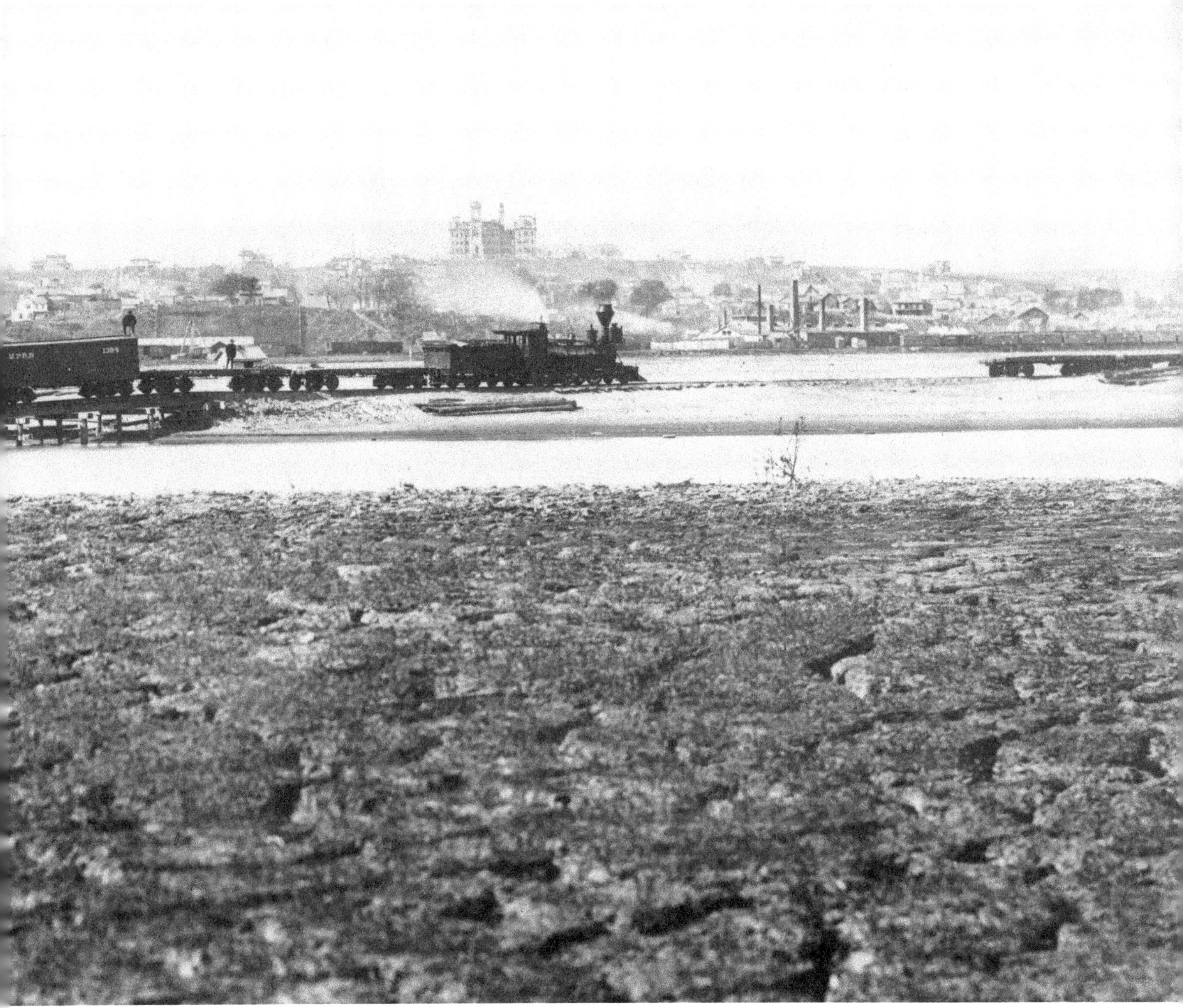

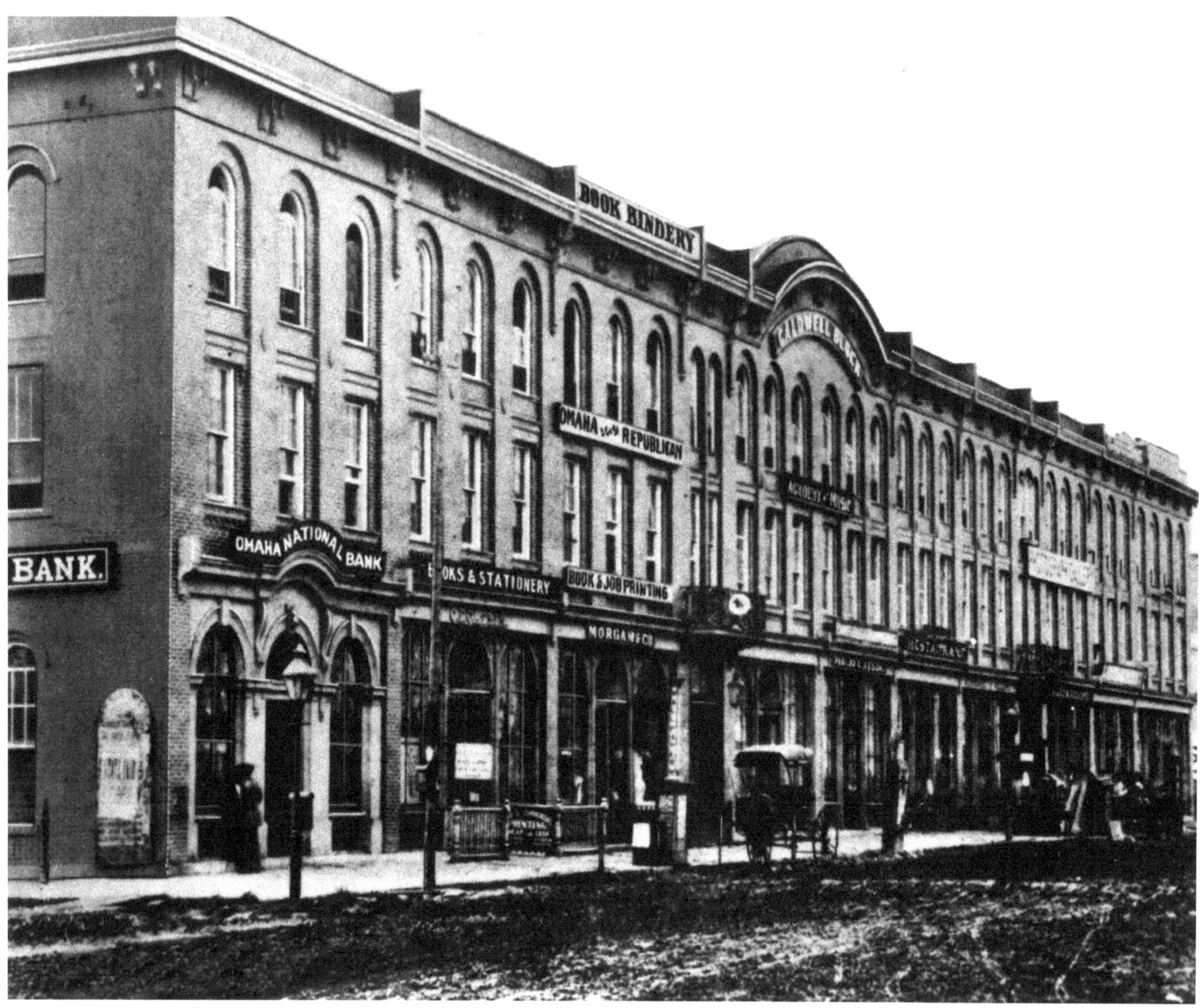

Shown shortly after its completion in 1867, the Caldwell Block was a business area located on the south side of Douglas between 13th and 14th streets. This block contained the Academy of Music, the Omaha National Bank, the Omaha *Republican* newspaper and job printer, a restaurant, a book bindery and a photographic gallery. The Academy of Music, which had a large auditorium, was the only permanent venue for stage productions in Omaha until the opening of Boyd's Opera House in 1881.

The congregation of the First Presbyterian Church, organized in 1857, built the large, brick building shown here in 1868, on the northwest corner of 17th and Dodge streets. The building was razed in 1915, and the land sold for commercial development. The congregation relocated to 34th and Farnam streets and is still there today in an elegant and spacious church building that was dedicated in 1917.

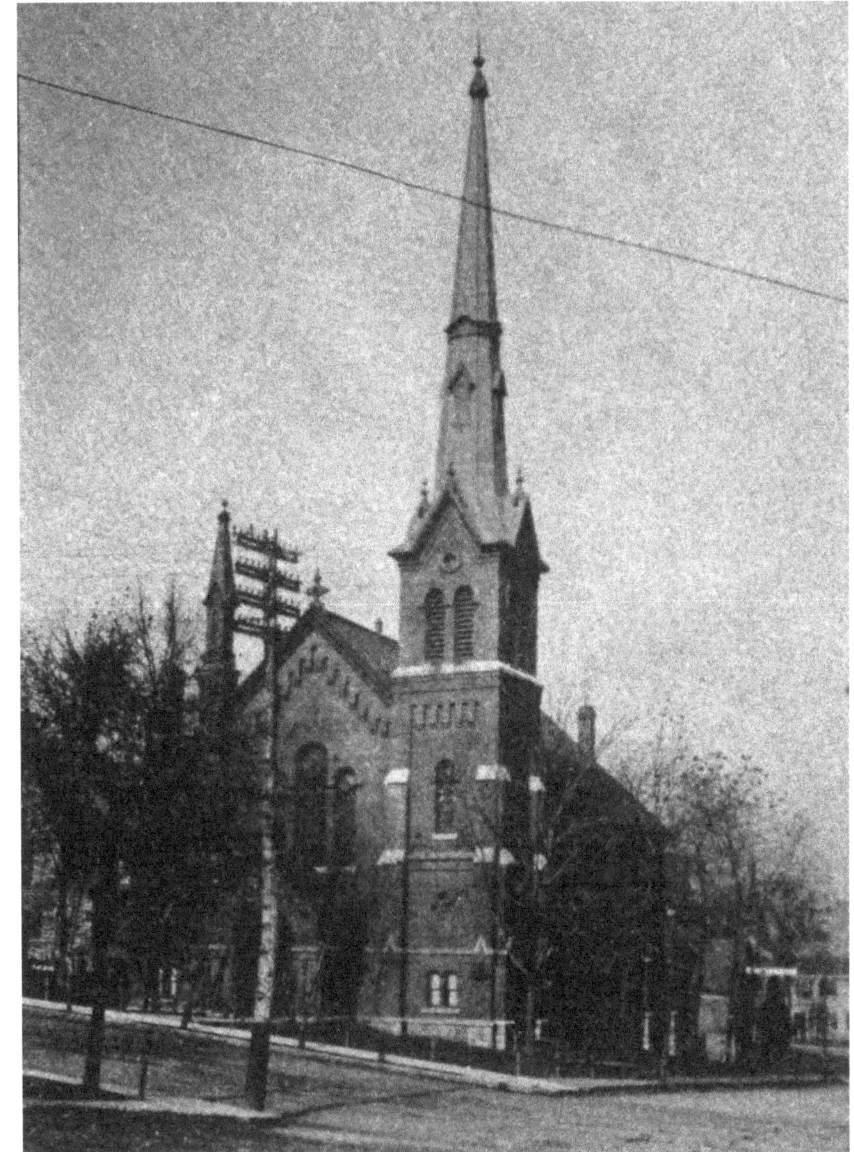

The Missouri River Bridge at Omaha was completed in March 1872, when this view was taken. Each of its eleven spans was 250 feet long. The approach on the Omaha side was situated at the foot of Mason Street. The bridge was rebuilt after being struck by a tornado in 1877. It was rebuilt again and reinforced in 1916.

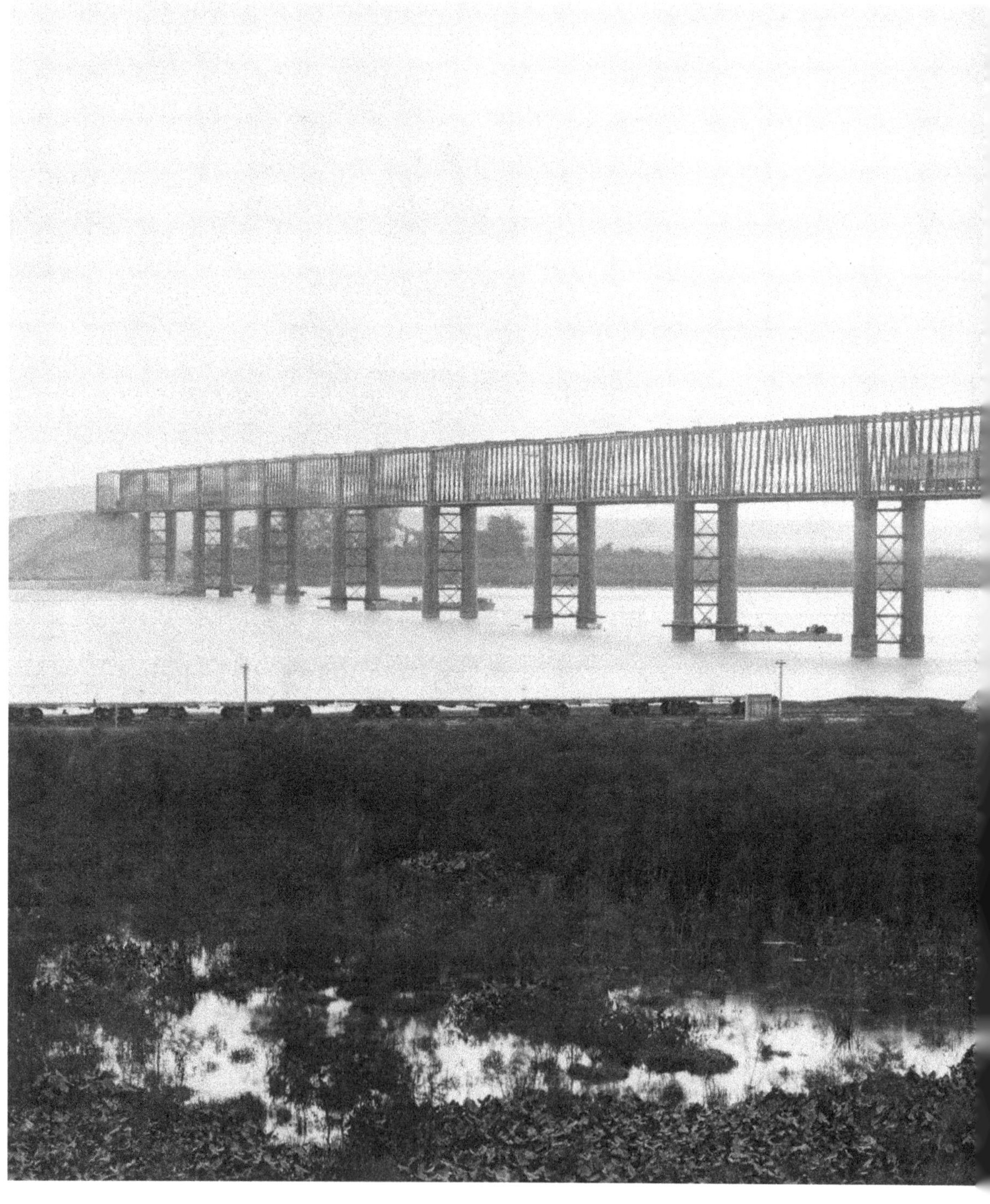

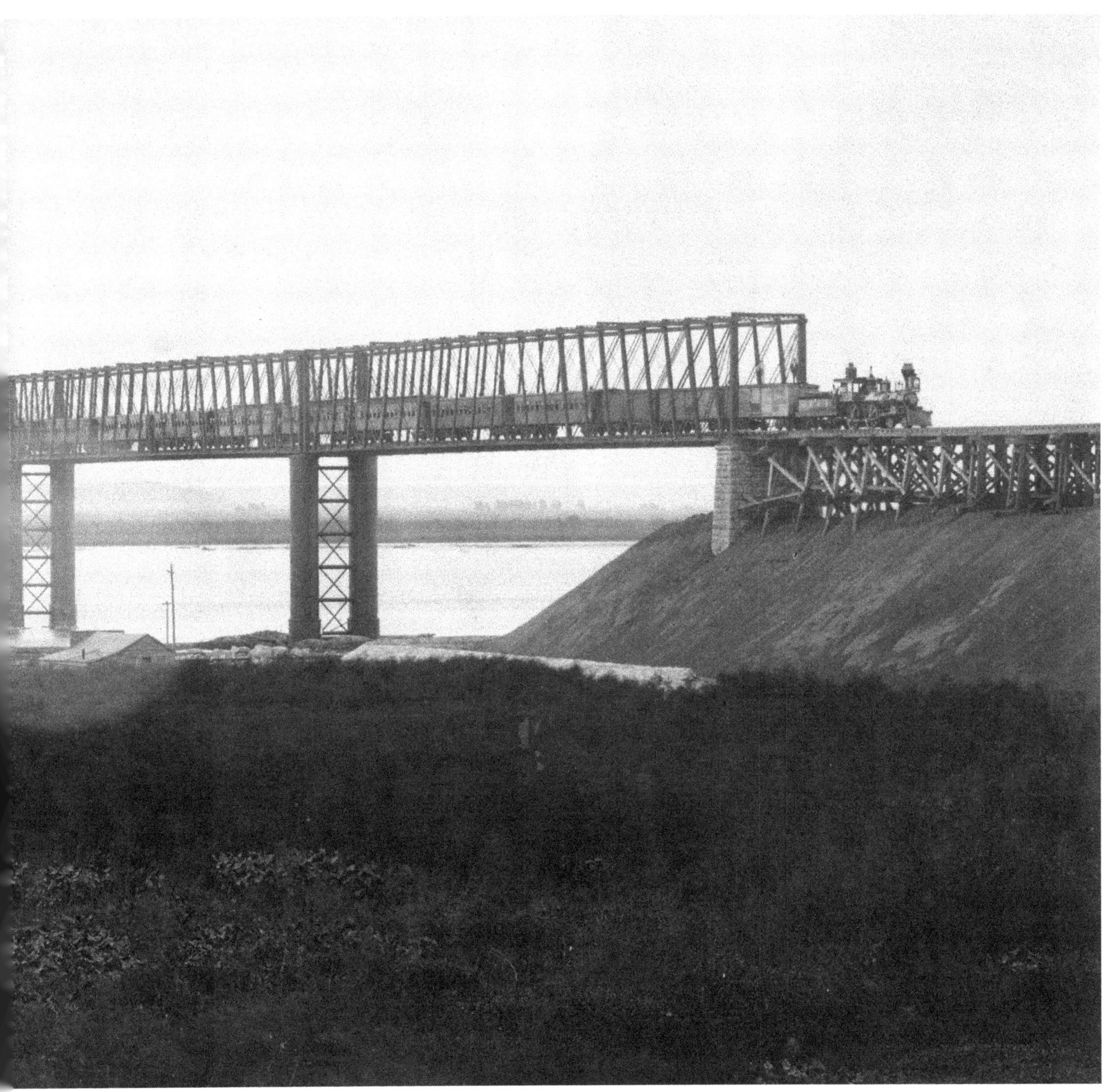

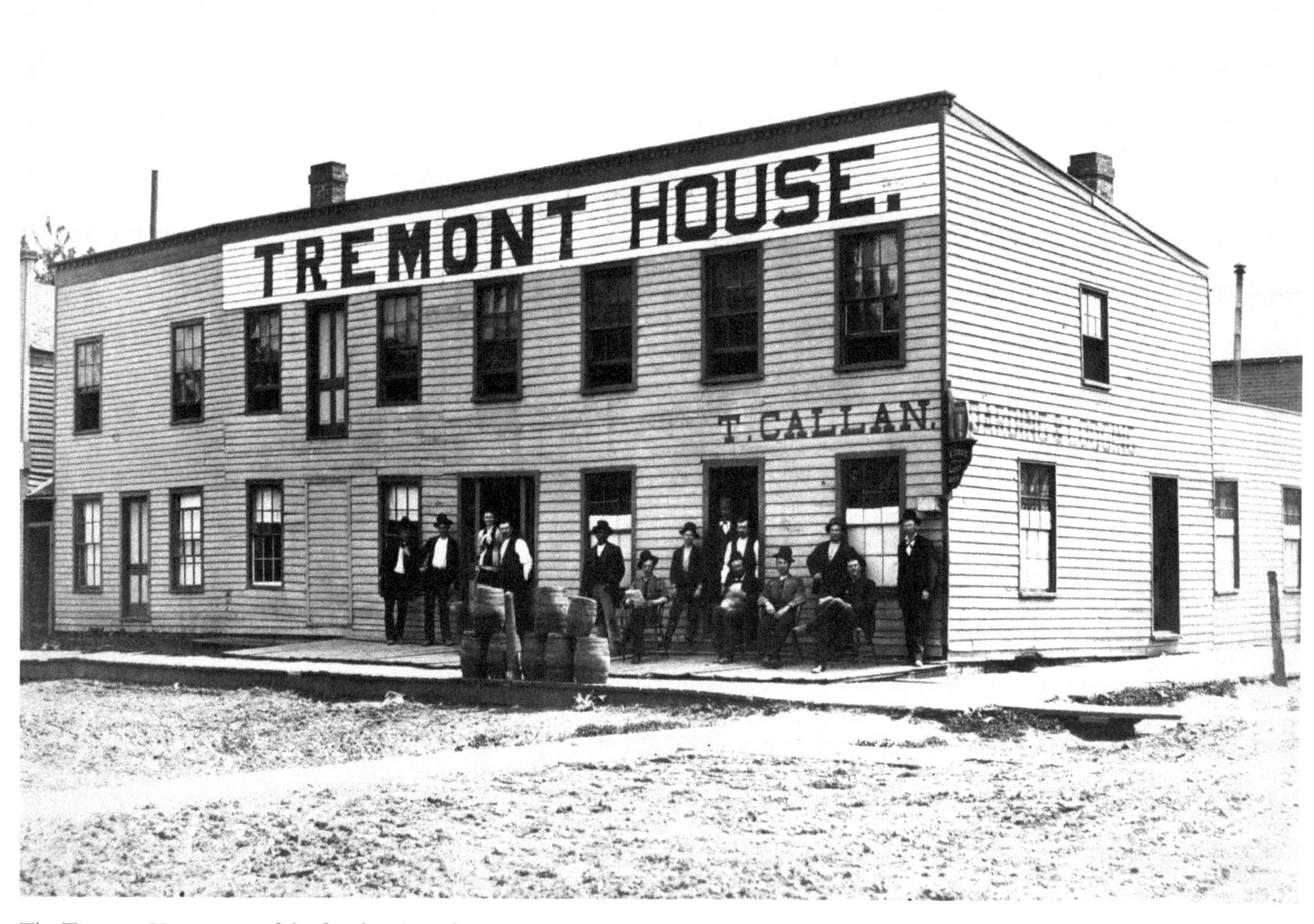

The Tremont House, one of the first hotels in the city, opened in October 1856, on the south side of Douglas between 13th and 14th streets. It was operated by William F. Sweesy and Aaron Root until 1865. At that time, the hotel was sold and the building moved to the southeast corner of 16th and Capitol streets. This photograph was made about 1878, after it had moved to the new location.

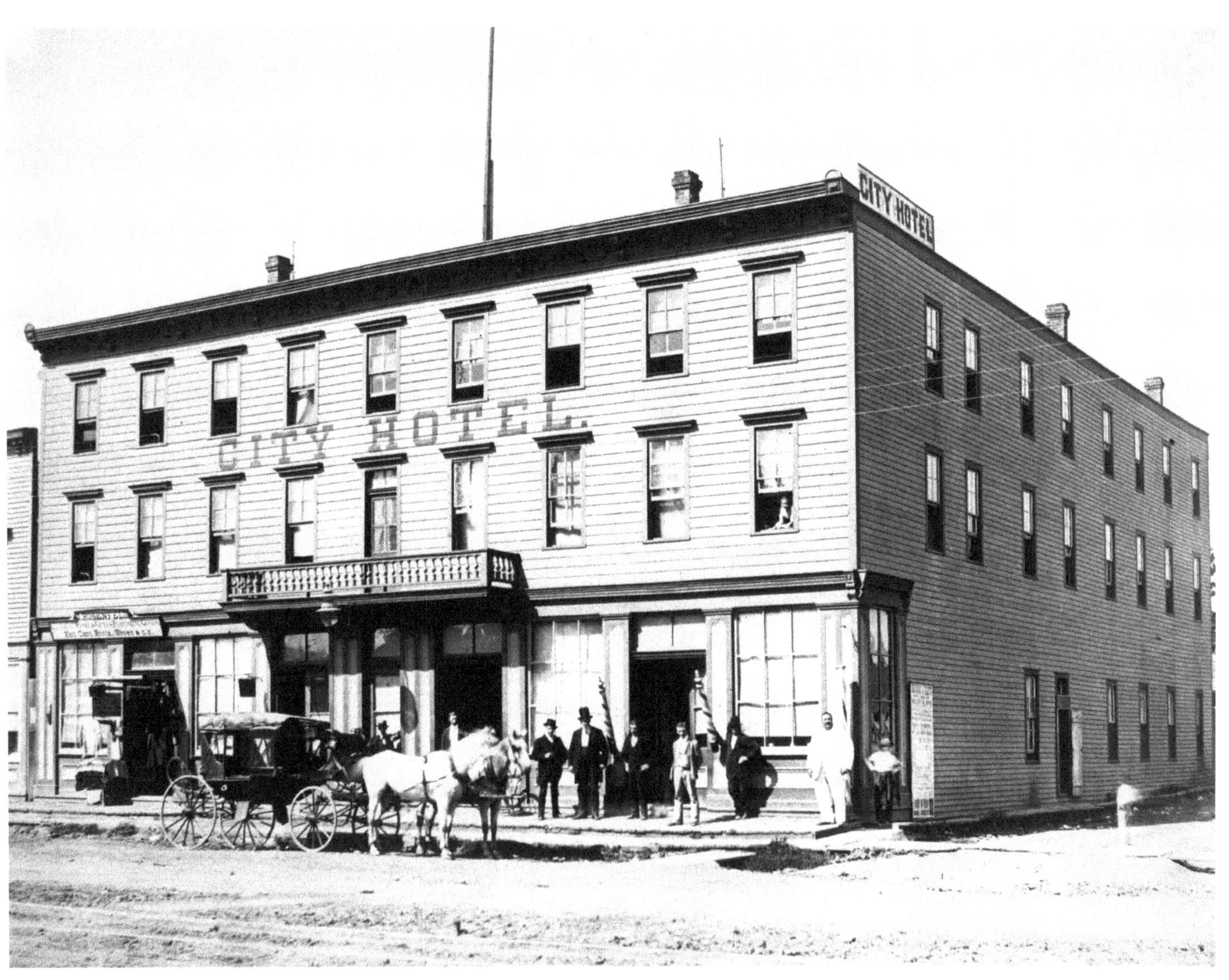

The City Hotel, shown here around 1877, on the west side of 10th Street between Farnam and Harney was Omaha's second hotel. Prior to 1860, there were few brick structures because there were no brick yards here. Building materials had to be brought across the river from Council Bluffs, Iowa.

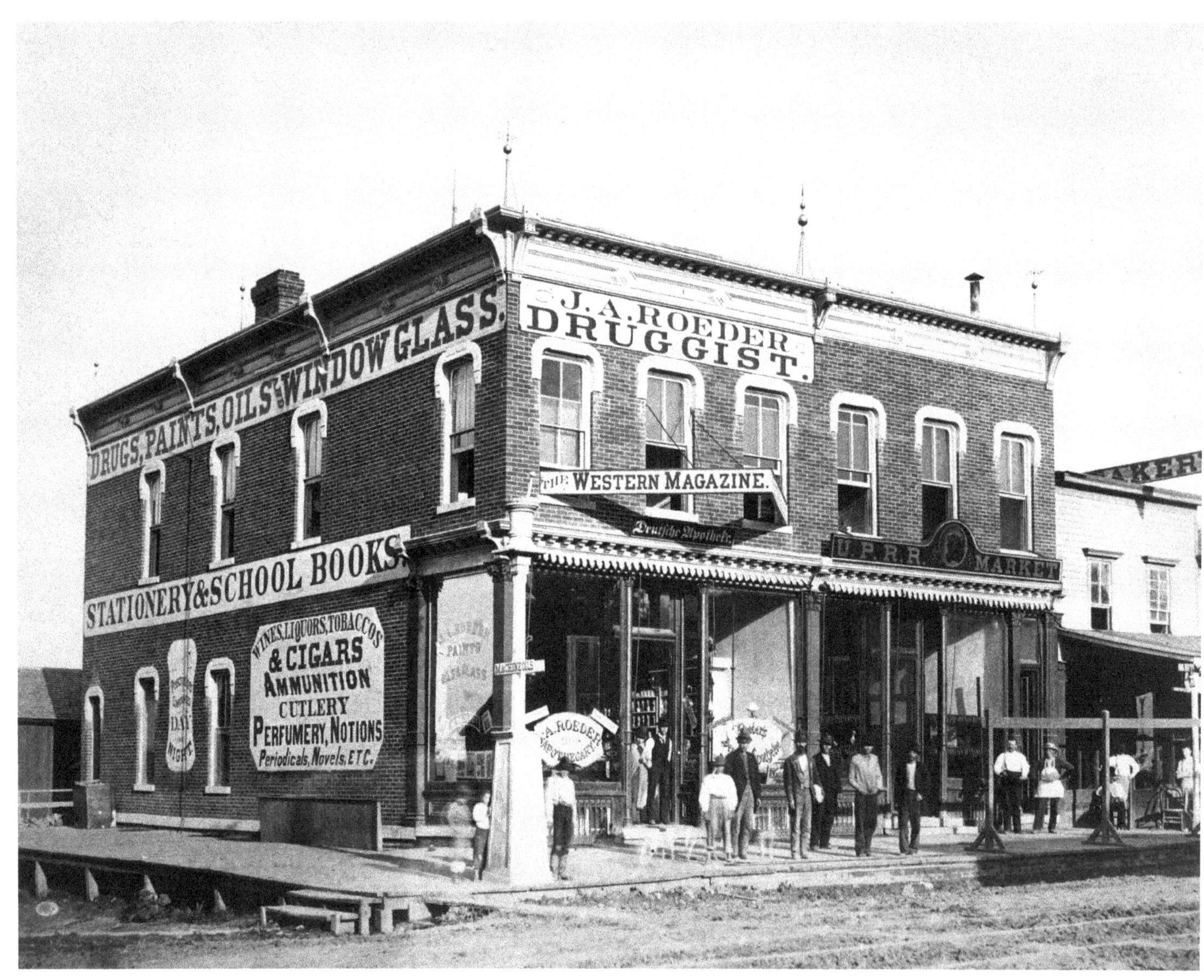

Druggist Julius A. Roeder's business was located on the southeast corner of 16th and Webster streets. Next door is the Union Pacific Block building, 621 North 16th Street, home to the Union Pacific Railroad Market, a company store operated by the railroad for the benefit of its employees. This photograph was taken about 1879.

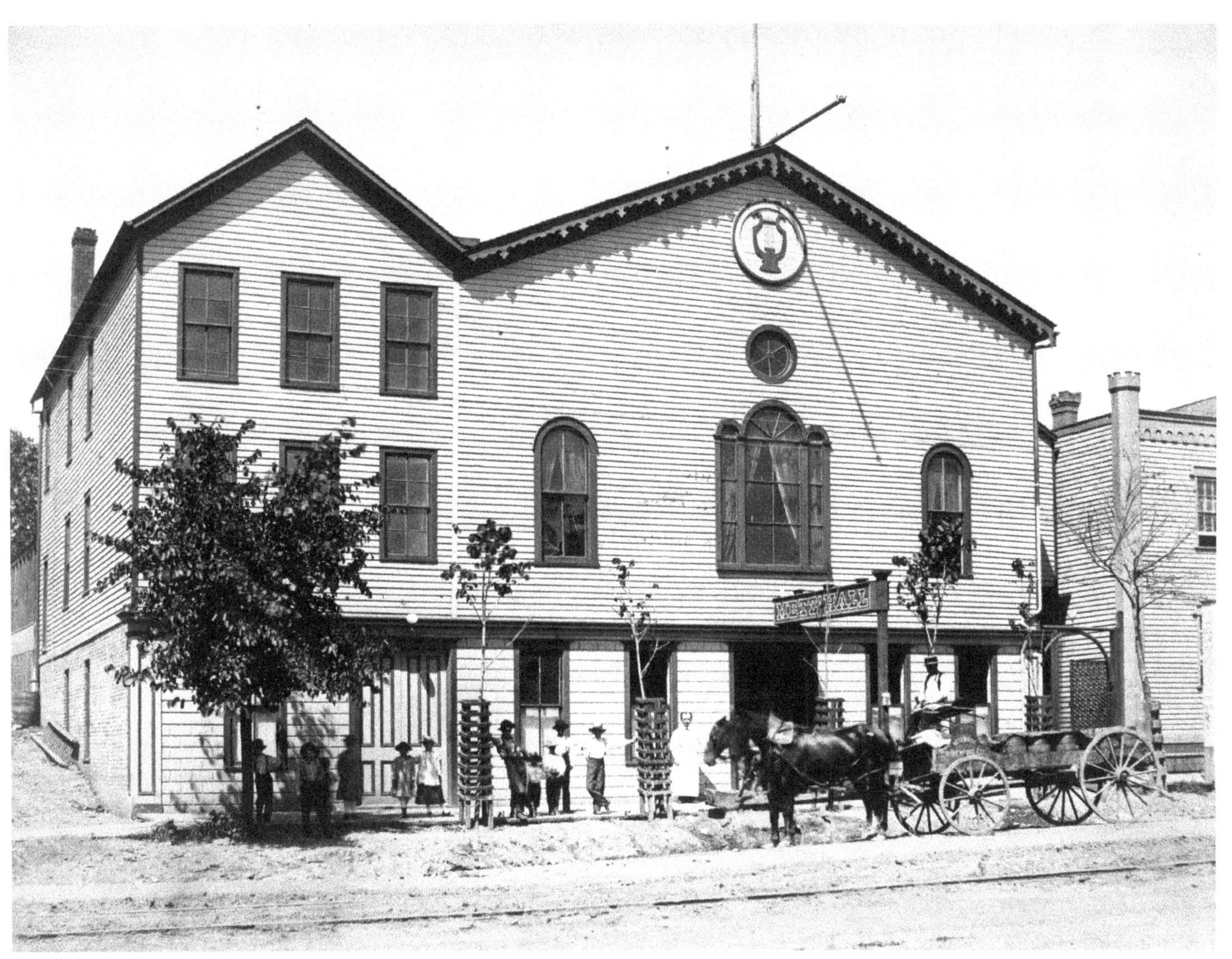

This view of Metz Brothers Beer Hall, 510–512 South 10th Street, was taken in 1879. Metz Brothers Brewing Company was one of the earliest breweries in Omaha, with headquarters at 6th and Leavenworth. Germans were the largest immigrant group in Omaha, and brothers Charles and Fred Metz arrived early on to establish their business. At one time, there were nine large breweries operating in the city.

General view of Omaha to the northwest in 1879, taken from the tower of Omaha High School on Capitol Hill. Creighton College, at the upper left, is Creighton University today, one of the leading Catholic universities in the United States. This view gives a clear idea of the rapid development of the city during this period.

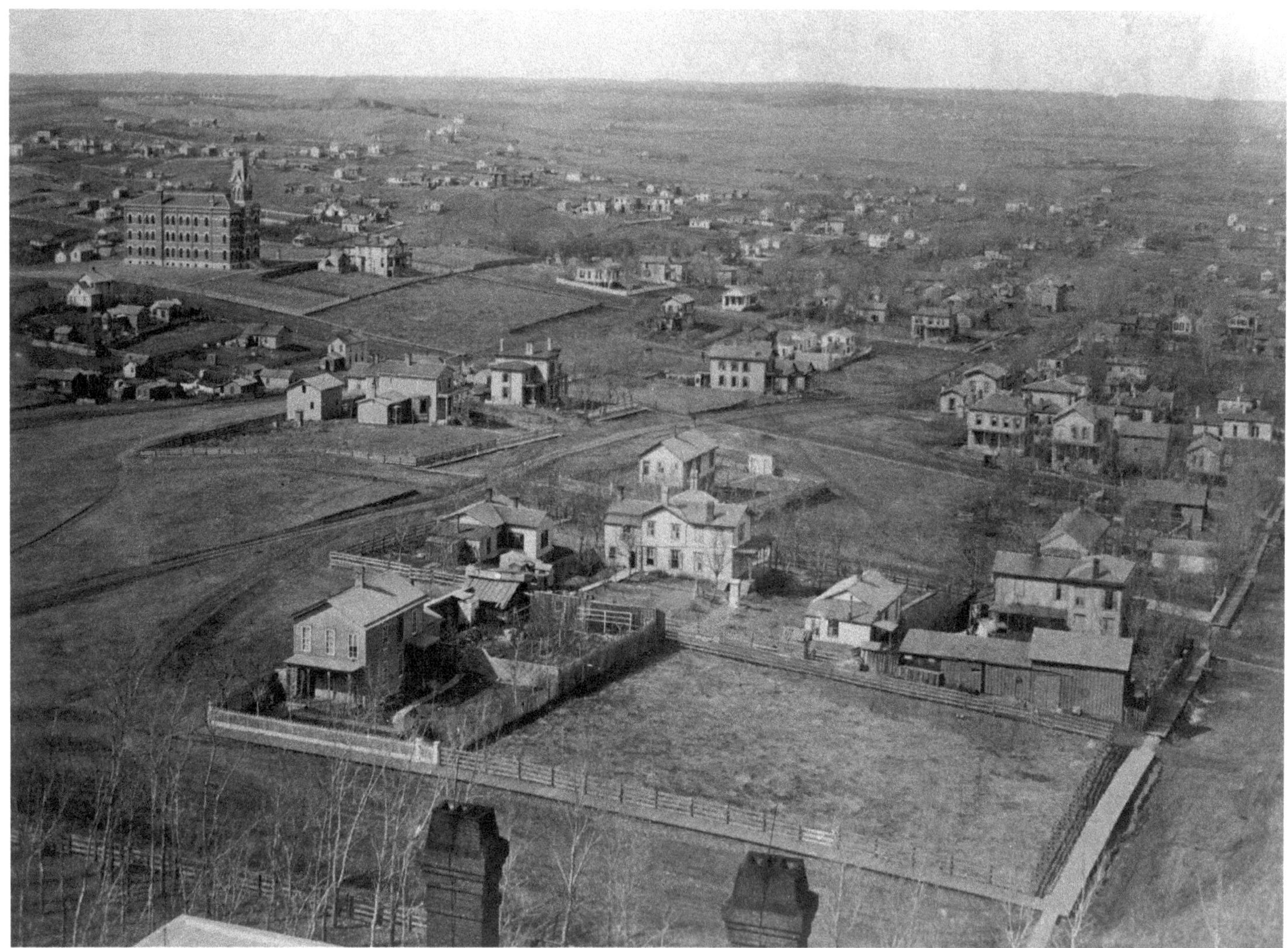

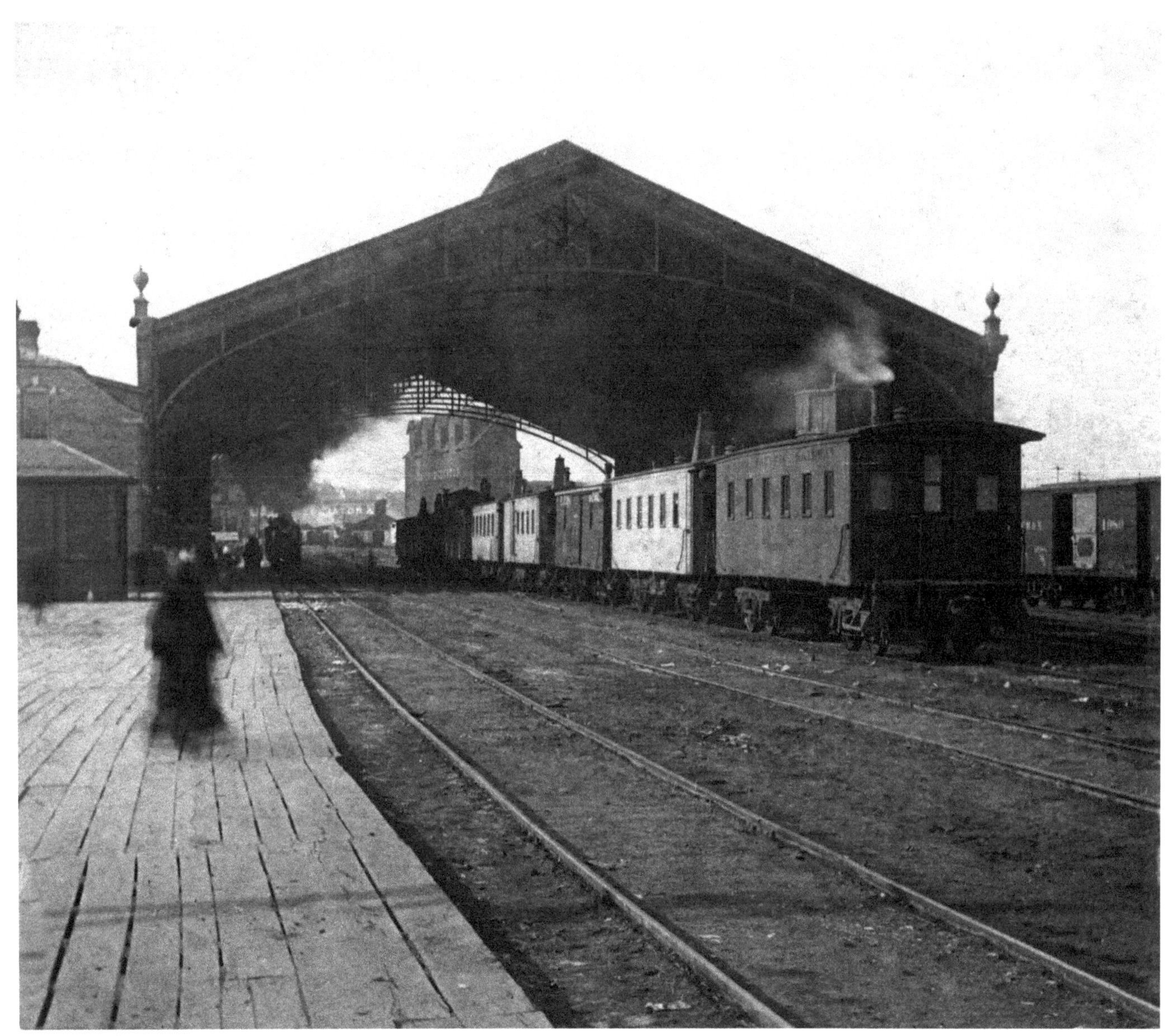

Pioneer Omaha photographer George Heyn captured this image of the Union Pacific railroad depot in 1882. Built at 9th and Mason streets in 1871, it was called a "cow shed" because it was open at both ends. In 1889, the Union Pacific Depot Company was formed to replace this structure with a more permanent one. After many delays, a new depot was finally opened in 1897.

This view, taken in the early 1880s, shows the Paxton Hotel, located on the southwest corner of 14th and Farnam streets. When it opened in 1882, it was considered Omaha's finest hotel. It was torn down in 1927 to make way for the elegant New Paxton Hotel, which opened June 26, 1929.

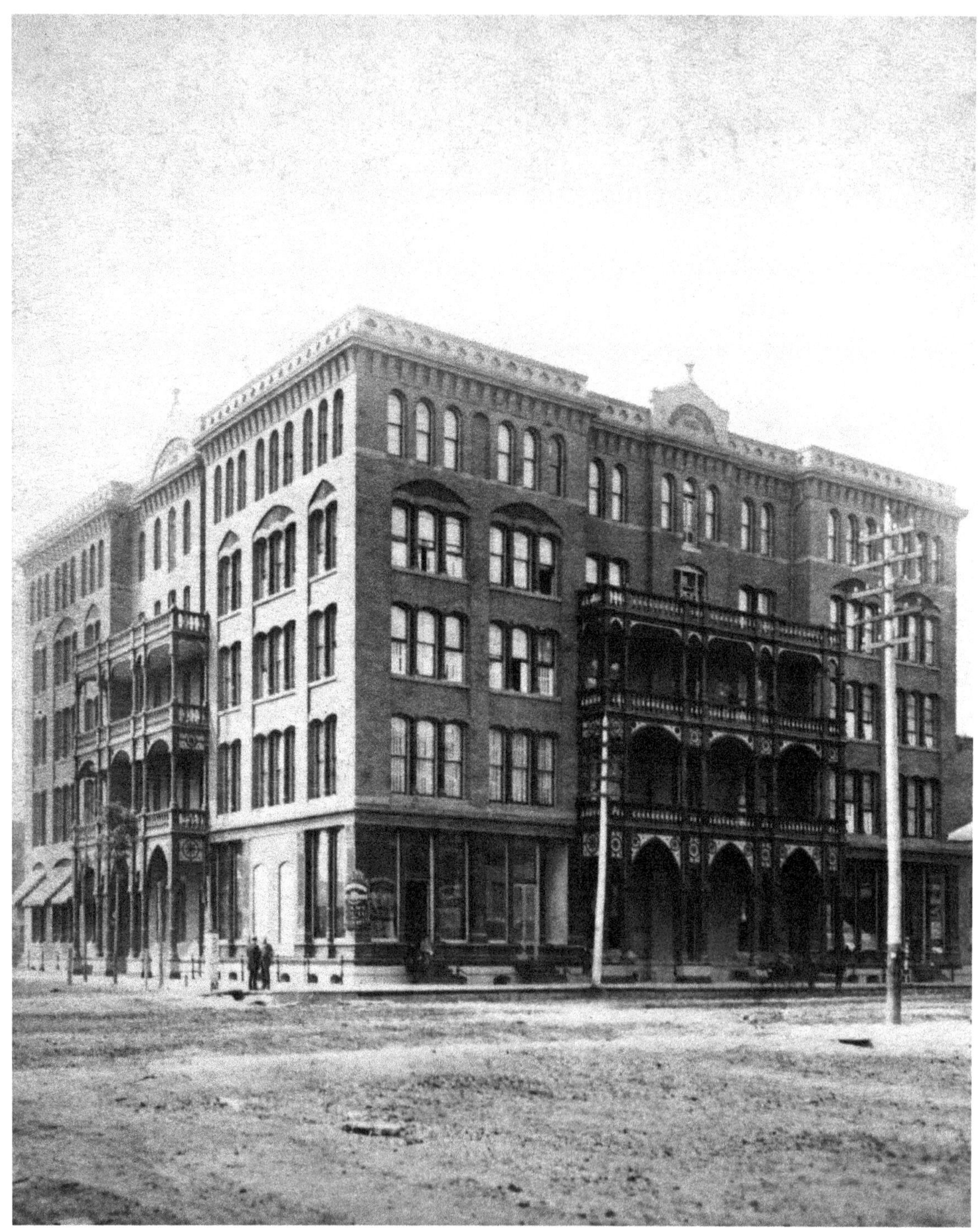

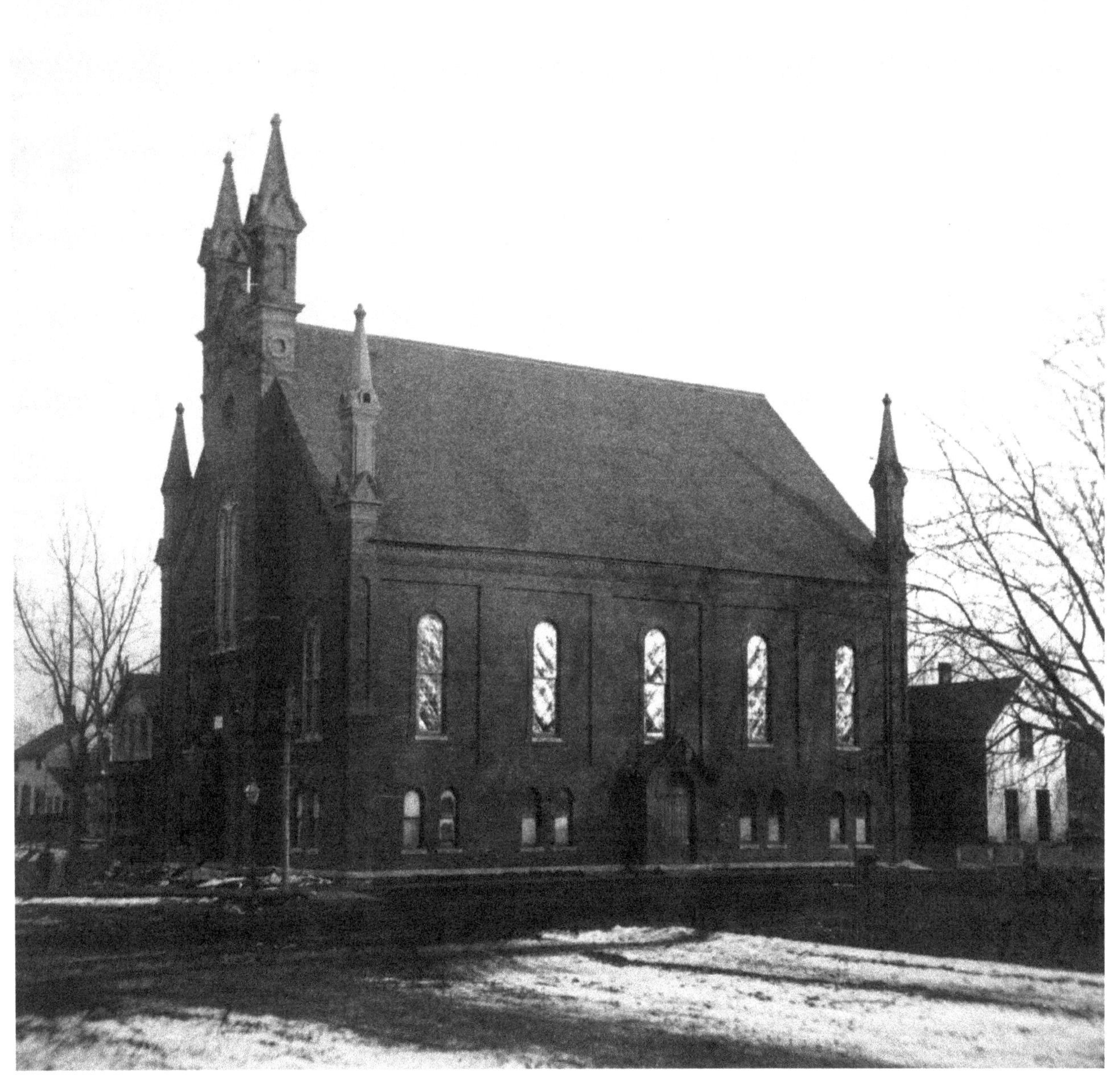

First Baptist Church on the corner of 15th and Davenport streets. The lower section was built in 1870 and the upper floor added in 1881. This view was taken in the early 1880s. Fire destroyed the building on December 4, 1894, and the congregation relocated to its present location at 29th and Harney streets. A beautiful new church was completed there in 1904.

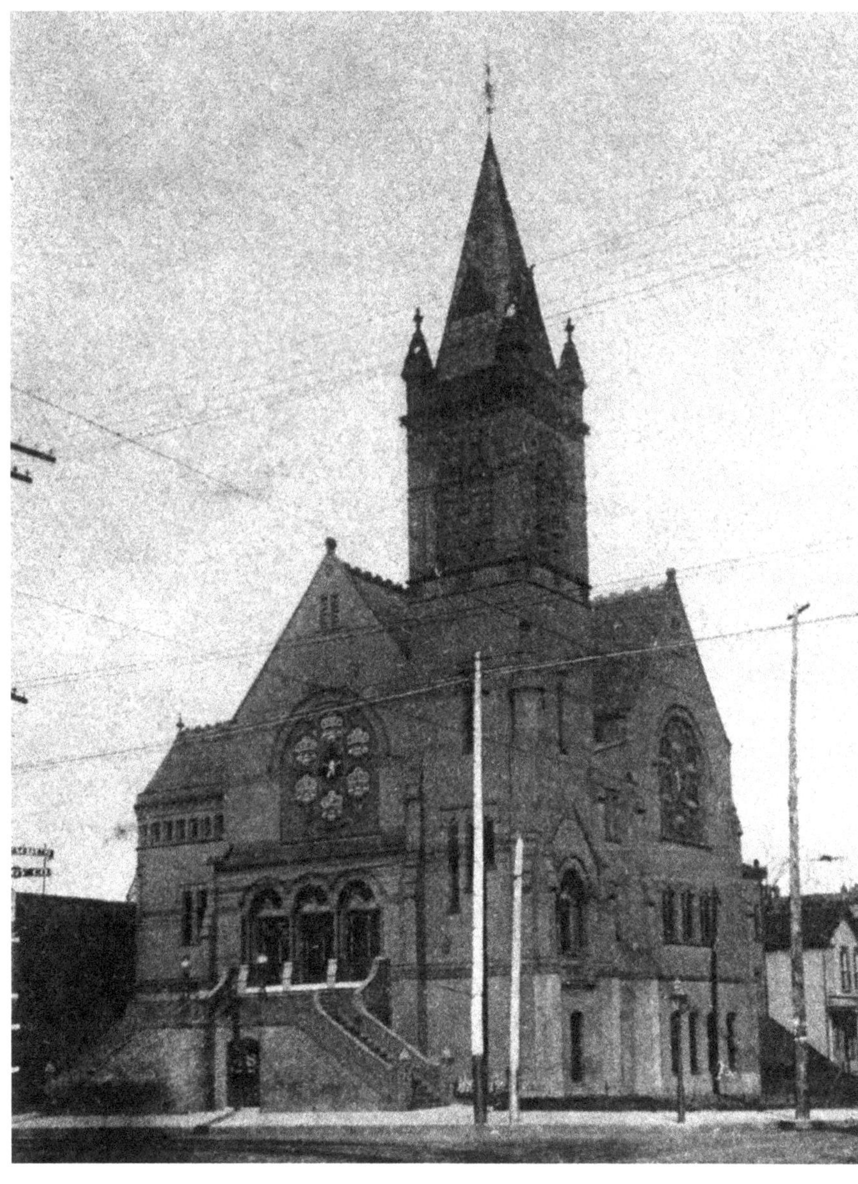

In 1880, the Lutheran congregation, which had a church on Douglas Street, sold their property and bought lots on the northeast corner of 16th and Harney. One of their members, Augustus Kountze, promised to match any amount raised for construction of a new building. The church was named the Kountze Memorial Lutheran Church in honor of his deceased father. The structure cost $50,000 when completed in 1882. This view dates to about 1885. Later, when 16th Street became a commercial area, the congregation sold this property and relocated to 29th and Farnam, dedicating a magnificent new church building there in 1906.

Boyd's Opera House was built by local businessman James F. Boyd in 1881 at 1422 Farnam Street. It had a seating capacity of 1,700 and was the first large building in Omaha heated entirely by steam. This view was taken shortly after it opened. Later the name was changed to the Farnam Street Theatre. Although considered "fireproof," it was totally destroyed by fire on October 2, 1893. One Omaha firefighter was killed.

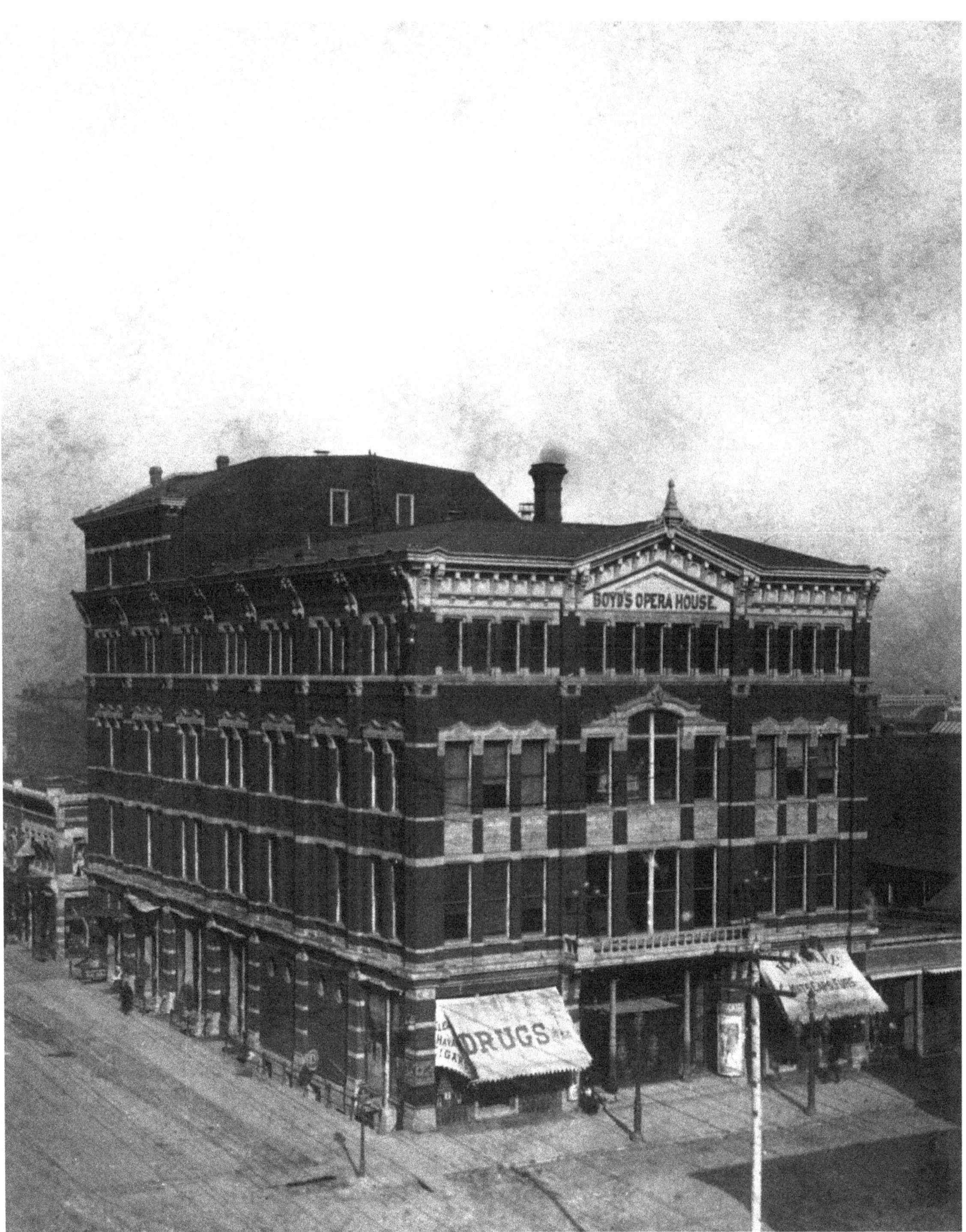

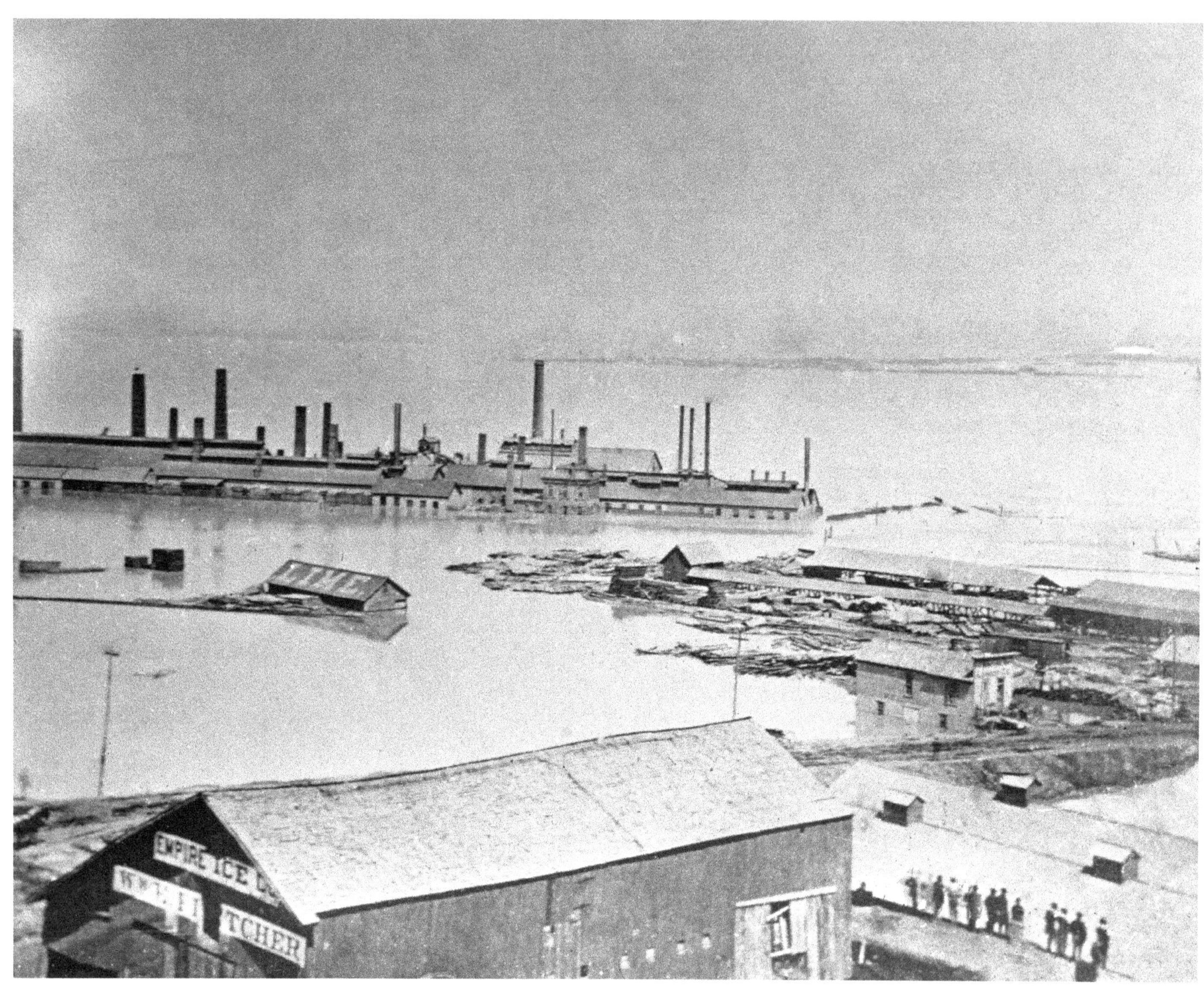

In April 1881, the entire Missouri River valley flooded, reaching Omaha April 6. A temporary dam built to protect downtown businesses failed. On April 7, the flood waters crested at twenty-three-and-a-third feet, two feet above the previous high water mark. This view shows the Omaha Smelting Works and the Union Pacific Railroad shops under water.

Omaha Comes of Age

(1891–1900)

The decade between 1890 and 1900 was a period of unprecedented growth for the City of Omaha. Paved streets, improved city utilities and services, a rapidly expanding transportation system, and significant architecture all indicated that Omaha was here to stay.

A system of parks and boulevards was transforming the physical appearance of the city, features which continue to define the landscape of Omaha even today. The population had also grown to slightly more than 100,000 and future prospects were good. An elegant new city hall was built on the northeast corner of 18th and Farnam streets. Many large and ornate commercial and public buildings lent an air of substance and prosperity to the city.

During the first week of July 1892, the Peoples Party (Populist) held their national convention at the old Coliseum. This event centered national attention on Omaha. However, the next year, 1893, saw a serious downturn in the economy throughout the entire country. An economic depression took hold, and local business leaders sought a plan to improve the situation. In 1895, the Knights of AK-SAR-BEN (Nebraska spelled backwards) was founded to promote Omaha. For the next one hundred years, this was one of the most important associations in the city.

Finally, in 1897, at a meeting of the Trans-Mississippi Commercial Congress in Omaha, William Jennings Bryan proposed that an exposition be held in the city during the summer of 1898. Thus was born the great Trans-Mississippi and International Exposition and Indian Congress of 1898. If one were to look back over the entire history of Omaha to select the single most important event, it would undoubtedly be the Trans-Mississippi Exposition. The Exposition was expected to breathe new life into the community. There were, of course, positive results, but none were especially long lasting. While many came to view and visit, few relocated permanently. It was the service industry—hotel and saloon keepers, restaurants, and department stores—which saw the greatest benefit. When the fair closed on October 31, a new organization, the Greater America Exposition Company, took over and decided to hold another fair in 1899. This was to showcase the colonial possessions which had been gained by the United States as the result of its victory in the Spanish-American War. This fair was not successful, and the Exposition buildings were all sold—mostly to the Chicago House Wrecking Company—and demolished.

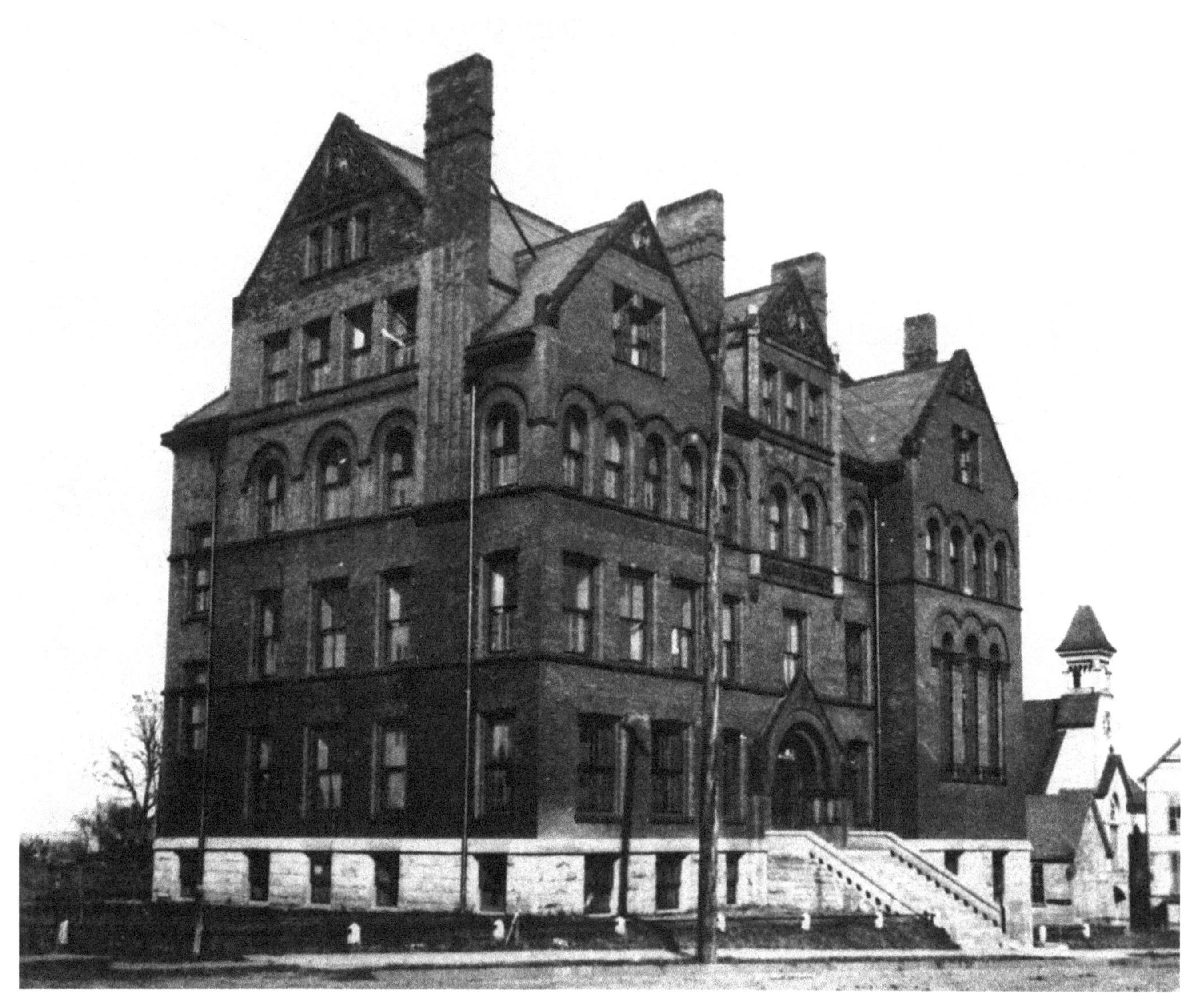

Constructed in 1888 at 1424 Castelar Street by the Sisters of Mercy, a teaching order, this imposing brick building was a prominent landmark in South Omaha. This Order maintained several schools in the city, including St. Catherine's Academy. This building served as the Mother House of the Sisters of Mercy in Nebraska. The photograph was taken in the mid-1890s.

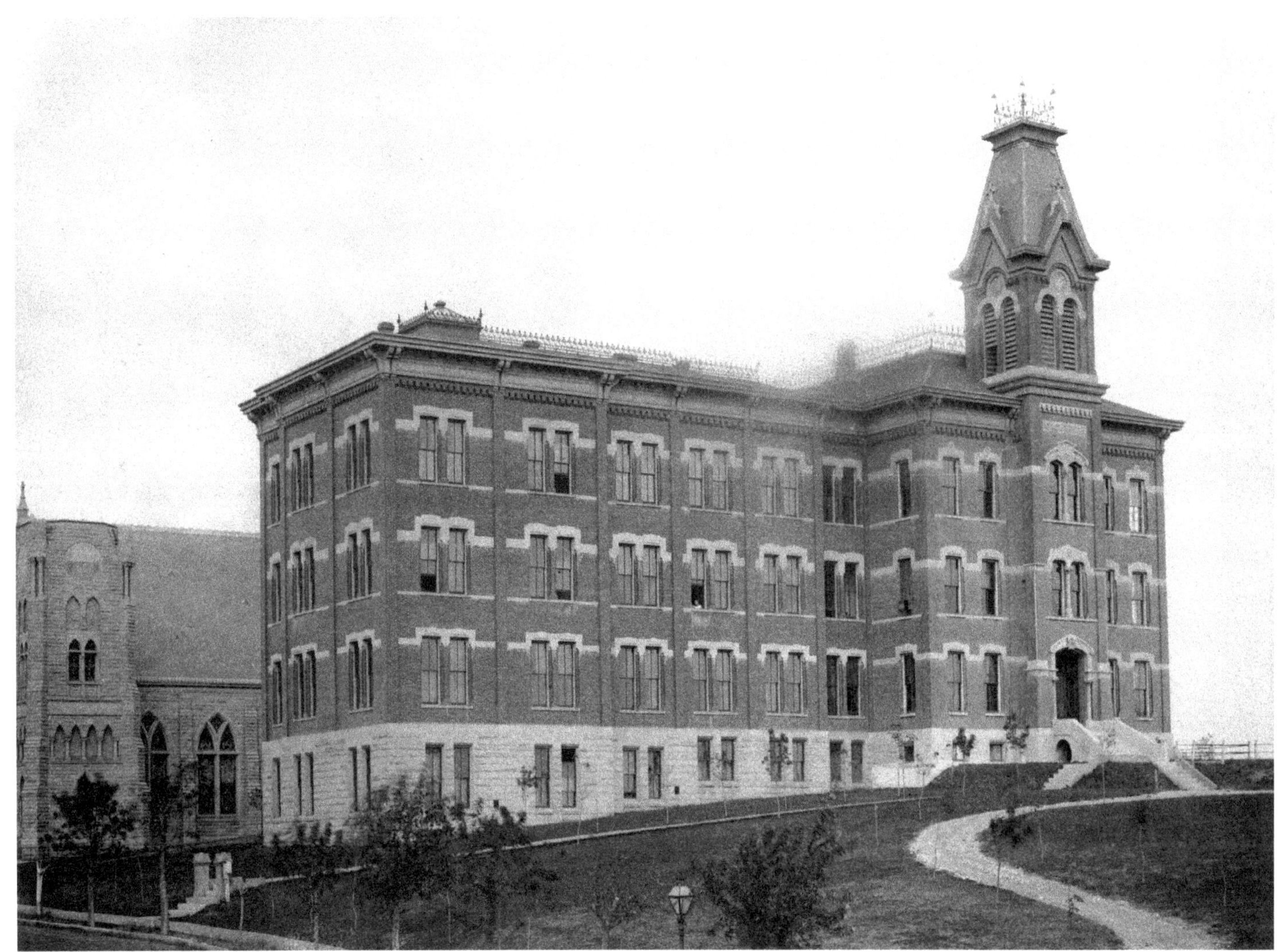

Creighton College, a private Catholic institution of higher learning, opened in Omaha on September 2, 1879. This photograph taken about 1892 shows the original brick structure which housed the school. It was located at 25th and California streets. Later, another wing was added. Today, Creighton University ranks as one of the outstanding private universities in the United States.

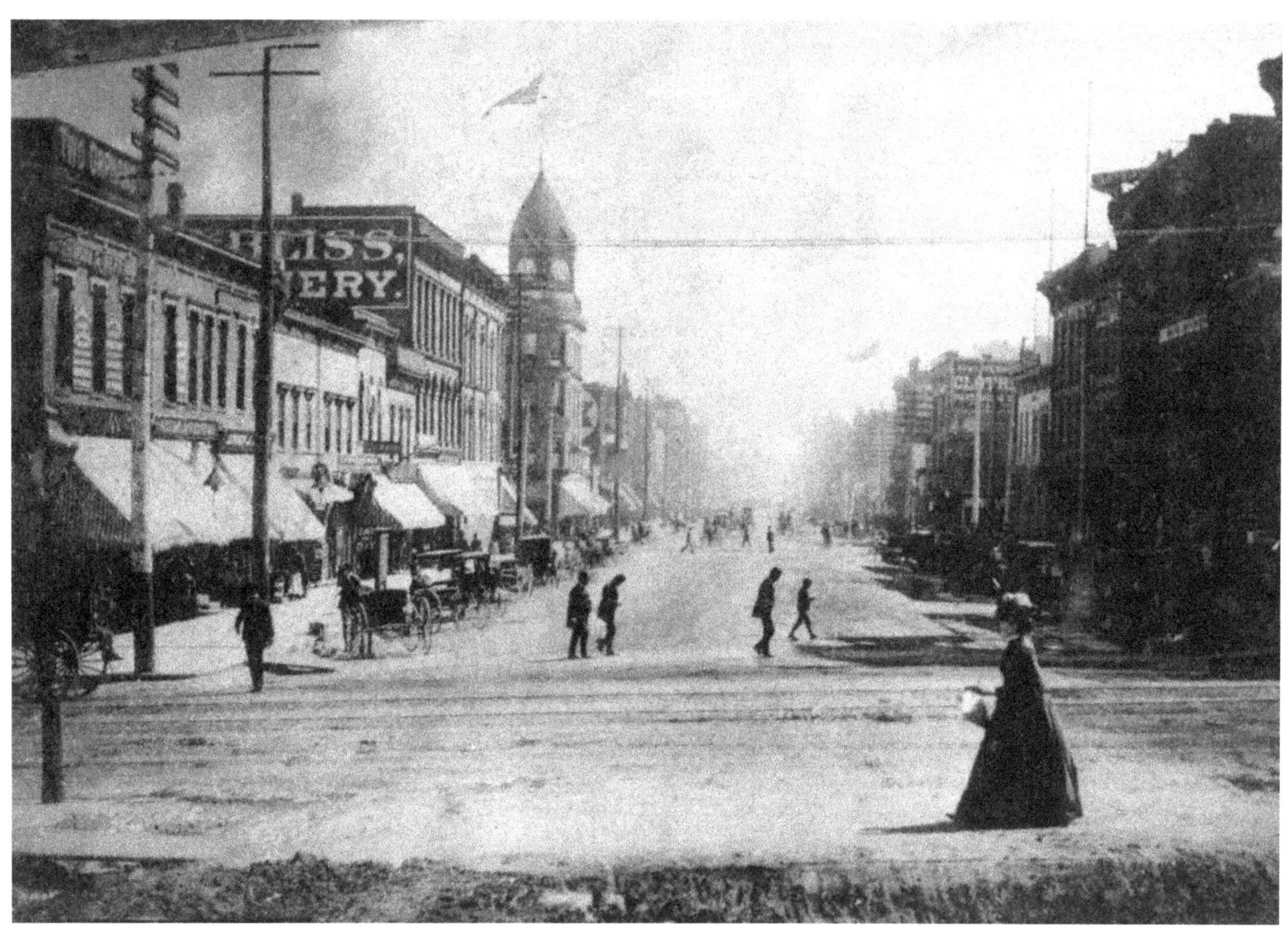

Looking east on Douglas Street from 16th, in a view taken in the mid-1890s. On the left is the Continental Block on the northeast corner of 15th and Douglas streets, which has a tall round tower surmounted by a banner. This served as general office building.

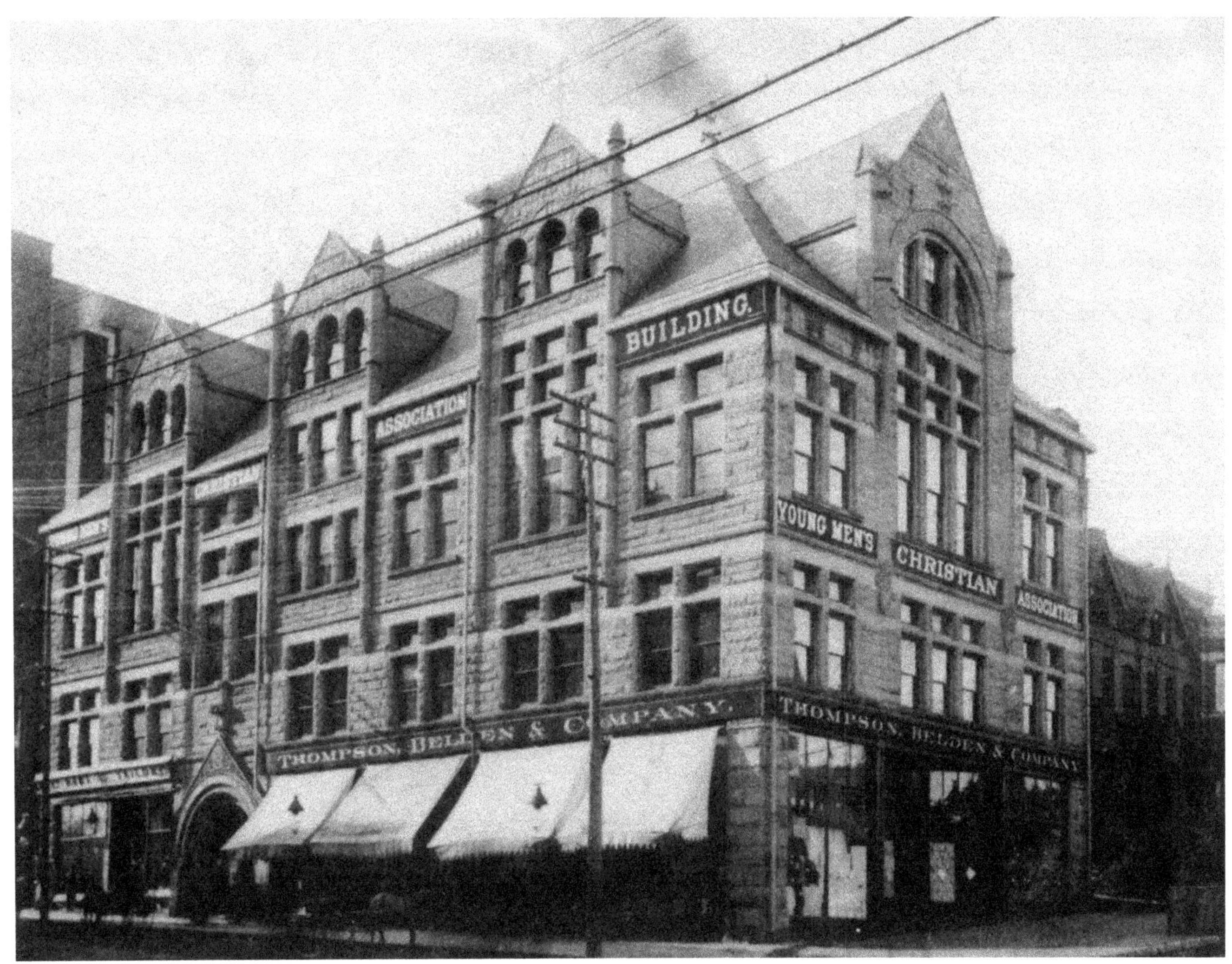

The Young Men's Christian Association (YMCA) building at 16th and Douglas streets, as it appeared in the 1890s. This building opened in July 1888 and cost $90,000 to construct. The YMCA used the upper floors and rented out the lower two. Later, the YMCA built a larger structure at 17th and Harney streets, and this site was replaced by the Brandeis Building.

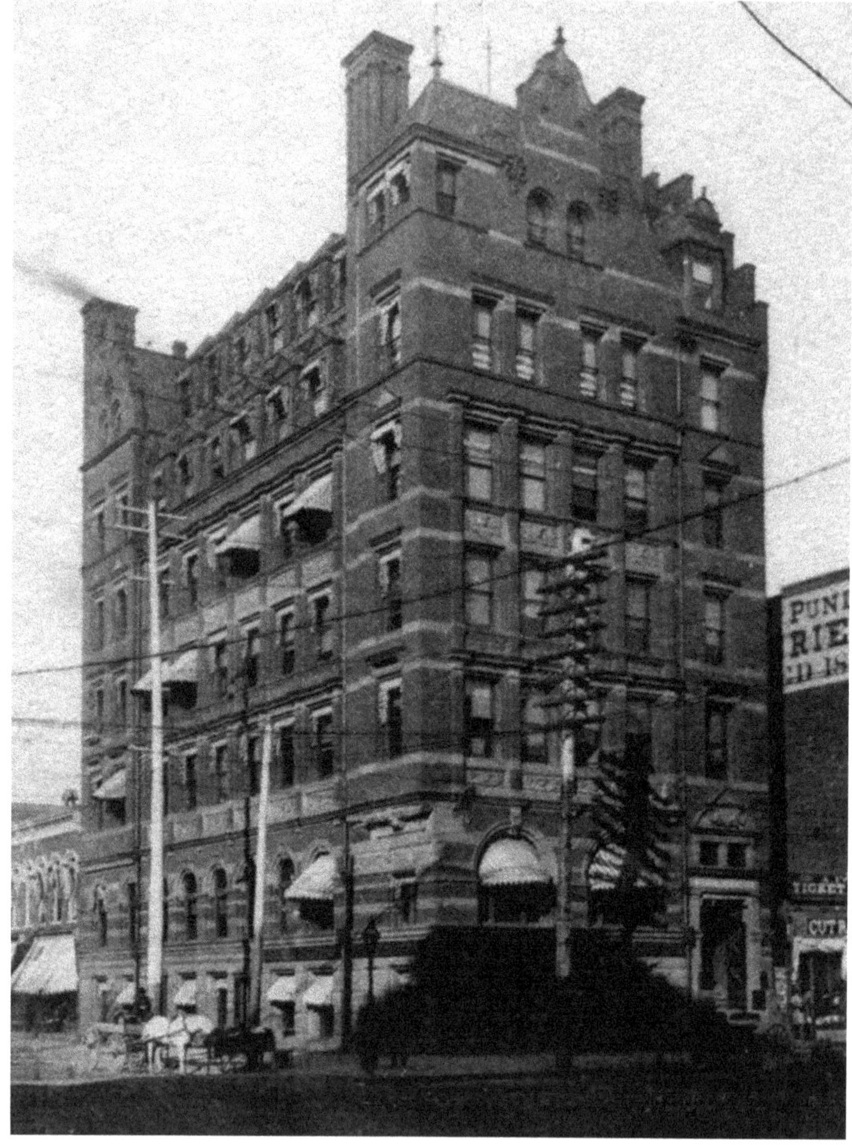

The Merchants National Bank building on the northeast corner of 13th and Farnam streets was designed by the local architectural firm of Mendelssohn, Fisher and Lawrie. In 1888, the year this building was constructed, the bank was capitalized at $500,000. This picture was taken in the early 1890s.

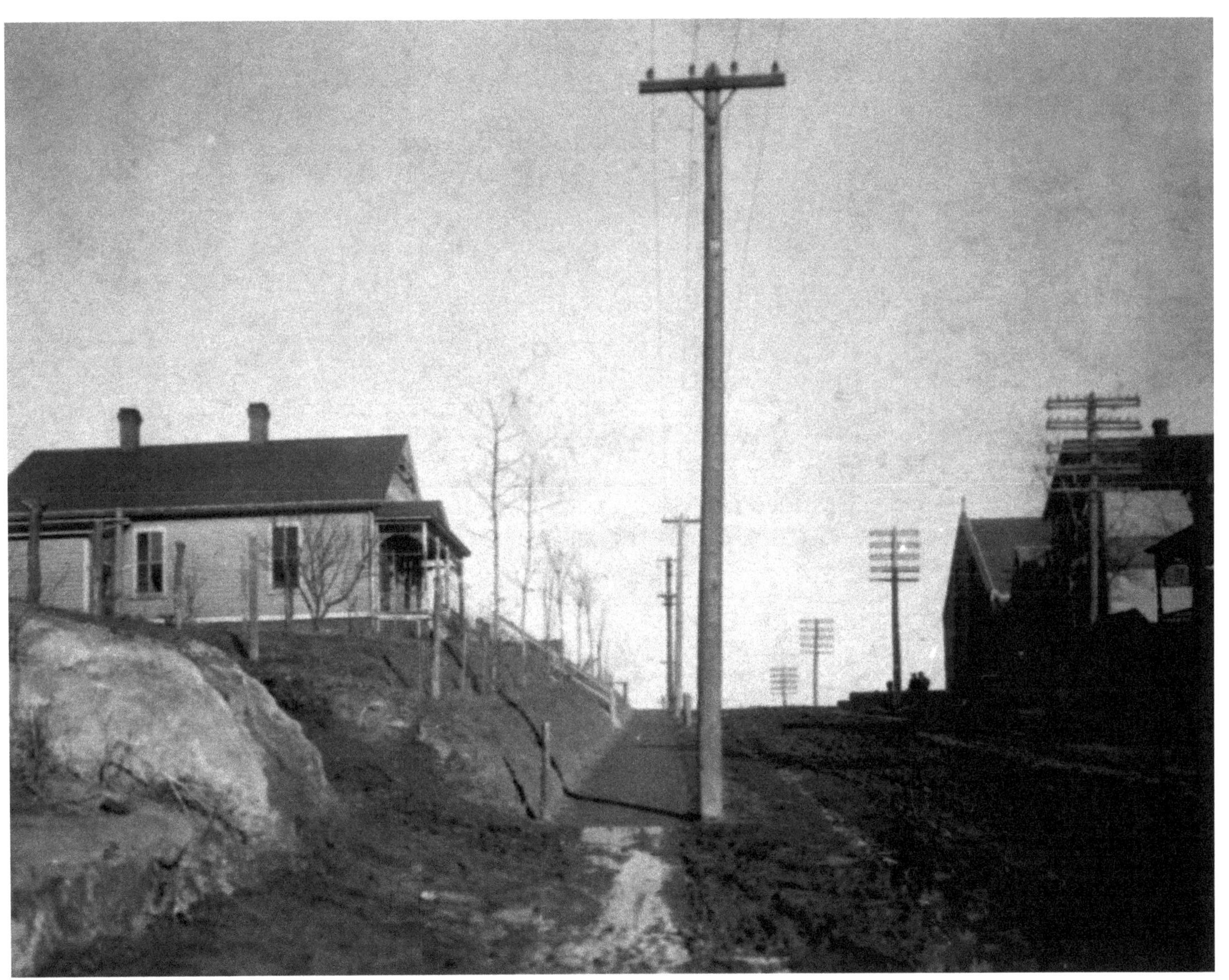

Beginning in the early 1890s and continuing through the mid-1920s, many of the streets in the central part of Omaha were lowered to reduce the steep hills west of downtown. The intersection of 11th and Pierce streets, for example, was lowered a total of 66 feet! This scene is looking east on Q Street.

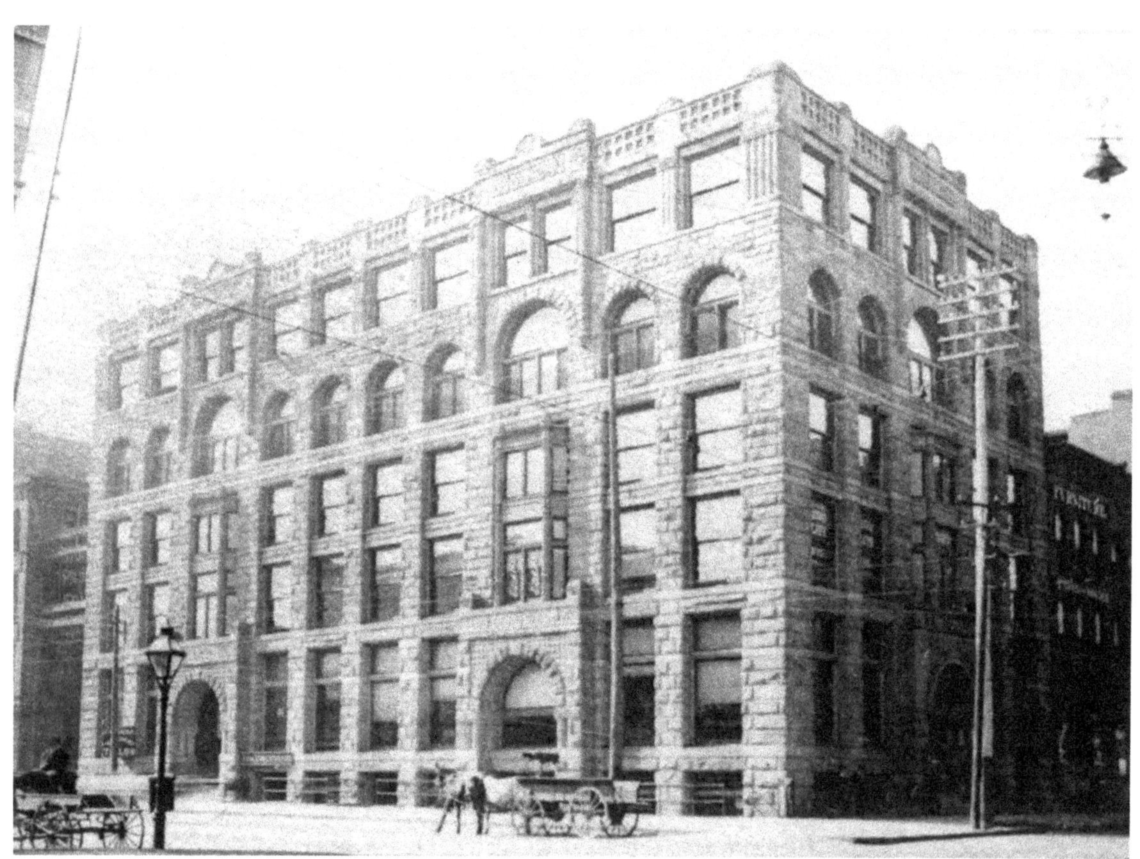

The oldest banking institution in Nebraska was the United States National Bank, the successor of a land company and exchange agency first opened in 1855 by the Joseph H. Millard Company. This company became the United States National Bank on October 2, 1883. The building was constructed in 1887, designed by Mendelssohn, Fisher and Lawrie and located at the southwest corner of 12th and Farnam streets. This photograph was taken in the mid-1890s.

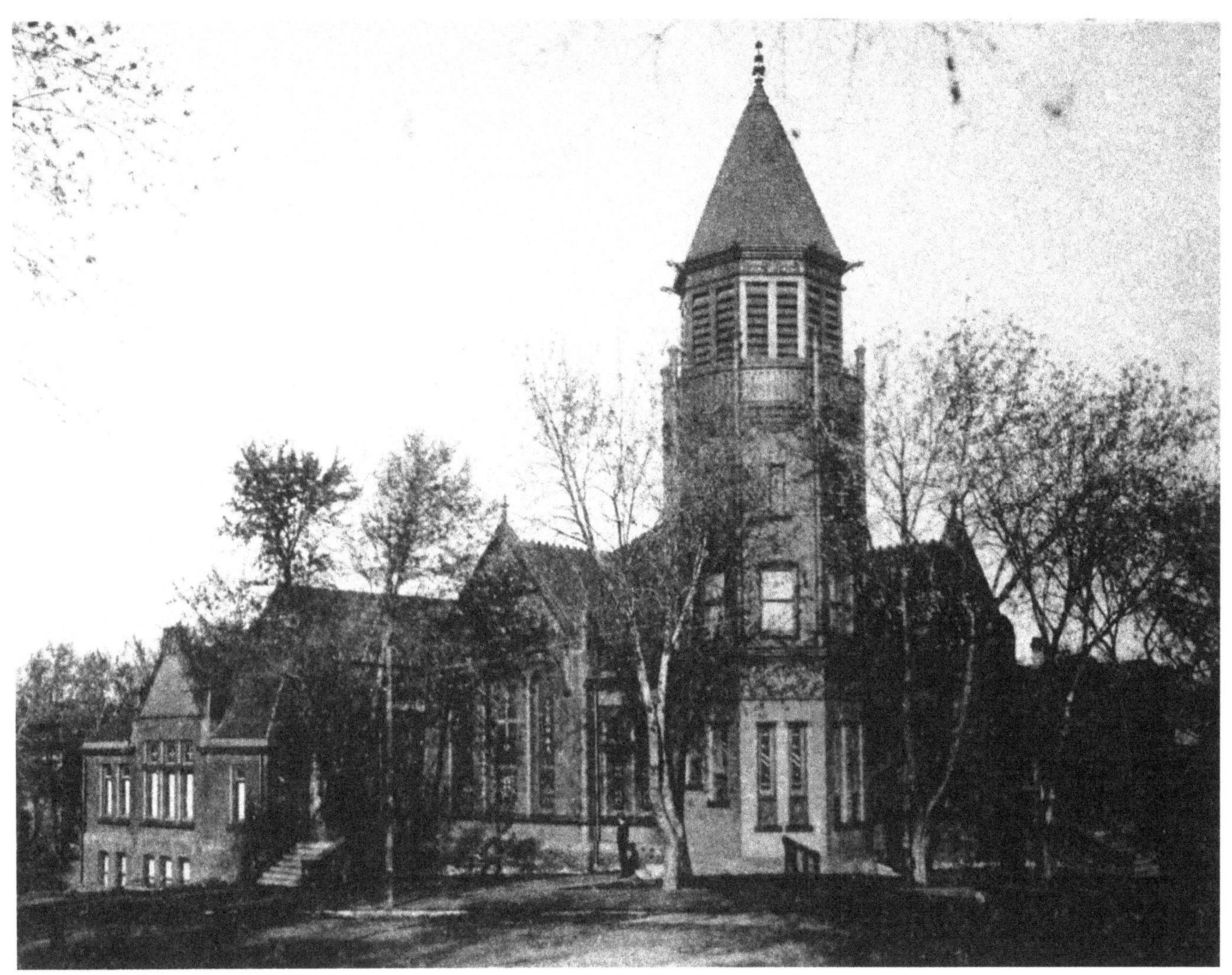

First Congregational Church, one of the oldest congregations in Omaha, built the first Protestant church in the city in 1856. The building shown here, on the northwest corner of 19th and Davenport streets, was the third church erected by this congregation and was constructed at a cost of $60,000 in 1888. This picture was taken a few years later. It served the congregation until it was sold in 1920 to the Labor Temple of Omaha. The structure was razed in 1954 to make way for the new Omaha City Auditorium.

This image of the Nebraska Territorial Capitol located in Capitol Square at 20th and Dodge streets, dates from about 1869. It was in use as the territorial capitol from approximately 1858 to 1867. The building was 137 feet × 93 feet, with the supreme court, library, and government offices on the first floor. The legislative and governor's offices were on the second floor. In 1867, when Nebraska became a state, the capital was moved to Lincoln. In 1869, the building and grounds were presented to Omaha. By 1870, it was completely torn down and by 1872, it was replaced by Omaha High School.

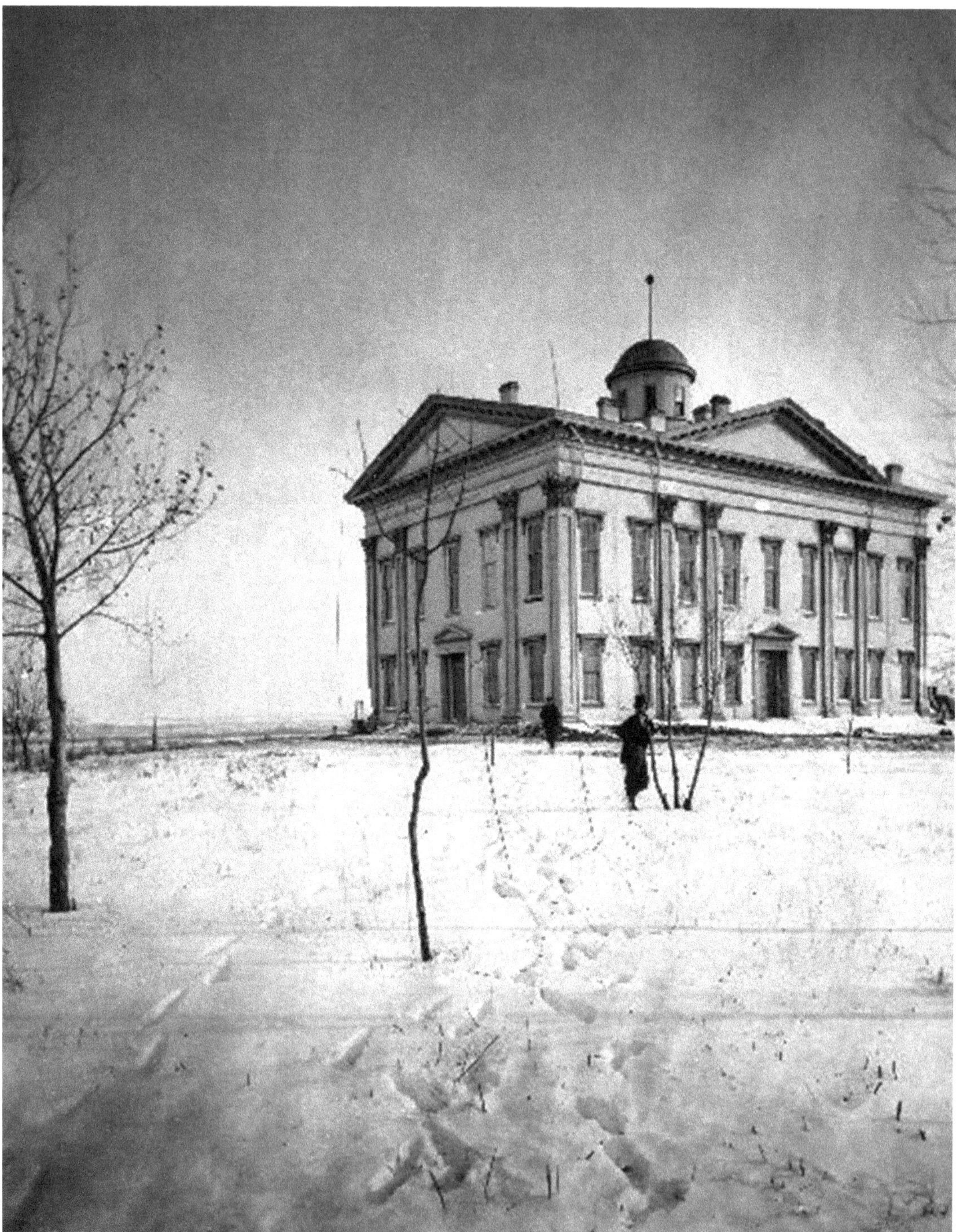

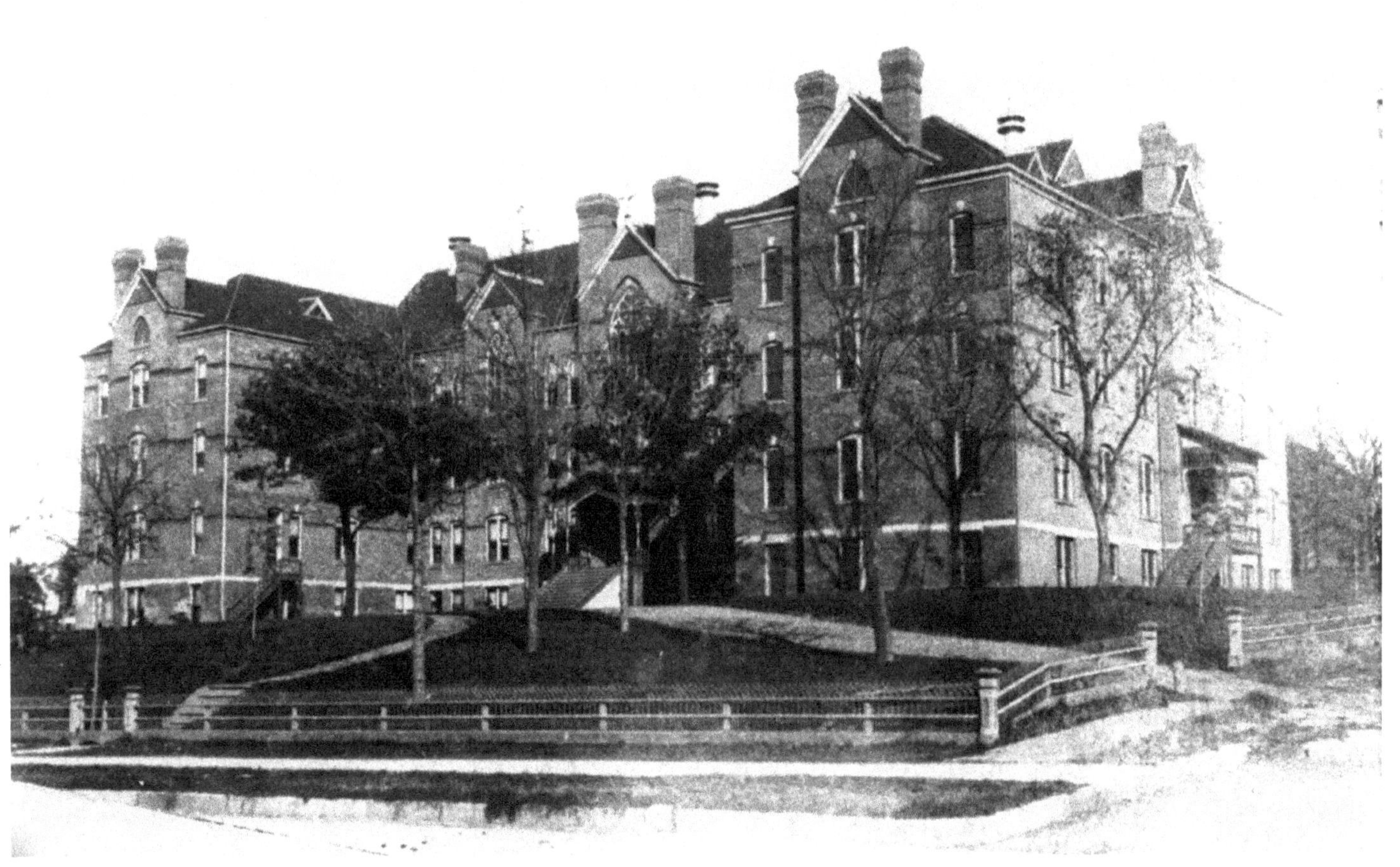

Construction of the new Brownell Hall began in 1886 and was completed in January 1887, on property donated by Herman Kountze at 10th and Worthington. This was originally a private school for young ladies, under the direction of the Episcopal Church in Nebraska. This fine, brick building was 40 feet × 100 feet and designed in the shape of an H. In the early 1920s, this property was sold, and the school relocated to the old Happy Hollow Club at 55th and Underwood Avenue. The school is now known as the Brownell-Talbot School. The building pictured here in the 1890s was razed in the summer of 1997.

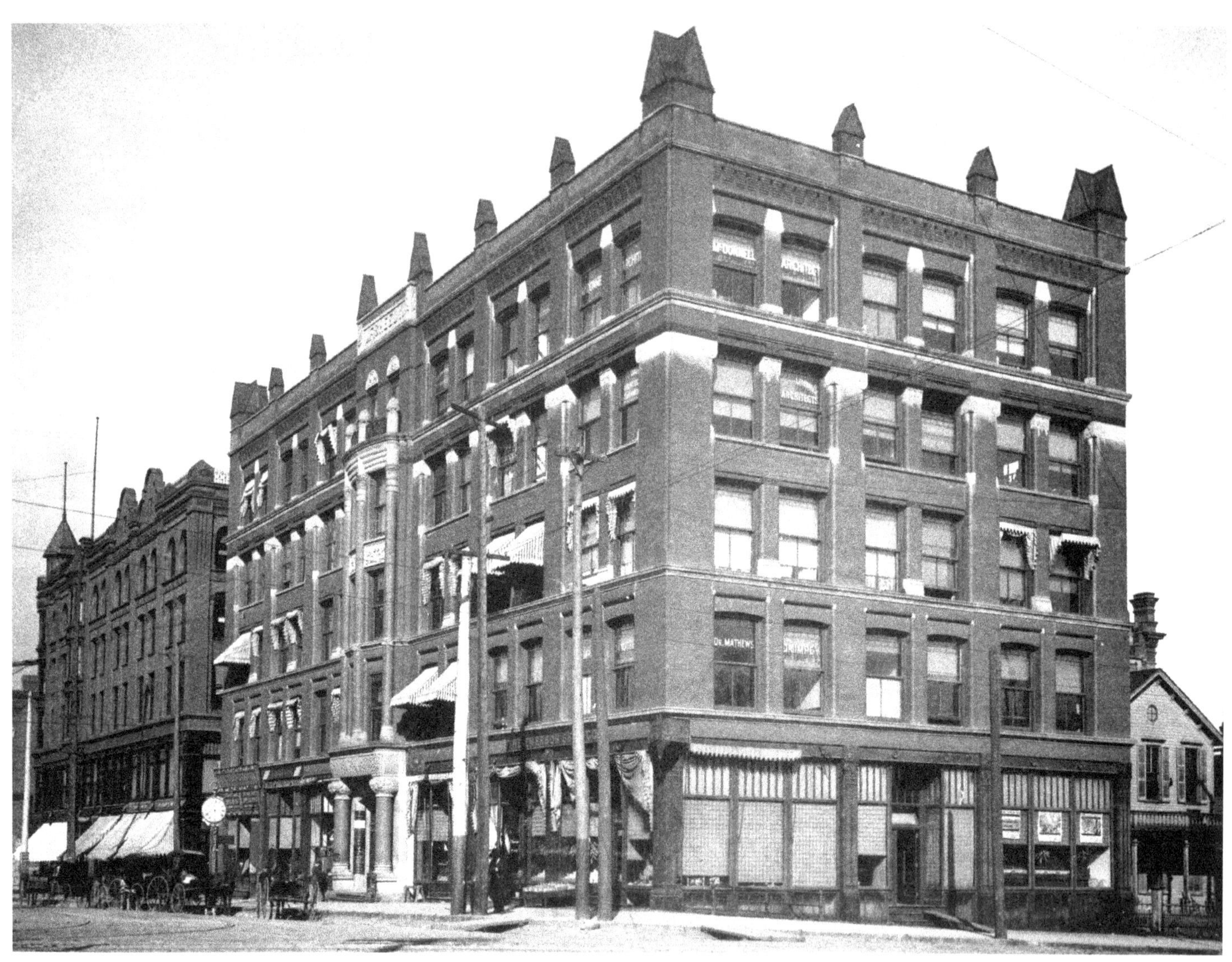

The Sheely Block, 419 South 15th Street. This office building was designed by prominent local architects Mendelssohn, Fisher and Lawrie and was built in 1887 at the northeast corner of 15th and Howard streets. The original cost was $116,000, and at the time the structure was considered one of the finest business blocks in the city. This is the building as it looked in the 1890s.

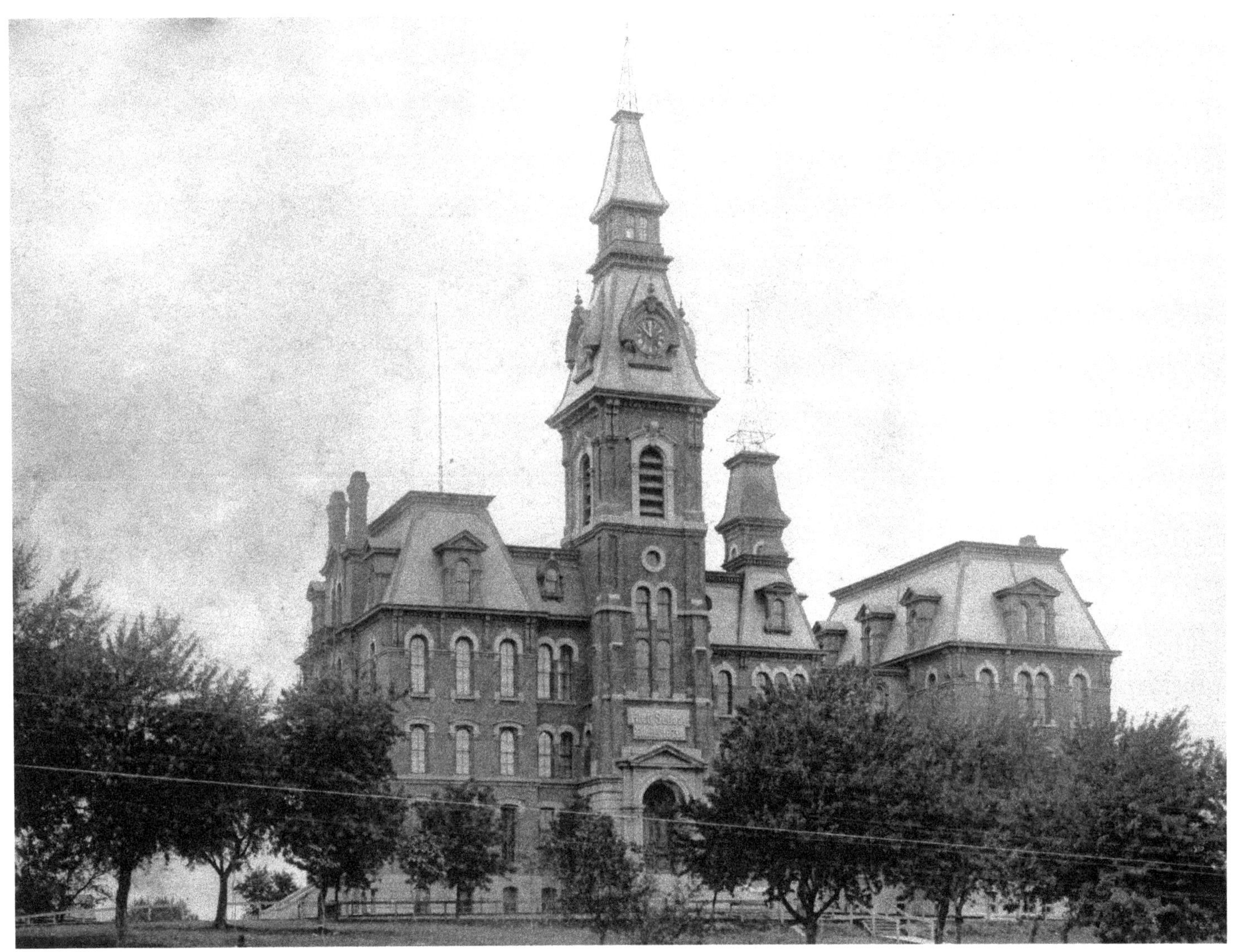

Omaha High School was constructed between 1869 and 1872 at a total cost of $225,000. This picture was taken about 1895. Designed by Chicago architect G. R. Randall, it was built on Capitol Hill, the site of the Nebraska Territorial Capitol building. On November 1, 1875, when President and Mrs. Ulysses S. Grant visited, they came to this building to meet a large group of Omaha schoolchildren. This structure was torn down after 1900, when a new high school was built on the same site. Today, Omaha's Central High School occupies this location.

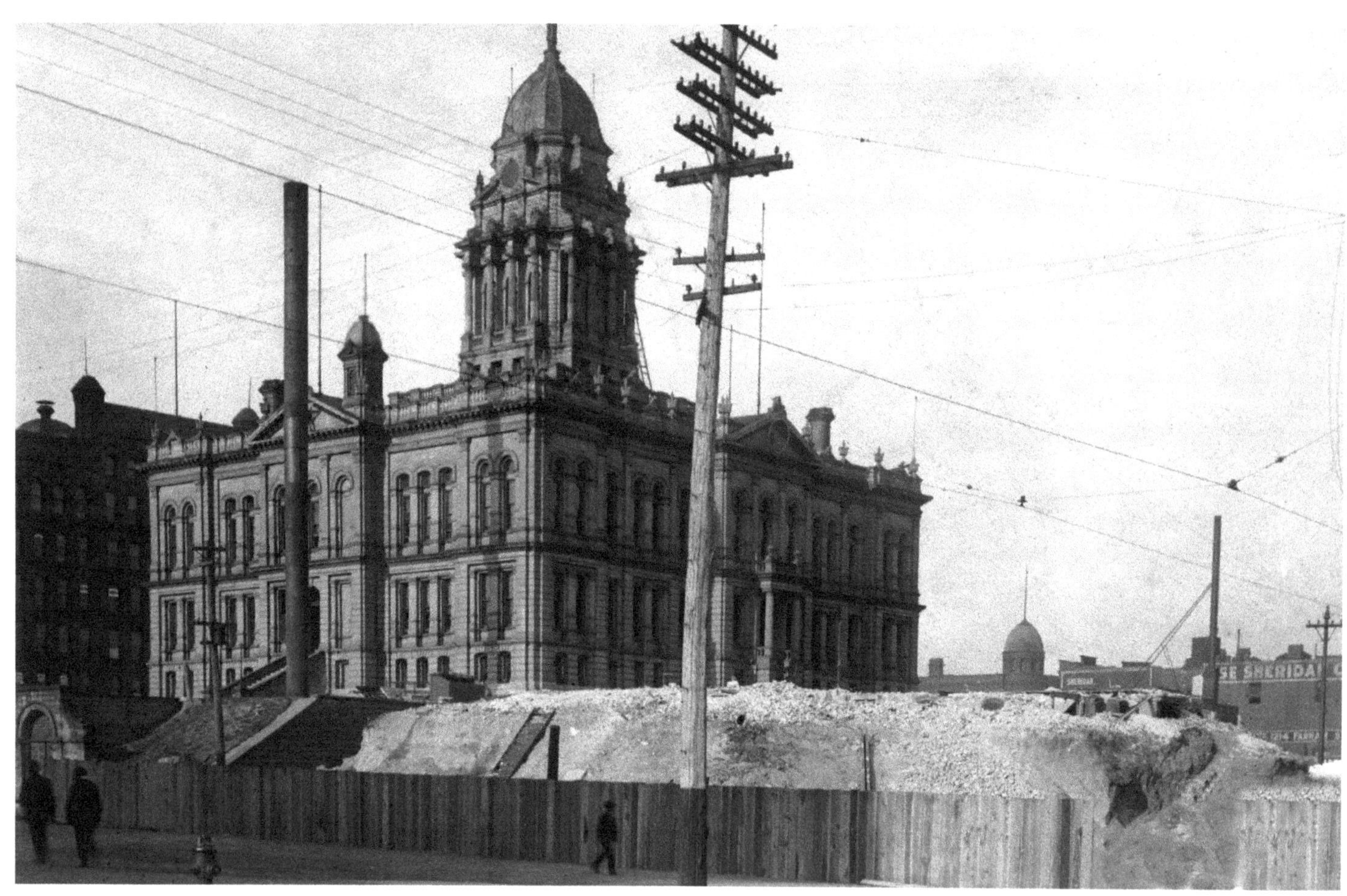

The Douglas County Court House, designed by E. E. Meyers of Detroit, as it appeared in the 1890s. The wooden retaining wall holds back earth being removed as the street was lowered to cut down the hill on which the courthouse was built. The location was between 17th and 18th streets on Farnam. It was completed in 1885 at a cost of $200,000 and opened with a large public reception that year on May 28. The building was razed in 1908 for the construction of a new courthouse at the same location.

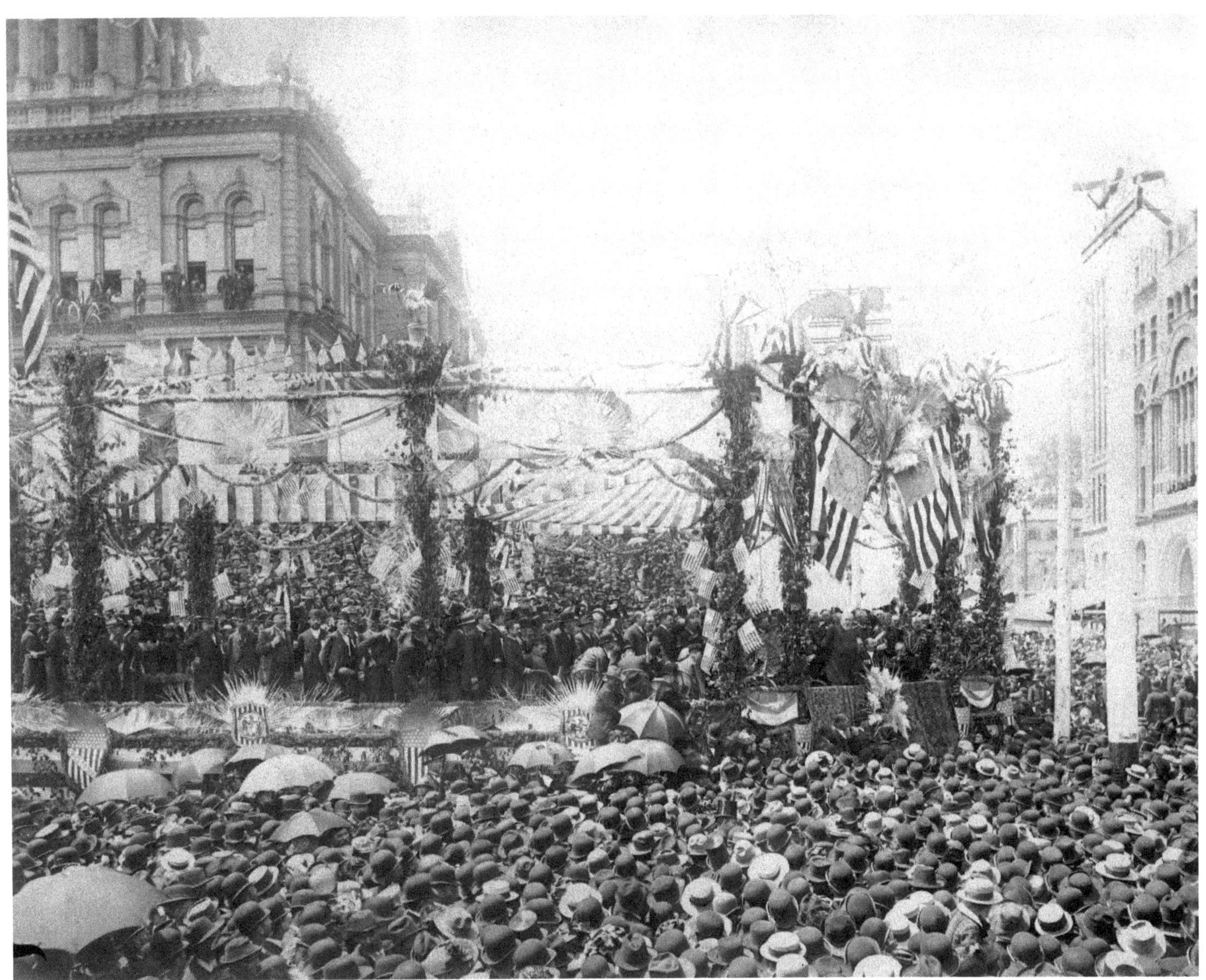

On May 13, 1891, President and Mrs. Benjamin Harrison visited Omaha. The presidential party proceeded by carriage to 17th and Farnam streets, where a speaker's platform had been constructed. This large crowd gathered in front of the Douglas County Court House to hear him. Later, a public reception was held in the atrium court of the Bee Building. Afterwards, the president visited Omaha High School and Creighton College before returning to Union Station.

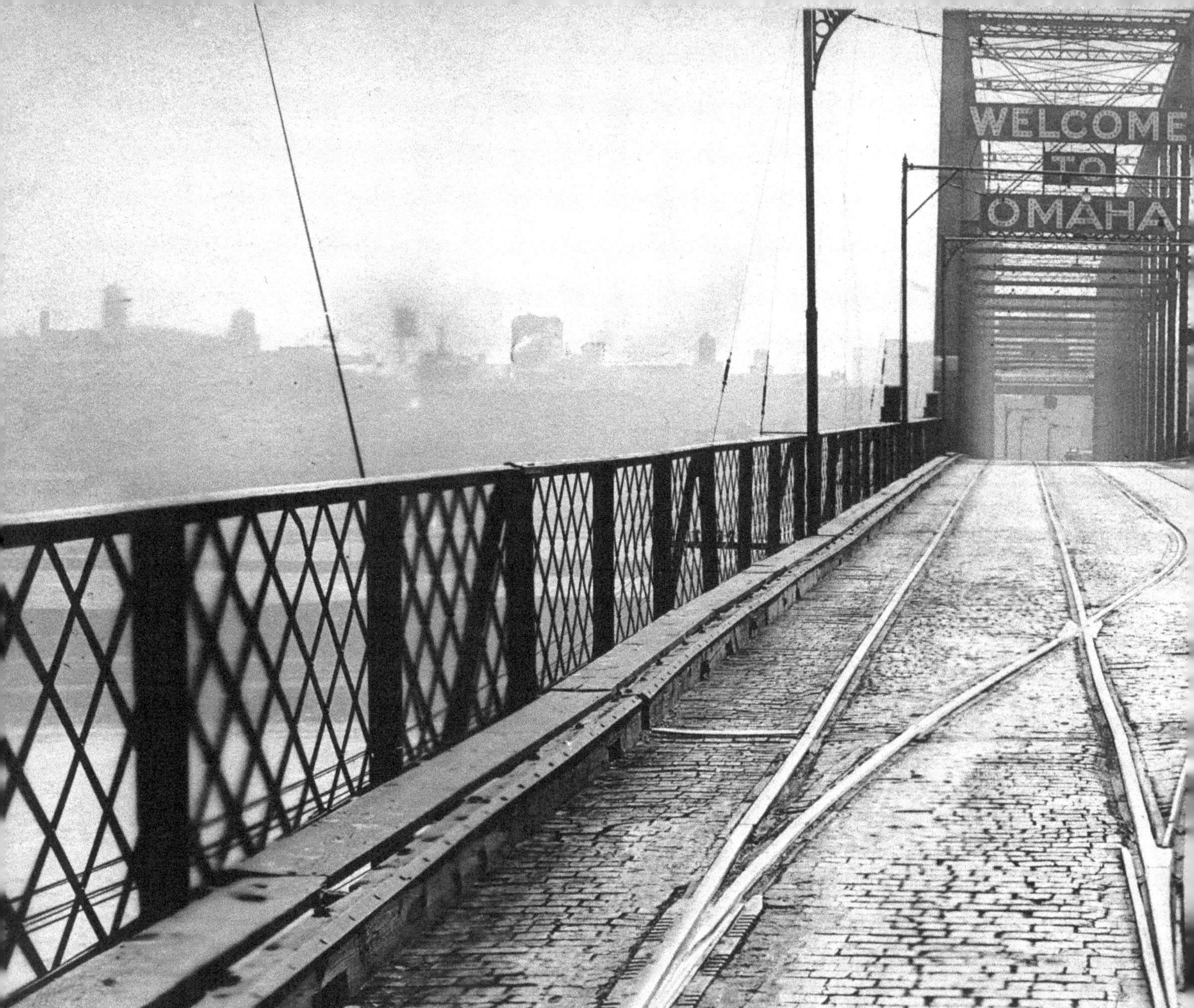

On April 1, 1887, the Omaha and Council Bluffs Railway and Bridge Company was organized to build a street railway bridge across the Missouri River at Douglas Street between Omaha and Council Bluffs, Iowa. The new bridge and an electric streetcar motor line opened on November 1, 1888. This view was taken in the 1890s, looking toward Omaha from the Council Bluffs side. The bridge stood until the late 1960s.

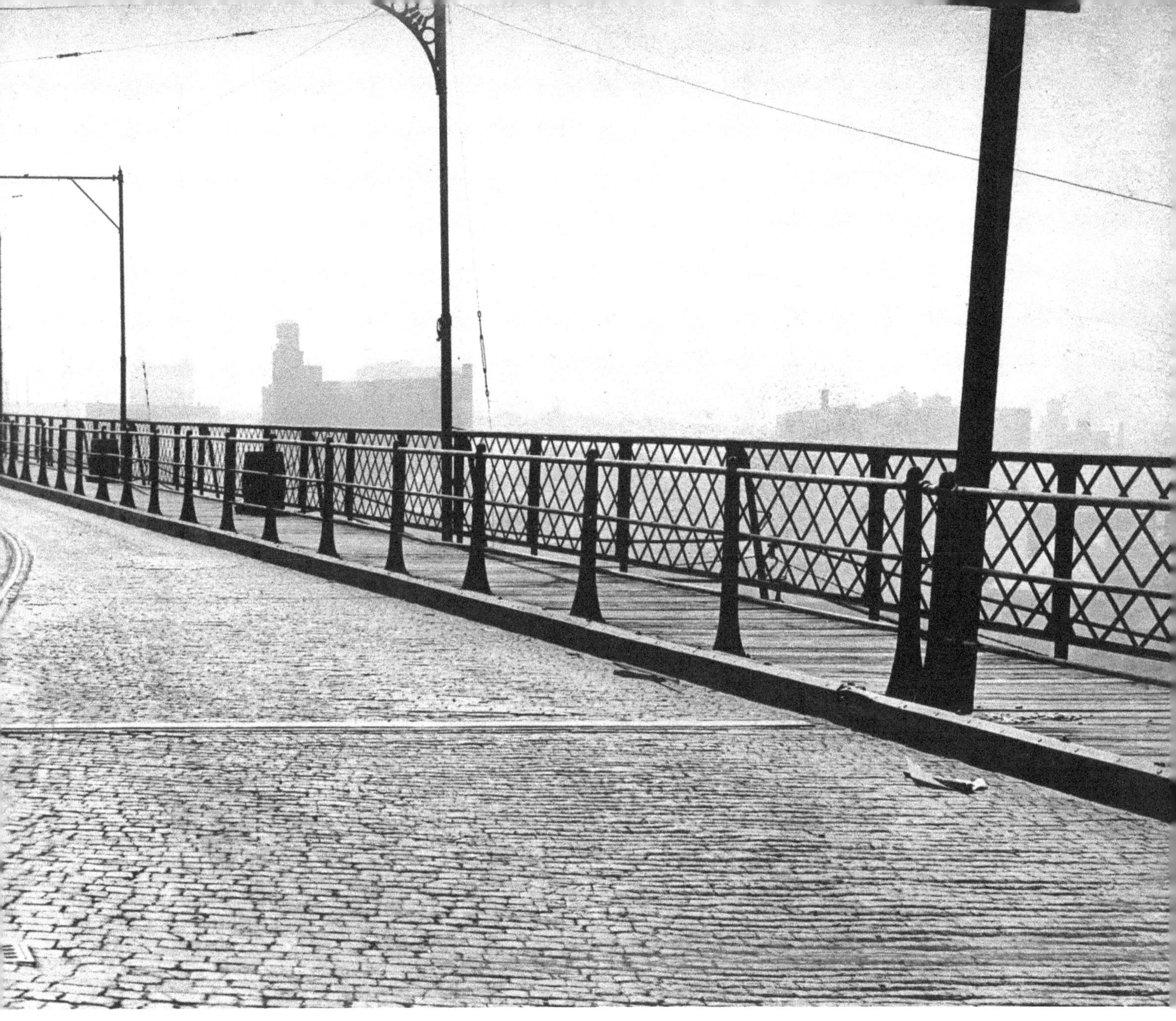

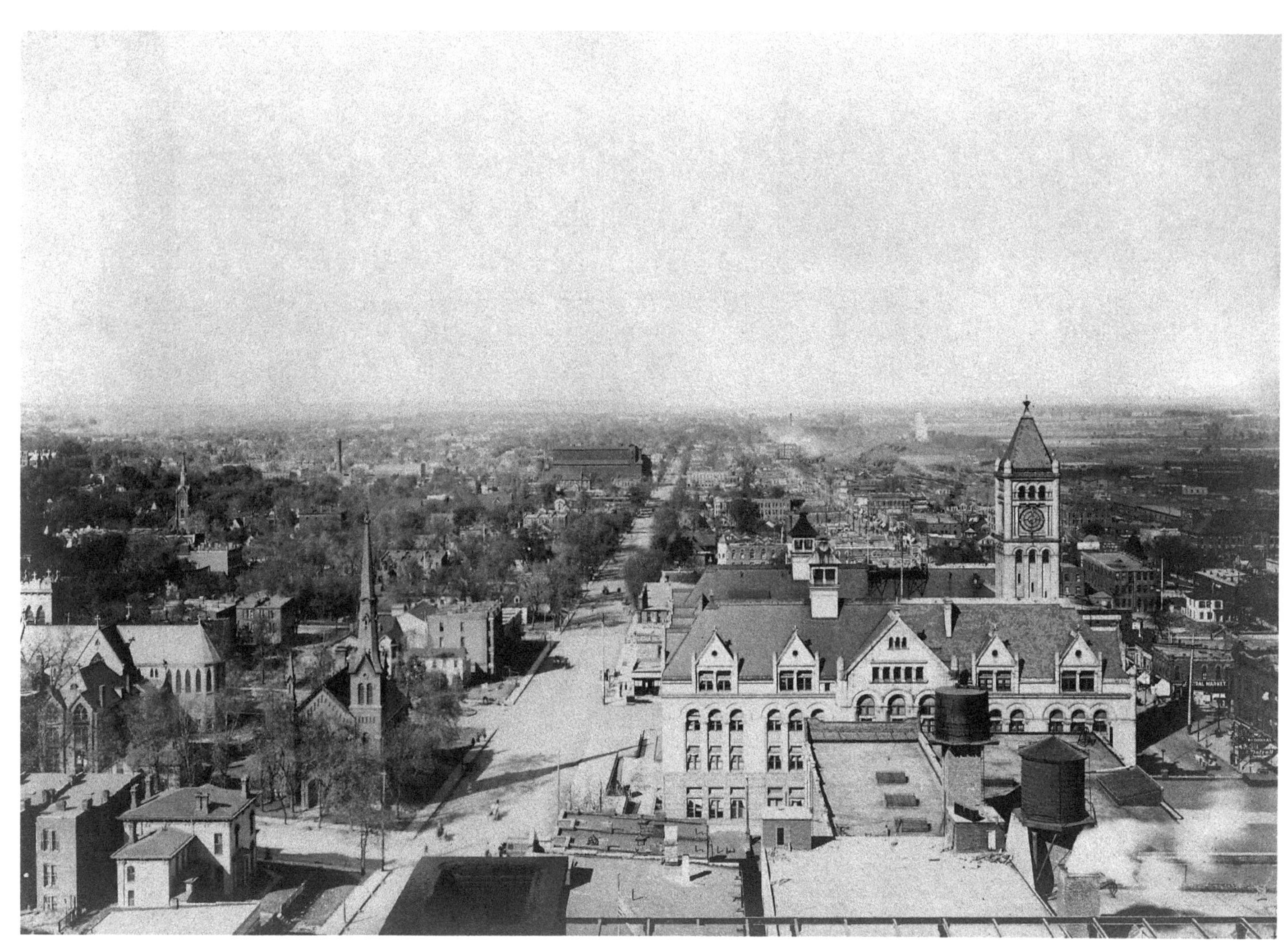

Omaha, viewed north along 17th Street. On the right is the new United States Post Office and Customs House. Trinity Episcopal Cathedral appears at the far left and to the right of that is the First Presbyterian Church.

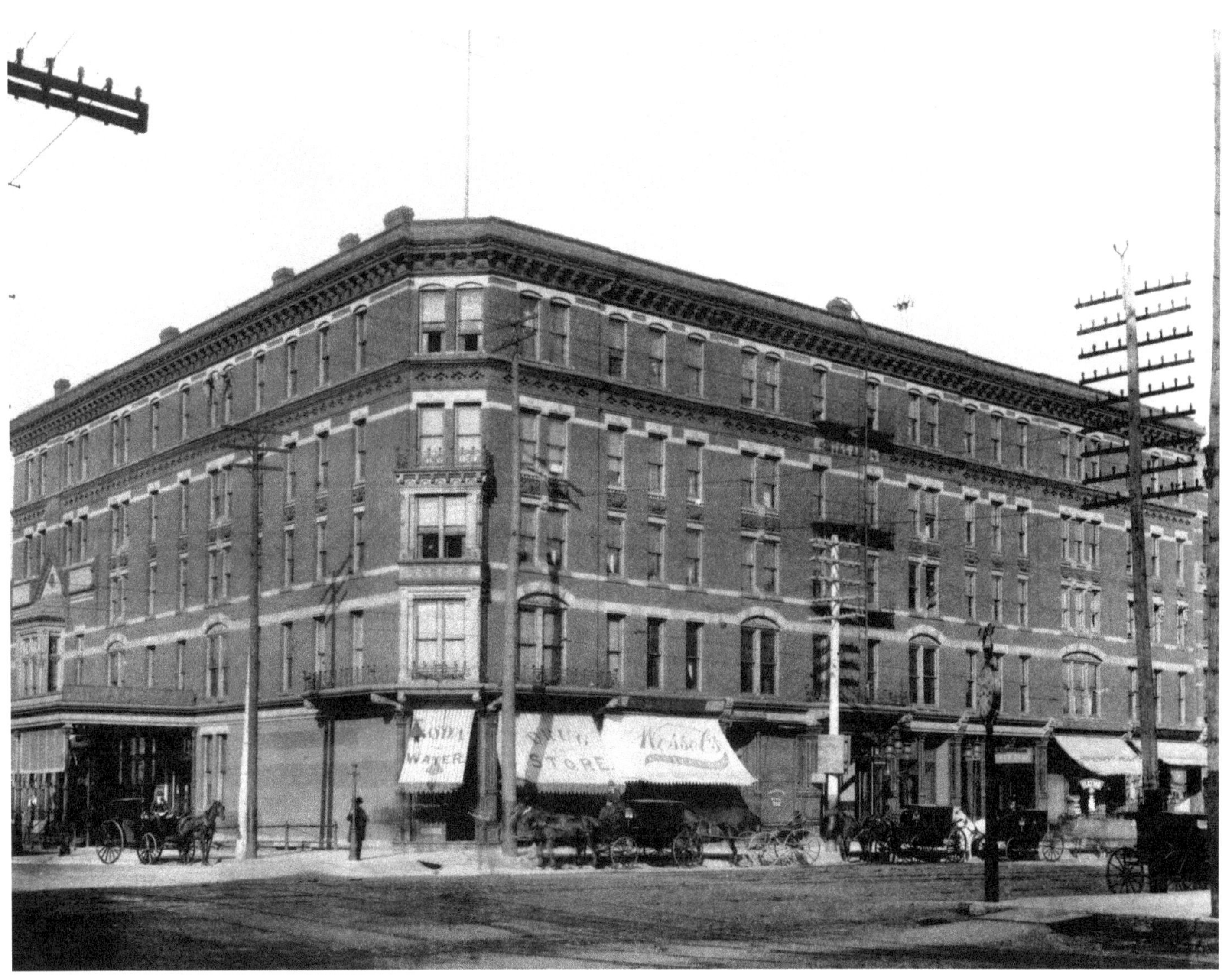

The Millard Hotel on the northeast corner of 13th and Douglas was a five-story, brick building that opened to the public in July 1882. Considered one of the best hotels in Omaha, it was the site of many community events. Although touted as "absolutely fire-proof," it was destroyed in a spectacular blaze on February 8, 1933, when temperatures reached 15 degrees below zero. Seven Omaha firefighters lost their lives, and twenty-two others were injured.

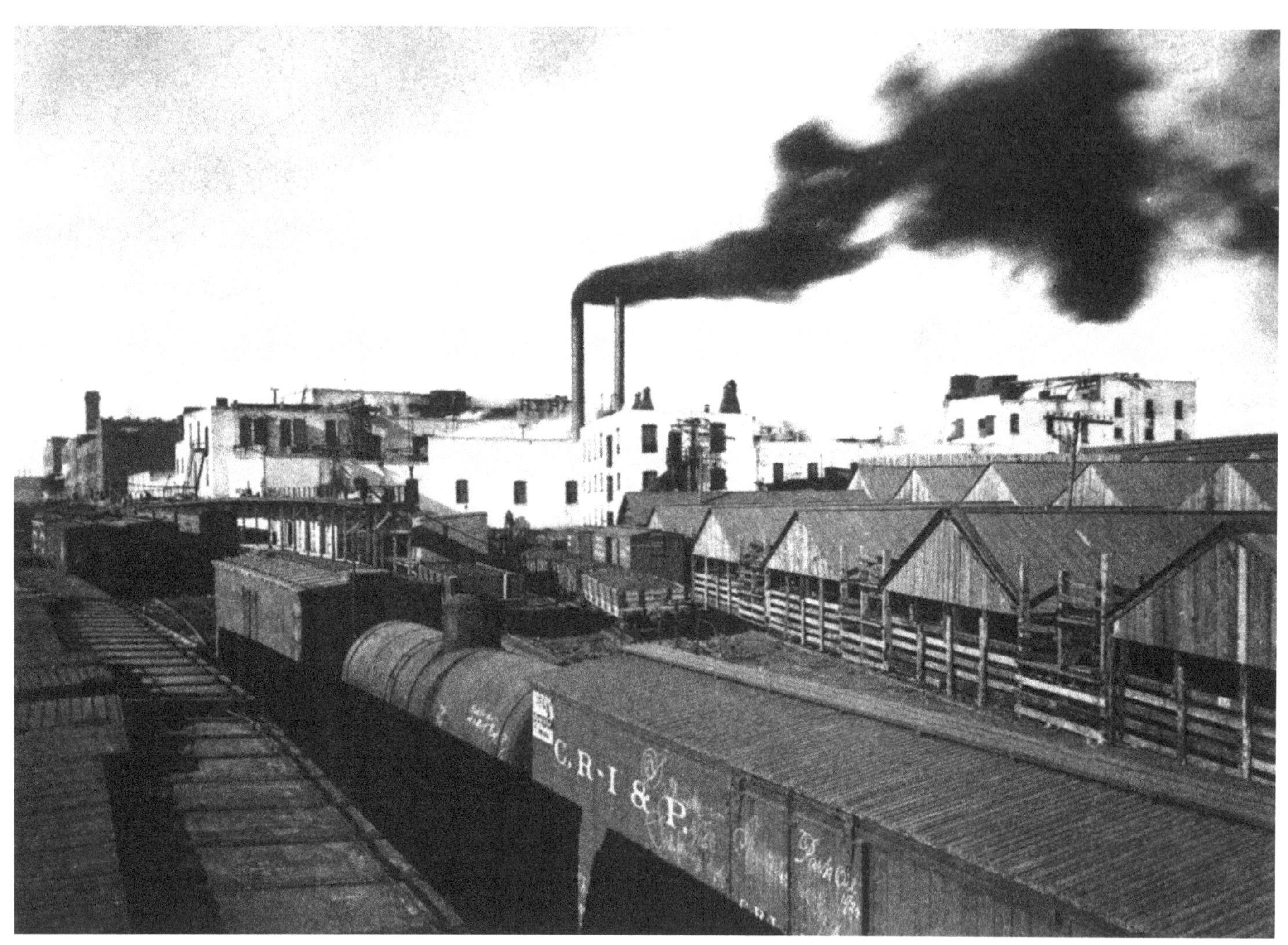

The Cudahy Packing Company cold storage plant, 33rd and O streets, in the late 1890s. Michael and Edward Cudahy started their meatpacking business in Omaha in 1887, when they built a large plant here. Reorganized in 1890, the Cudahy Packing Company became one of the largest meat processors in the country. The building shown in this view was destroyed by fire May 25, 1908.

This palatial, twenty-three-room, red brick mansion was built by Dr. Samuel D. Mercer at 3920 Cuming Street in 1885 for $60,000. It contained many costly and unique architectural features. Dr. Mercer had come to Omaha as chief surgeon of the new Union Pacific Railroad. In 1920, the house was divided into apartments and is still owned by the Mercer family.

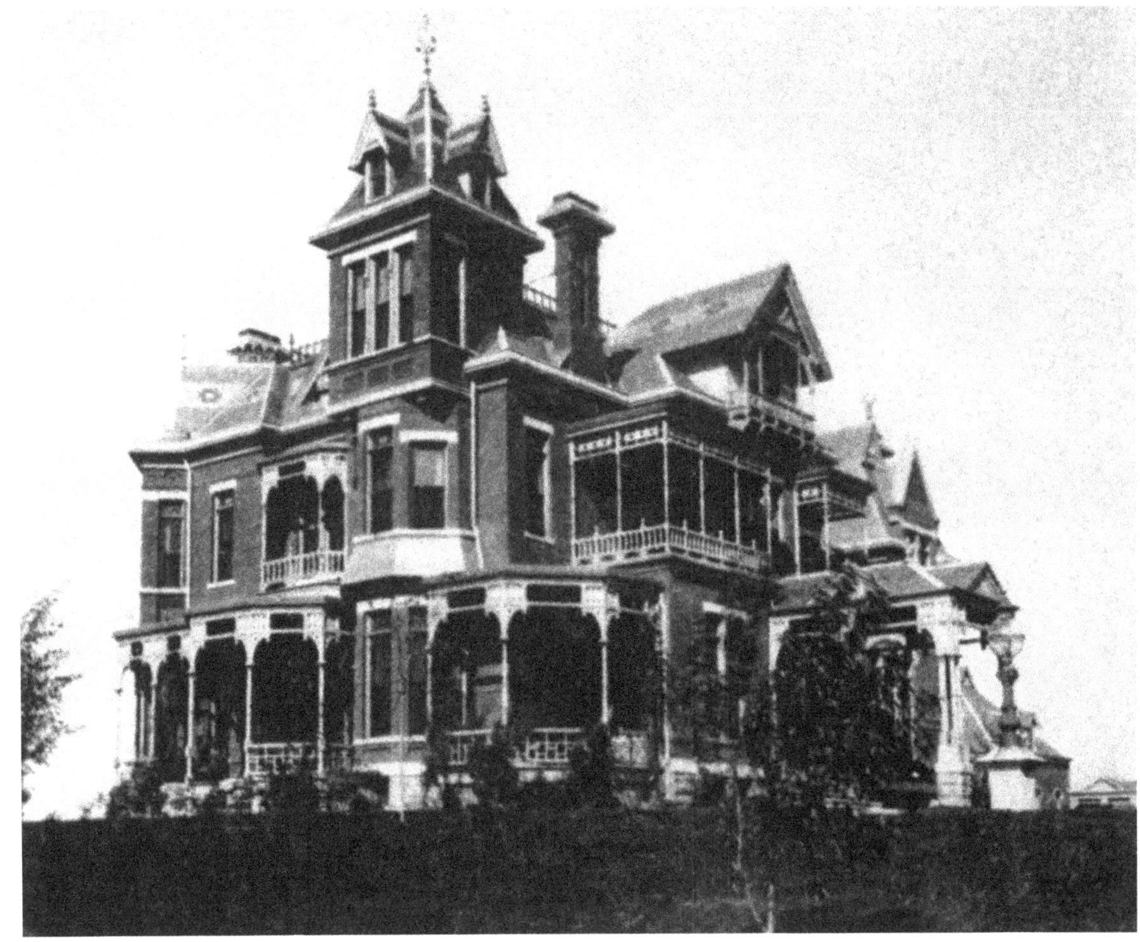

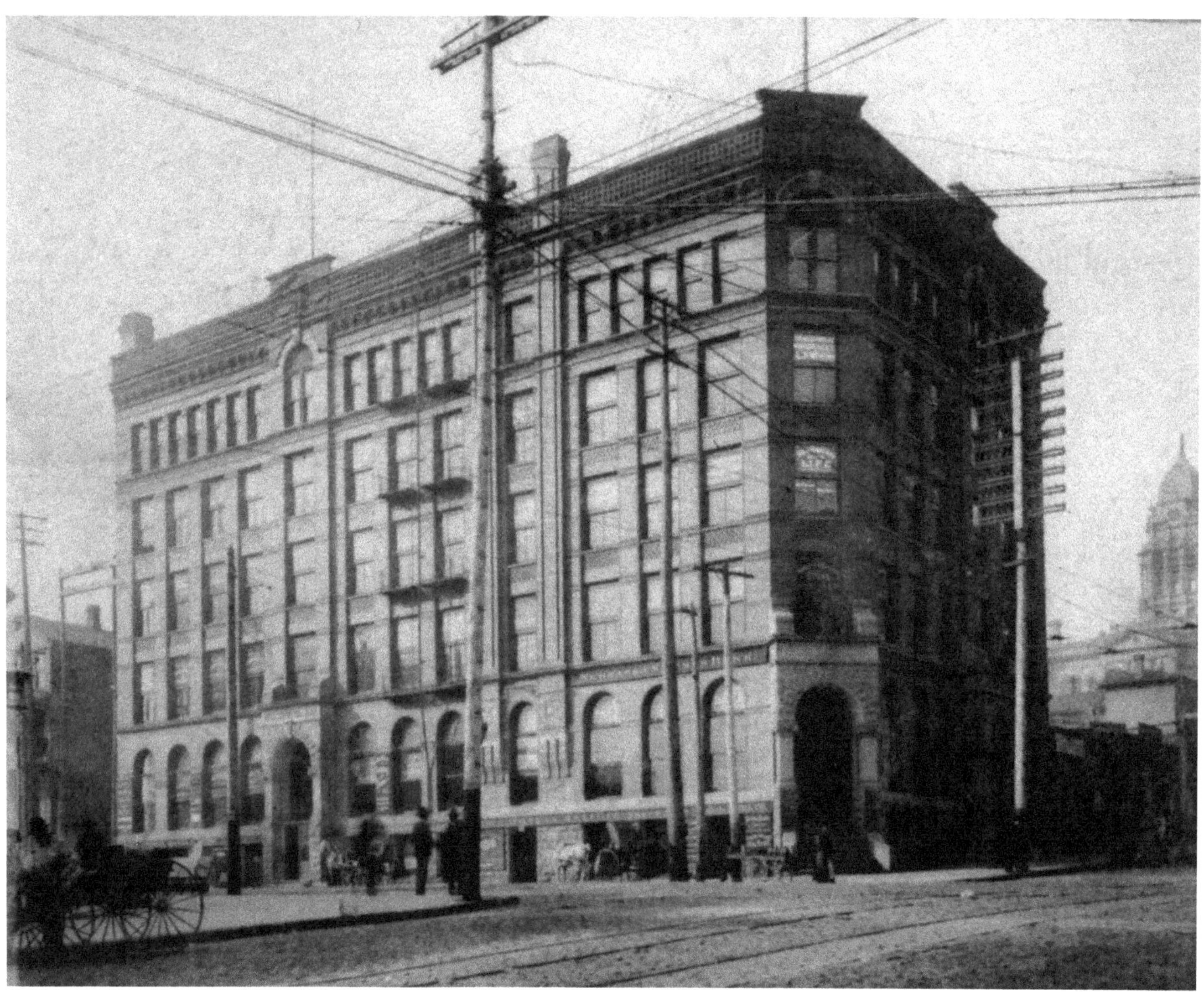

The Omaha Board of Trade building on the southwest corner of 16th and Farnam streets was completed in 1885. It was designed by local architects Mendelssohn, Fisher and Lawrie. Destroyed by fire on February 16, 1915, the property was then sold to the First National Bank, which built its new offices there. This photo is from the 1890s. The Omaha Board of Trade later became the Omaha Chamber of Commerce, which serves the city today.

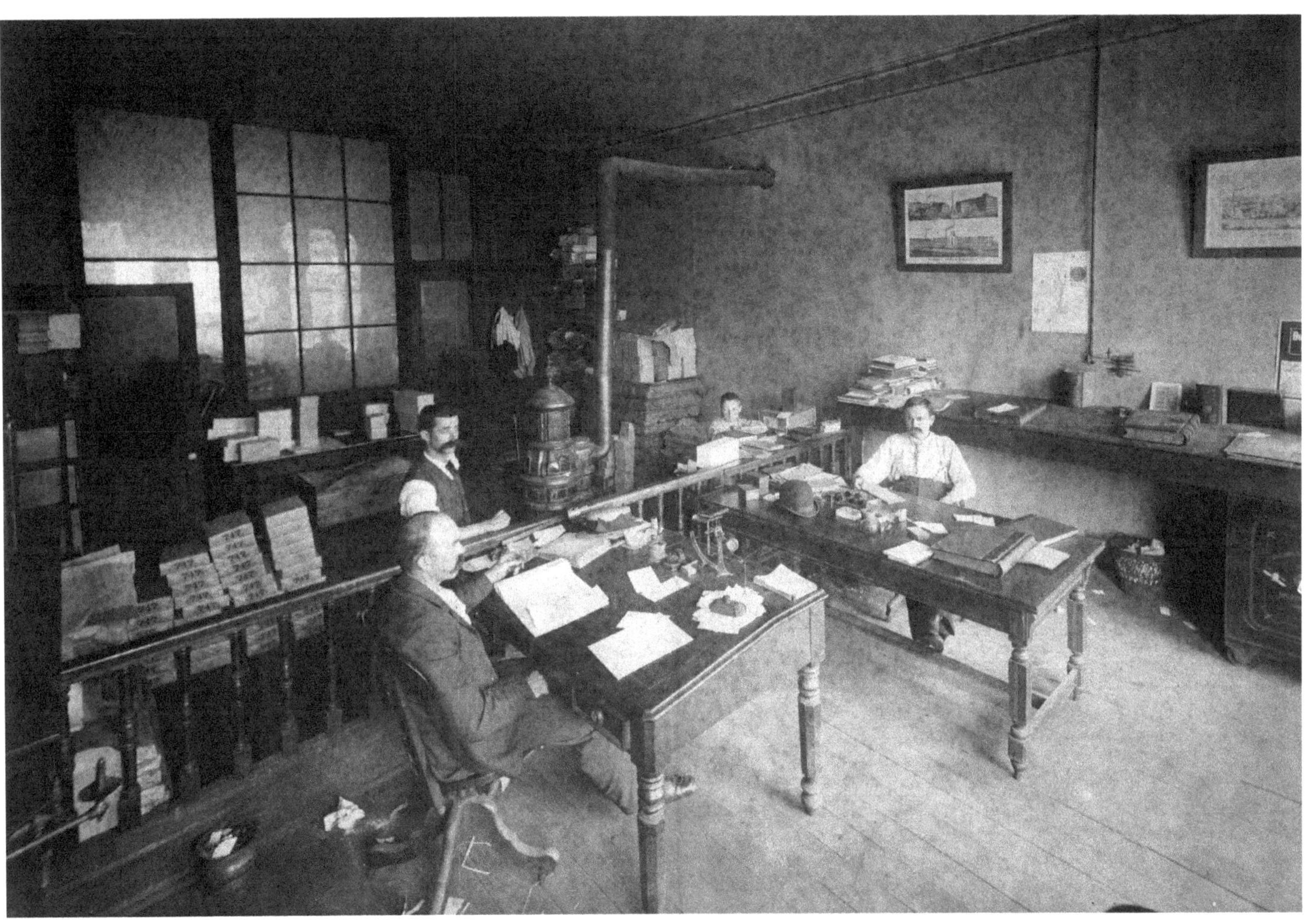

Interior view of the offices of Klopp, Bartlett and Company in the late 1890s, a large commercial and job printing firm located at 1114 Farnam Street. This company was organized in 1885, having taken over an earlier printing concern, and at that time they moved to the location shown here. Klopp, Bartlett and Company became one of the largest printing companies in the region.

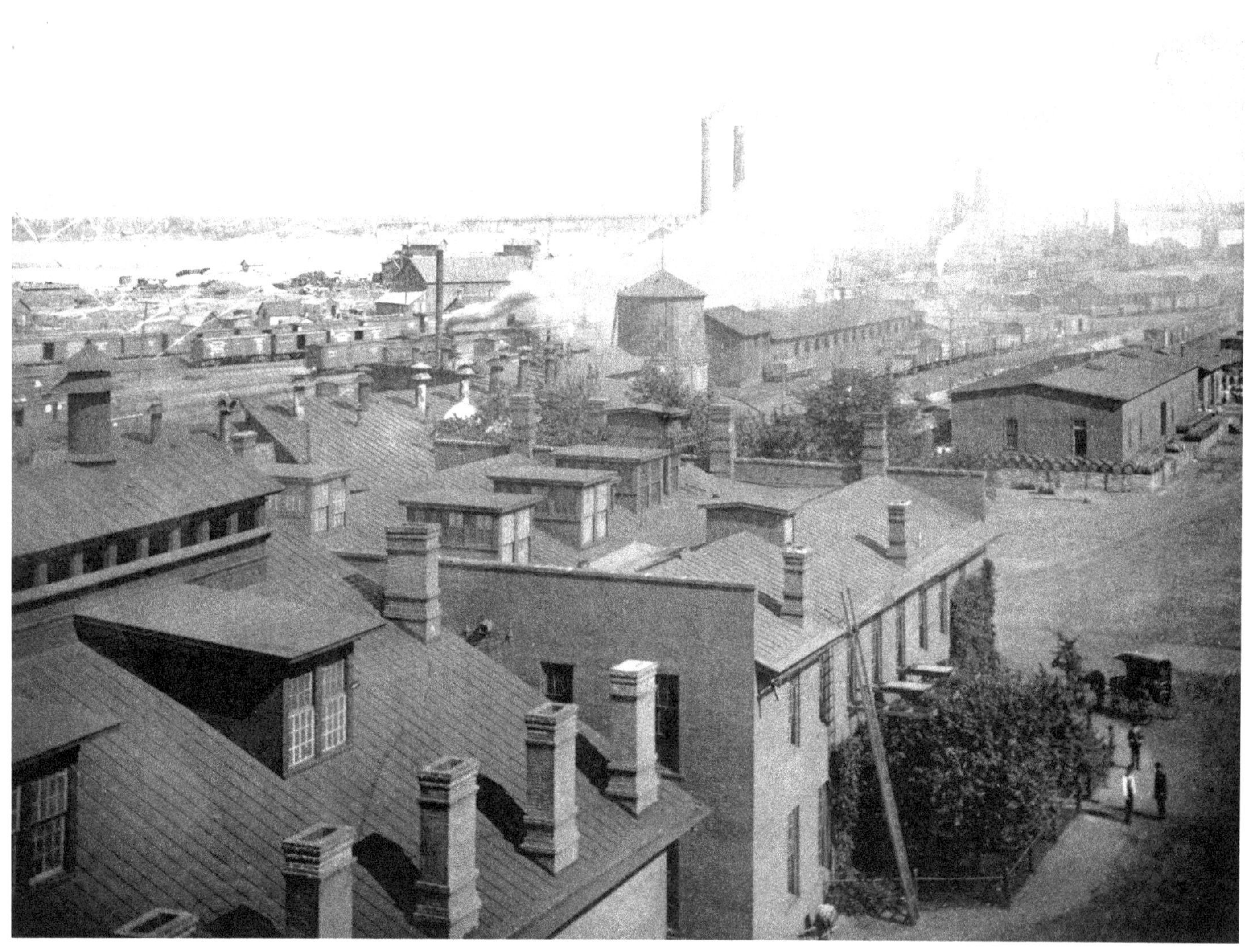

Photograph of the Union Pacific Railroad shops in the 1890s, looking east toward the Missouri River. The shops, located between 8th and 13th streets along Davenport Street, serviced all the rolling stock of the Union Pacific Railroad, which had its headquarters in Omaha.

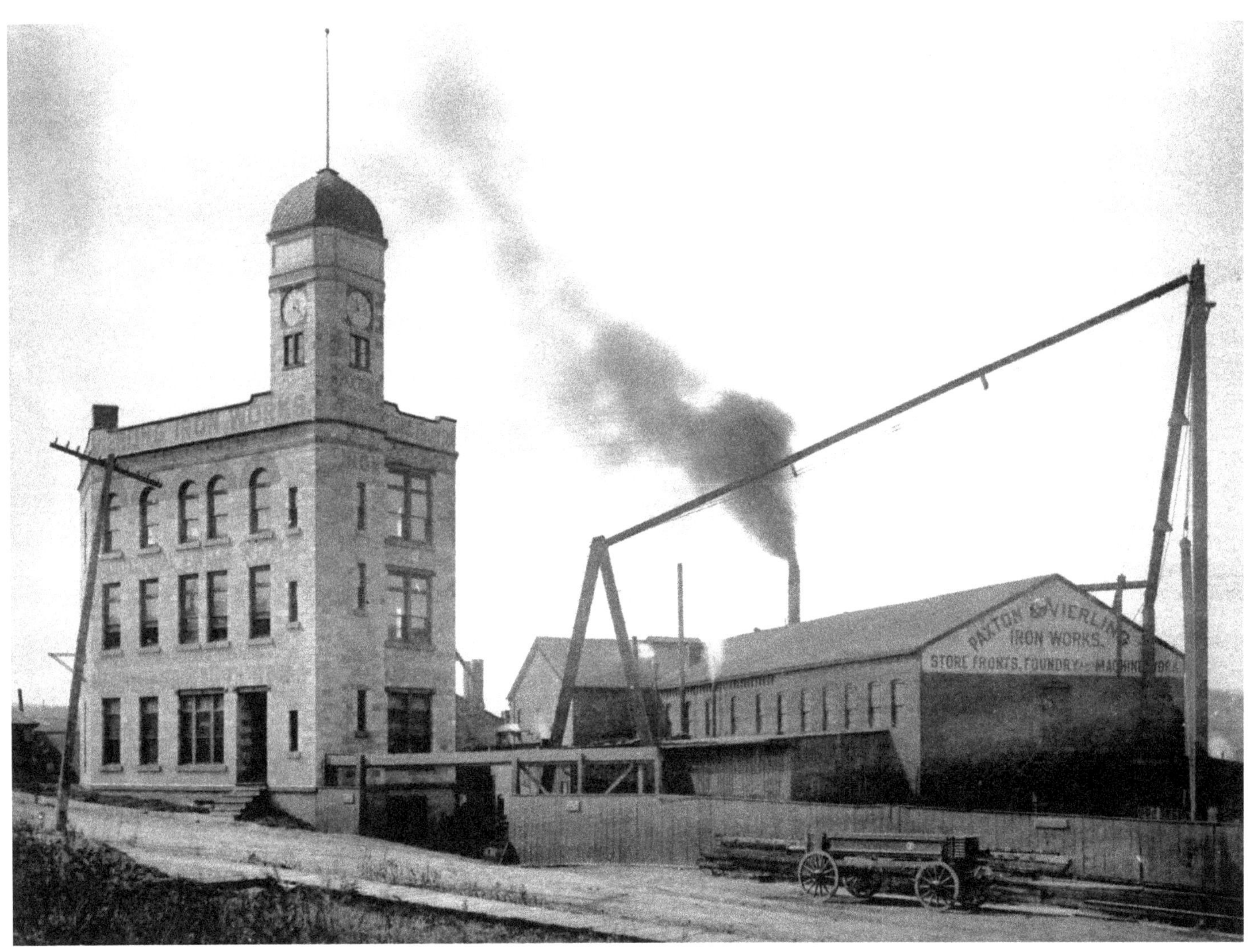

Paxton and Vierling Iron Works, located on 17th Street by the Union Pacific Railroad tracks, was organized and financed by capitalist William A. Paxton, in partnership with brothers Robert, Louis, and A. J. Vierling in 1886. This was one of the largest iron works in the region. This photograph shows the business as it appeared in the late 1890s.

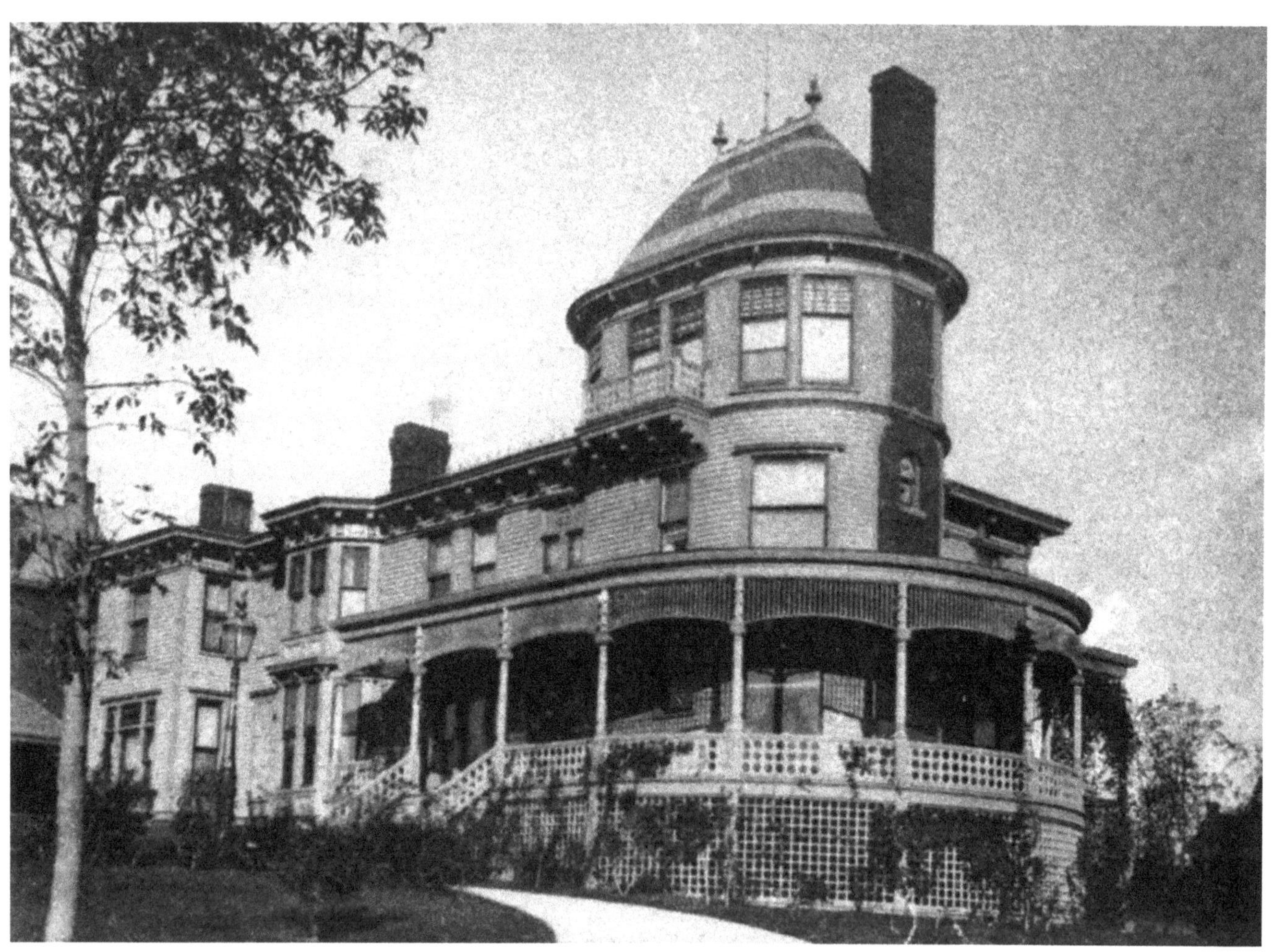

A photograph of the large residence of Joseph Hopkins Millard, located on the northwest corner of 24th and Harney streets. J. H. Millard came to Omaha in 1856, engaging in the real estate business. In 1867, he became associated with the Omaha National Bank, becoming its president in 1884. Elected mayor in 1872, he served as a United States senator from Nebraska 1901–1907. He died in Omaha in 1922.

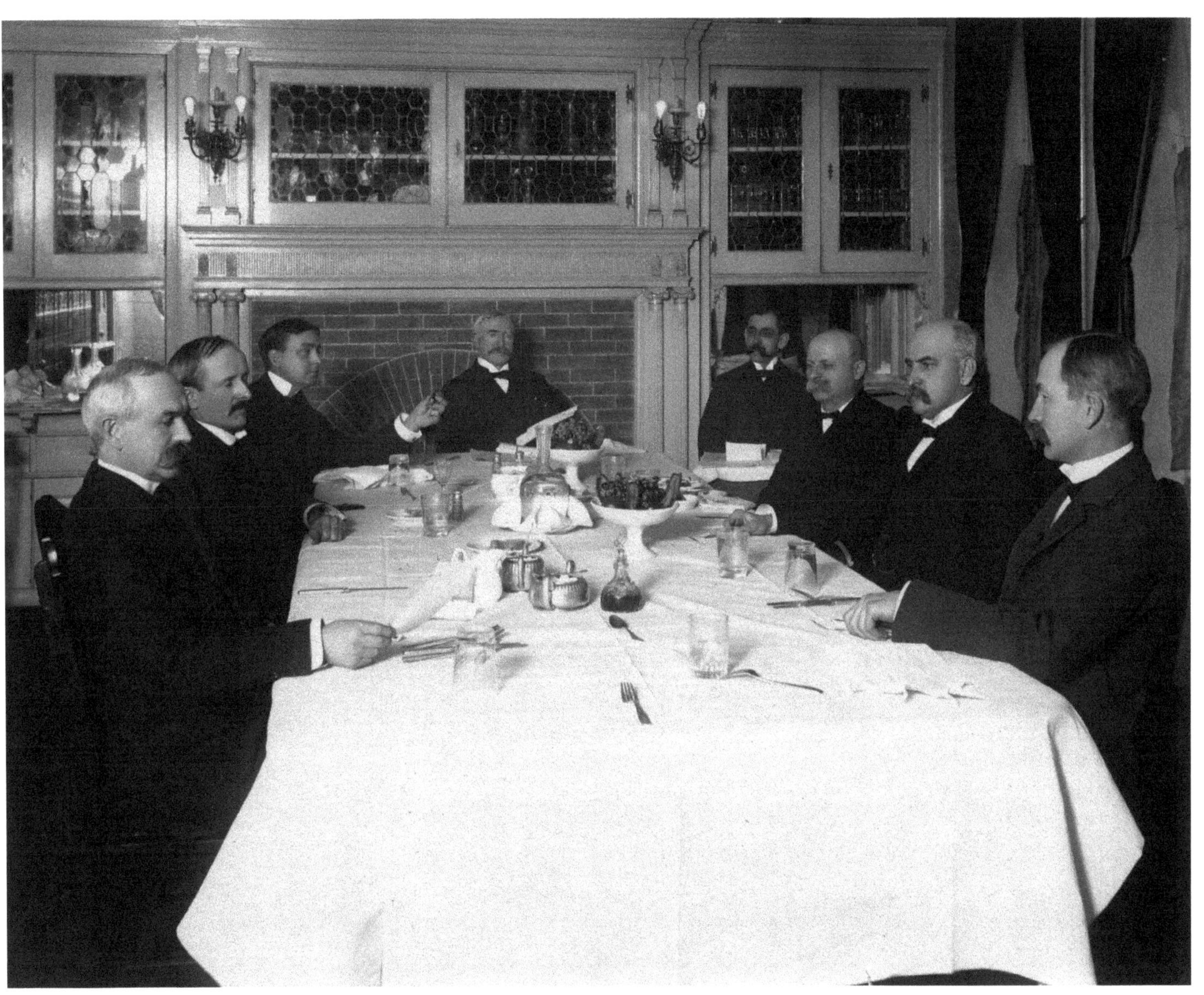

The Executive Officers of the Trans-Mississippi Exposition, meeting in executive session at the Omaha Club on 20th and Douglas streets in 1898. Left to right: Freeman P. Kirkendall, Edward E. Bruce, Abraham L. Reed, Chairman Zachary T. Lindsey, Secretary John A. Wakefield, Edward Rosewater, William N. Babcock, and President Gurdon W. Wattles.

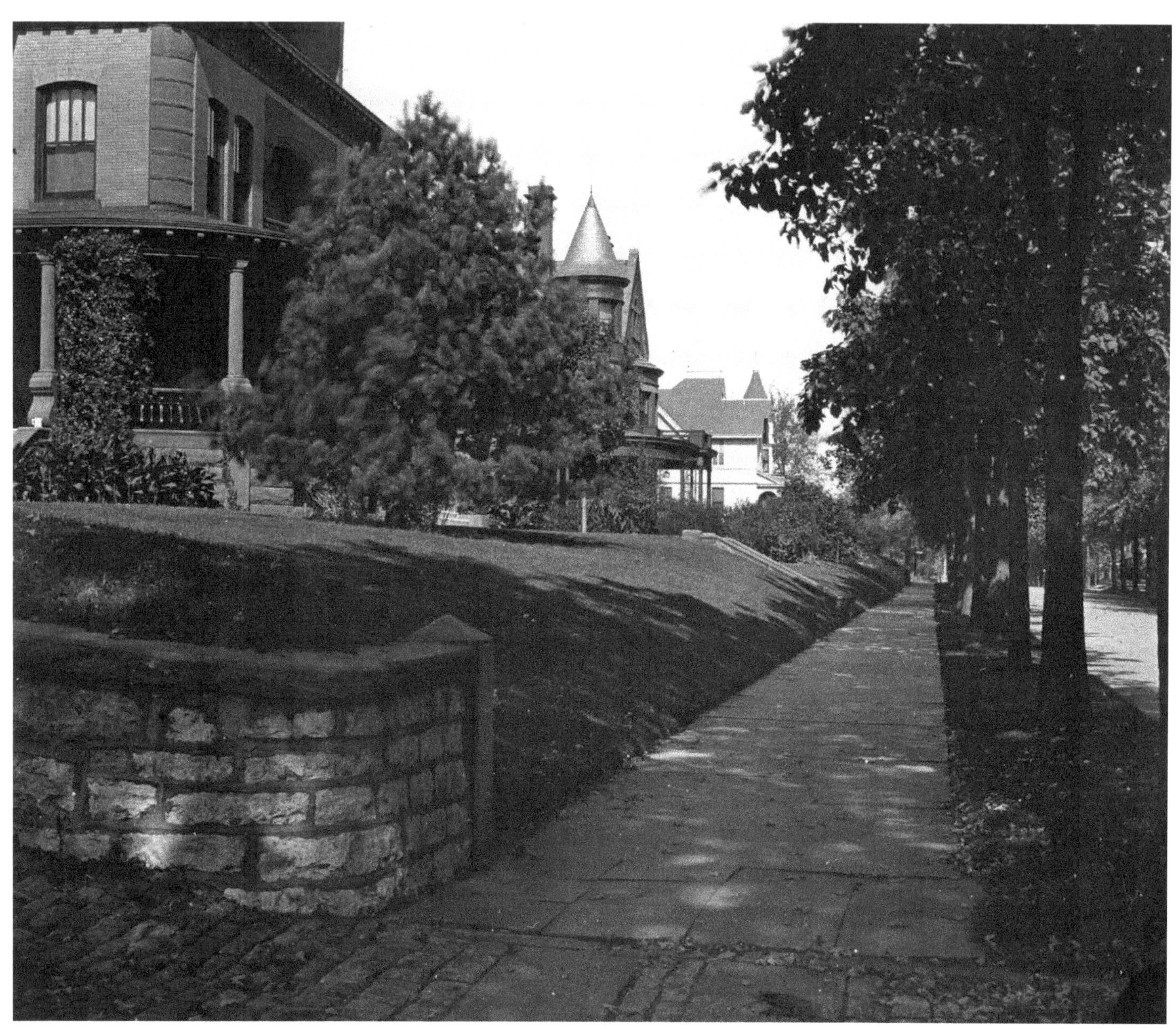

This was a residential street in the affluent "Gold Coast" neighborhood where many prominent families relocated, beginning near the end of the nineteenth century. The conical tower of the Charles Turner residence is visible in the middle of the block. Today, this area contains many of Omaha's architectural landmarks.

The first United States Post Office building in Omaha was located on the southwest corner of 15th and Dodge streets. Construction began in 1870 and was completed in 1874 at a cost of $300,000. It was built entirely of limestone. When a new and much larger post office opened in 1898, this structure became the Army Building, utilized for the headquarters of the U.S. Army Department of the Platte. It was later razed to provide the site for a new Federal Building in 1930.

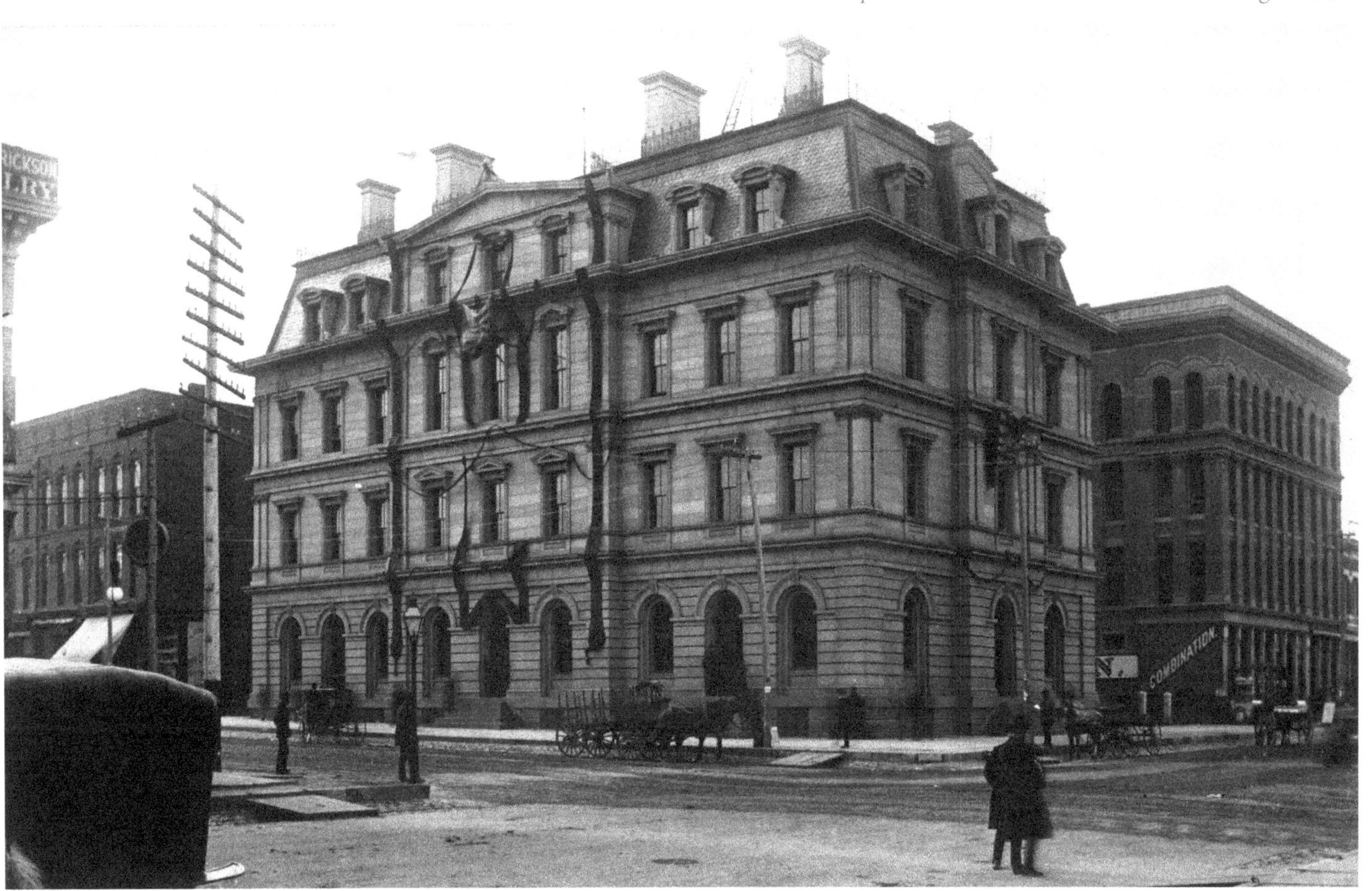

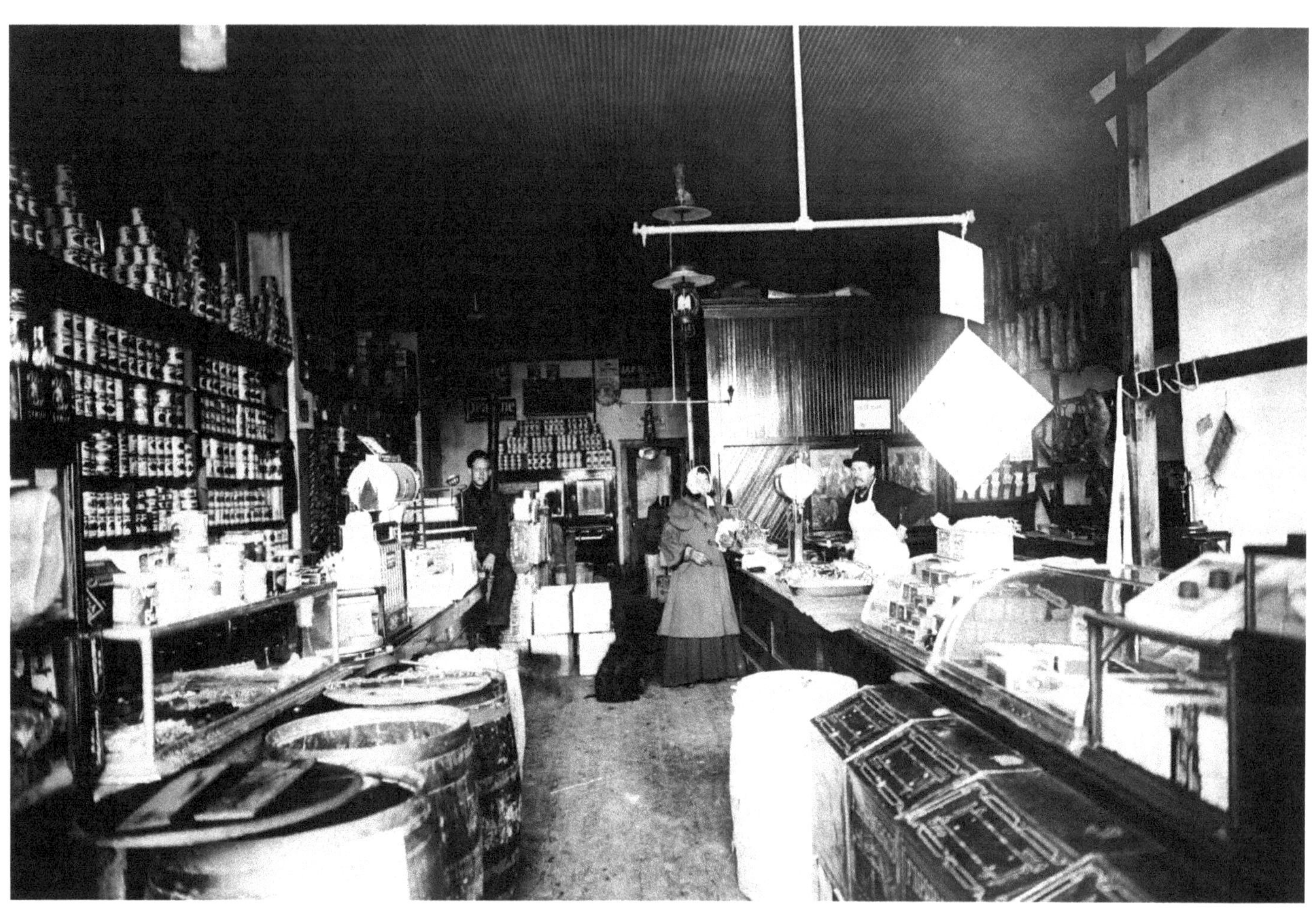

A typical interior view of a late-nineteenth-century grocery, Larson's Store, at 27th and Lake streets. At the time, almost all businesses providing goods and services were small, independent, neighborhood establishments such as this. Note the bins and barrels for holding various commodities. Individual packaging was rare.

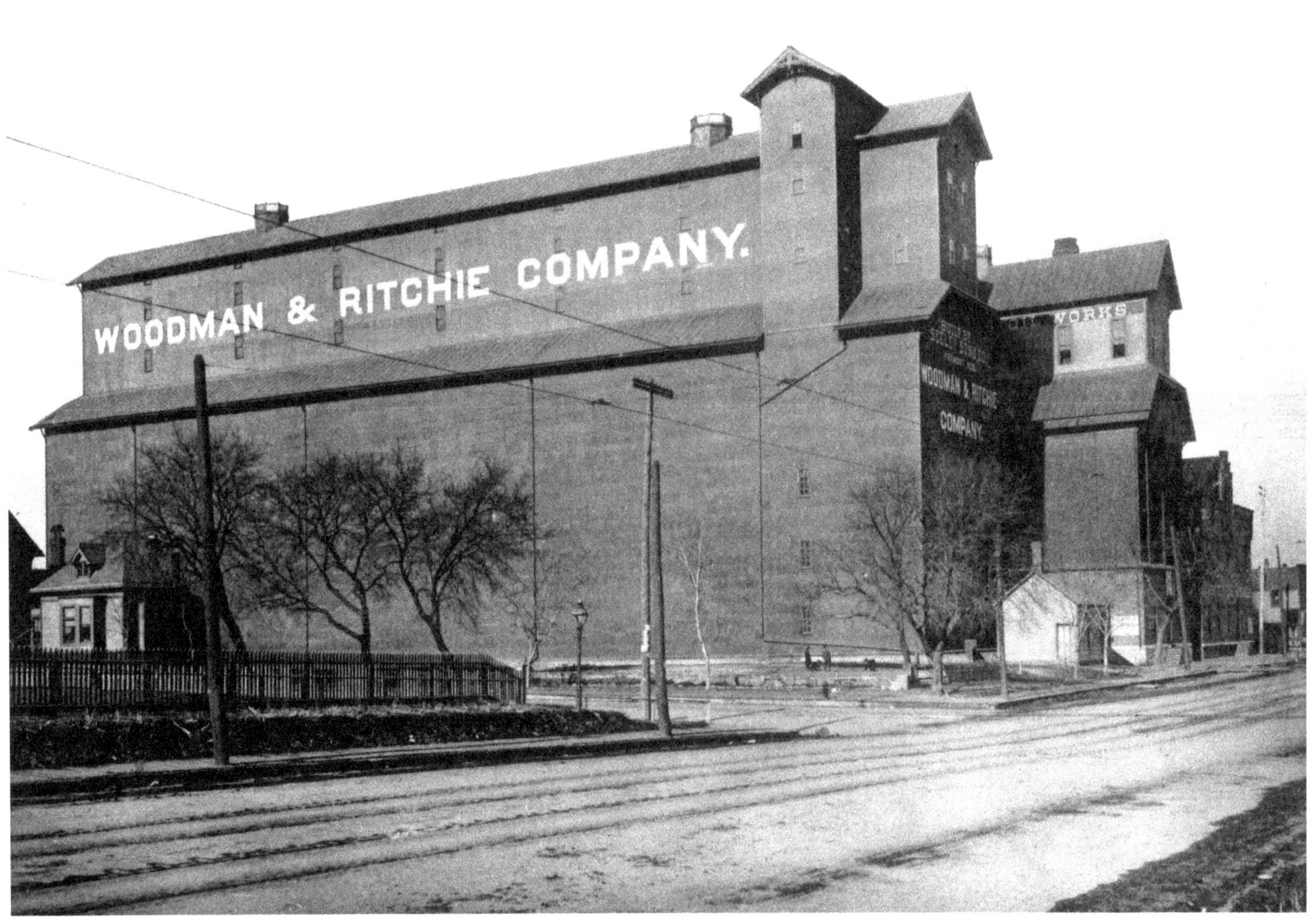

The Woodman and Ritchie Company, located on the corner of 17th and Nicholas streets. This large grain elevator with a capacity of 600,000 bushels was opened September 1, 1890, and operated by Clark Woodman and Frank E. Ritchie. The elevator was 140 feet high, one of the largest and most successful in the area. After the death of Woodman in 1891, Ritchie continued the business as sole proprietor. This picture was made in the late 1890s.

Portable bandstand being moved in Hanscom Park, 32nd and Woolworth streets, in the late 1890s. Hanscom Park is the oldest park in Omaha, established in the fall of 1872. It was named for pioneer Andrew Jackson Hanscom, one of the original donors of a 57.5-acre tract of land. With a lagoon, a large pavilion, and numerous walkways decorated with artistic arrangements of plants and flowers, it was an oasis of beauty in early Omaha.

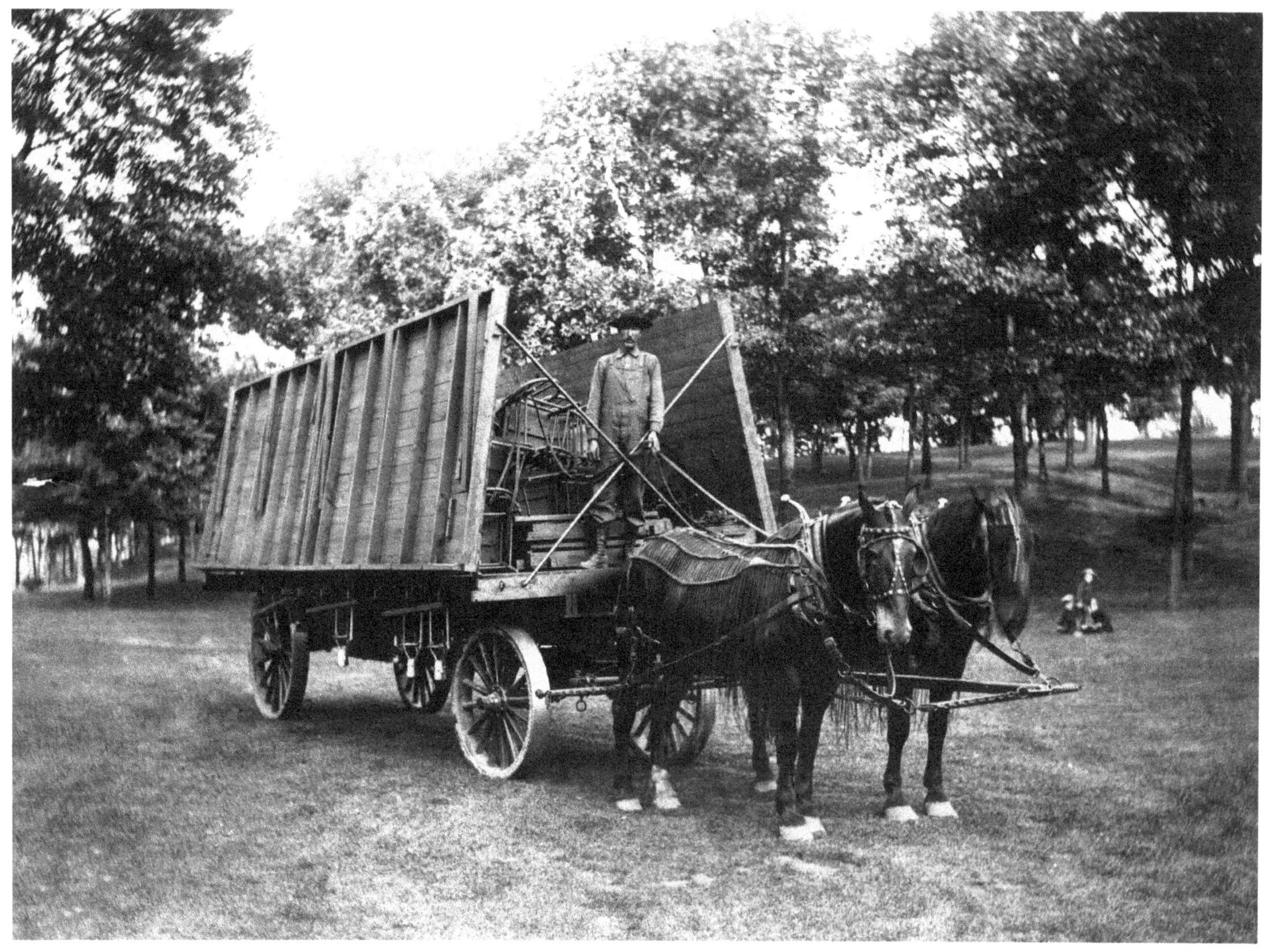

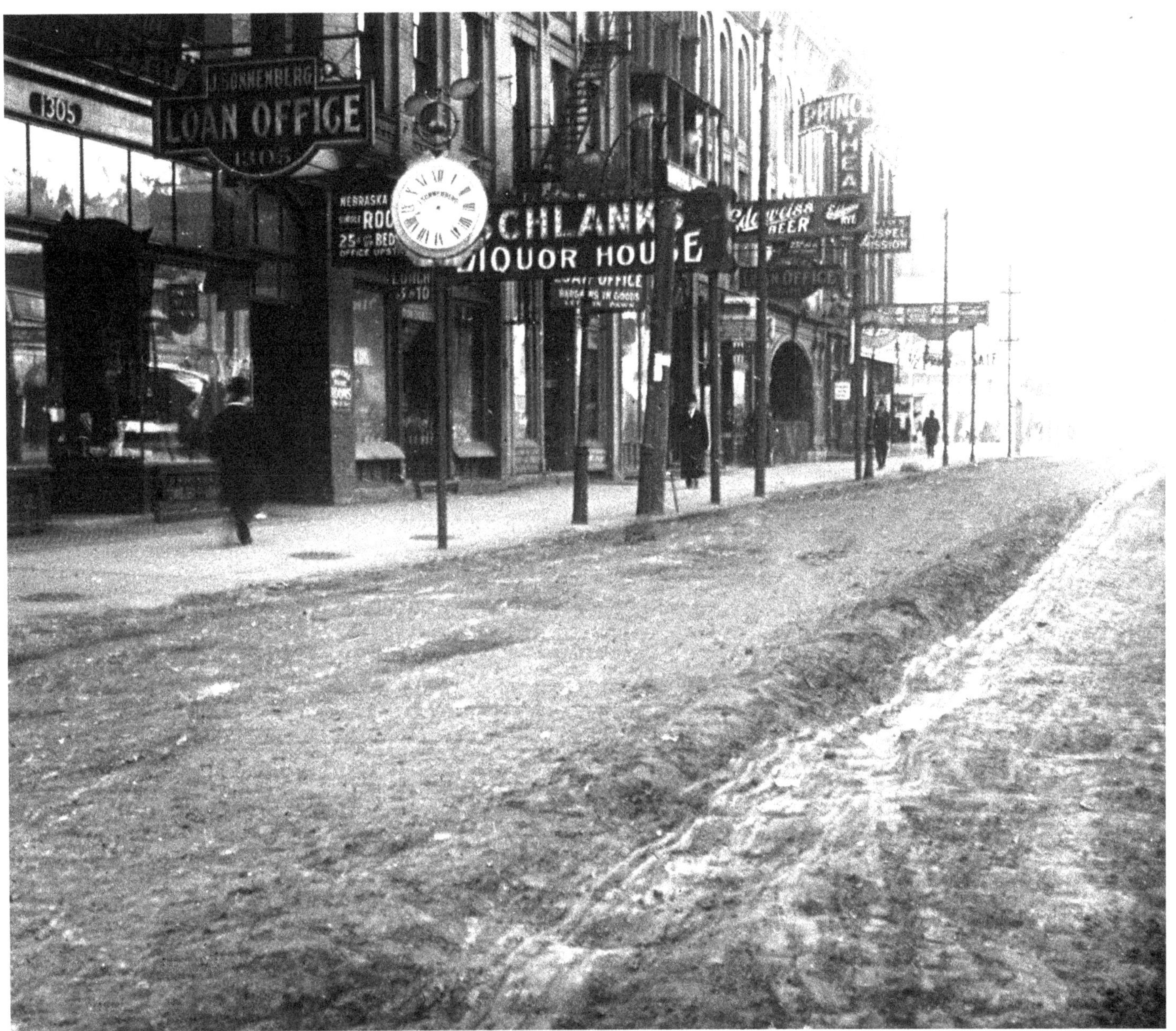

This view west along 13th Street at Douglas in the late 1890s shows the unpaved streets which turned into mud after a rain. The bad condition of Omaha streets was a continual problem well into the twentieth century. This section of the city, part of the infamous "Third Ward," held many saloons and "entertainment" establishments.

Workers excavating to install a sewer line between 16th and 20th streets, Paul to Nicholas streets, one of Omaha's early public works projects. In 1881, a large waterworks plant began operation, and for the next fifteen years Omaha undertook to construct an adequate system of drains and sewers to improve sanitation. Usually these projects were managed by independent contractors working for the city.

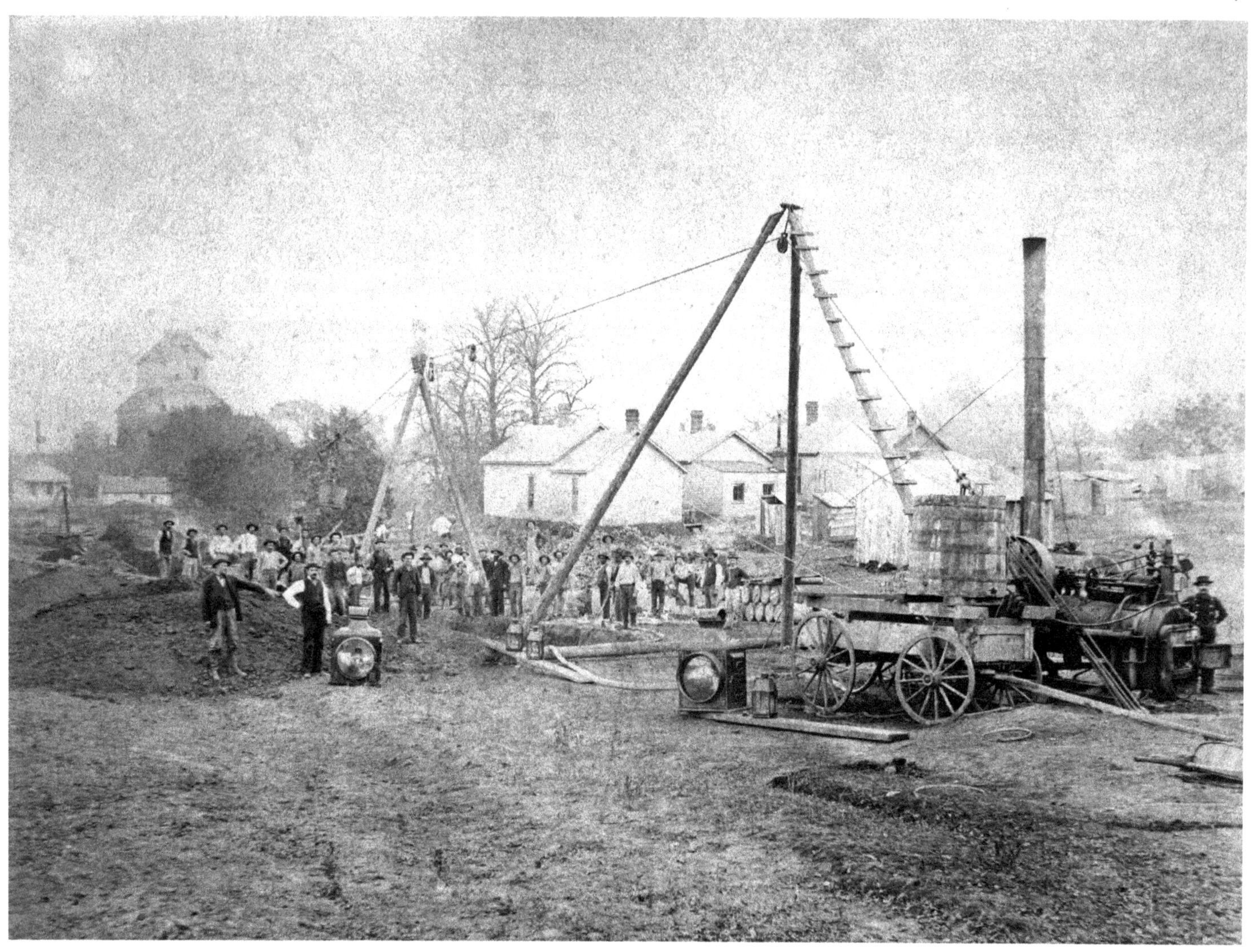

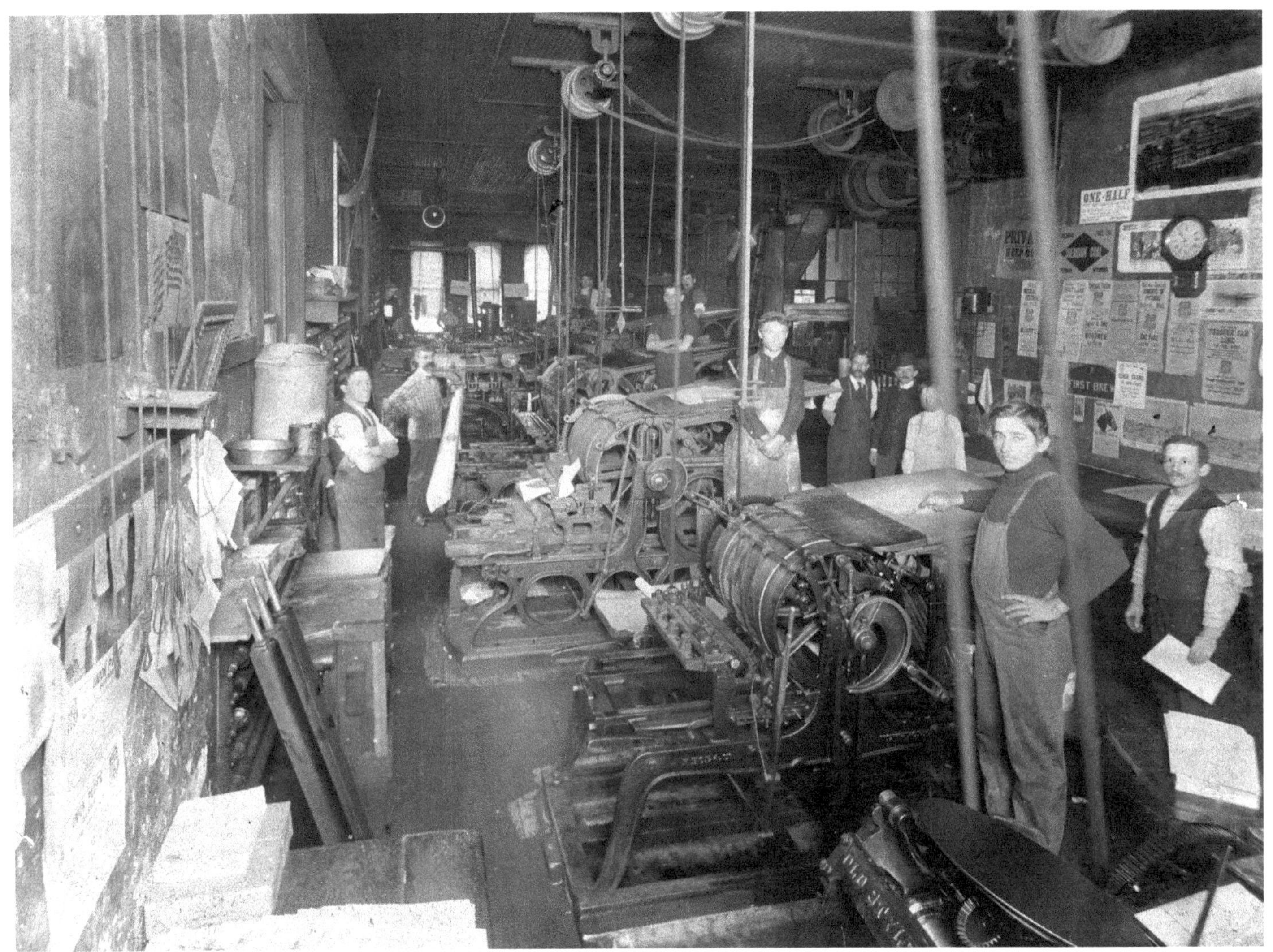

Klopp, Bartlett and Company was a large commercial printing company. Shortly after Klopp and Bartlett took over the business in 1885, the premises were badly damaged by fire, and they relocated to the building shown here at 1114 Farnam Street. Continuing to expand, they were soon also operating a large book bindery and a lithography department. This is their press room in the late 1890s.

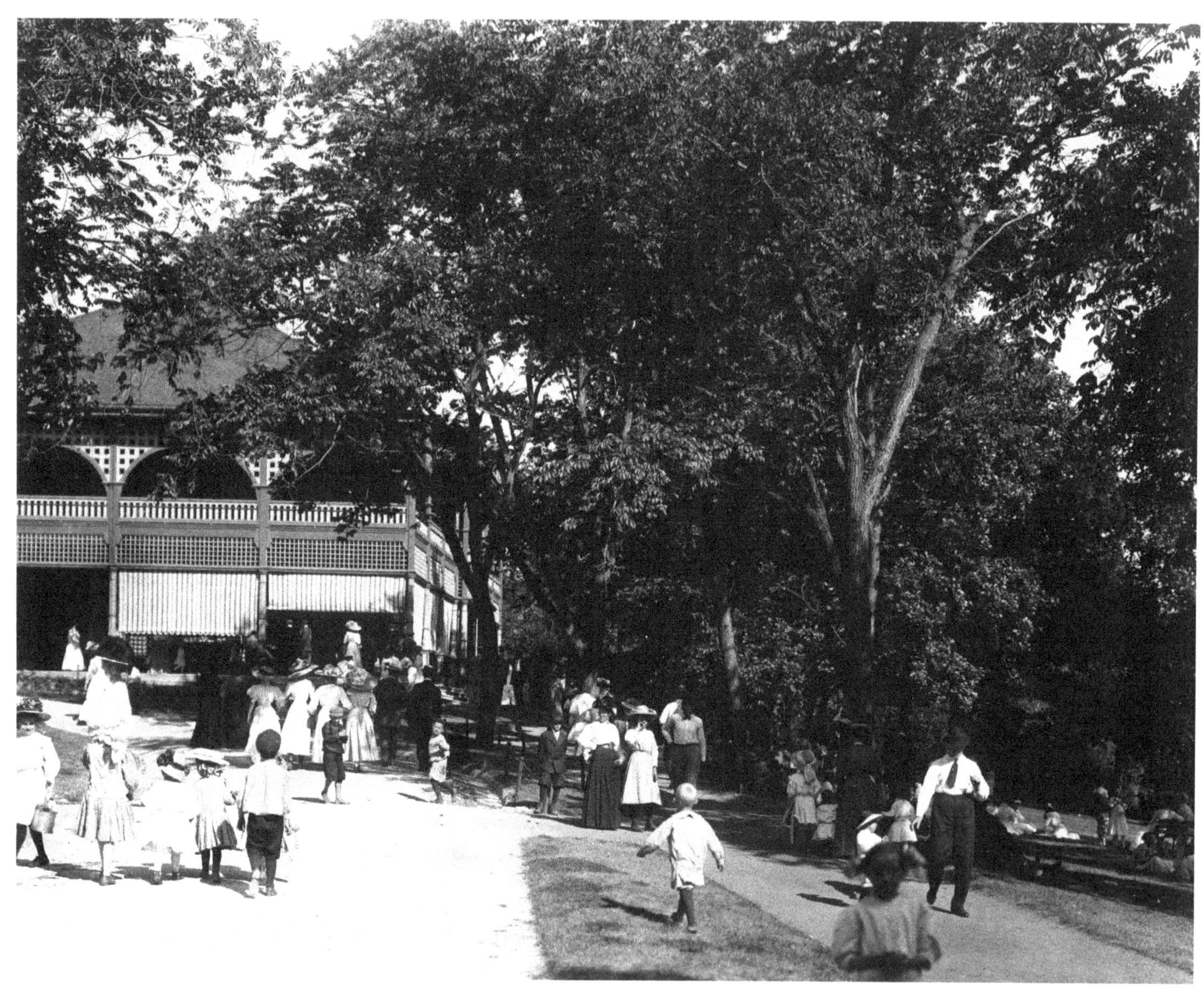

A large pavilion with striped awnings stood in Hanscom Park, 32nd and Woolworth, in the late 1890s. Band concerts held in an elegant bandstand, picnics, fishing in the lagoon, and winter ice skating in the park were all sources of entertainment for local citizens.

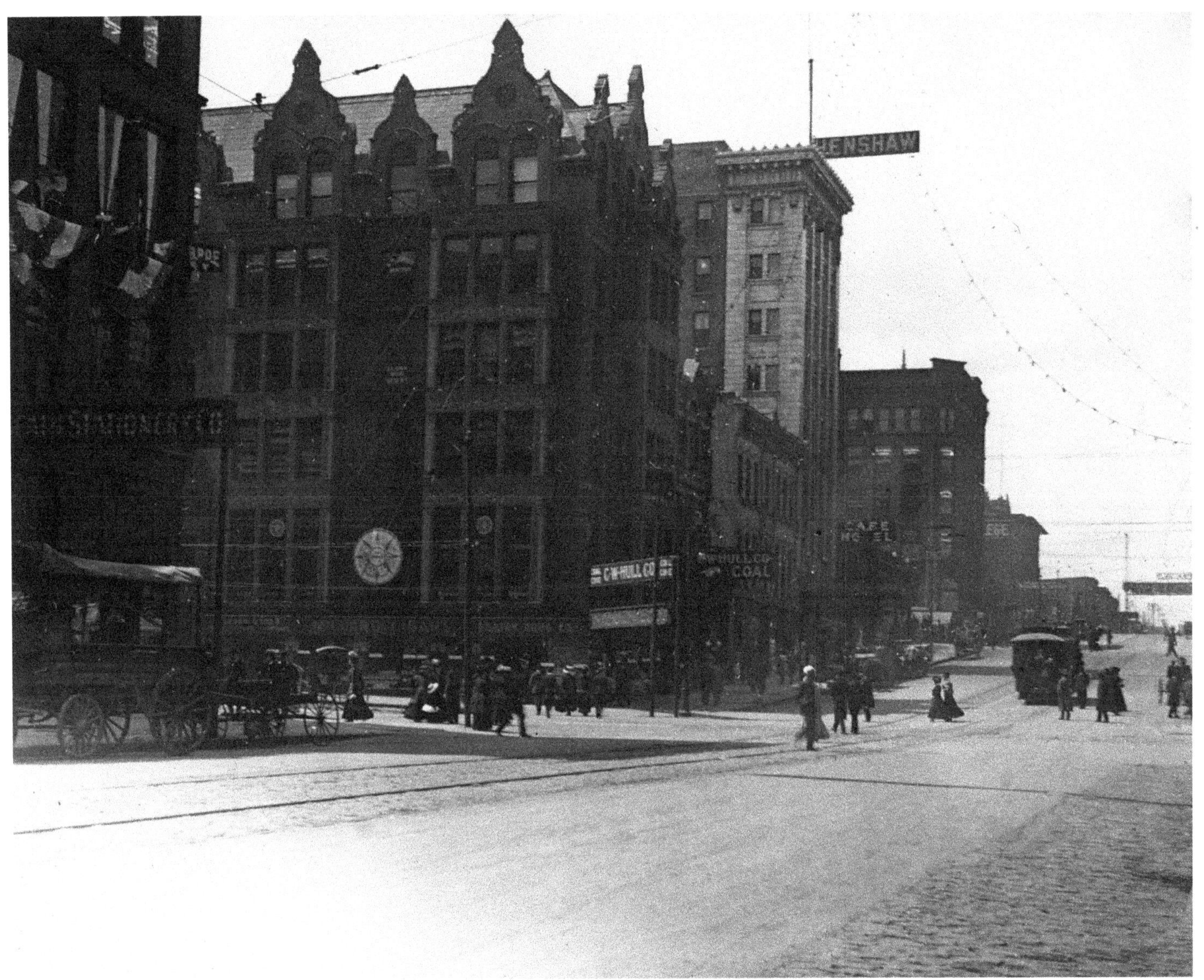

A view of downtown Omaha as it appeared in the late 1890s, west on Farnam Street from 14th. The Barker Building, southwest corner of 15th and Farnam, is in the center. Just to its west is the Henshaw Hotel. Pedestrians, horse-drawn vehicles, and a streetcar share the brick-paved streets.

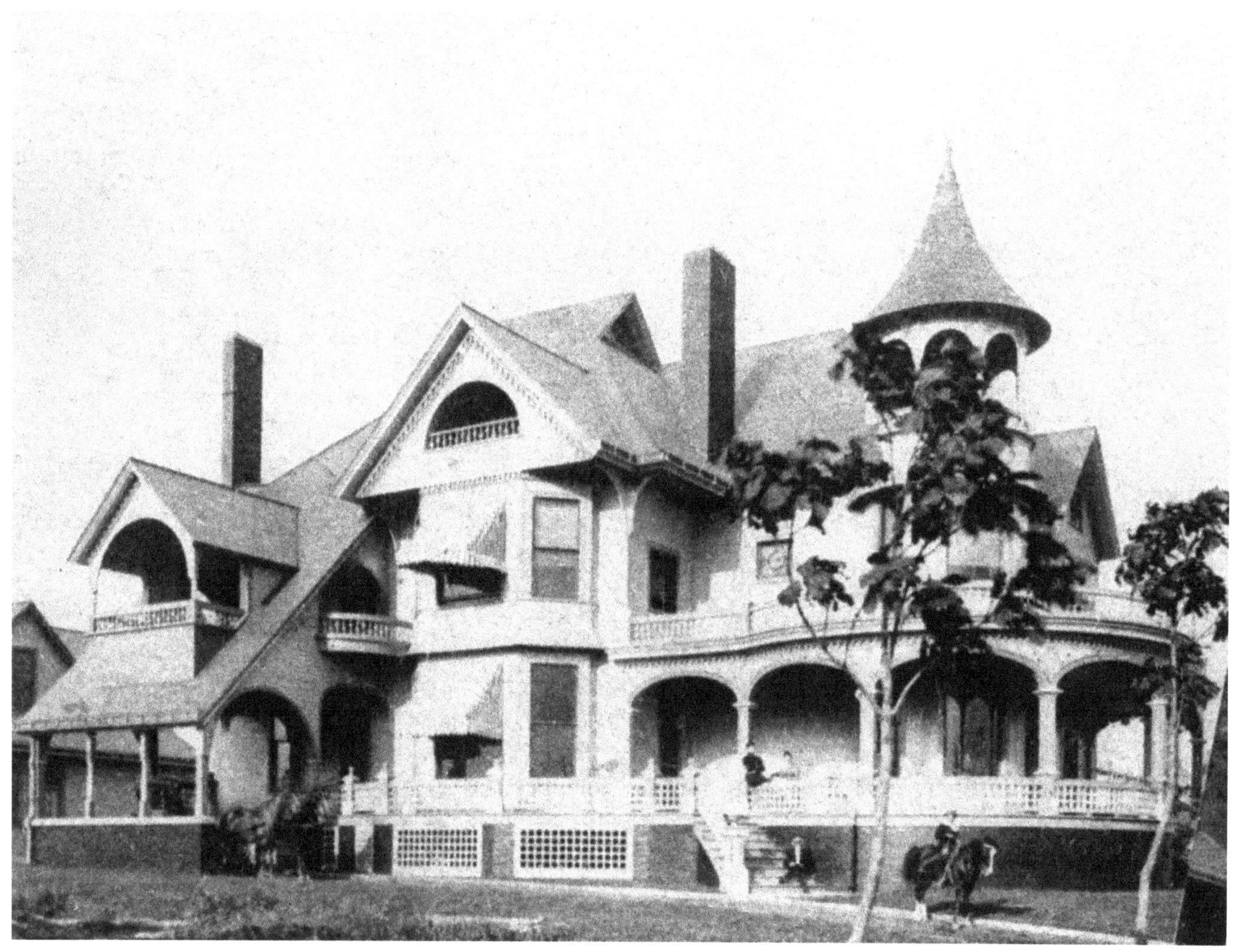

Large and elegant residence of Christian Hartman, 3411 Farnam Street. This home was originally built about 1889. Hartman served in Company D, 1st Nebraska Infantry, during the Civil War. He held many elected city offices and in the 1870s established the first beef canning and packing house in Omaha. He was also very prominent in the Masonic Lodge. This view was made in the late 1890s.

Around 1890, students of the Central Elementary School were photographed on the front steps of Omaha High School. The classes for the Central School at that time were being held in a temporary location, until their new school building was completed in 1891 at 21st and Davenport streets, adjacent to the Omaha High School building.

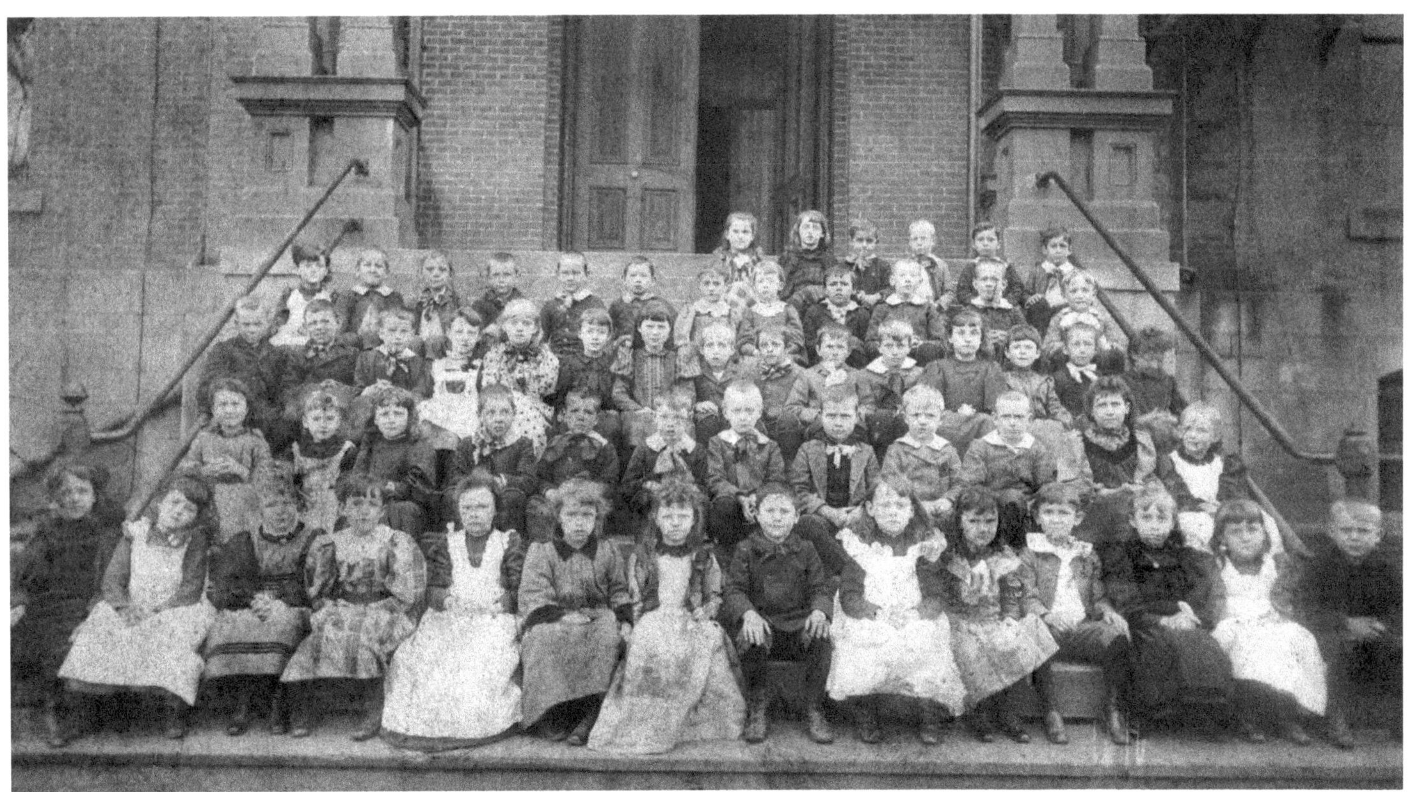

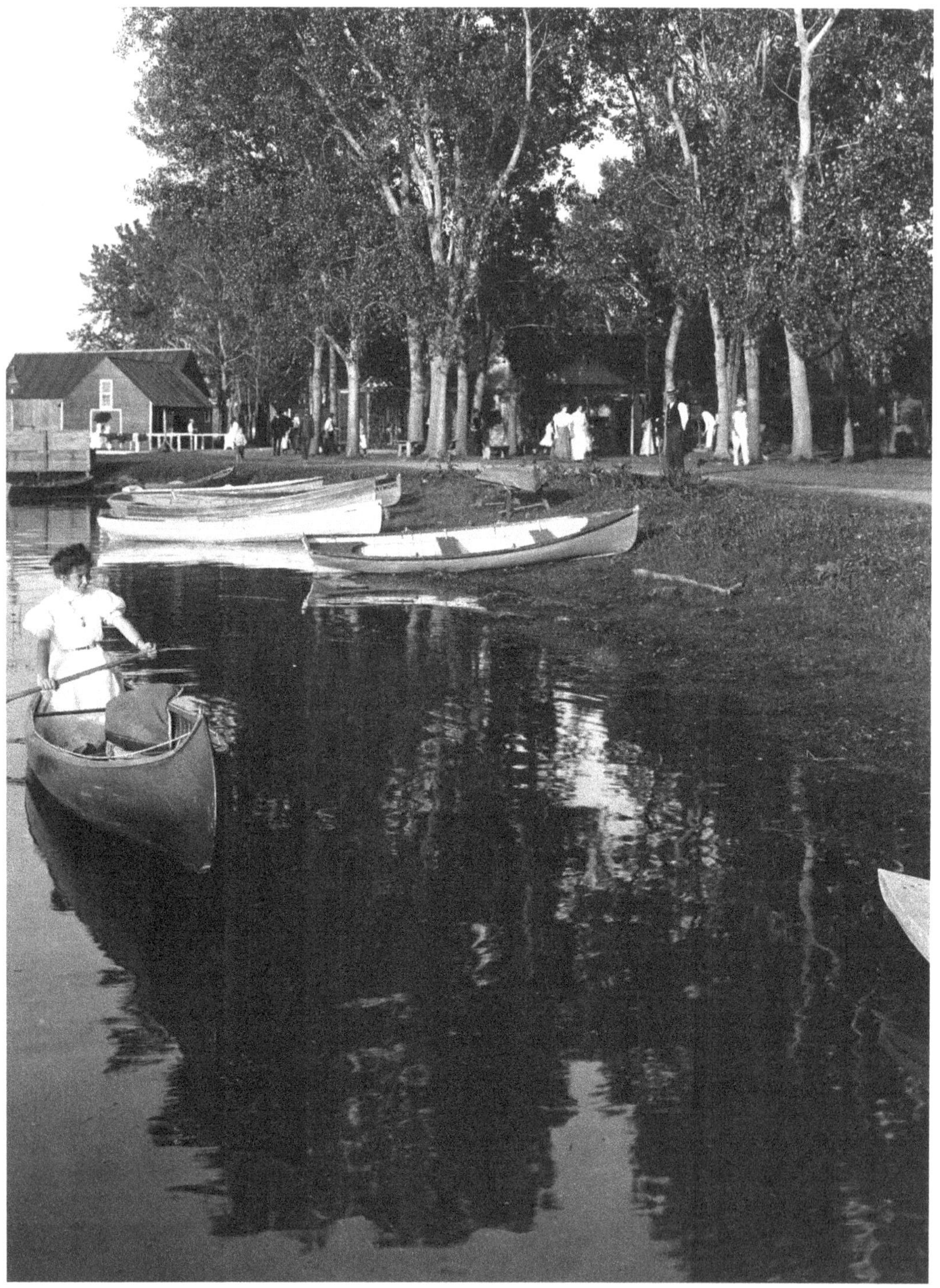

Lake Nakoma, originally named "Cut-Off Lake," formed in 1877 as the result of a flood which caused the Missouri River to reroute its channel. In 1908, this lake was renamed Carter Lake, in honor of pioneer Levi P. Carter. At that time, his widow donated $50,000 for the improvement of the area as a recreational facility.

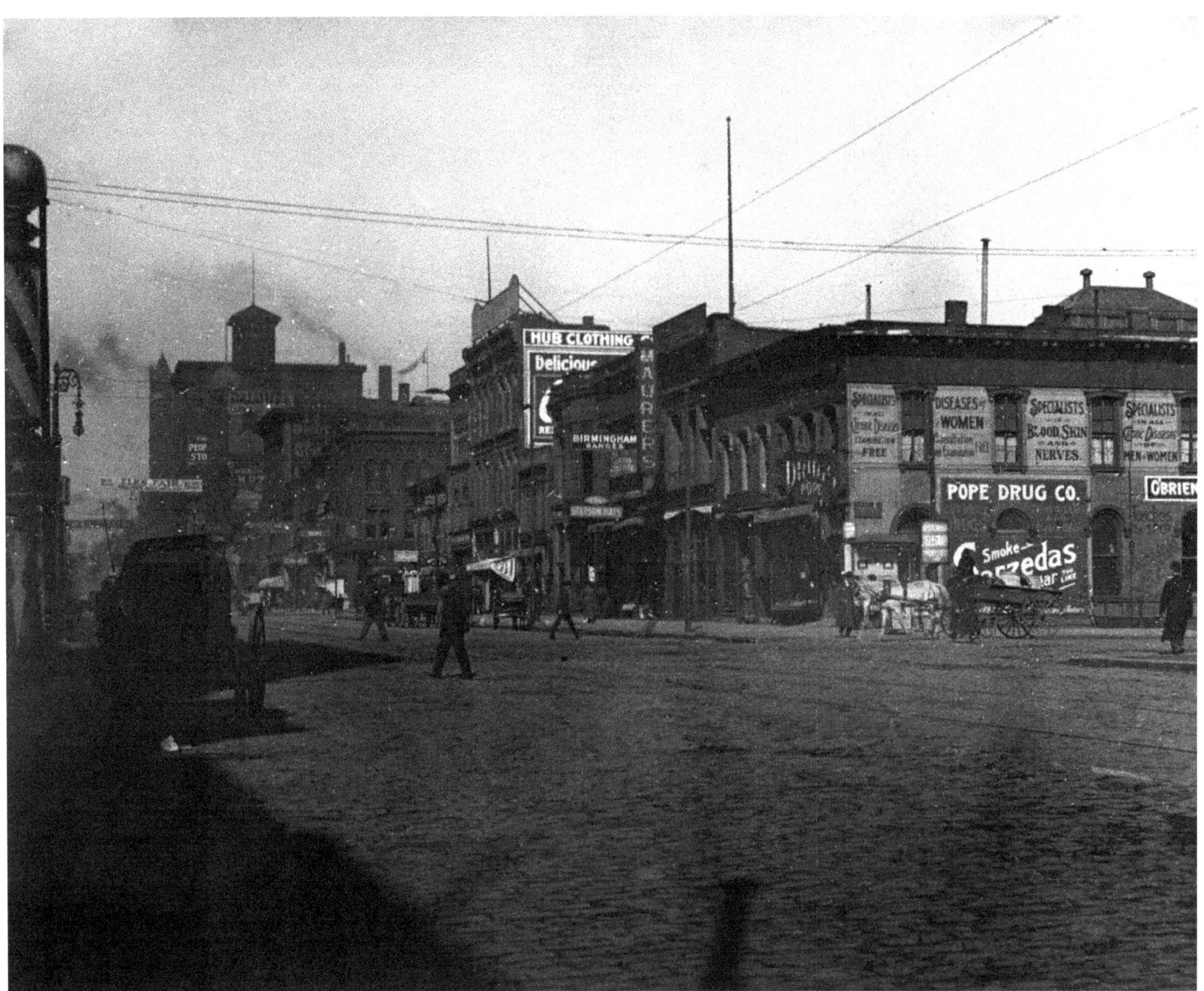

Farnam Street west from 13th Street about 1890 included The People's Store, which dealt in general merchandise (in background beyond Elks Fair banner); Ed Maurer's Restaurant, one of the finest in Omaha; and the Nebraska Clothing Company. All were on Farnam's north side.

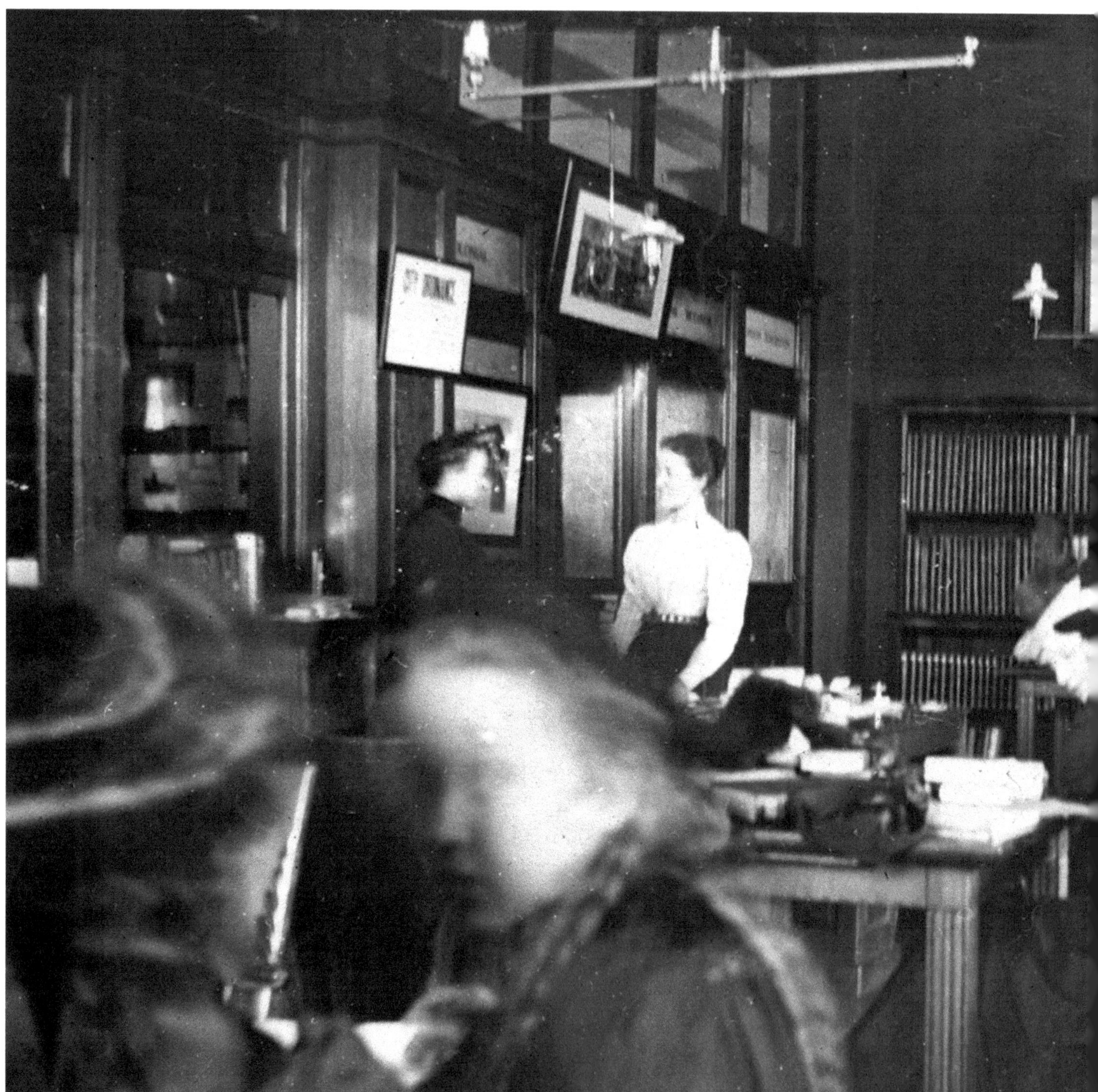

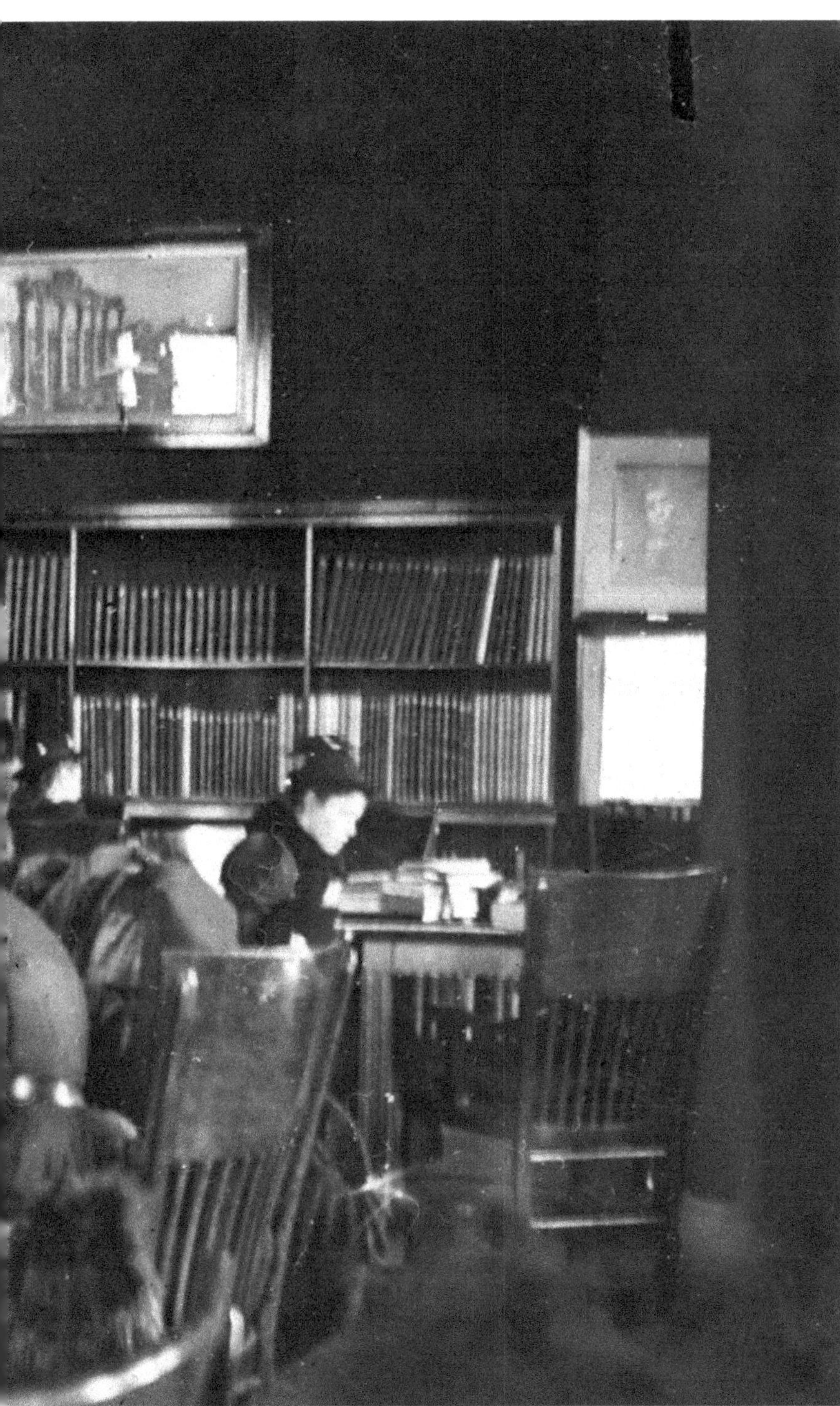

Photograph of the Reference Room inside the old Omaha Public Library building on the southeast corner of 19th and Harney streets about 1898.

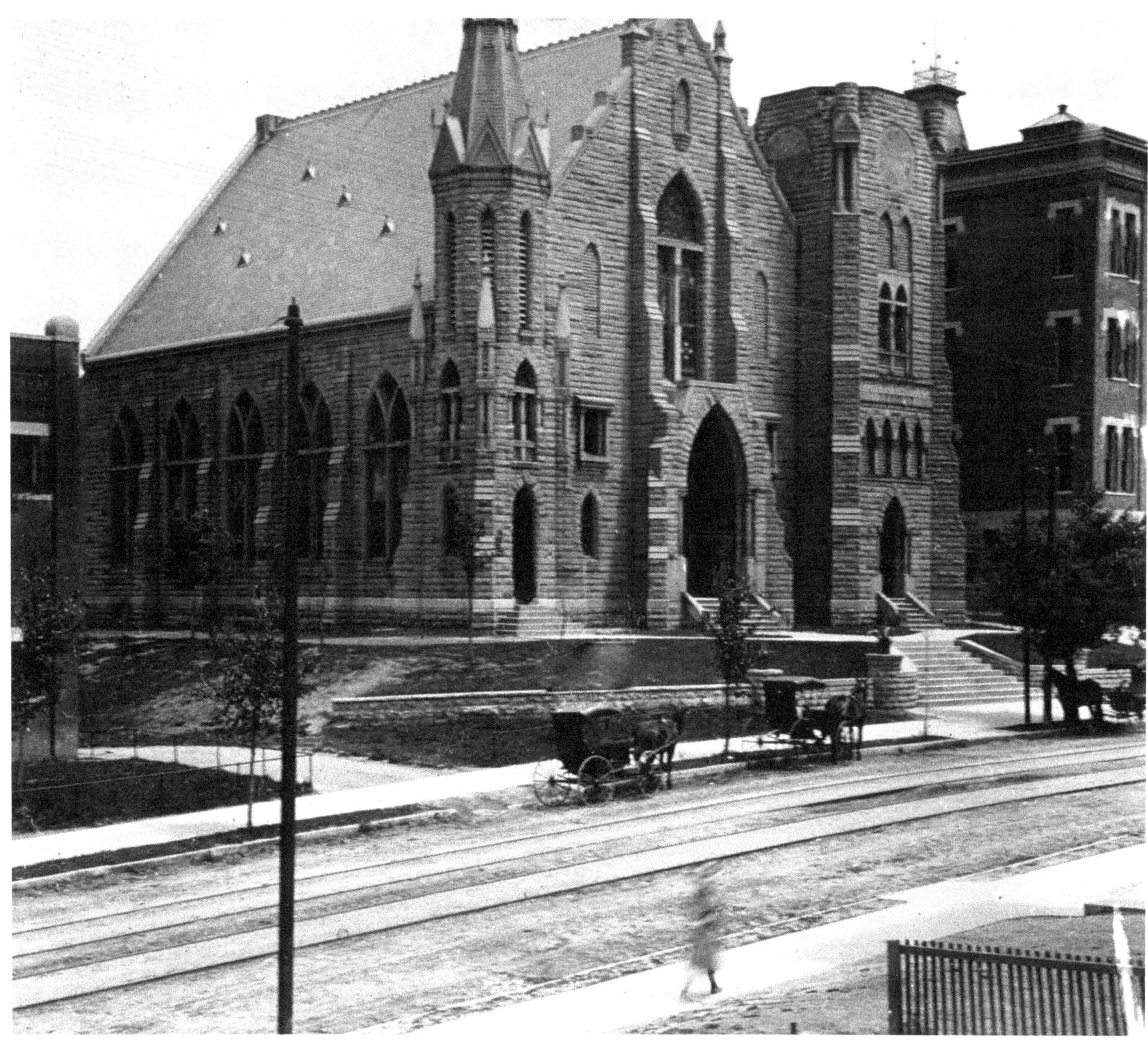

St. John's Collegiate Church was the second structure built on the campus of Creighton College. This Romanesque-style church at 2506 California Street, built of gray stone, is one of the most beautiful edifices in the city. The interior contains many memorials to members of the Creighton family. This image was made about 1890.

This neighborhood grocery store was owned and operated by Henry Moeller, located on the northwest corner of 13th and Jones streets. It is typical of the small businesses which served the needs of local residents. This picture dates to approximately 1890.

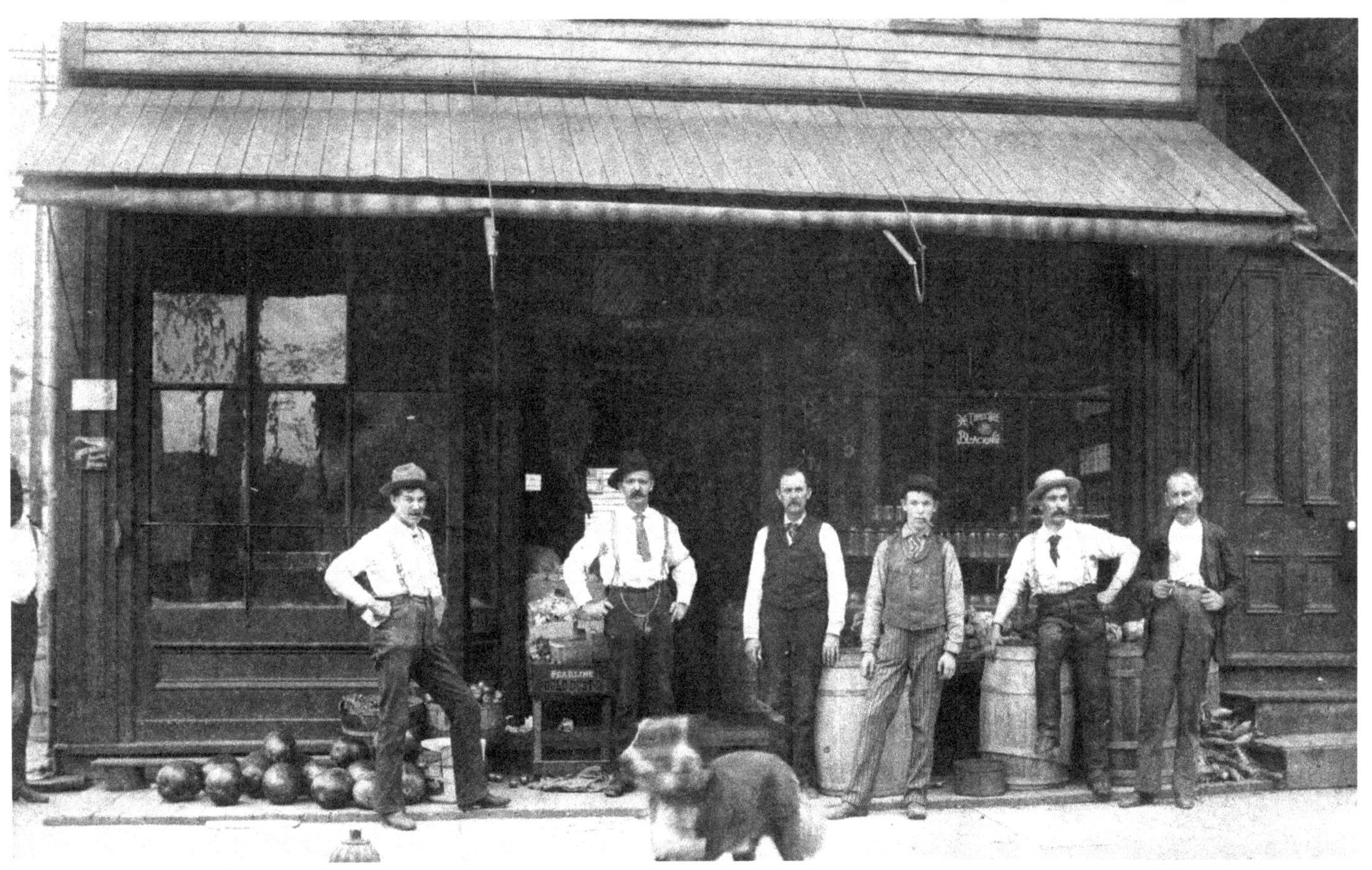

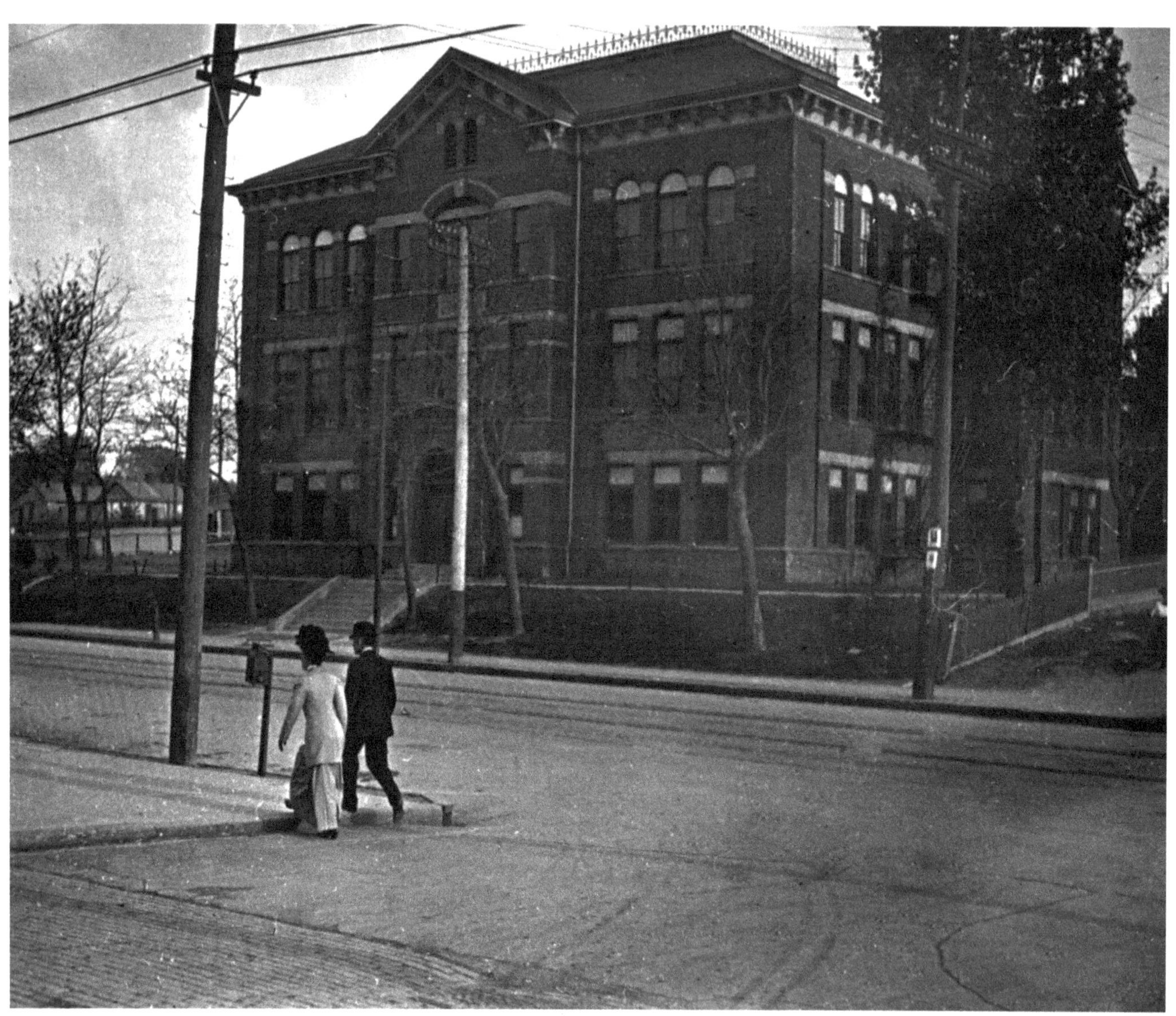

The Farnam School (elementary) was located at 2915 Farnam Street, one of several substantial brick school buildings erected in Omaha in the 1880s and 1890s. It was torn down in the 1920s.

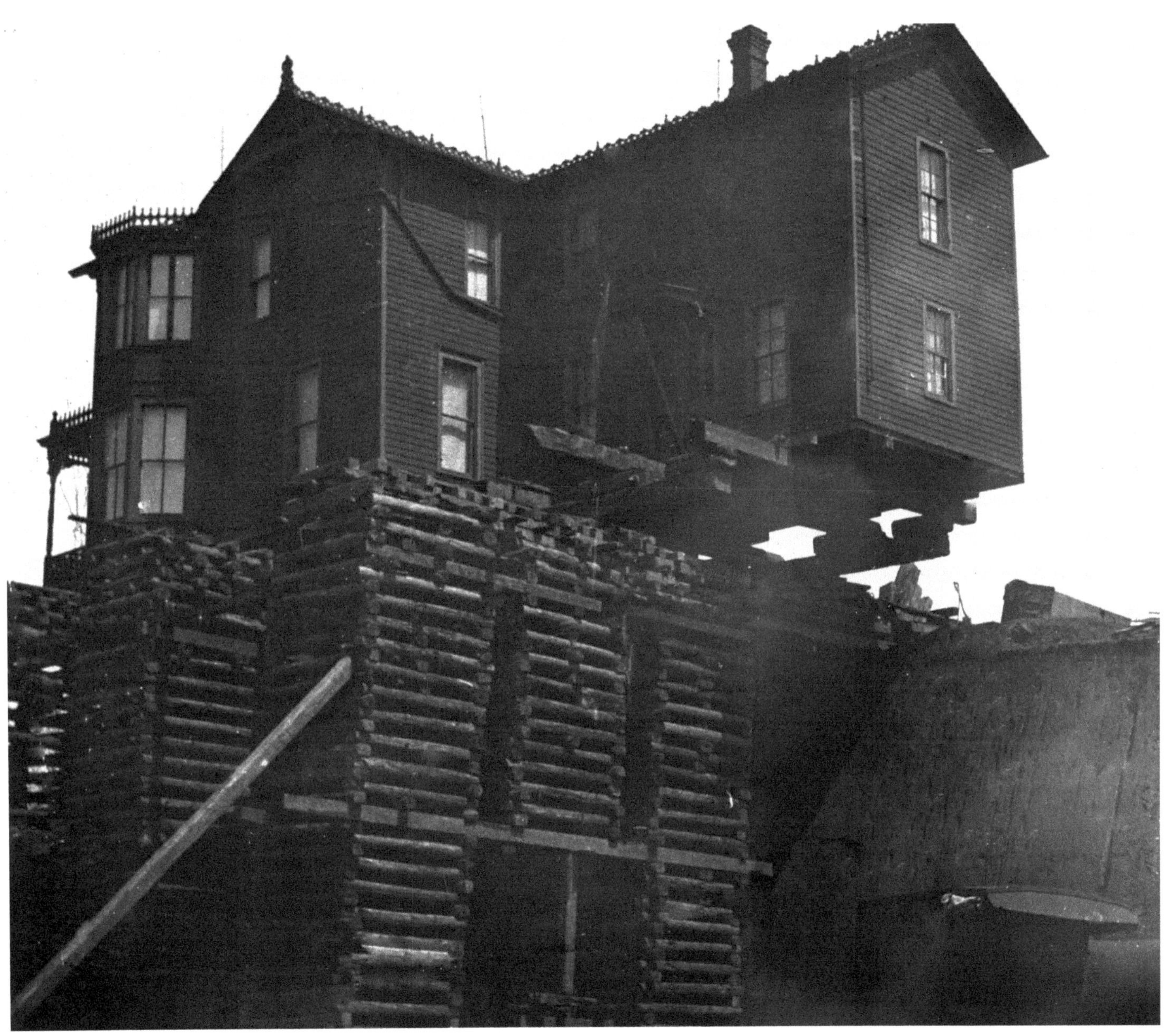

Around 1892, the Falconer residence at 1821 Douglas Street was lowered to the new street level which had been excavated as part of the municipal engineering project to reduce the steep grade of Omaha's streets.

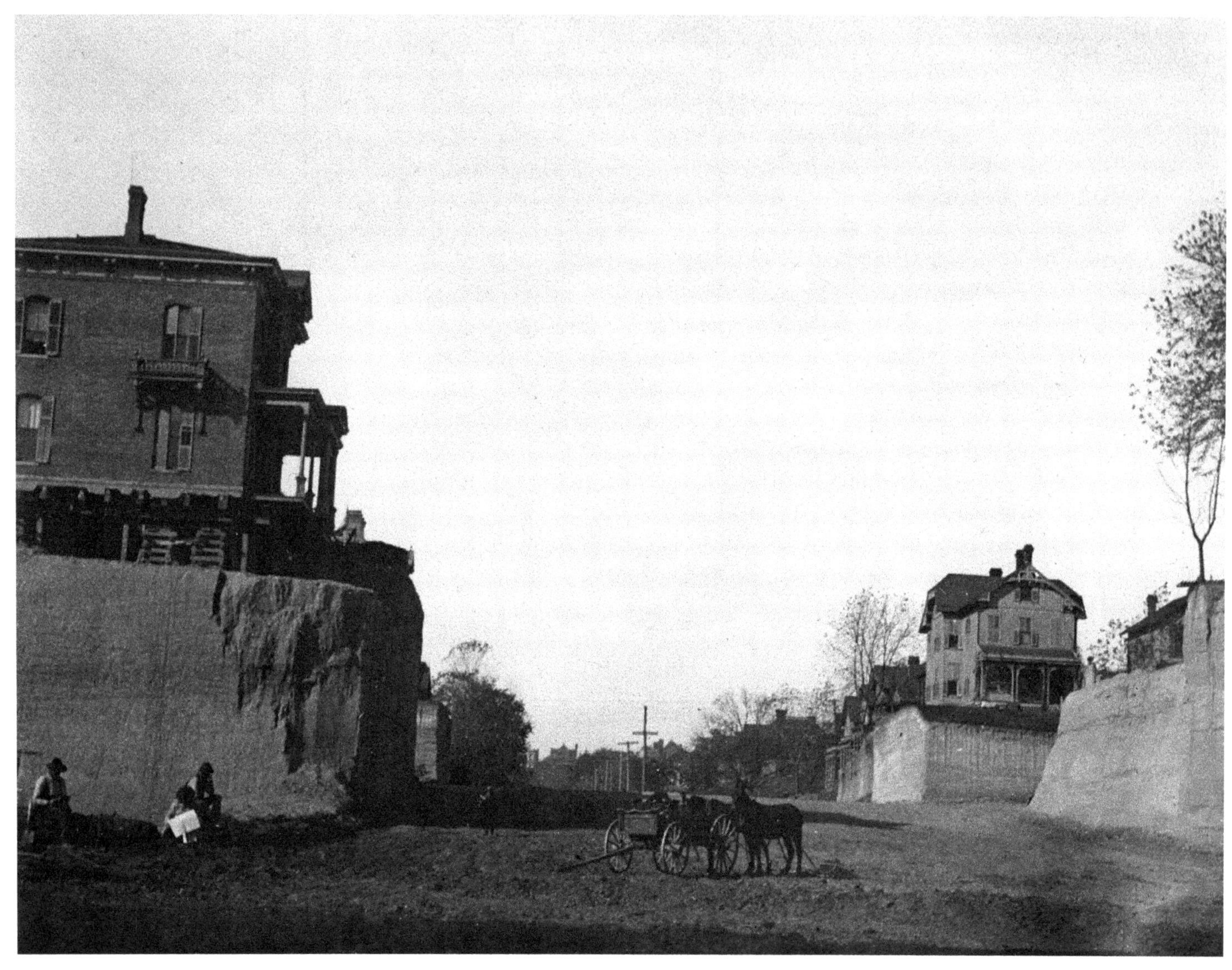

An 1892 view of the street-lowering project shows residences along Douglas Street at 18th. The street obviously was lowered a considerable amount. These projects were undertaken to allow for the installation of street railway service, which could not run easily on steep grades.

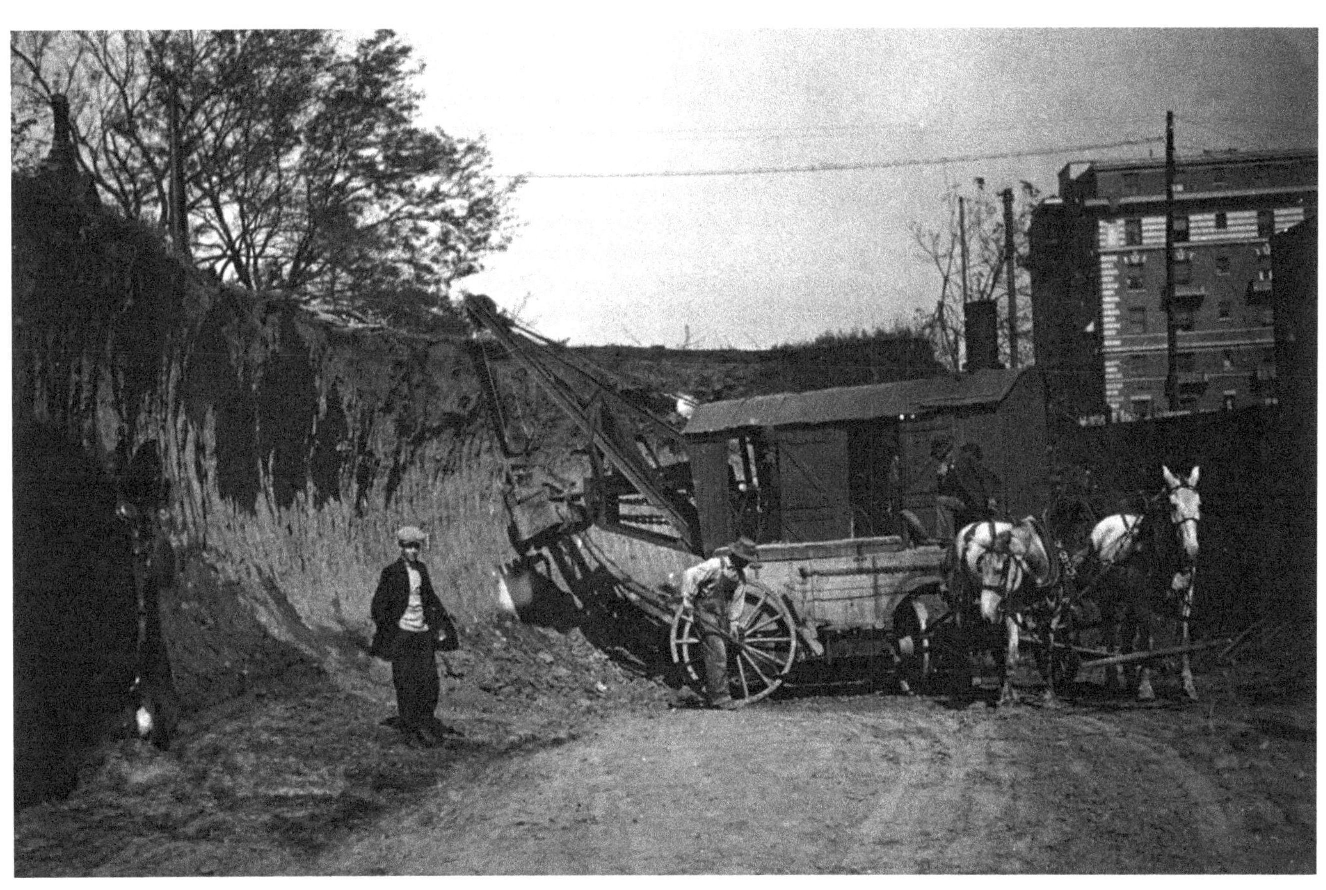

Street regrading was the first large-scale engineering project in the city. Many independent contractors were employed to work on various sections. This crew is working near 2420 Harney Street in the early 1890s.

An audience watches cavalry maneuvers in the late 1890s at Fort Omaha, a military post north of the central city. Tents have been set up by the parade ground. Established in 1868, it was administered by the U.S. Army Department of the Platte during the Indian Wars. Today, many original buildings house the North Campus of Omaha's Metropolitan Community College at 30th and Fort streets.

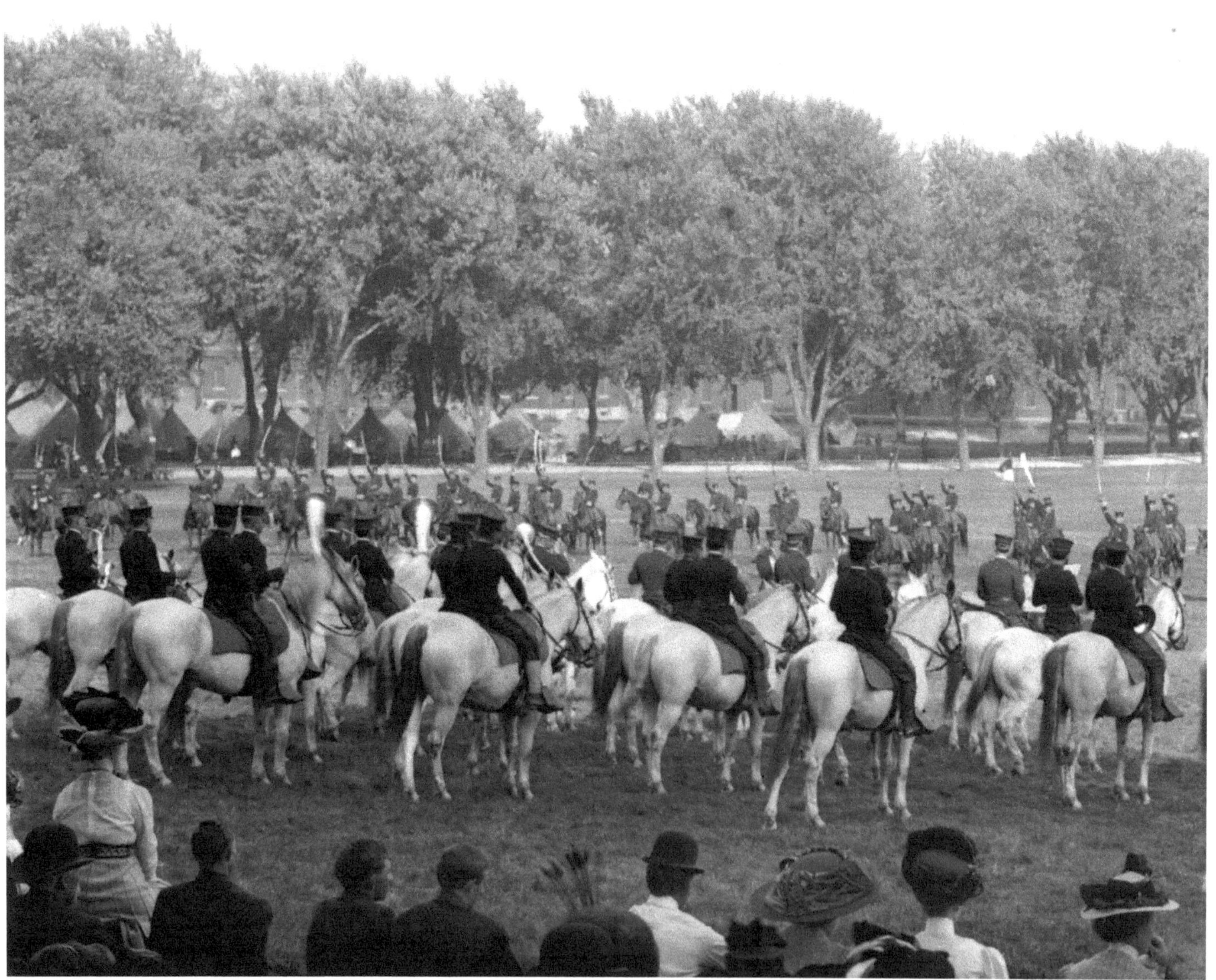

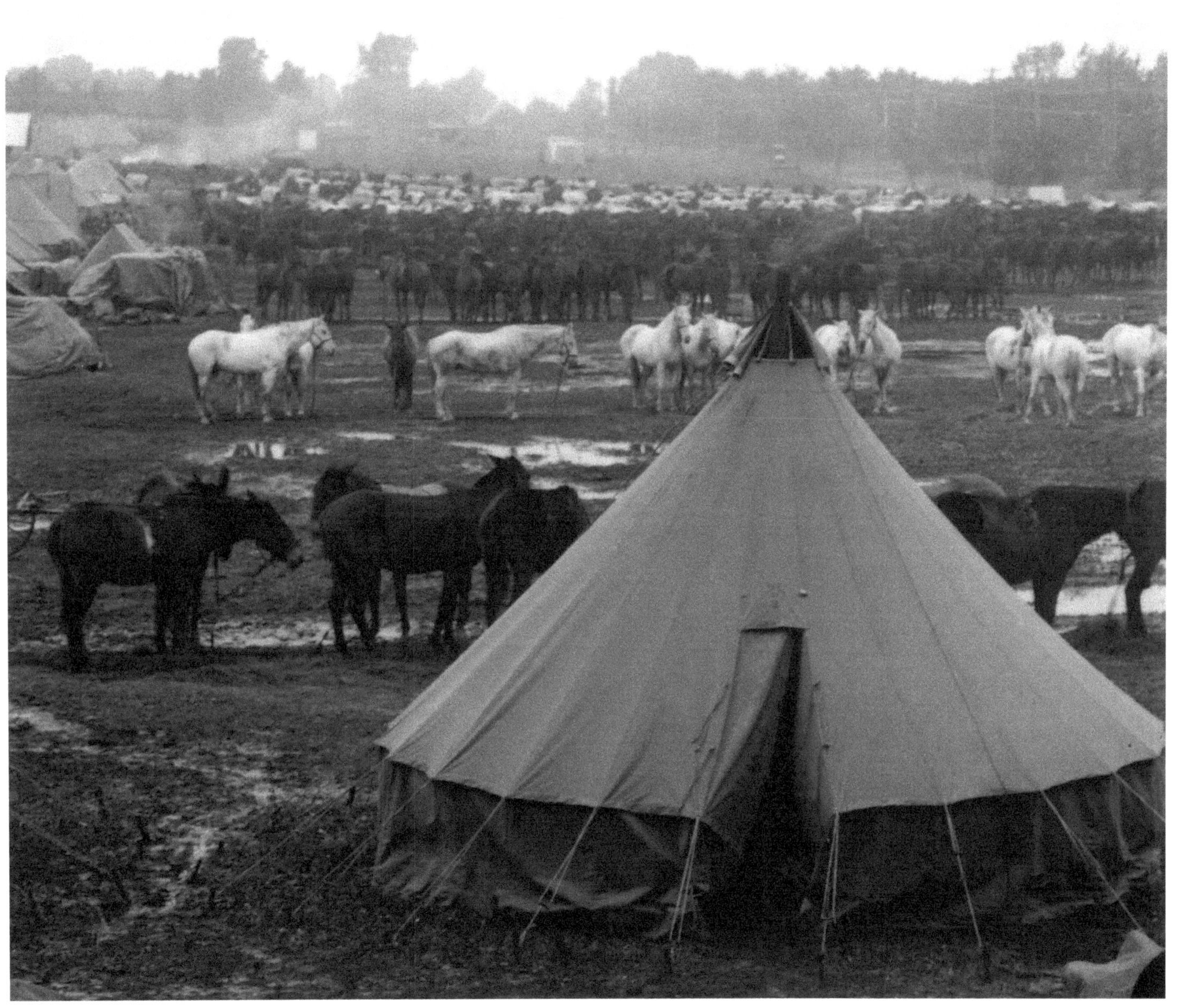

Army horses stand beyond a large tent set up beside the parade ground at Fort Omaha, 30th and Fort streets, during cavalry maneuvers in the late 1890s. This fort is now the site of the North Campus of Metropolitan Community College.

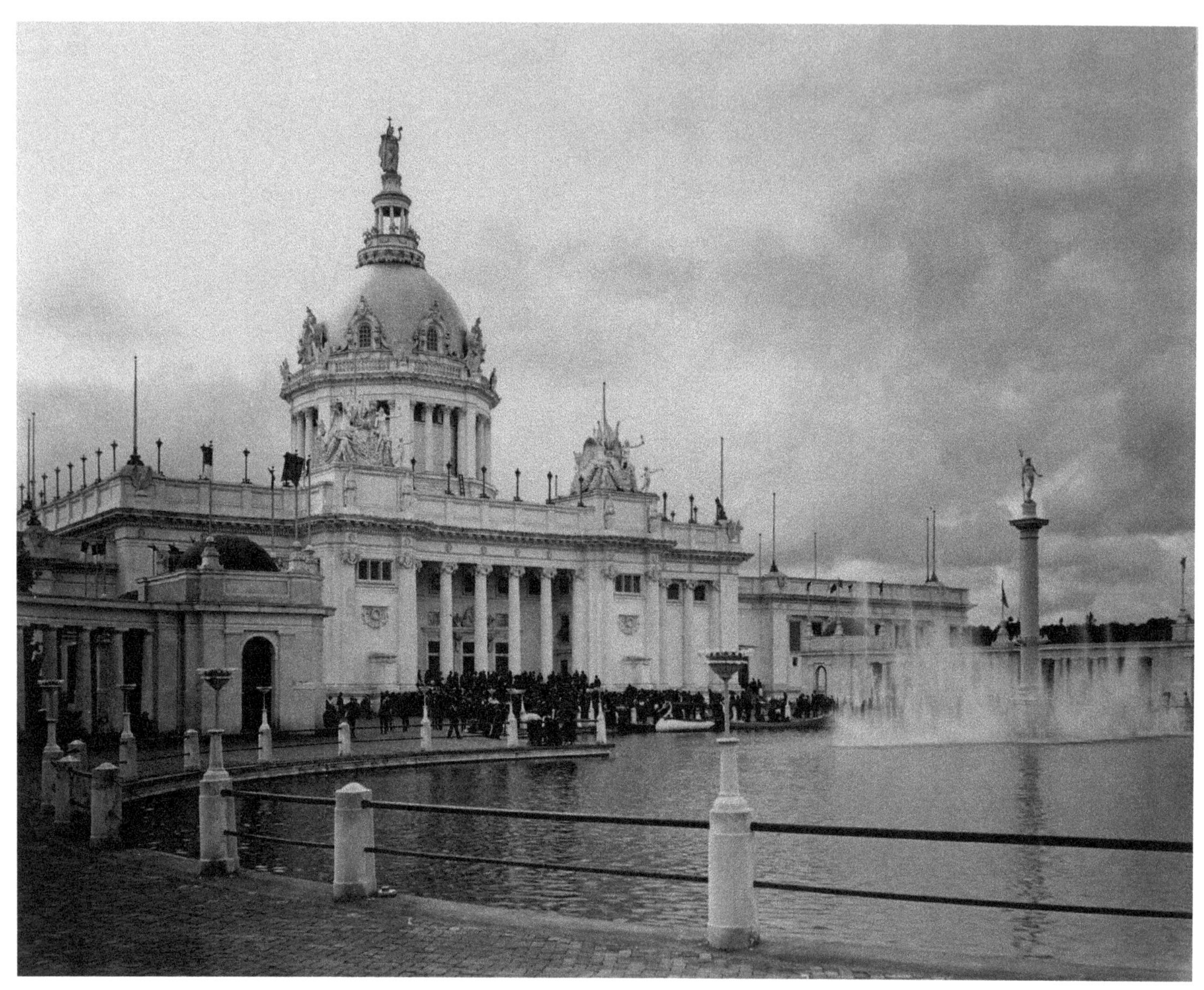

A view of the United States Government Building at the Trans-Mississippi and International Exposition and Indian Congress, held in Omaha June 1st through October 31st, 1898. This building was located at the west end of a large man-made "lagoon," which was eight city blocks long and more than 300 feet wide.

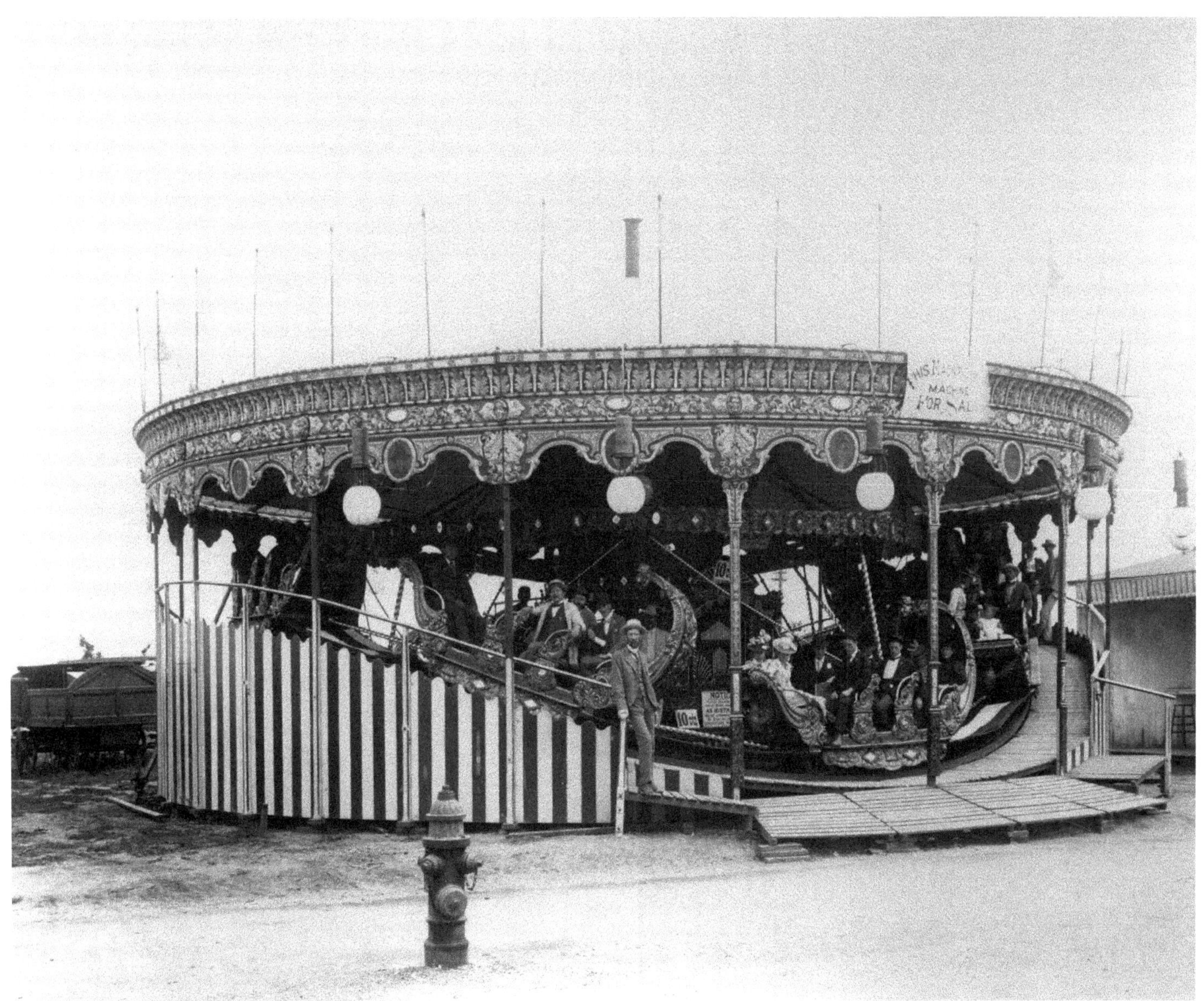

This "Mini Roller Coaster" was one of the Midway attractions at the Trans-Mississippi Exposition. Many such small concessions were transported by rail to the fairgrounds where the operators leased space. Admission for most of the attractions was 5 or 10 cents, and the operators had to pay a percentage of their profits to the Exposition Company in addition to the rental fee. A sign advertises, "This Magificent Machine for Sale."

The main entrance to the Agricultural Building, Trans-Mississippi Exposition, 1898. One of the large "palaces" which surrounded the Lagoon, or Grand Court area, it was more than 400 feet long and about 150 feet wide. This building was designed by the famous architect Cass Gilbert. It contained many exhibits related to agricultural production.

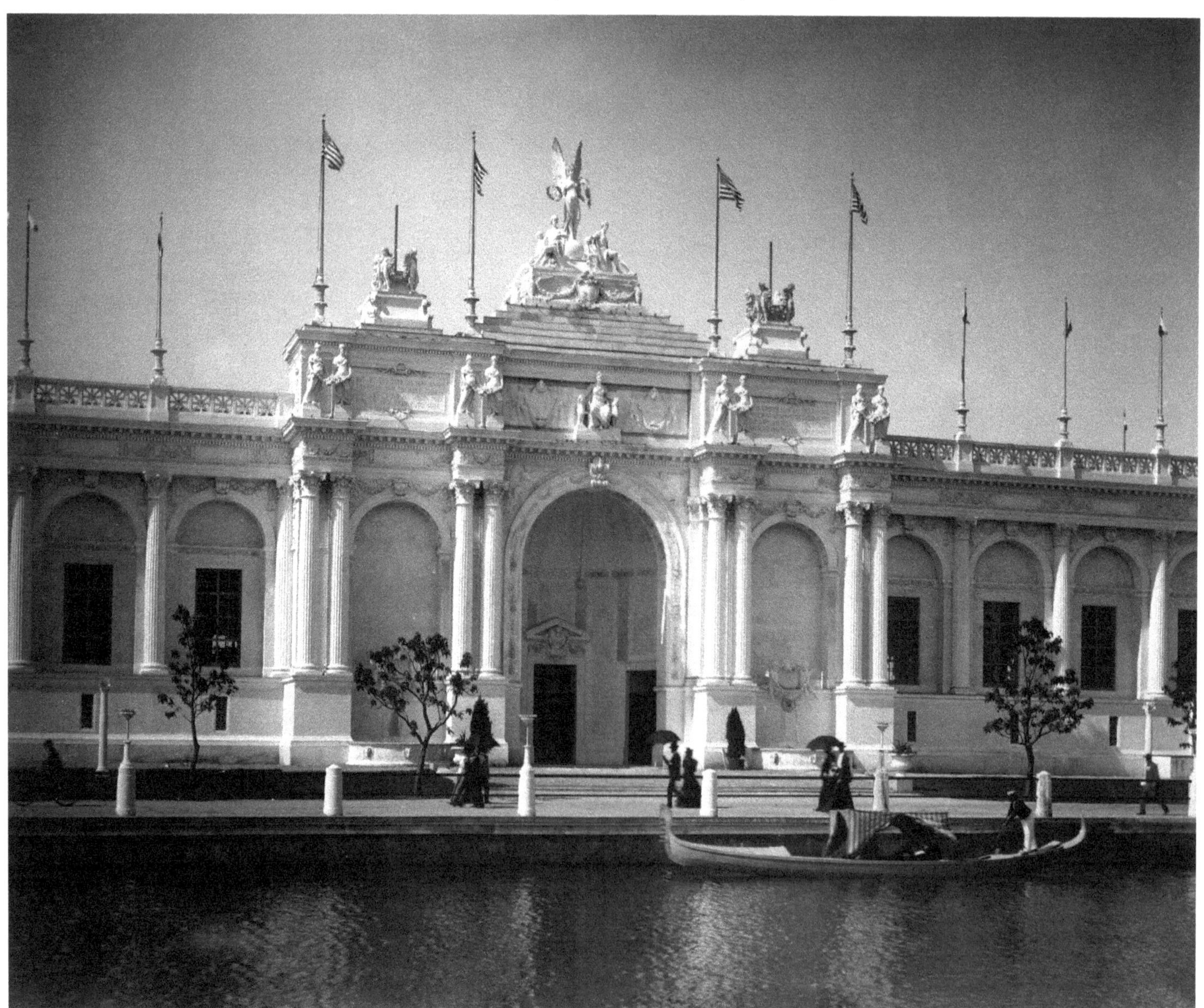

General Electric Company hosted this large exhibit in the Machinery and Electricity Building, located on the Grand Court. Electricity was in its infancy and was a noted feature of the Trans-Mississippi Exposition, which was one of the first major events in the United States to be entirely illuminated by electricity. Thomas Edison himself designed the electrical features of the Omaha fair.

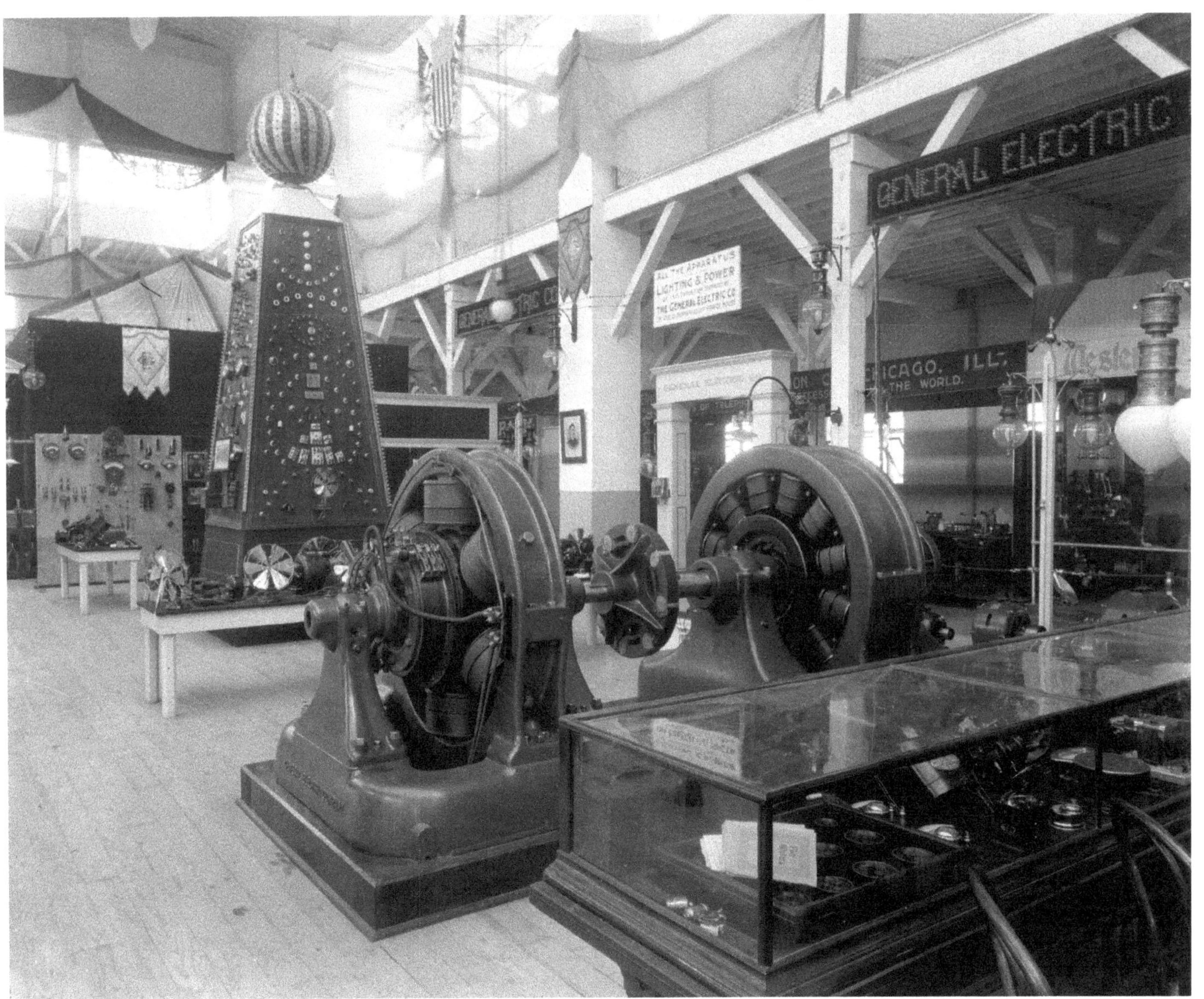

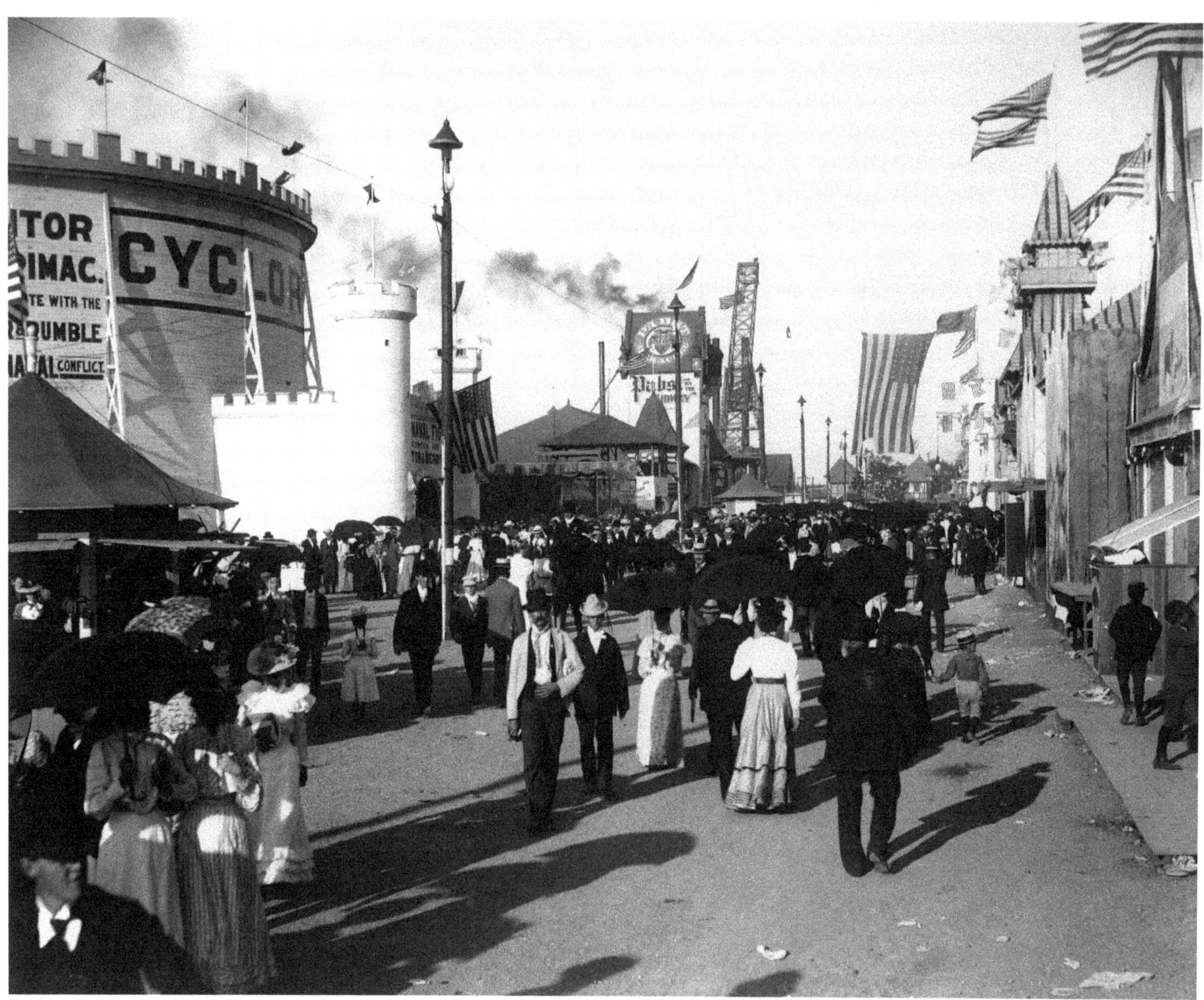

The North Midway at the Trans-Mississippi Exposition. The Cyclorama on the left featured a large, panoramic painting depicting the first naval battle between ironclads. In the upper center of the photo is the Pabst Pavilion, which was operated by the Pabst Brewery as a restaurant and beer garden. To its right is the outline of the Giant See-Saw, a very popular feature of the Midway.

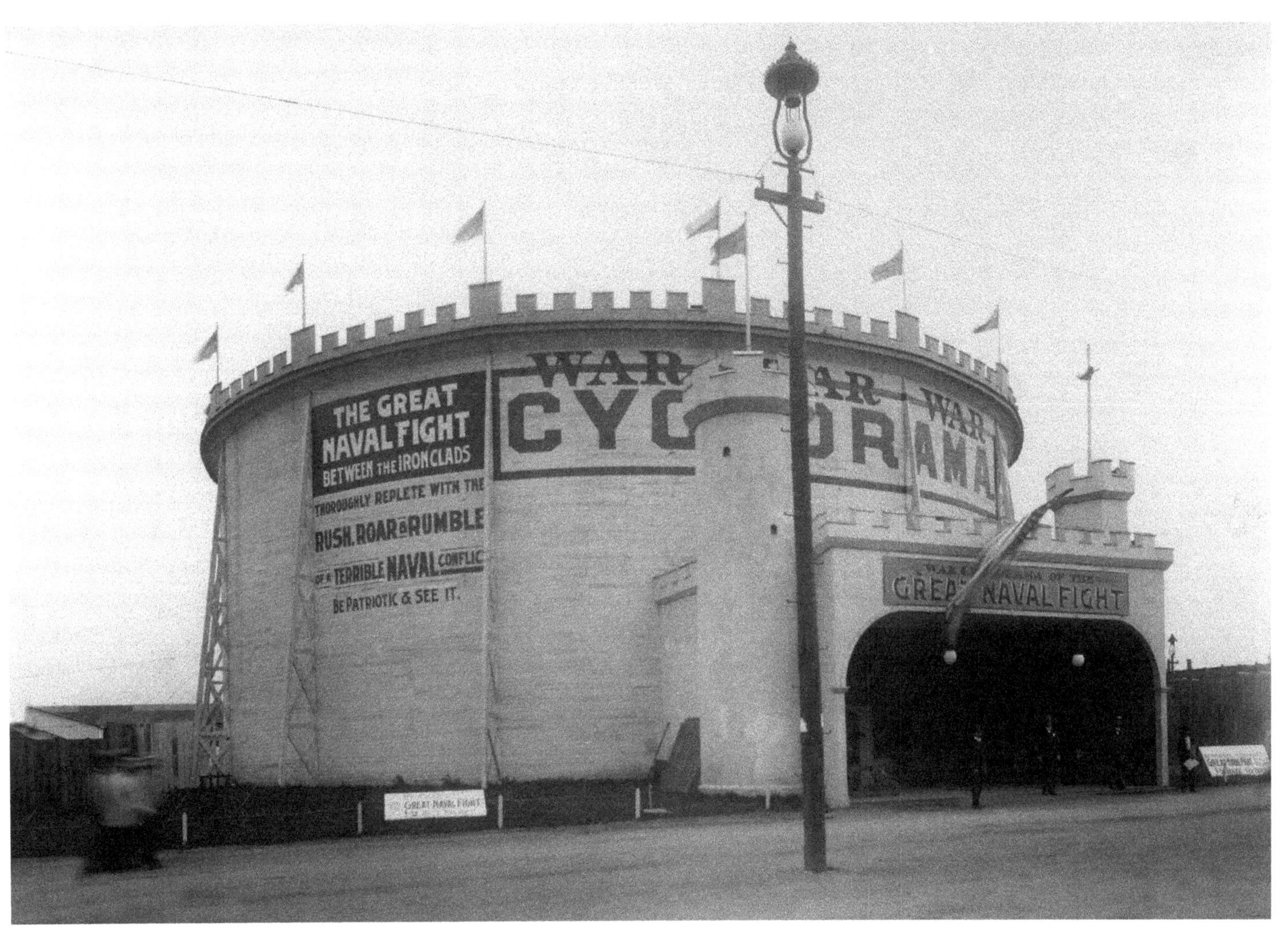

The Cyclorama on the North Midway held a large, circular panoramic painting of the famous naval battle between the ironclads USS *Monitor* and CSS *Virginia* (formerly named USS *Merrimac*) at Hampton Roads during the Civil War. Patrons entered the enclosure and walked around an elevated wooden platform to view the painting. The white signs outside entice viewers with admission prices that are "½ Rate To-day."

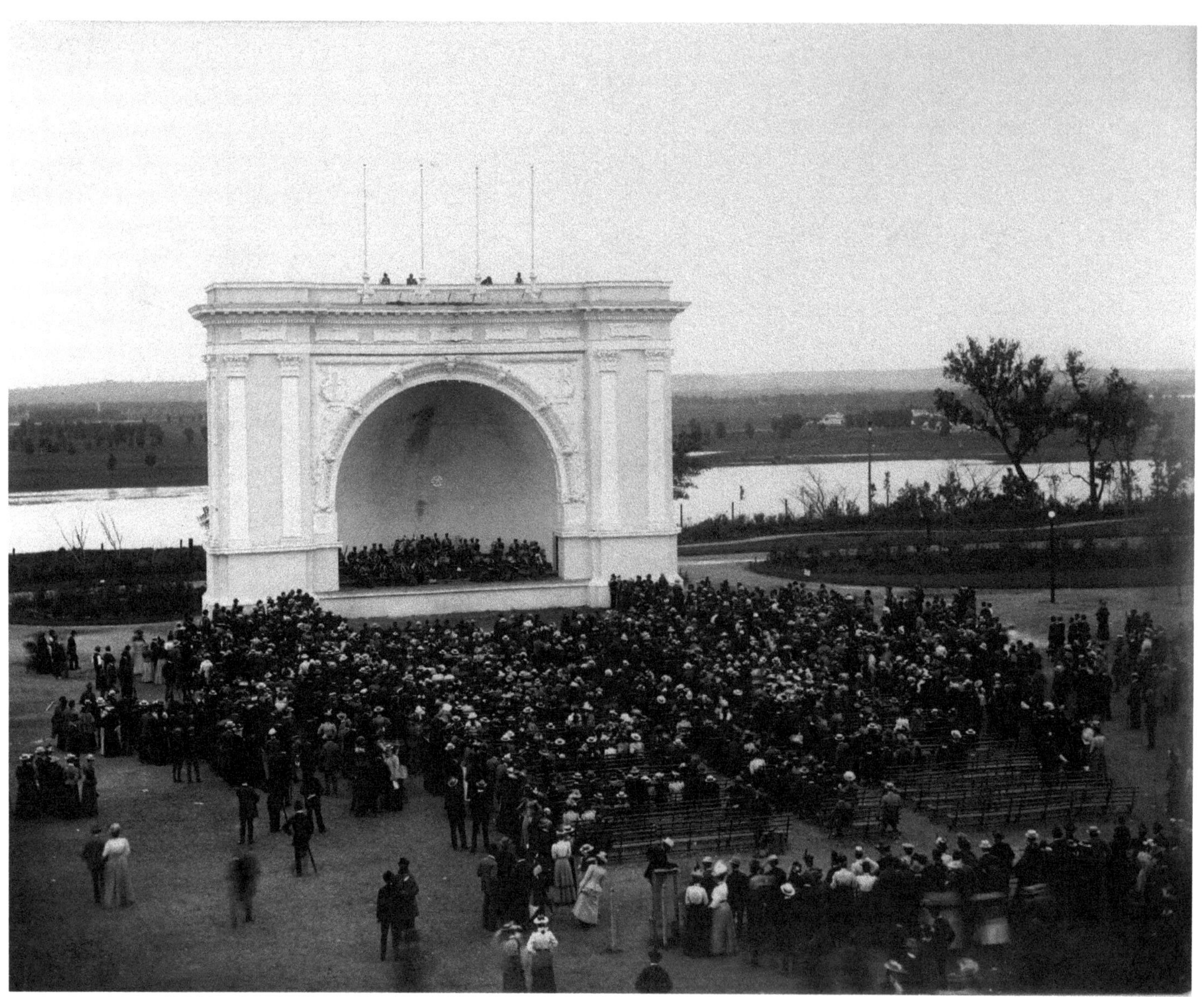

A crowd assembled to hear the Unites States Marine Band perform at the band shell located on the Grand Plaza of the Bluff Tract at the Trans-Mississippi Exposition. The Missouri River, behind the band shell, ran below this section of the Exposition grounds. The entire area of the fairgrounds was a little less than 200 acres.

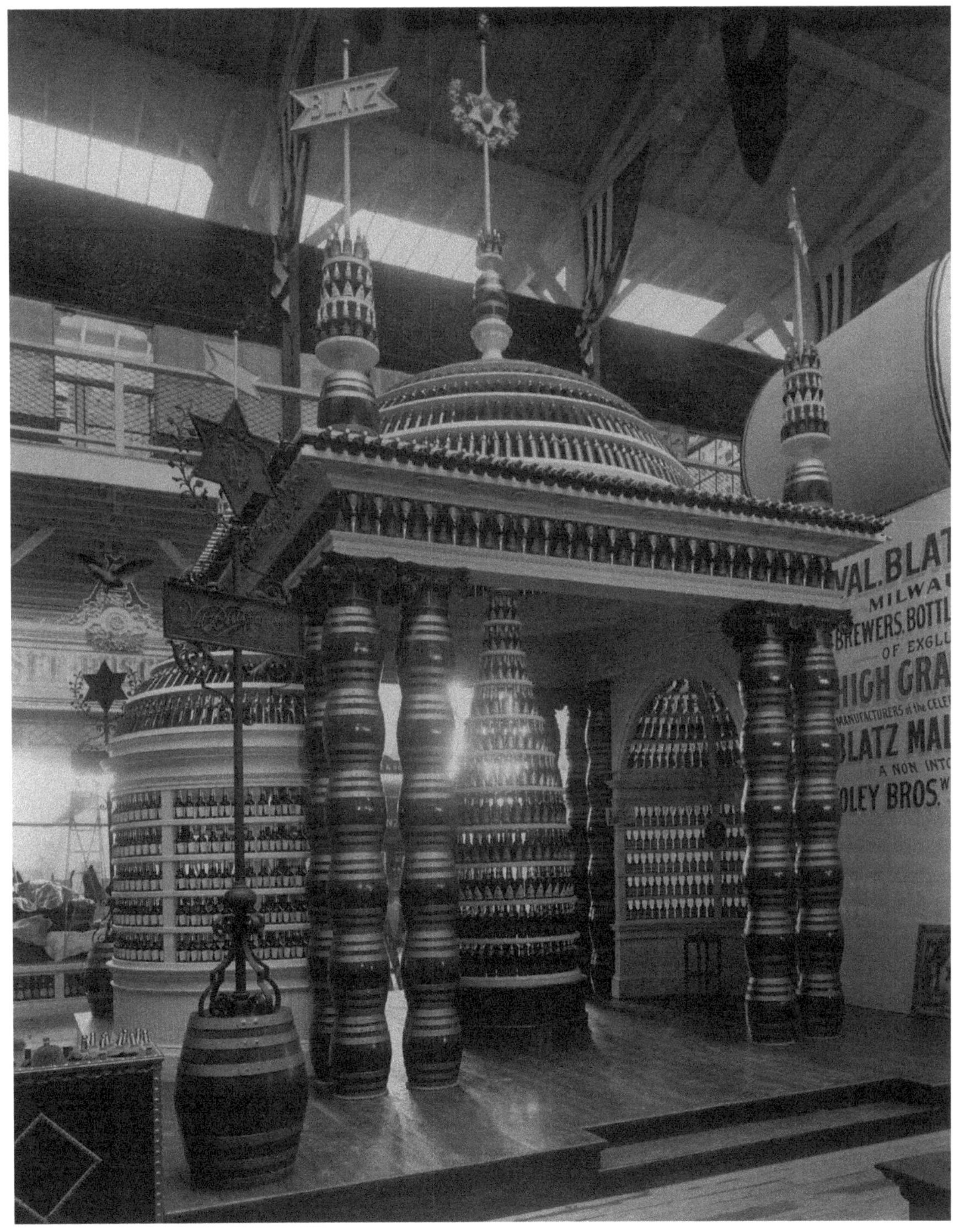

The Trans-Mississippi Exposition featured more than 5,000 individual exhibits. This one for Blatz Beer would have been in the Manufacturers Building located on the Grand Court, one of the largest exhibition buildings. All the structures were built using temporary materials. A combination of plaster, ground hemp (rope) fiber and Portland cement were mixed together to form a substance called "staff." This was formed in sections using molds and attached to a wooden superstructure.

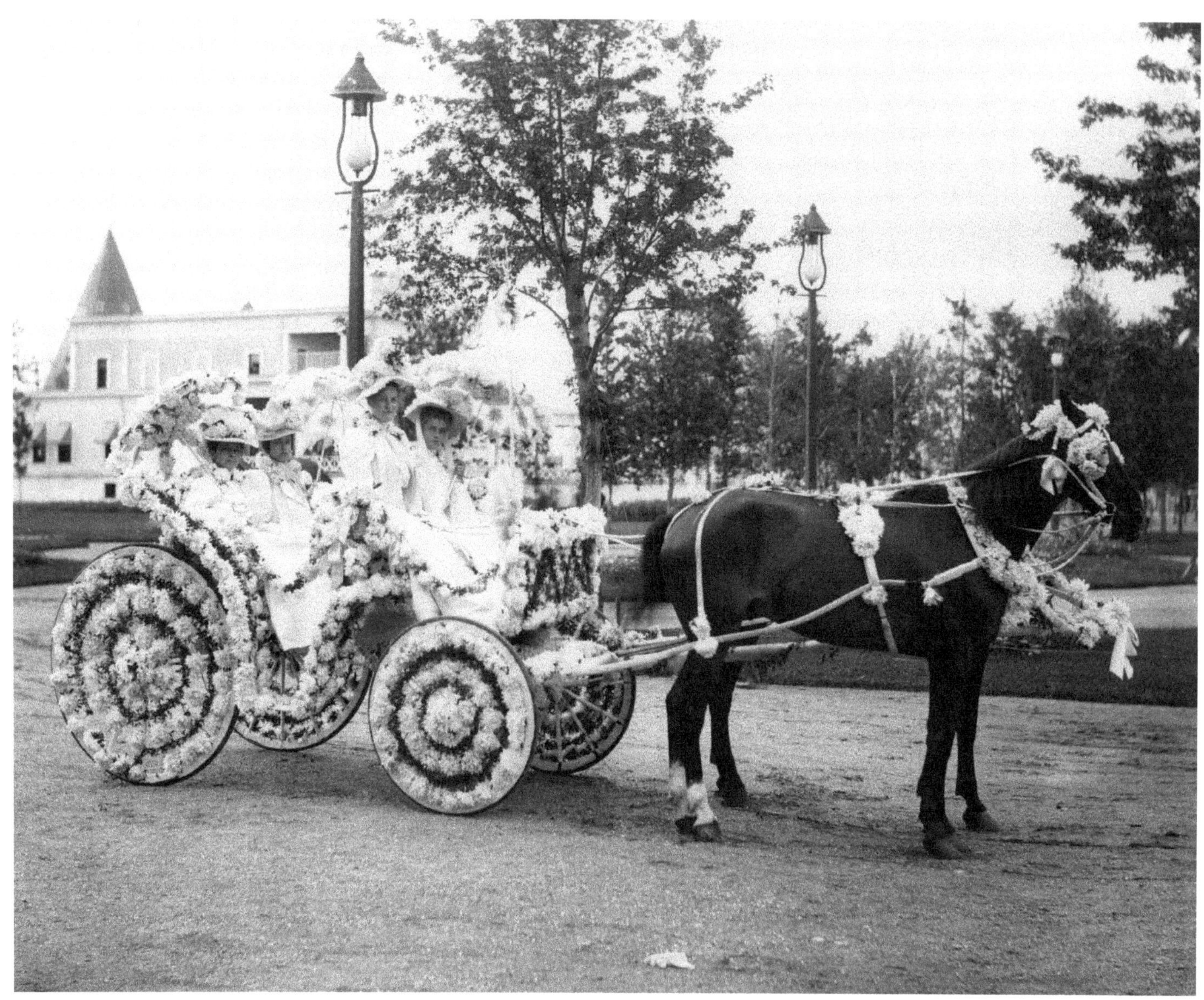

Tuesday, August 2, 1898, was "Flower Day" at the Trans-Mississippi Exposition. About forty horse-drawn vehicles were transformed into parade floats, decorated entirely with fresh flowers. This proved to be a very popular event.

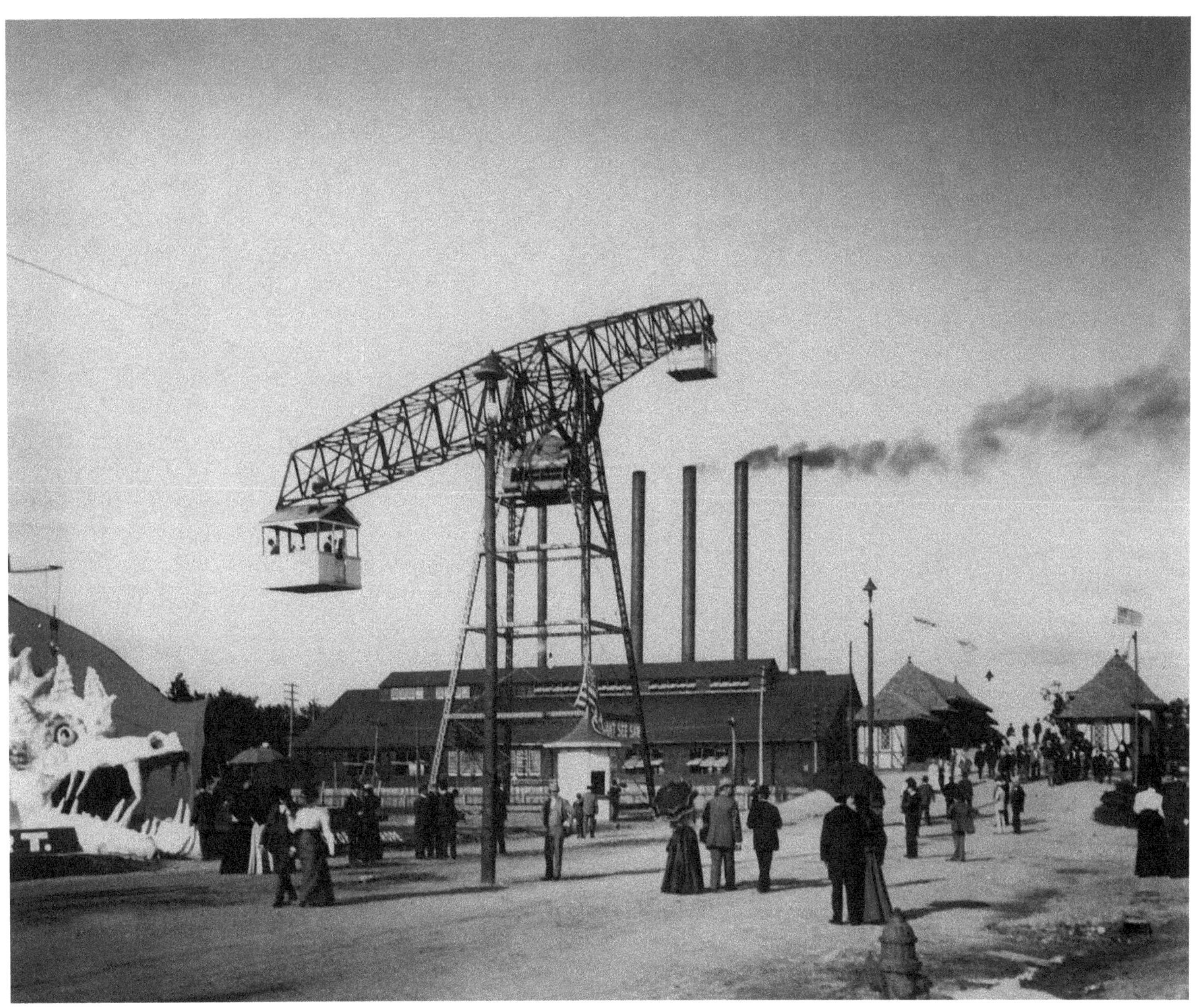

The Giant See-Saw located on the North Midway was one of the most popular attractions. This concession was brought to Omaha from Nashville after the close of the 1897 Tennessee Centennial Exposition. For an admission of 10 cents, passengers were elevated almost 200 feet above the ground. Several couples were married in the cars as they were raised to the highest point.

The display of the American Wringer Company, located in the Manufacturers Building, is an example of the type of exhibit that was very popular with those who attended the fair. World's Fairs were considered important venues for information and education. Modern technology was eagerly sought after by those who came to view these exhibits.

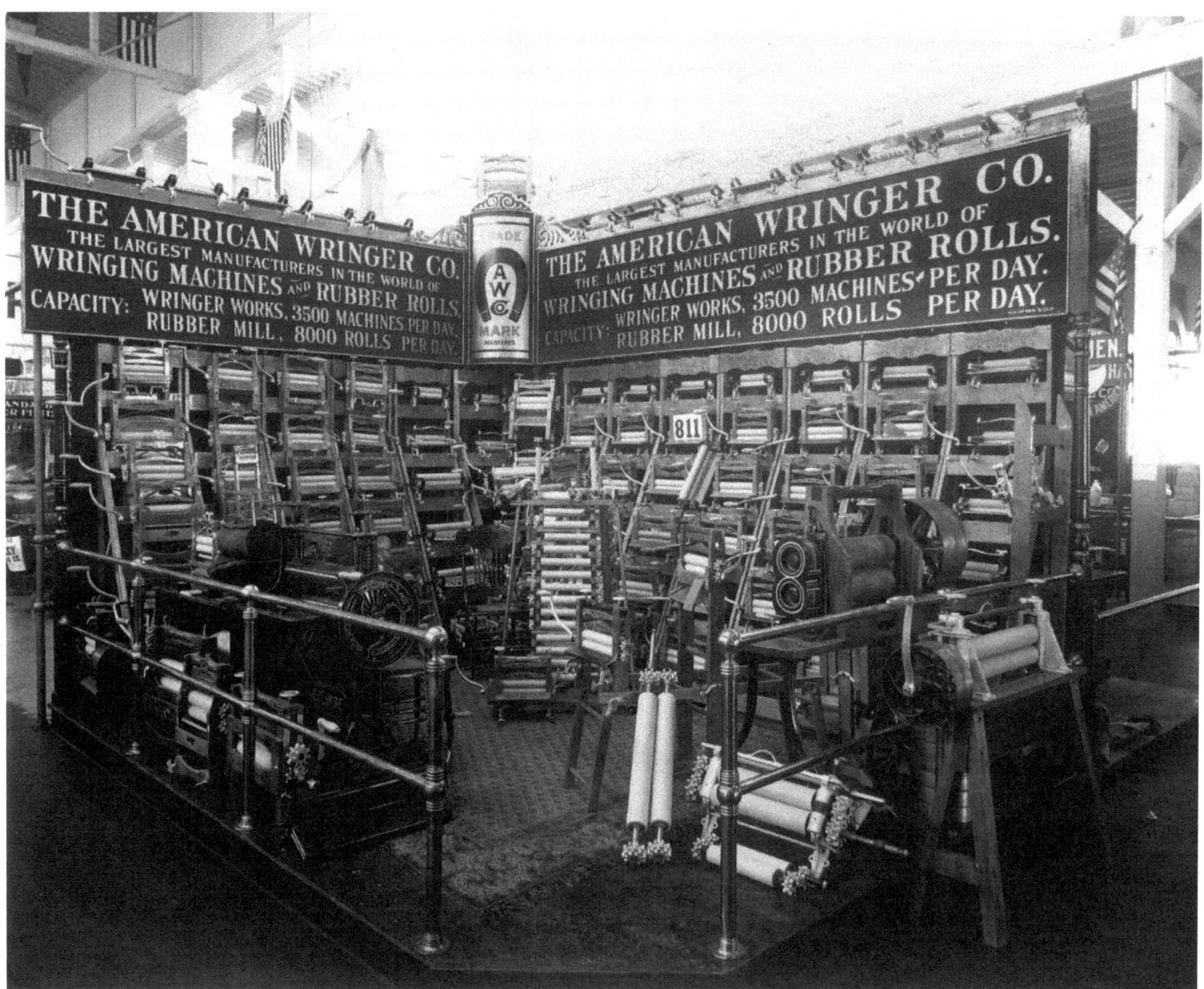

The Streets of Cairo was a large Midway attraction located on the Bluff Tract. It was a conglomeration of "Eastern" exoticism and architecture. The café, shown here, offered unusual teas and other Oriental treats for the enjoyment of fairgoers. These displays were very popular, as most people in the region had never traveled outside the United States.

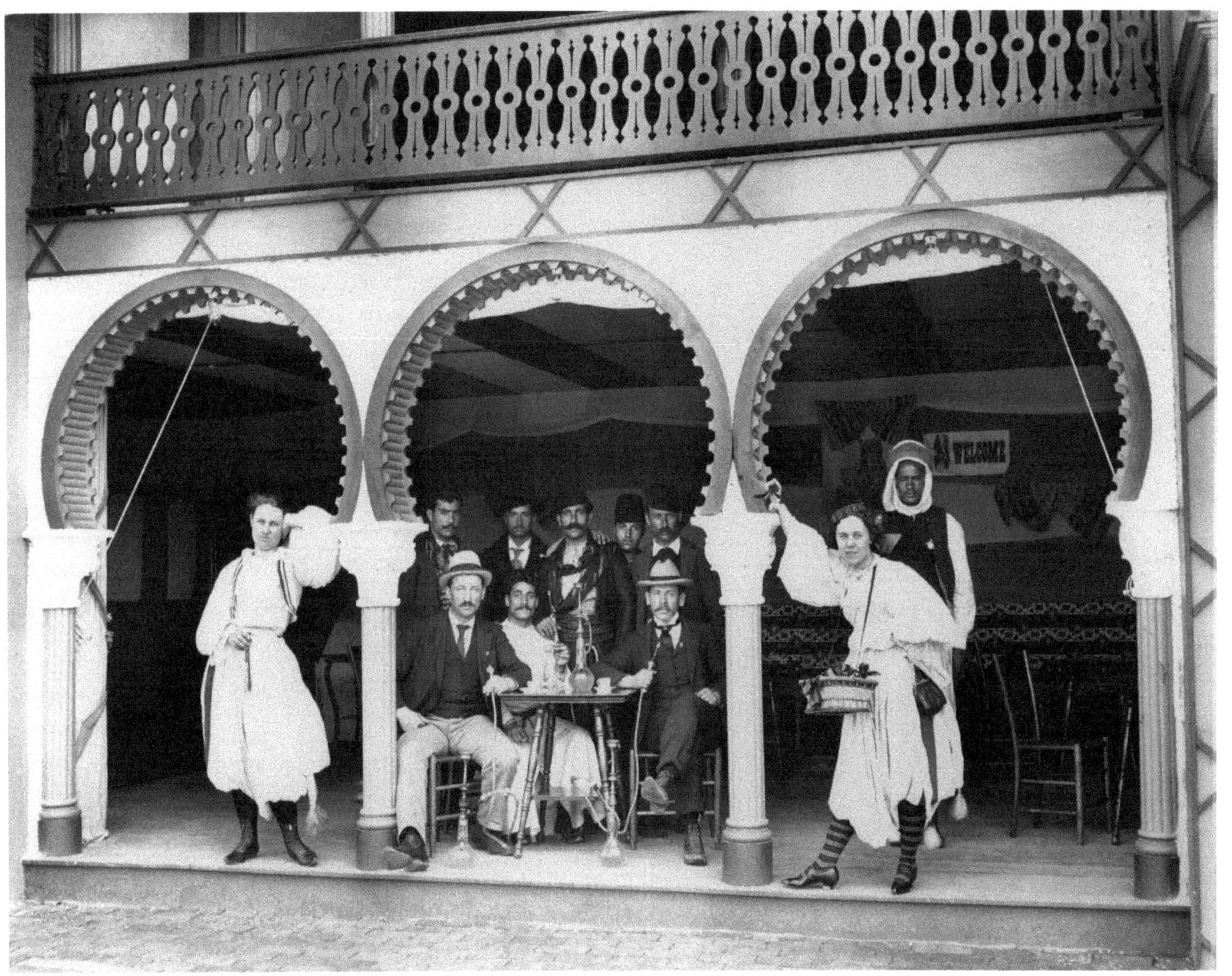

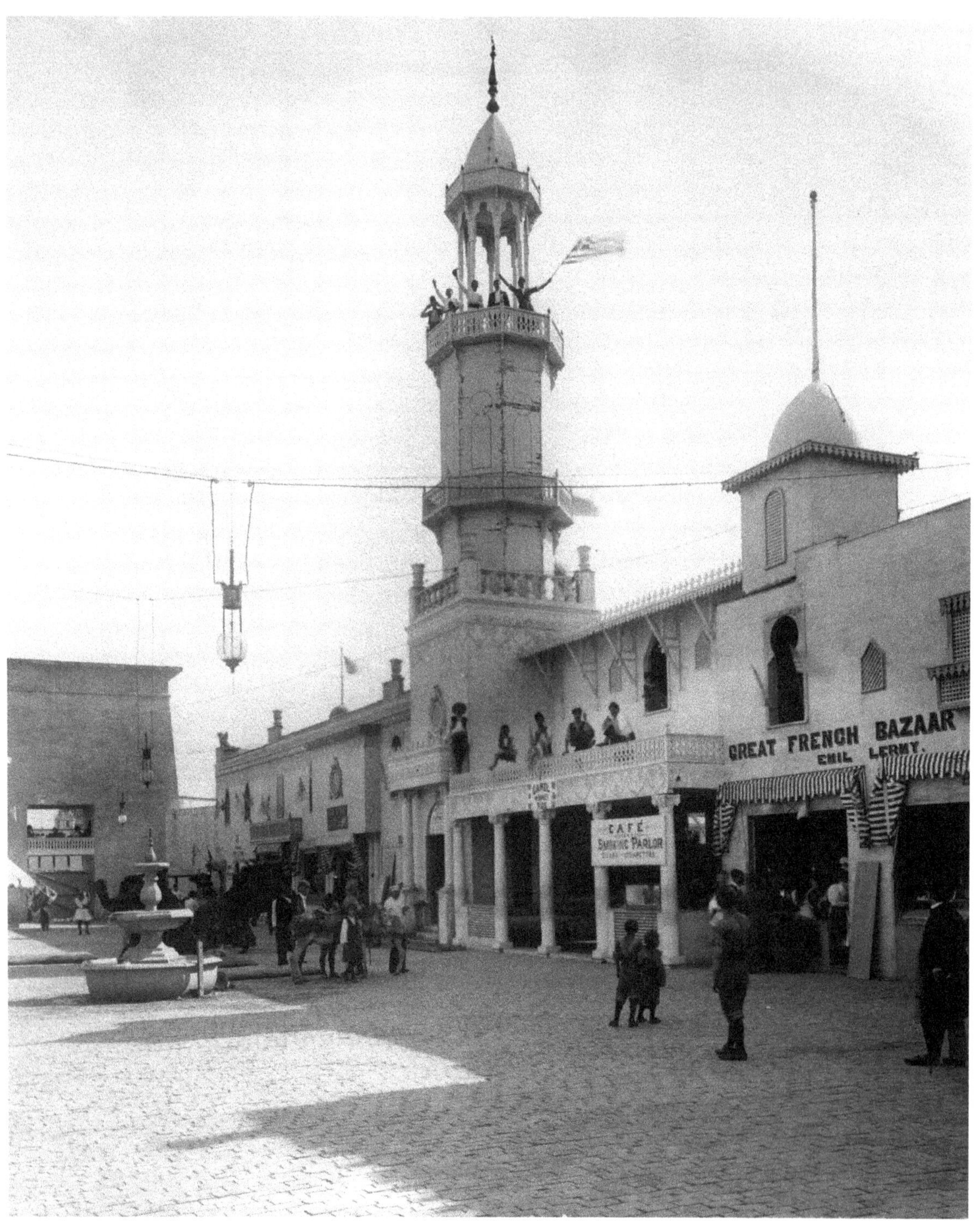

The Streets Of All Nations on the North Midway was an even larger assemblage of exotic designs, displays and entertainment. For an admission charge of 15 cents, visitors could pass through an imposing Egyptian-style entrance to view a wide assortment of displays. Camel rides, exotic dancers, impromptu athletic competitions, varied native costumes, and performances in the Streets Of All Nations Theatre were among the attractions waiting inside.

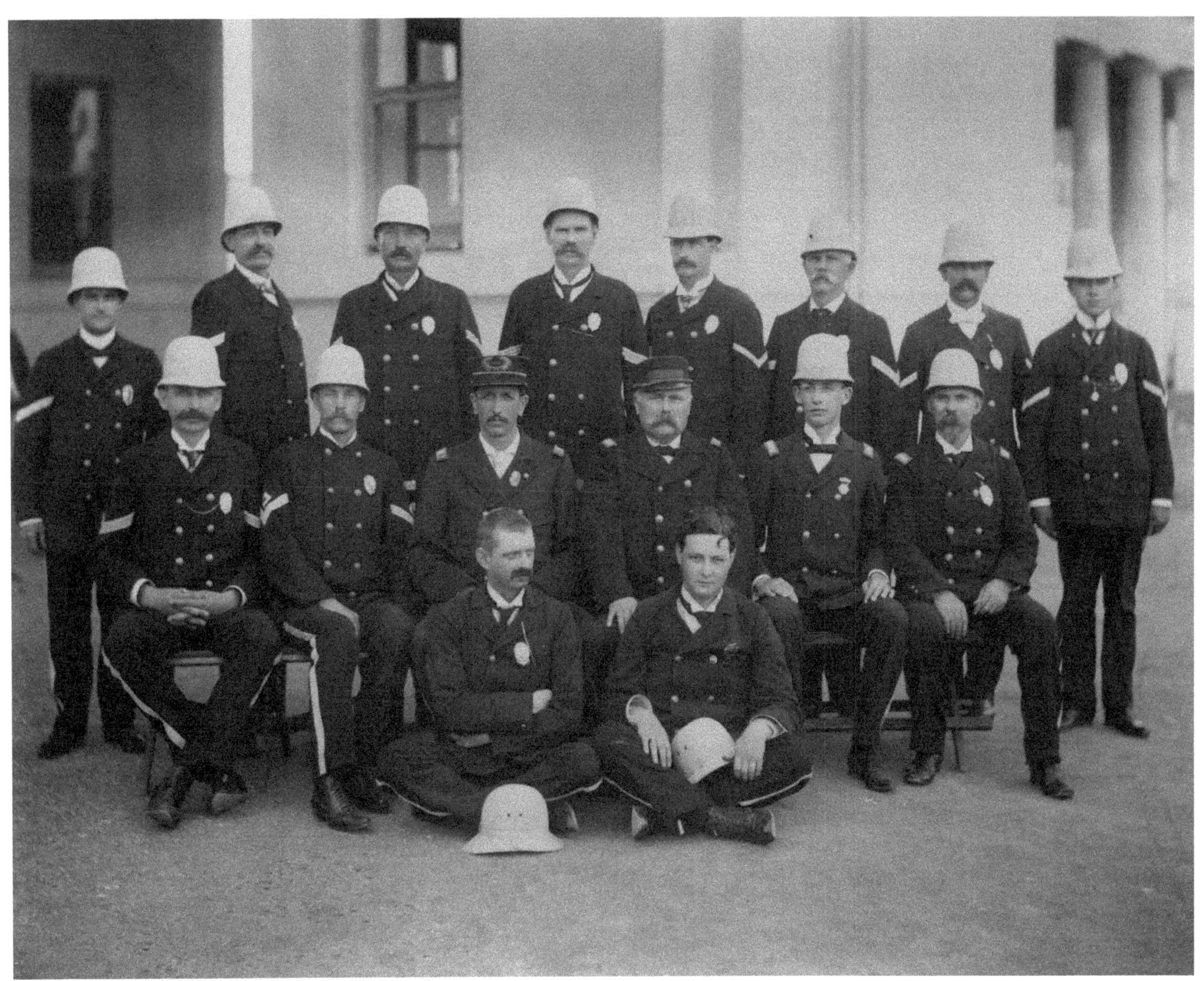

The Trans-Mississippi Exposition was a very large event, and security was an on-going concern. Besides special guards for the United States Government Building, there was a general security staff employed by the Exposition Company. The Chief of the Exposition Guards and his staff are shown here. The Exposition had more than 2.5 million visitors during its period of operation.

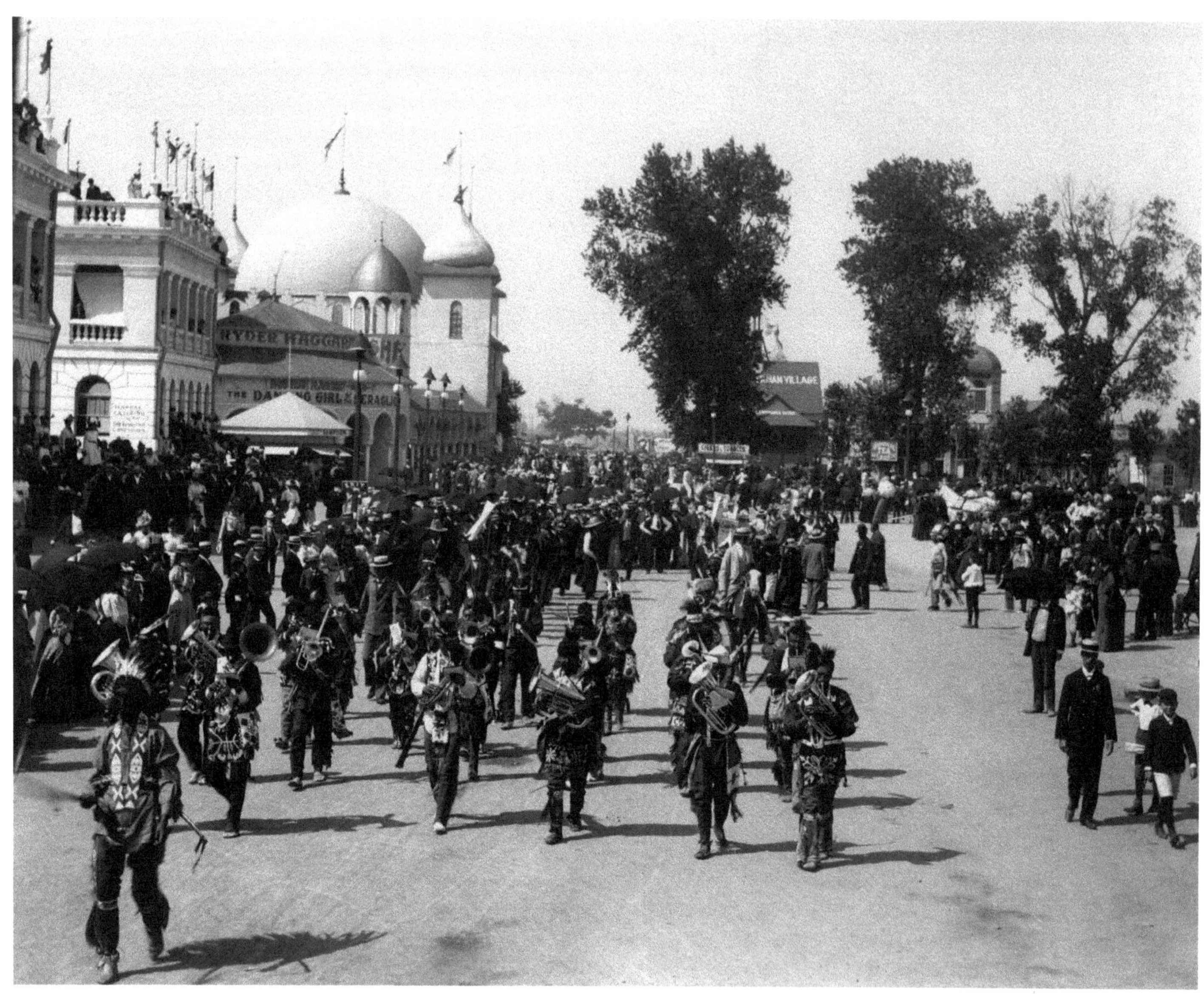

August 4, 1898, was "Indian Day," and this parade of Native Americans marched through the fairgrounds. One of the outstanding features of the Exposition was the Indian Congress, which brought together five hundred Native Americans, representing many different tribes and nations. This was the last time that such a gathering took place before most were resettled on reservations established by the federal government.

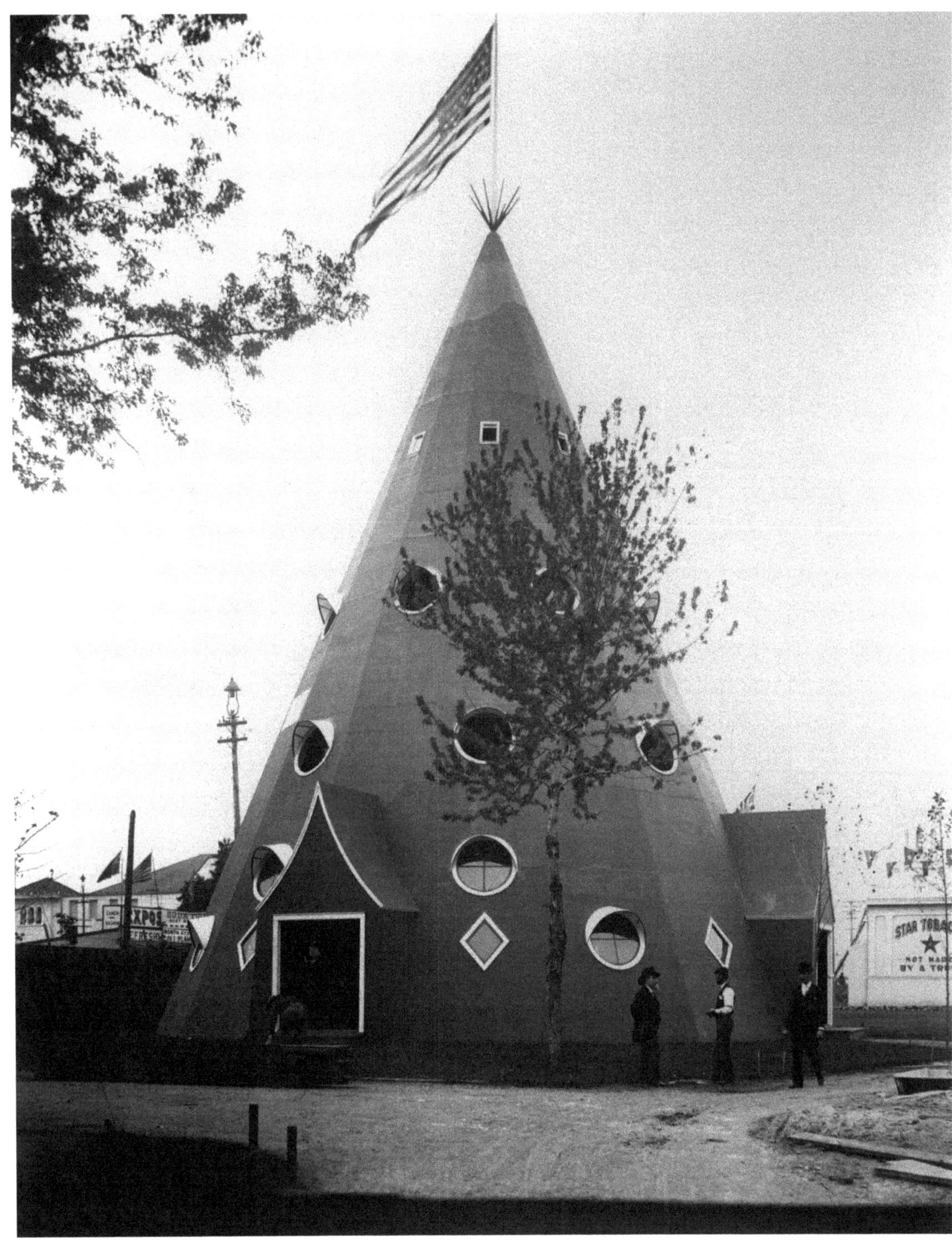

The State of Iowa was well represented at the Trans-Mississippi Exposition in Omaha. In addition to the elegant Iowa Building, Pottawattamie County, in which Council Bluffs is located, decided to have their own distinct building. They erected a giant "Wigwam" 83 feet tall. The first two levels contained displays and exhibits, while the third and fourth held parlors and sitting rooms for the convenience of fairgoers.

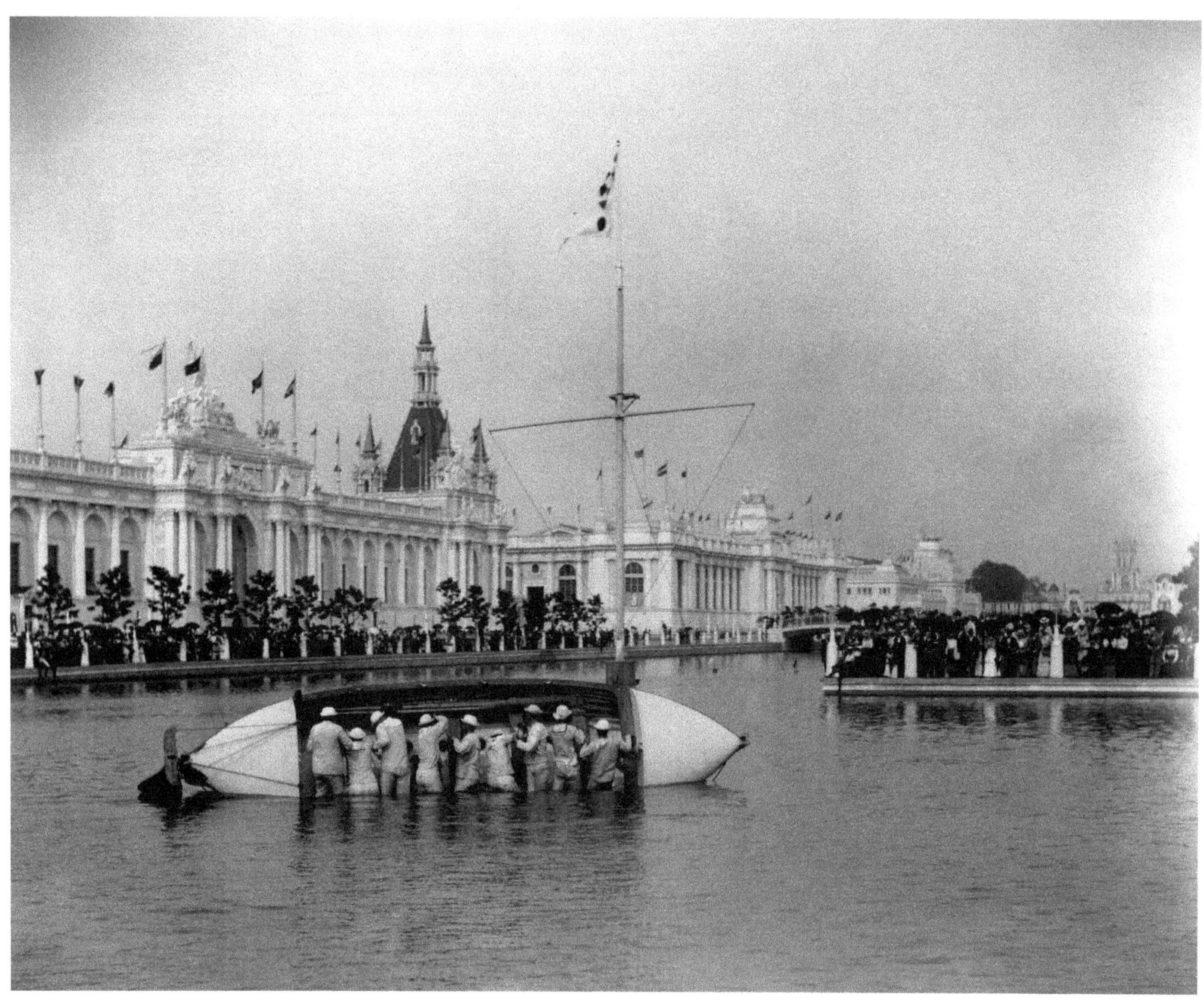

Drills conducted by members of the U.S. Government Life Saving Service were a special attraction. The demonstration shown here was held on Thursday, August 11th, the first day of their appearance. The maneuvers were held in the Lagoon and proved to be extremely popular. The Lagoon itself was a man-made excavation into which millions of gallons of water were pumped, filling it to a depth of nine feet.

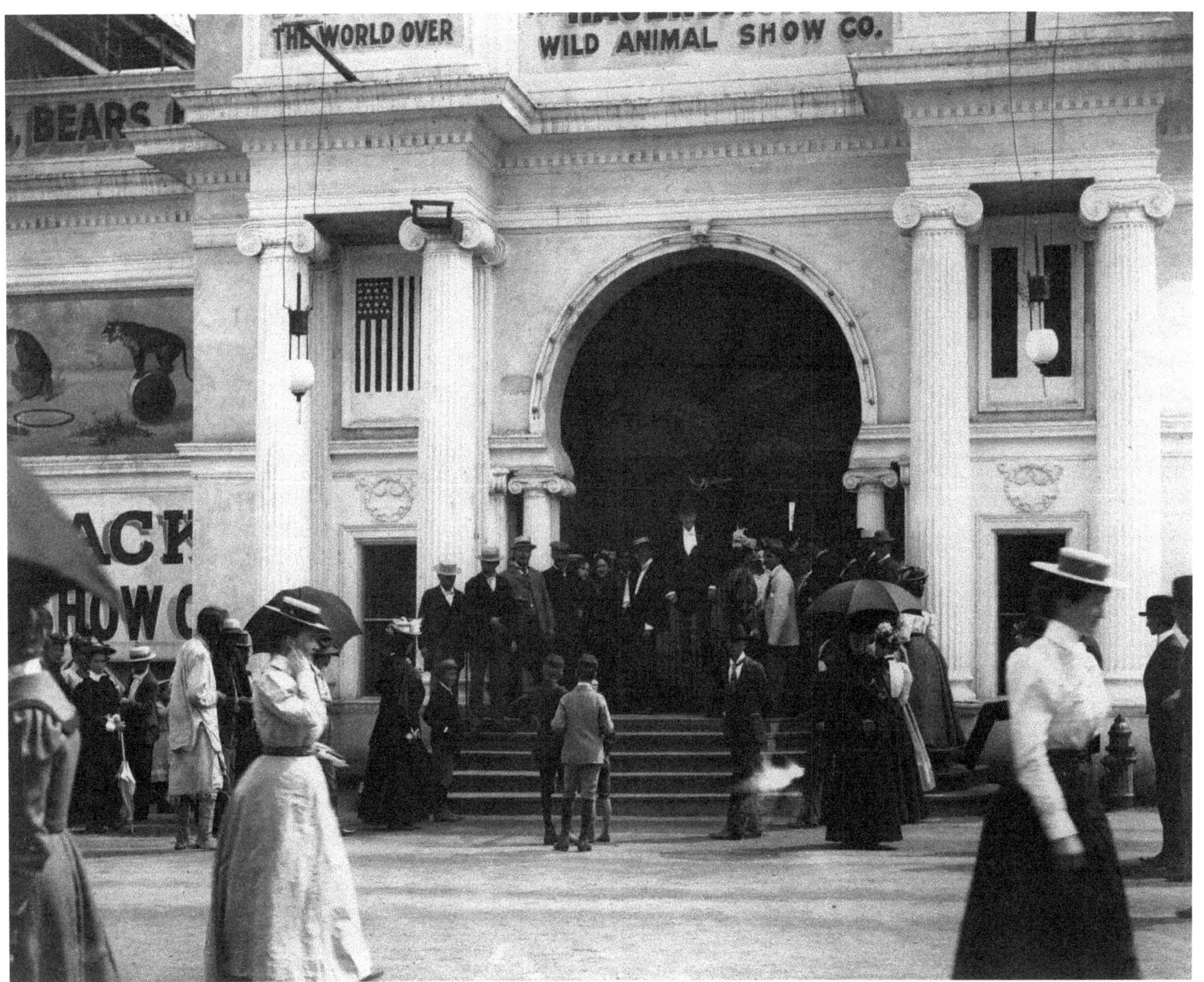

One of the most unusual features of the Exposition, located on the North Midway, was Hagenback's Wild Animal Show. Its pavilion held approximately five hundred different animals. More than twenty professional animal trainers accompanied this show, and there were almost continual performances throughout the entire run of the Exposition. Here, many visitors saw real lions, tigers, and elephants for the first time.

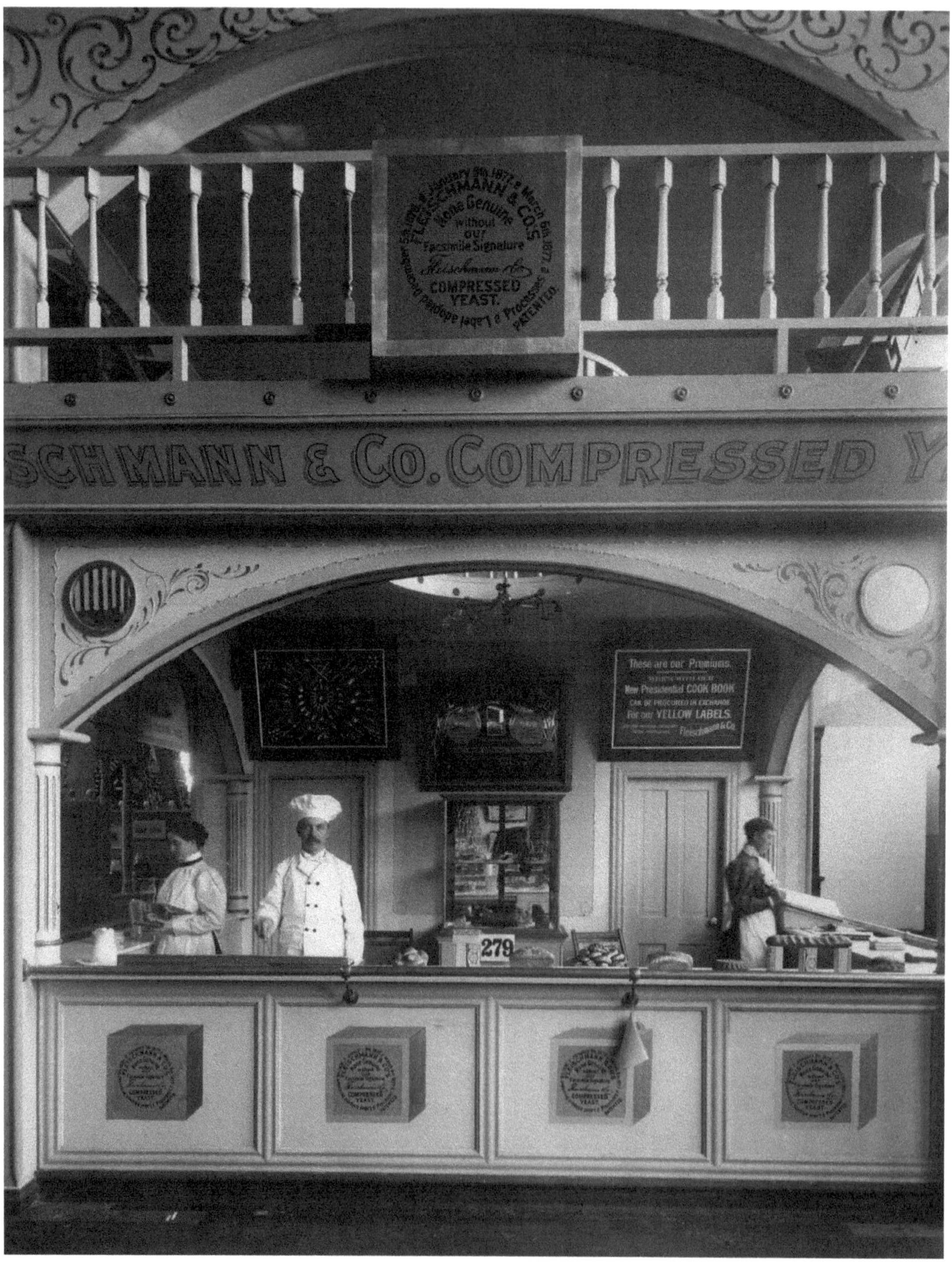

Many of the exhibits held in the Manufacturers Building demonstrated new and useful products for the home. At the Fleischmann and Company booth, visitors could see baking demonstrations and receive information and free samples of the company's revolutionary compressed yeast. A sign on the rear wall offers "our New Presidential COOK BOOK" in exchange for yellow Fleischmann labels.

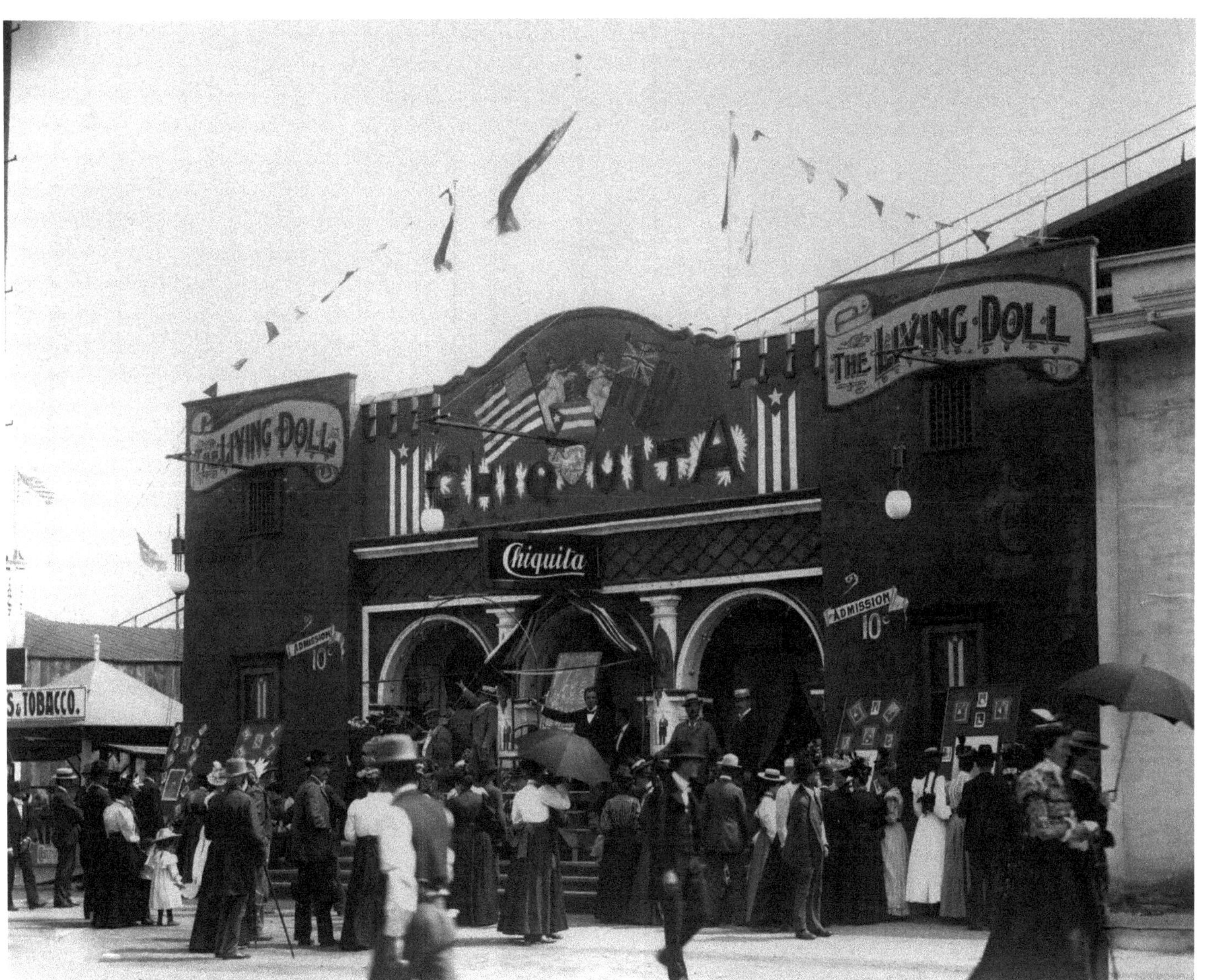

An unusual feature on the North Midway was "Chiquita—The Living Doll." Also known as the "Doll Lady" and the "Cuban Atom," Chiquita was billed as the "smallest woman in the world." Human anomalies were considered great curiosities in America at that time, so an exhibit such as this generated much interest. Not only could visitors view Chiquita in a miniature room setting, they could purchase her picture and autograph.

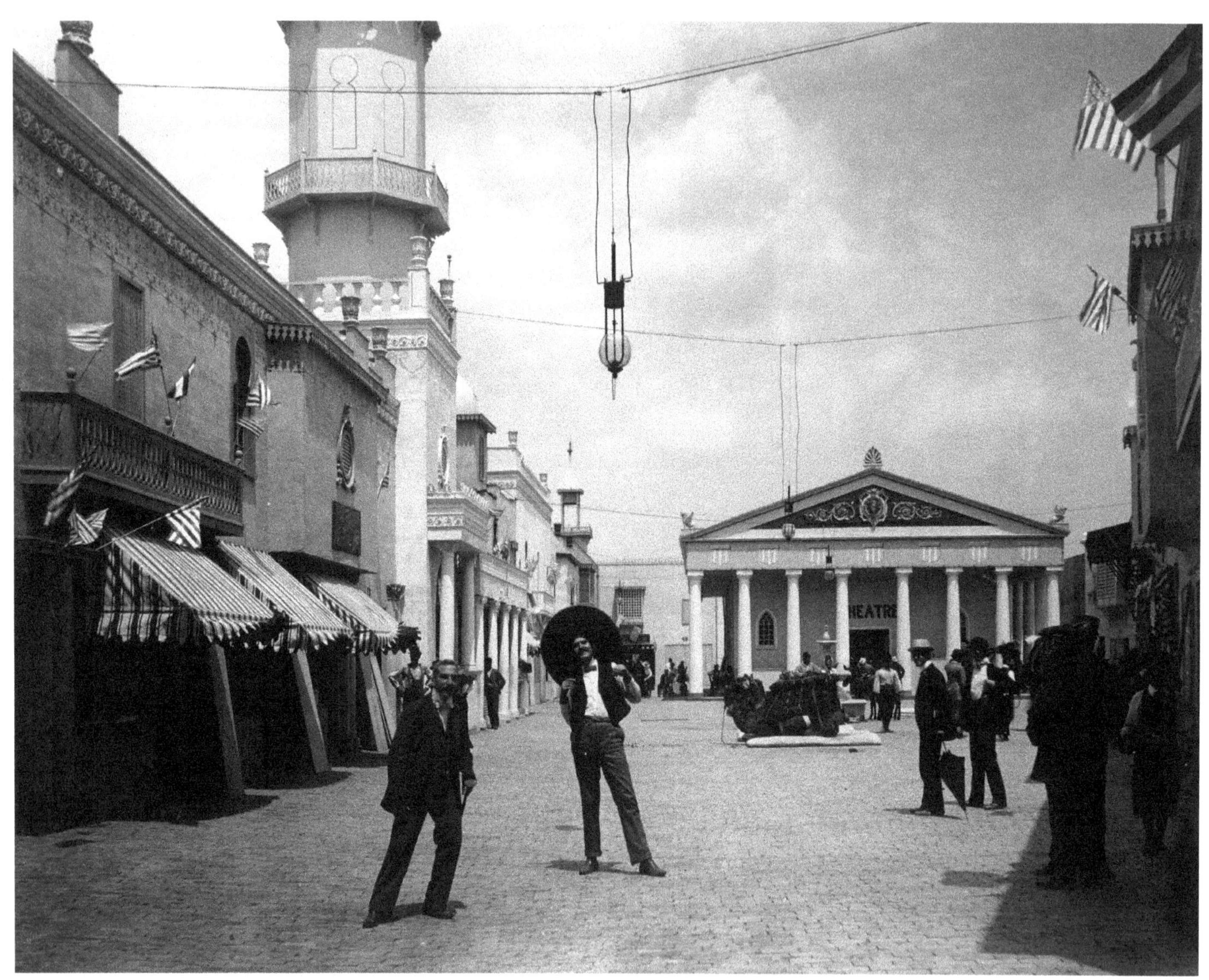

This view taken inside the courtyard of the Streets of All Nations depicts a row of small shops and "bazaars" on the left, which offered an assortment of exotic goods. In the center is the Theatre, styled after the Greek Parthenon. This was actually a small vaudeville theater, which held numerous live performances put on by the workers in the concessions.

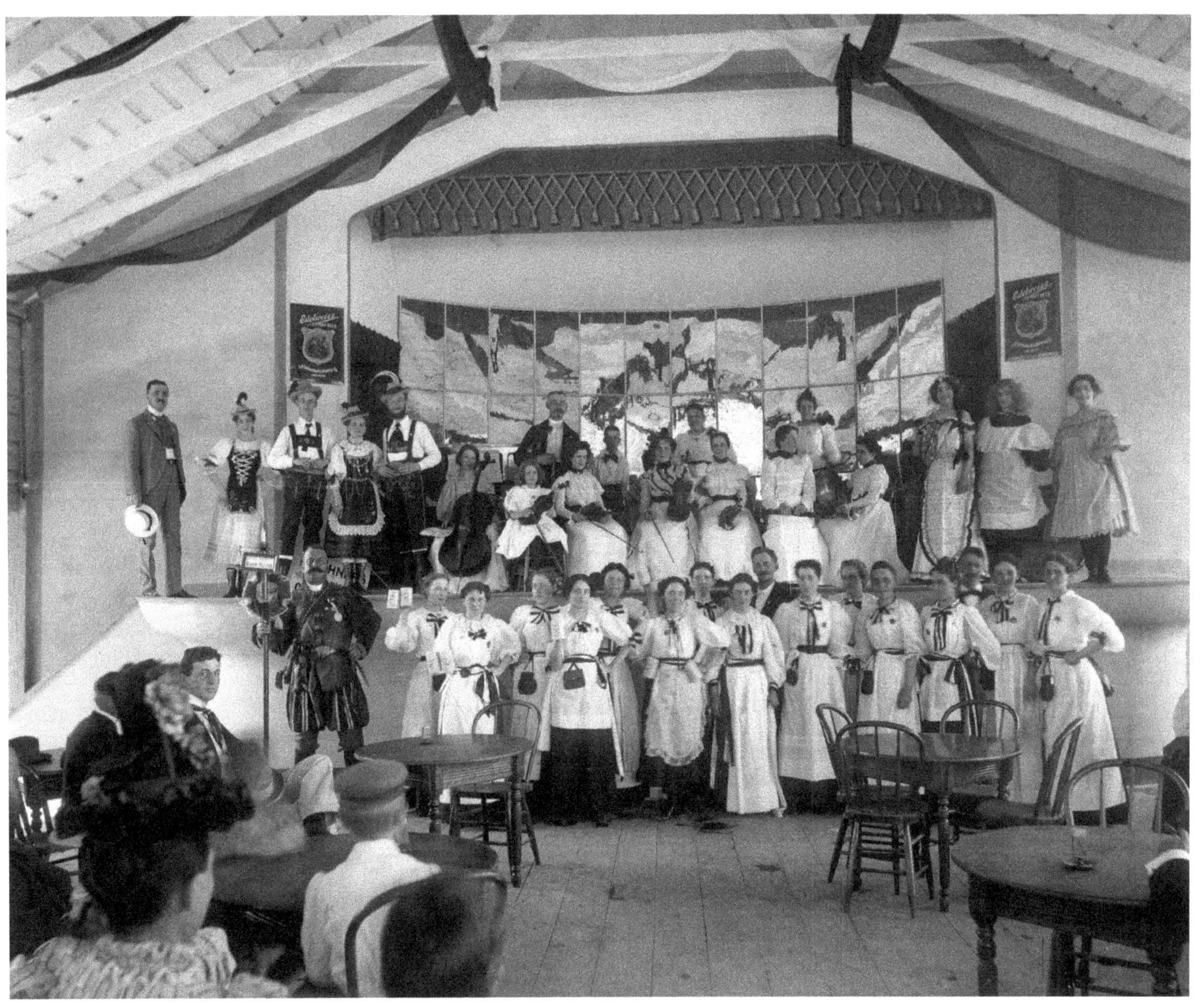

The German Village, located on the Bluff Tract, was another very popular attraction at the Exposition. The "Deutsches Dorf" was designed as a replica of the "Bratwurst Cloecklein," a historic inn at Nuremberg. This photo shows a group of waitresses working in the restaurant and beer hall which was a part of this concession. October 18th was "German Day."

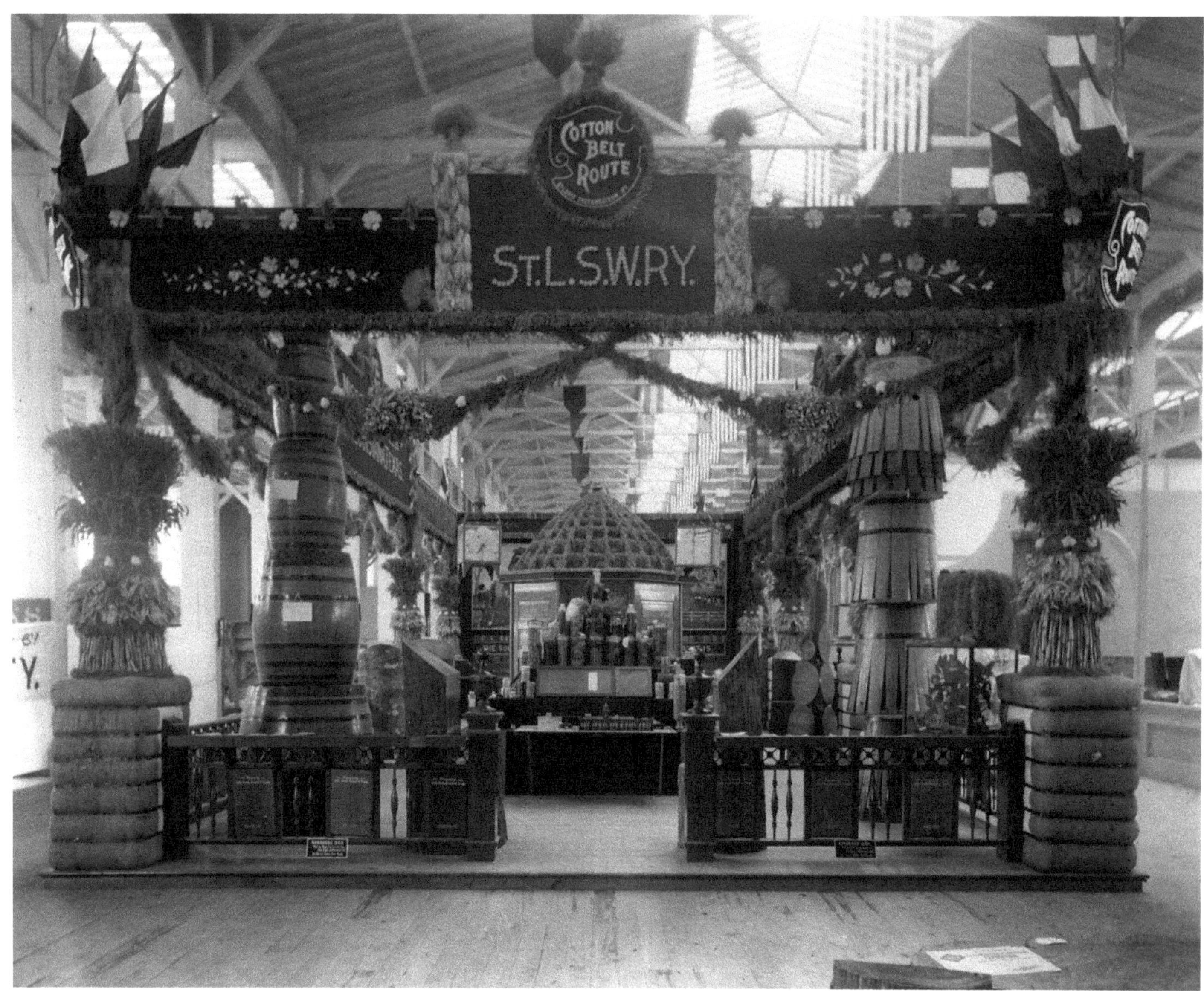

The St. Louis Southwestern Railway received a Gold Award Medal for its Cotton Belt Route Display, which featured agricultural products from the areas the railroad serviced in Missouri, Arkansas, Louisiana and Texas. Wood from those areas was also used to construct the framework.

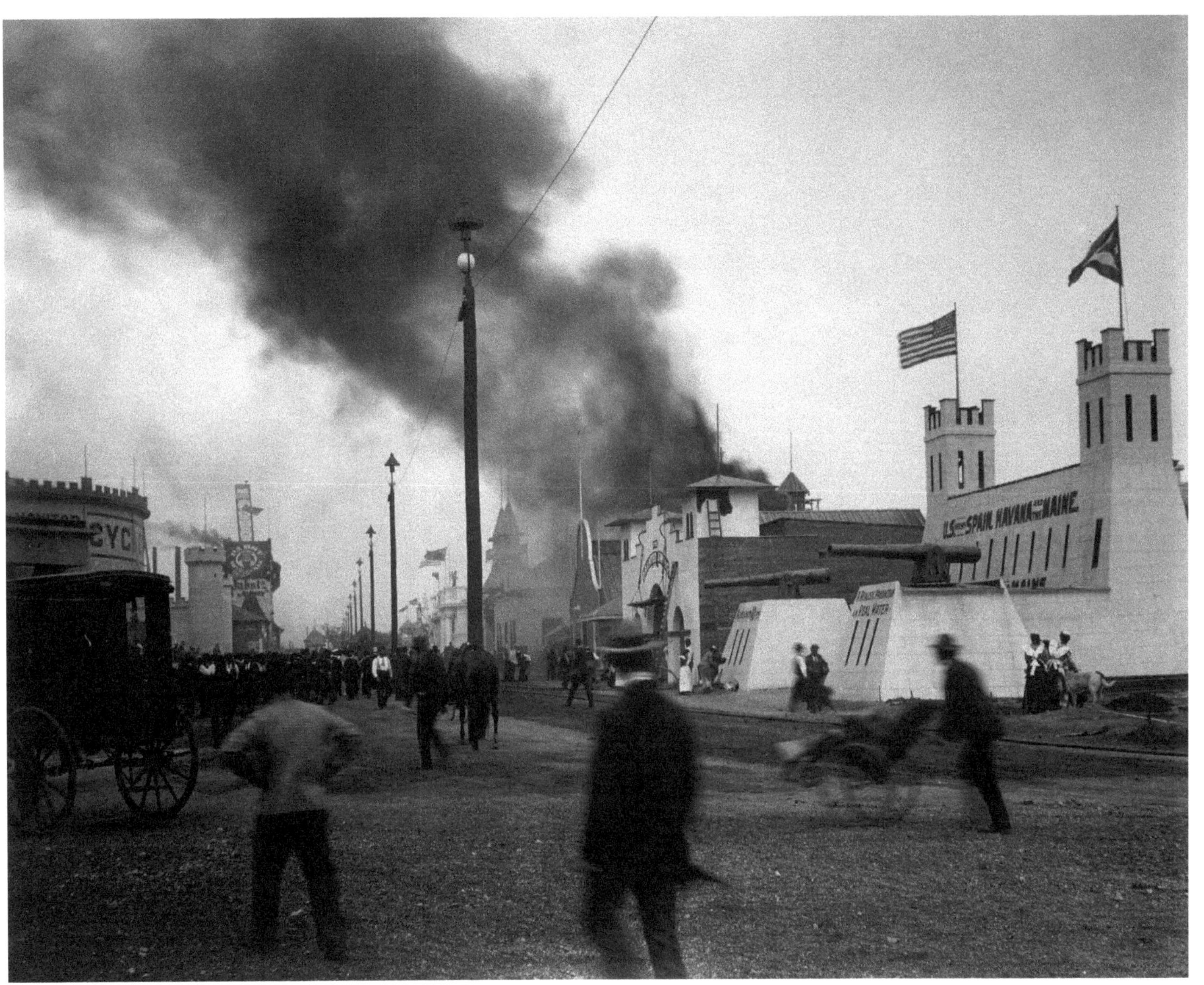

On June 3rd, a blaze started on the North Midway. All of the Exposition structures were made of wood and temporary materials, and fire was always a concern. A system of water lines and fire hydrants had been installed on the fairgrounds as a security measure. The exhibit on the right about the Spanish-American War ("A Realistic Production on Real Water") was not damaged in the fire. Next door, the Haunted Swing gave riders the impression of going to great heights and flipping completely over , but in reality they were barely moving.

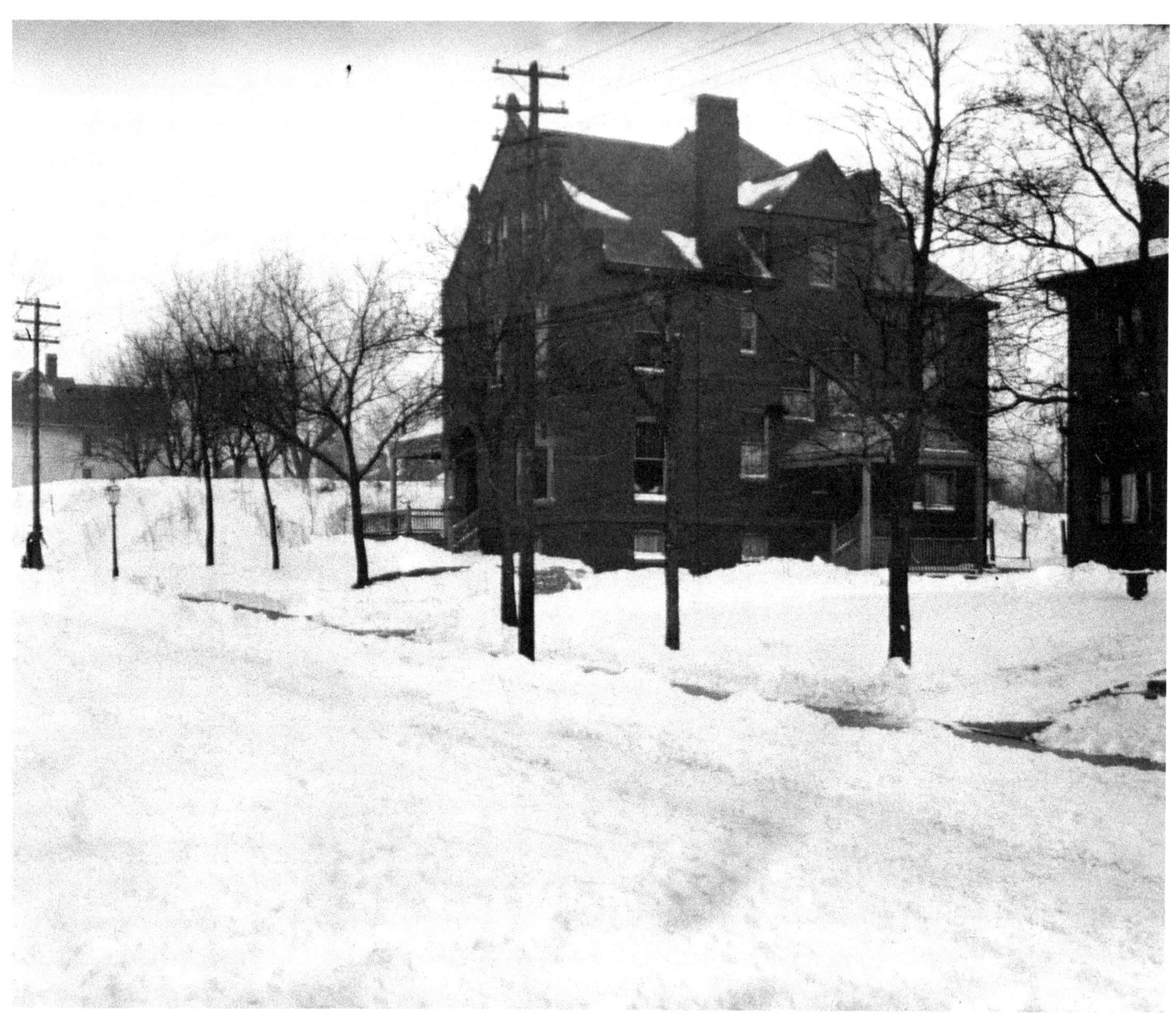

The William Wallace residence at 2420 Harney Street. Wallace was President of the Omaha Library Board and an officer of the Omaha National Bank, where he rose to be vice president, serving in that position to the time of his death in 1915.

A New Century

(1901–1920)

Although Omaha remained an important transportation center with numerous railroads, the economic base of the community was shifting. After 1900, great numbers of immigrants, mostly from Eastern Europe, poured into Omaha seeking work in the South Omaha packing houses. The growth of this industry sustained the general economy of the city.

The community marked its fiftieth birthday in 1904. Many made note of the progress since pioneer days, but other tensions were mounting. In 1909, an anti-Greek riot violently drove the majority of ethnic Greeks from the city. On Easter Sunday, March 23, 1913, Omaha was struck by a tornado. More than 185 people were killed in the area, and thousands of homes destroyed or heavily damaged. Between 1915–1917, a series of annexation fights ensued as the City of Omaha attempted to annex four contiguous communities. Dundee, Benson, South Omaha and Florence were absorbed into the boundaries of Omaha. This was not generally viewed in a positive way. Labor disputes led to a city-wide strike of street railway employees. Perhaps the lowest point in the history of the city came on September 28, 1919. A race riot resulted in the brutal death of a black man and two white men and included an attempt to murder the Mayor of Omaha. An angry mob of 4,000 went on a rampage, burning the Douglas County Court House and terrorizing the city. Federal troops were called in to restore order.

These decades provided more positive results as well. Mutual of Omaha, one of the most important insurance companies in the country, started here in 1909. In 1916, President and Mrs. Woodrow Wilson visited Omaha as part of the sesquicentennial celebrations hosted by AK-SAR-BEN. Father Edward J. Flanagan opened the Workingman's Hotel in January of 1916 and on December 12 of that same year rented a house at 25th and Dodge streets, officially opening his Father Flanagan's Home for Boys. By 1920, the population was approaching 200,000 due mostly to increases obtained by annexations and continued growth in the immigrant community as new job-seekers came into the city.

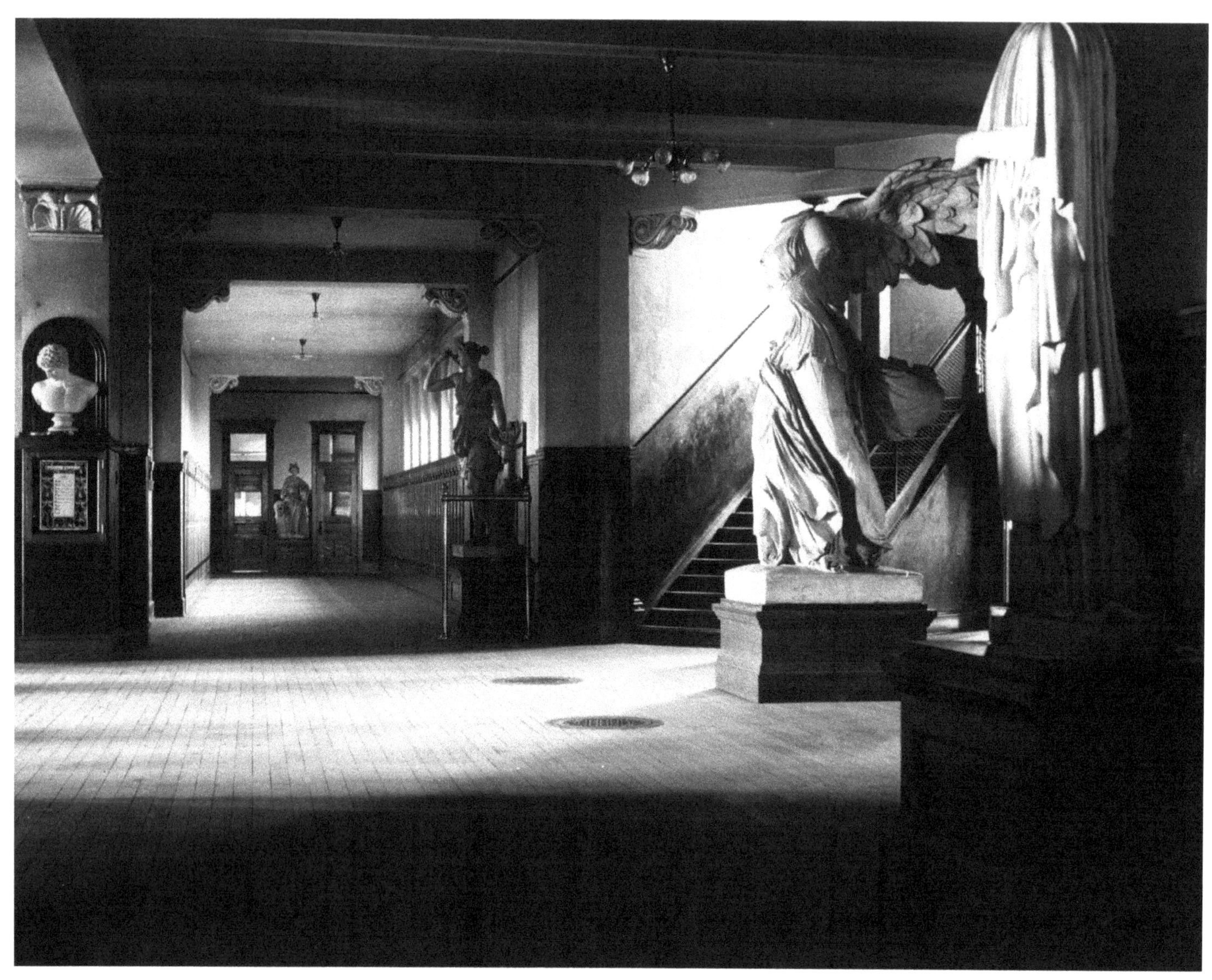

By 1899, the Omaha High School building at 20th and Dodge streets was deemed too small and obsolete. Plans were accepted for a new building that year, and ground was broken in 1901. This new high school was built in four sections over a period of about ten years at a cost of approximately $850,000. In this early 1900s shot, we see an interior corridor in the new building, displaying plaster copies of classical sculpture used by the art department.

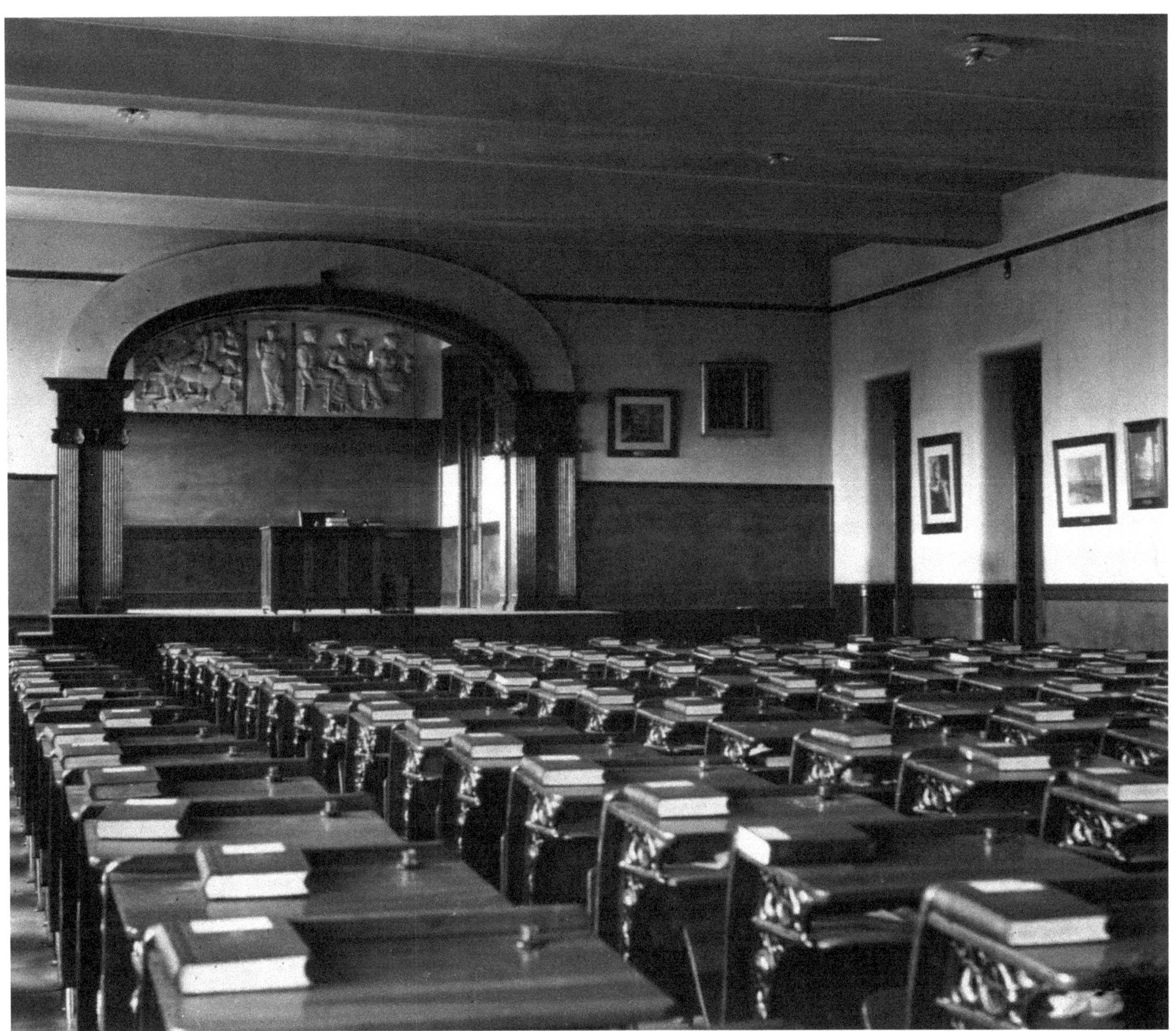

A view of the interior of study room 215, one of the largest in the new high school building at 20th and Dodge streets, as it appeared in the early 1900s, with rows of desks and at the far end a stage. This room was used as a general study hall and also for large class lectures.

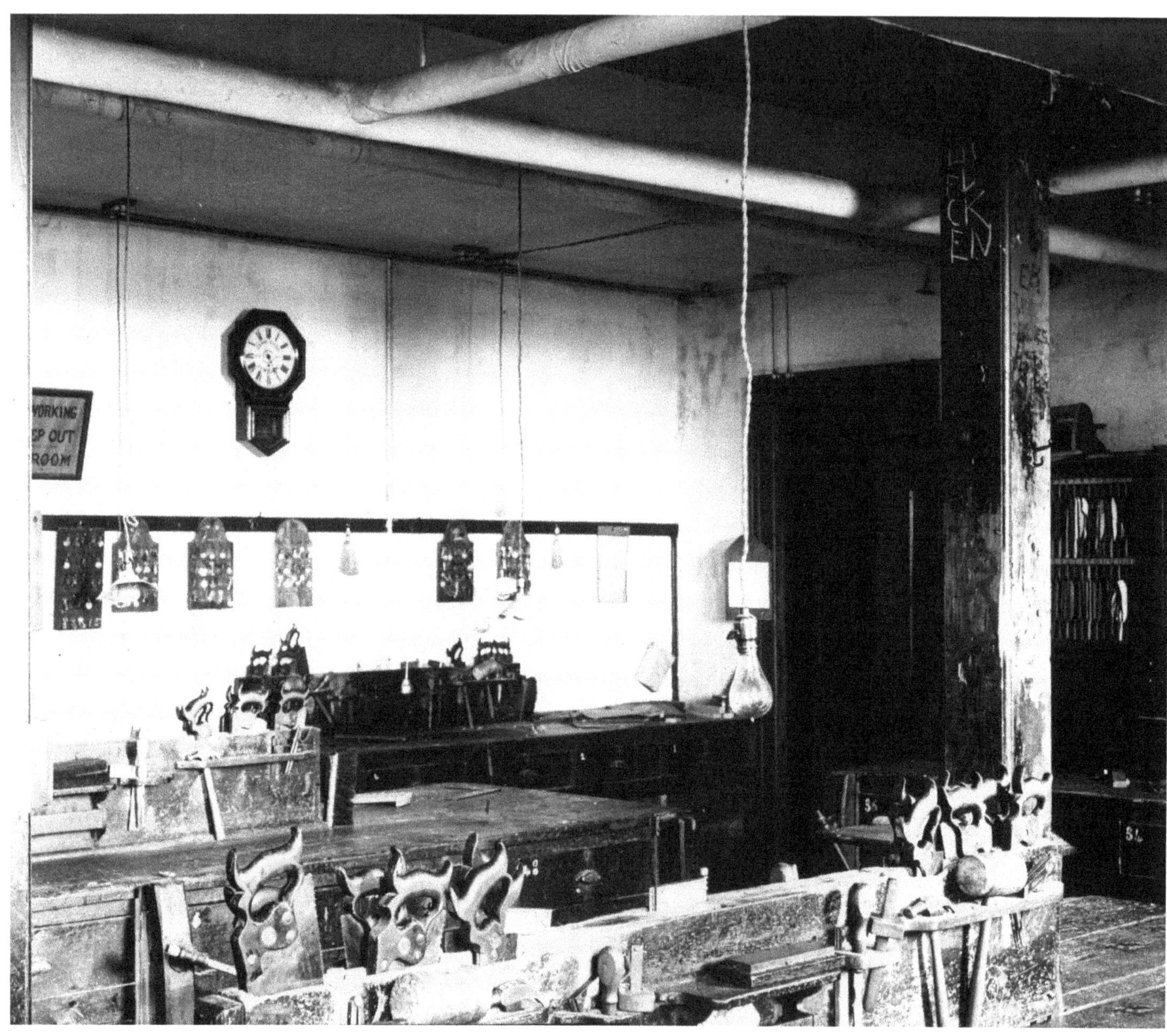

The manual training department, used for "shop" classes, was located in the basement of the new high school building at 20th and Dodge streets. Other courses included mechanical and architectural drafting, wood turning, joinery, and metal work. This view was taken in the early 1900s.

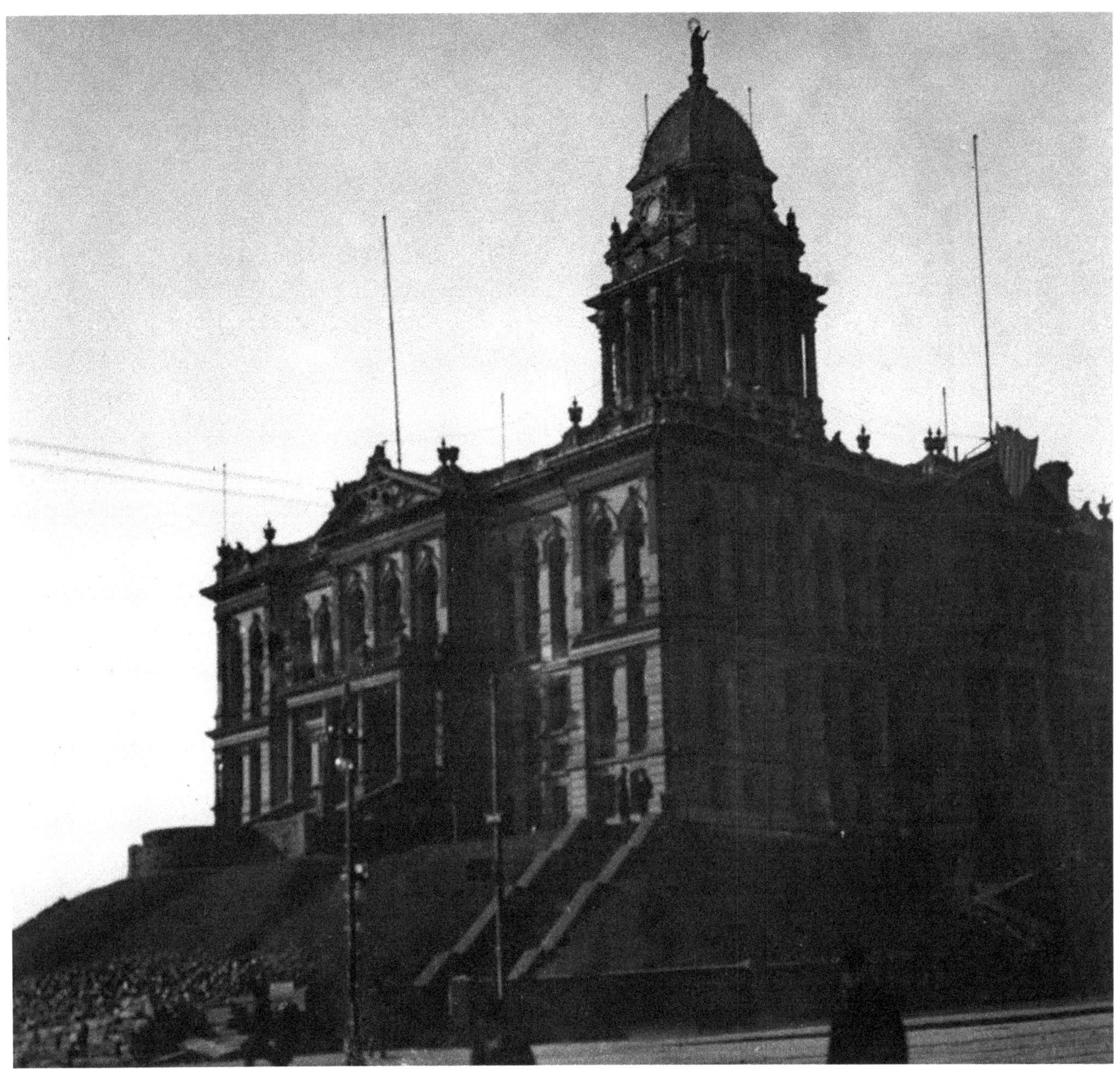

The original courthouse was built between 1857 and 1861 on a section of Washington Square, located between 15th and 16th streets on Farnam. Needing more space, the county purchased lots in 1878 between 17th and 18th streets on Farnam for the purpose of erecting a new courthouse. This image from early 1900s shows the second Douglas County Court House. It, too, was replaced by an even larger structure.

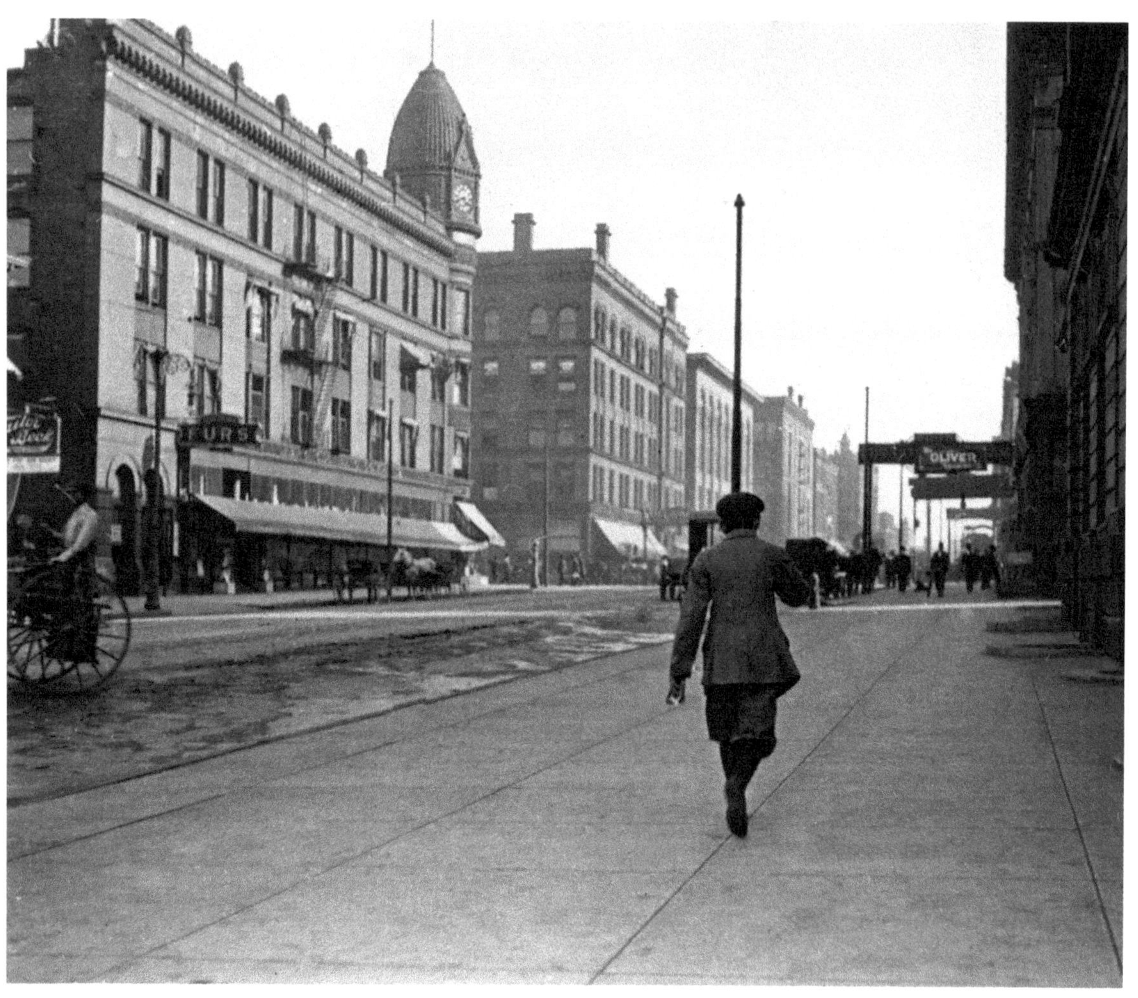

Looking south-southeast from the intersection of 15th and Dodge streets. The cupola visible at upper-center is atop the Continental Block, a large office building located at the northeast corner of 15th and Douglas.

The street railway viaduct on O Street in the vicinity of 33rd in South Omaha in the early 1900s. Beyond it are numerous meatpacking houses of the Union Stockyards Company, the economic backbone of the community for many years.

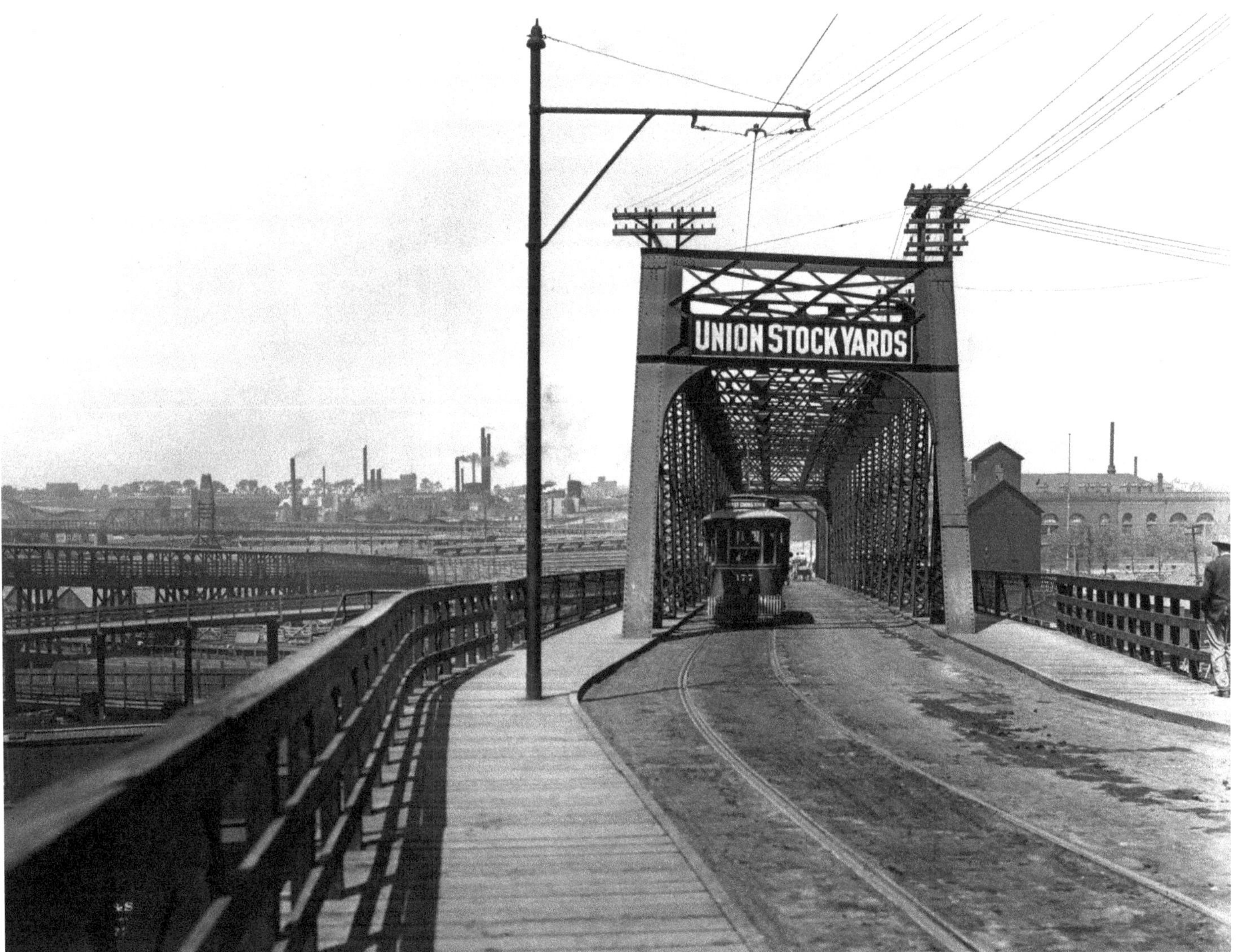

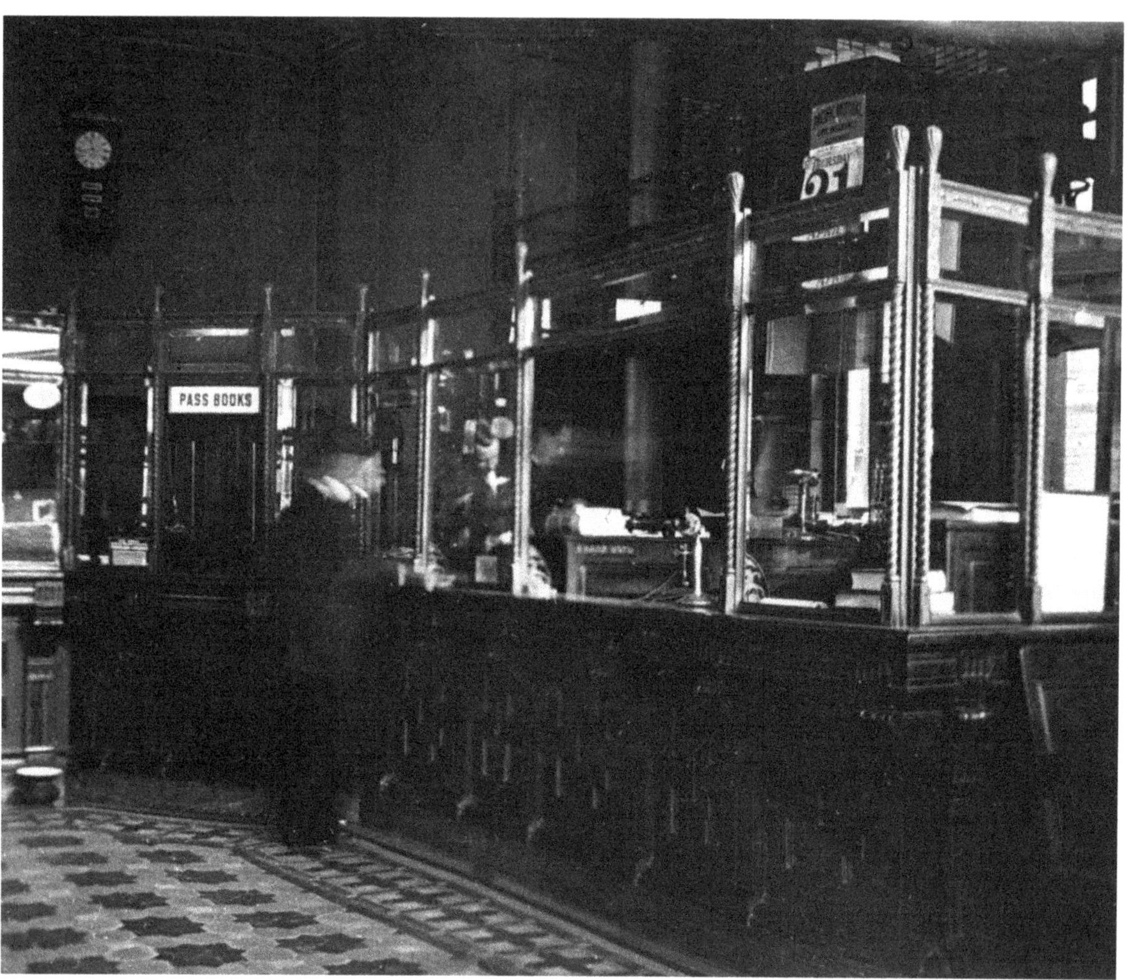

The lobby of the Omaha National Bank building at 212 South 13th Street, showing the teller cages where customers would conduct business. Interior views such as this were not common around the turn of the century, due to the technical difficulties of making photographs in an uncontrolled setting.

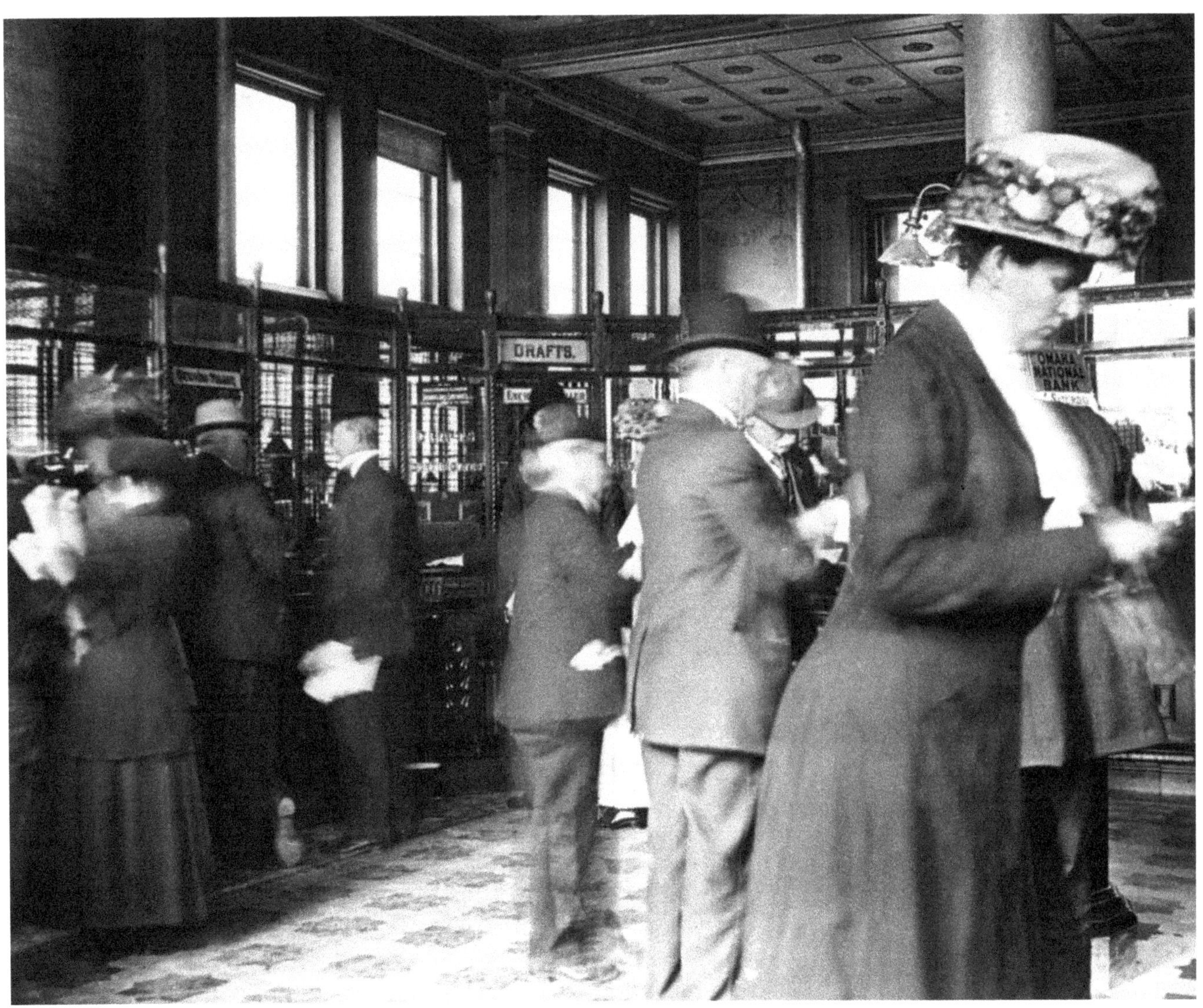

This picture from the lobby of the Omaha National Bank at 212 South 13th Street provides a window into daily life early in the twentieth century. Note the comparatively well-dressed appearance of the bank patrons, which was the norm in that more formal era.

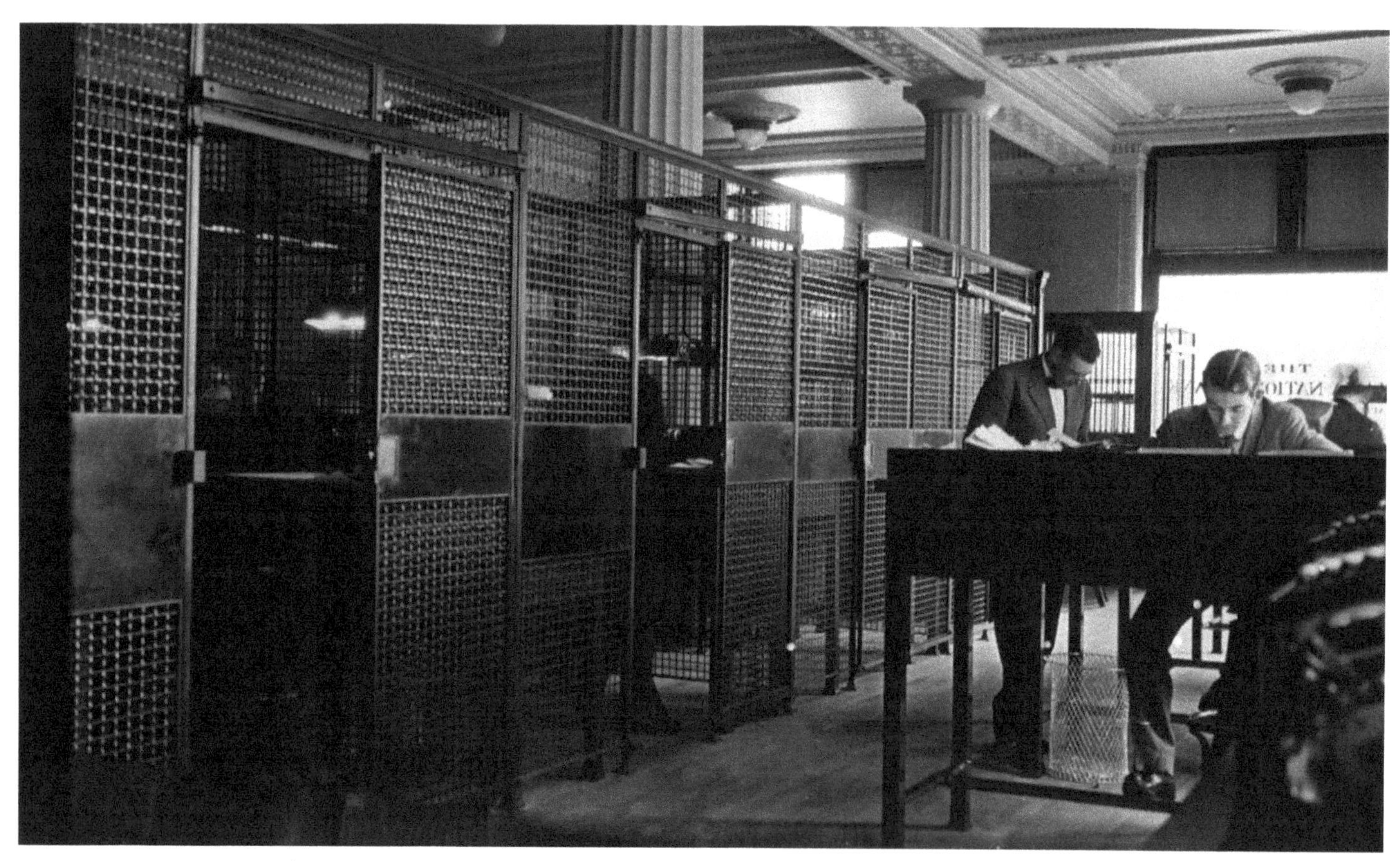

The working area behind the tellers' cages at the Omaha National Bank, 212 South 13th Street.

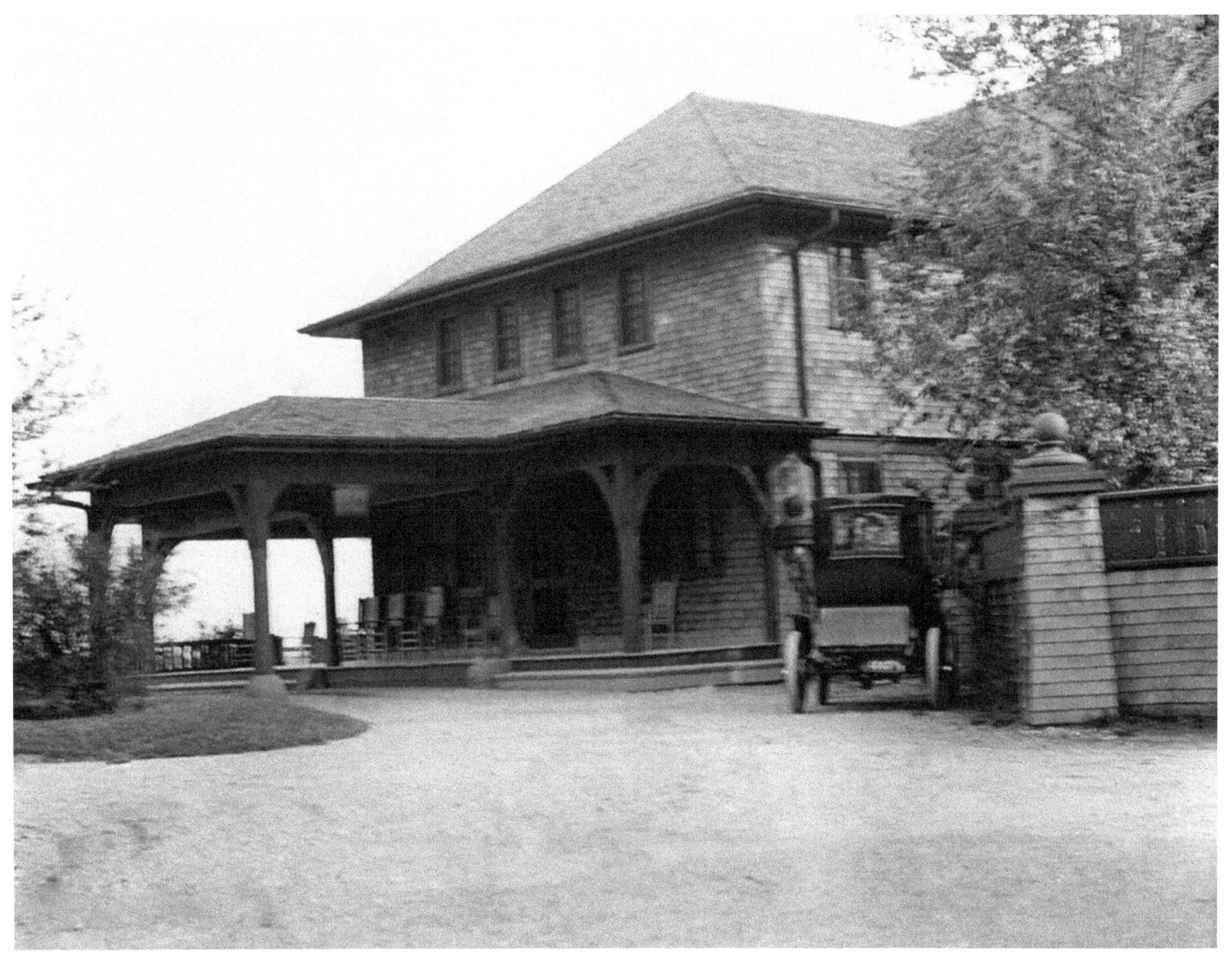

An early view of the original clubhouse of the Omaha Country Club, as it appeared about 1905. The club was organized in 1901 with E. A. Cudahy as its first president. Located on a one-hundred-acre tract adjacent to the community of Benson, the property was sold in 1916 for $130,000, and the club relocated in Northwest Omaha, where it remains today.

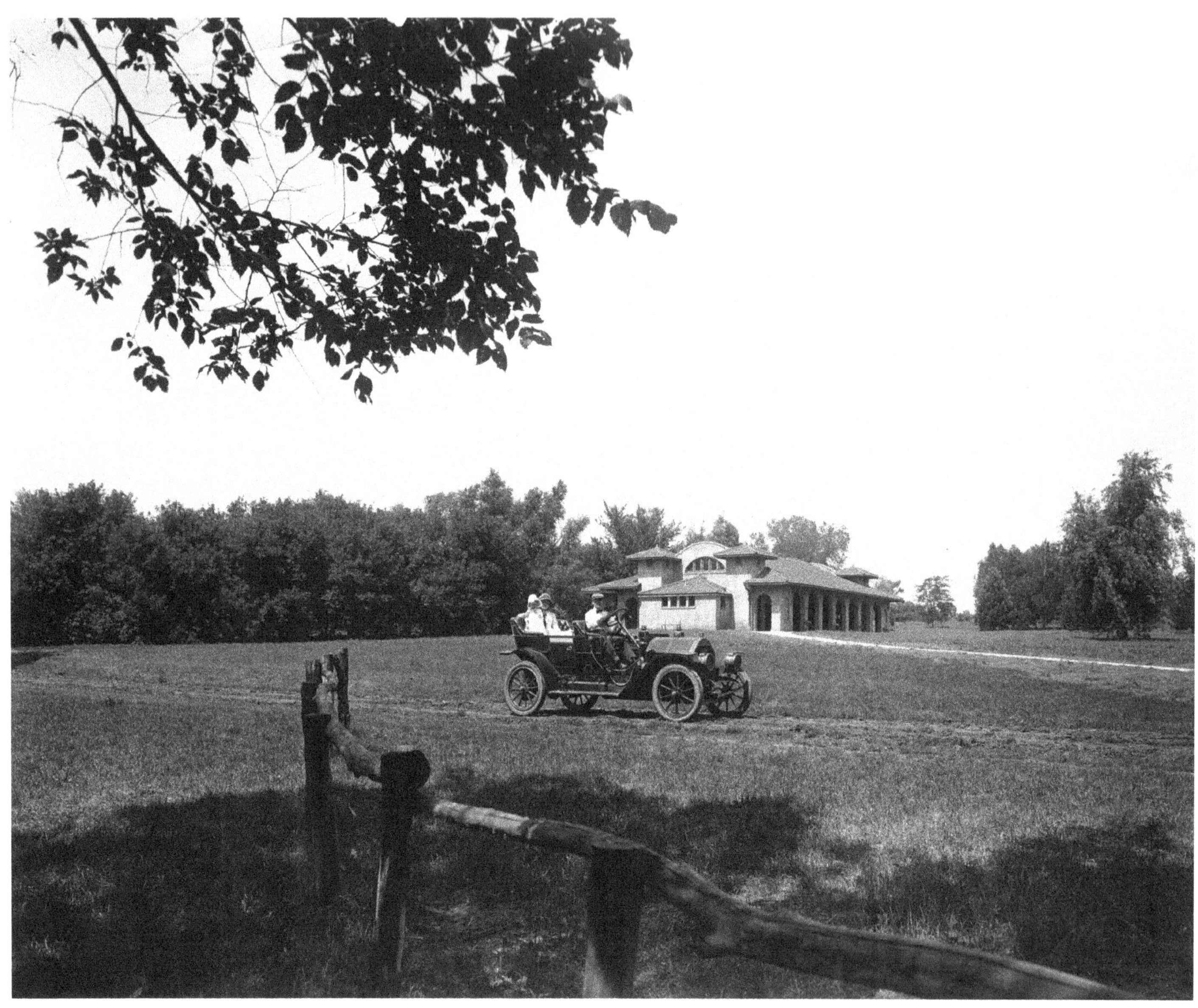

The pavilion at Elmwood Park was one of the first structures in Omaha built of cast concrete. Originally an open air structure, it was closed to the public in 1939. Later, it was repaired and enclosed. In 1987, $100,000 from a special bond issue was expended to refurbish it. This photo was taken around 1905.

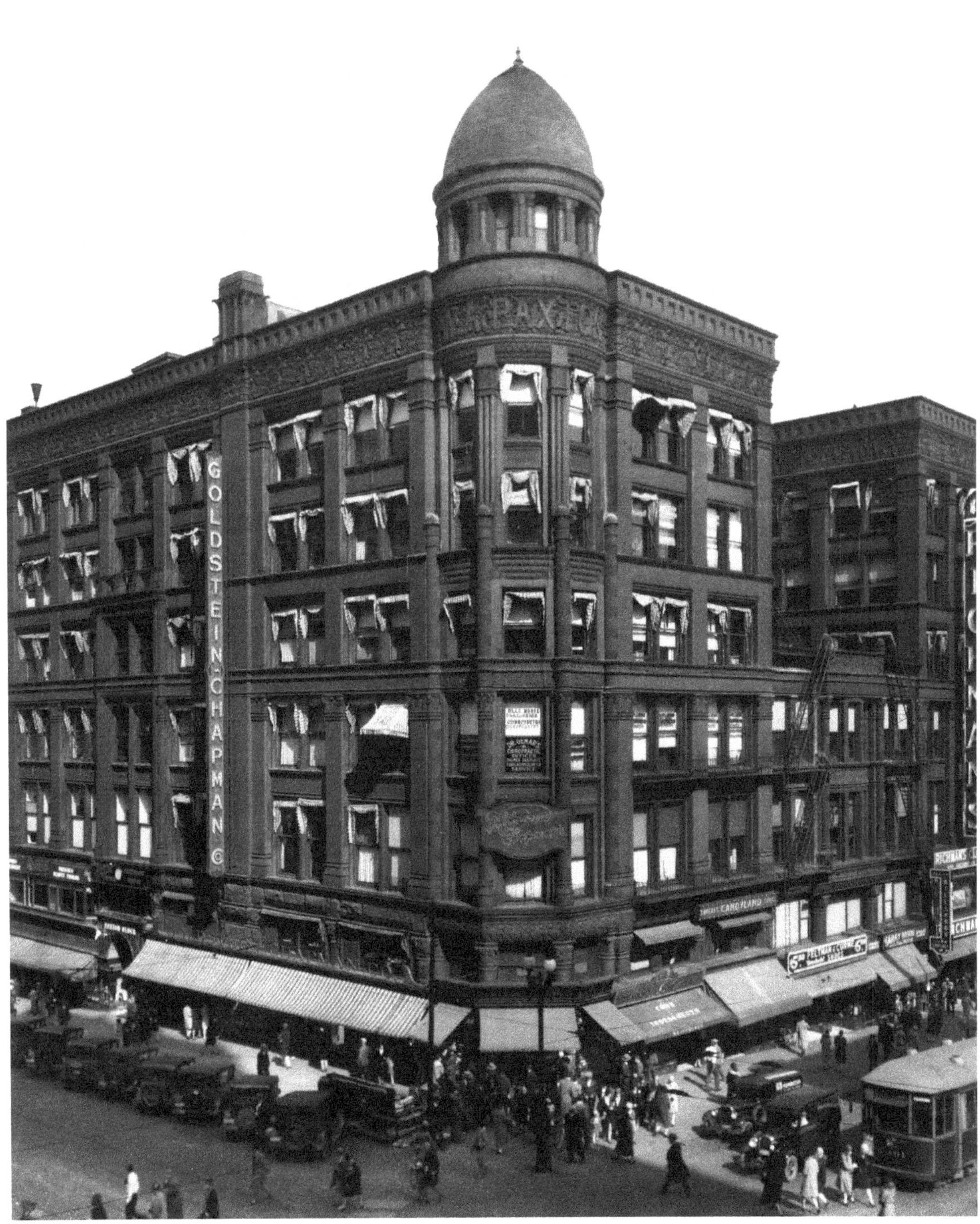

The Paxton Block, as it appeared in approximately 1905. Located at 16th and Farnam streets, this large office building was financed by Omaha capitalist William A. Paxton, whose name was associated with many local enterprises. He would usually provide the funds and take in other minority partners who would then manage the various businesses. Paxton died in Omaha in 1907.

Pavilion at Riverside Park, 3625 South 10th Street, about 1905. This outdoor pavilion was constructed of wooden architectural elements which had been salvaged from the Boys and Girls Building at the 1898 Trans-Mississippi Exposition.

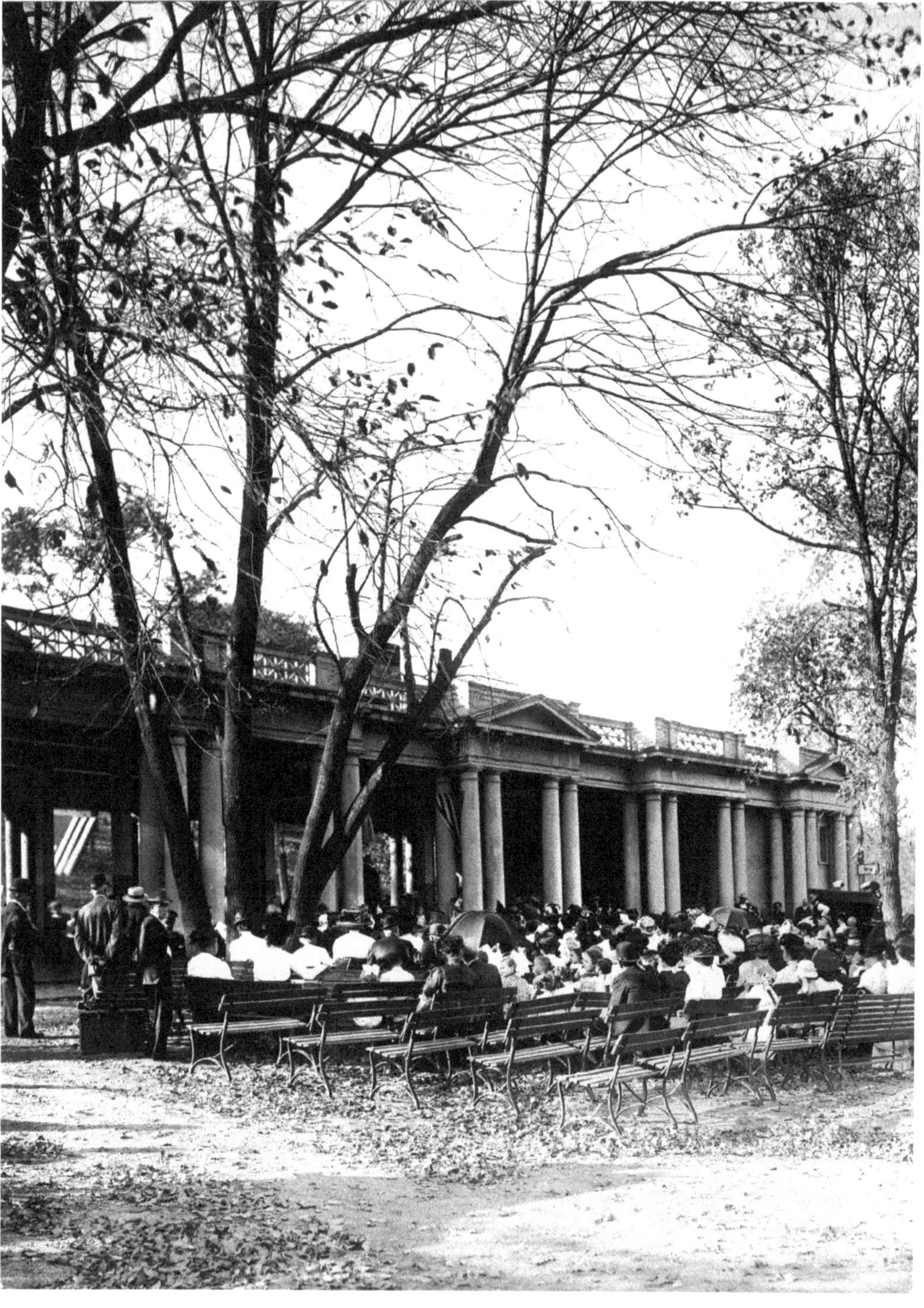

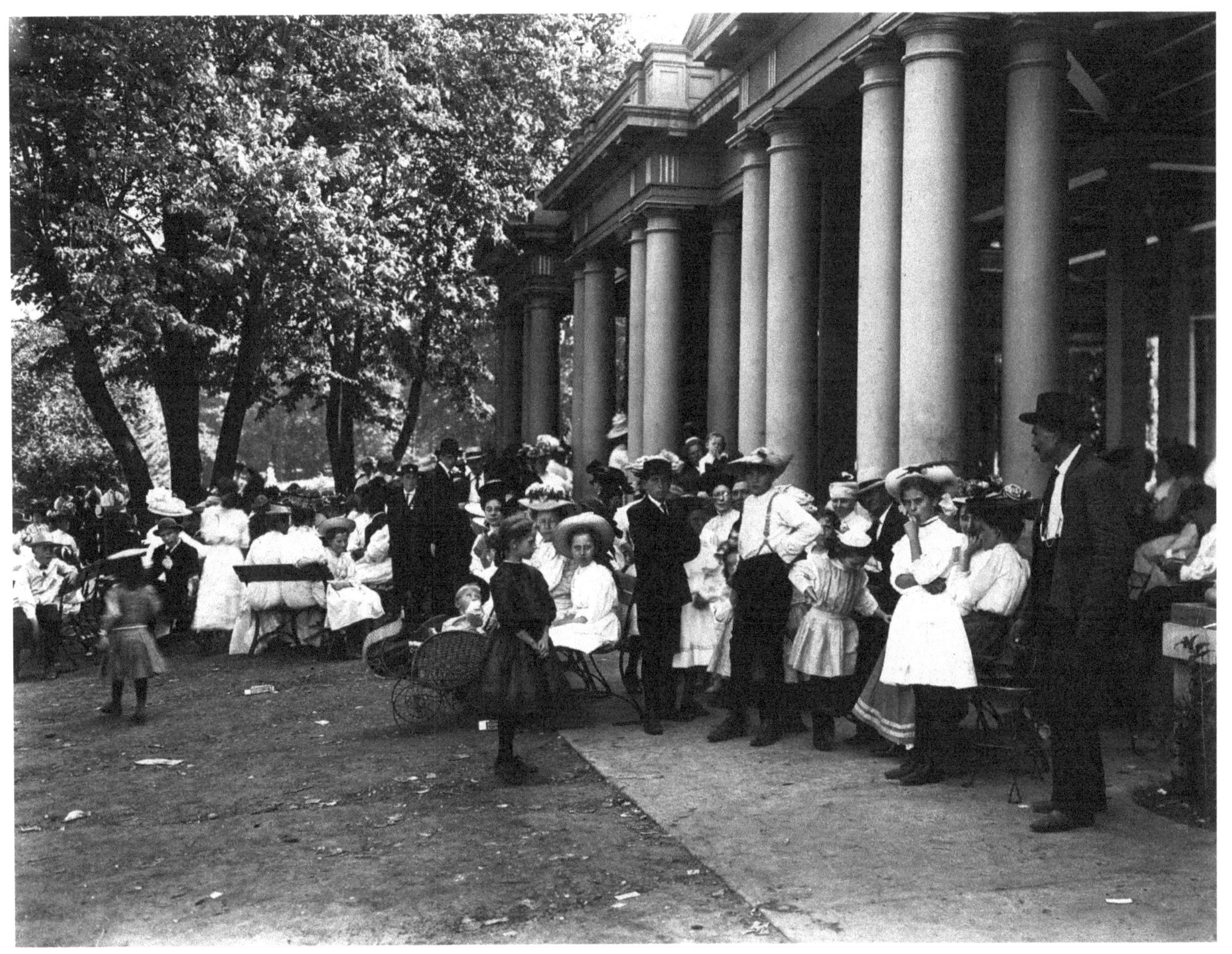

The Riverside Park pavilion, about 1905. Located in South Omaha, this park was a very popular location, featuring a lagoon and the first zoo in Omaha.

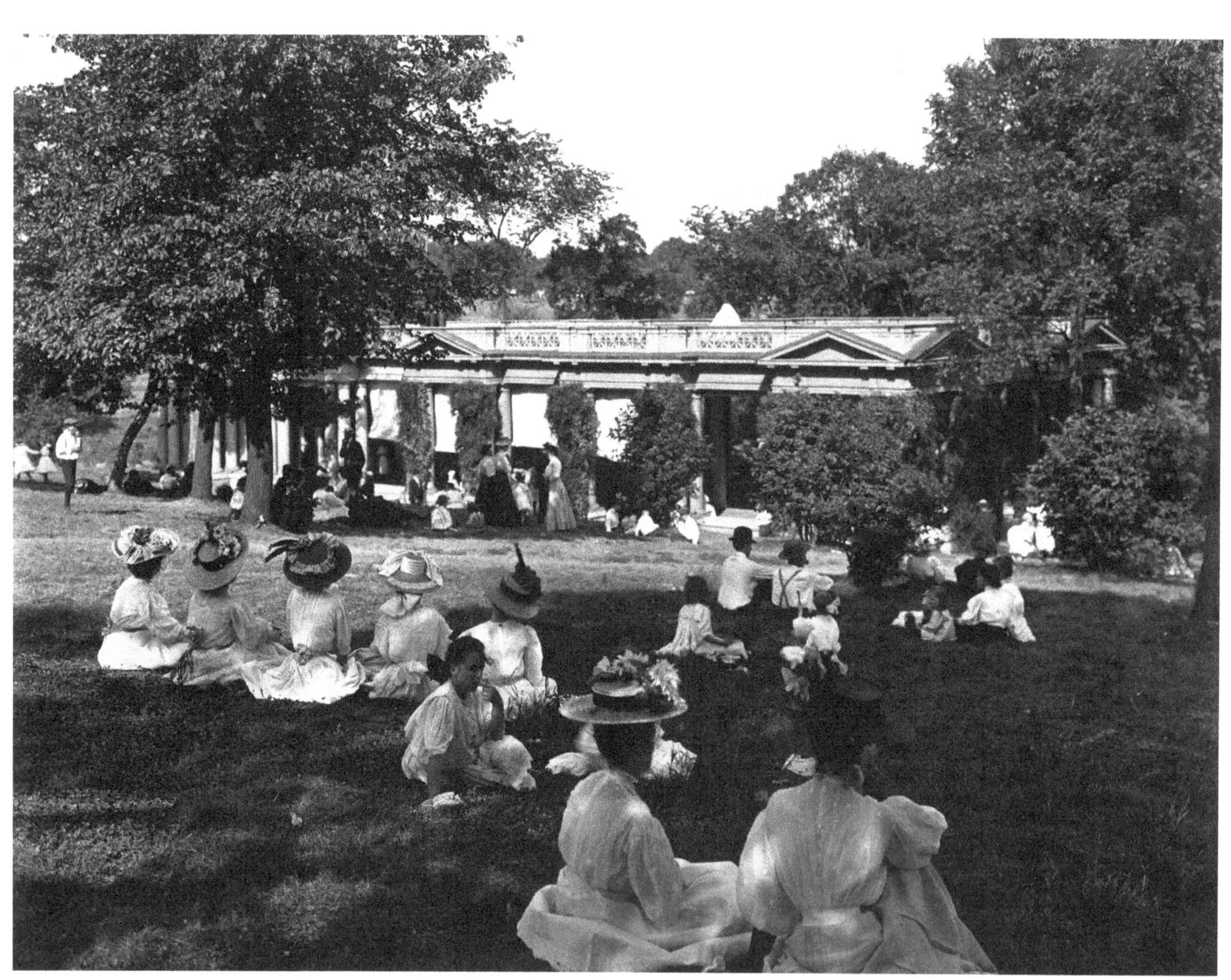

A crowd of well-dressed citizens enjoys an afternoon picnic at Riverside Park about 1905, with the park pavilion in the background.

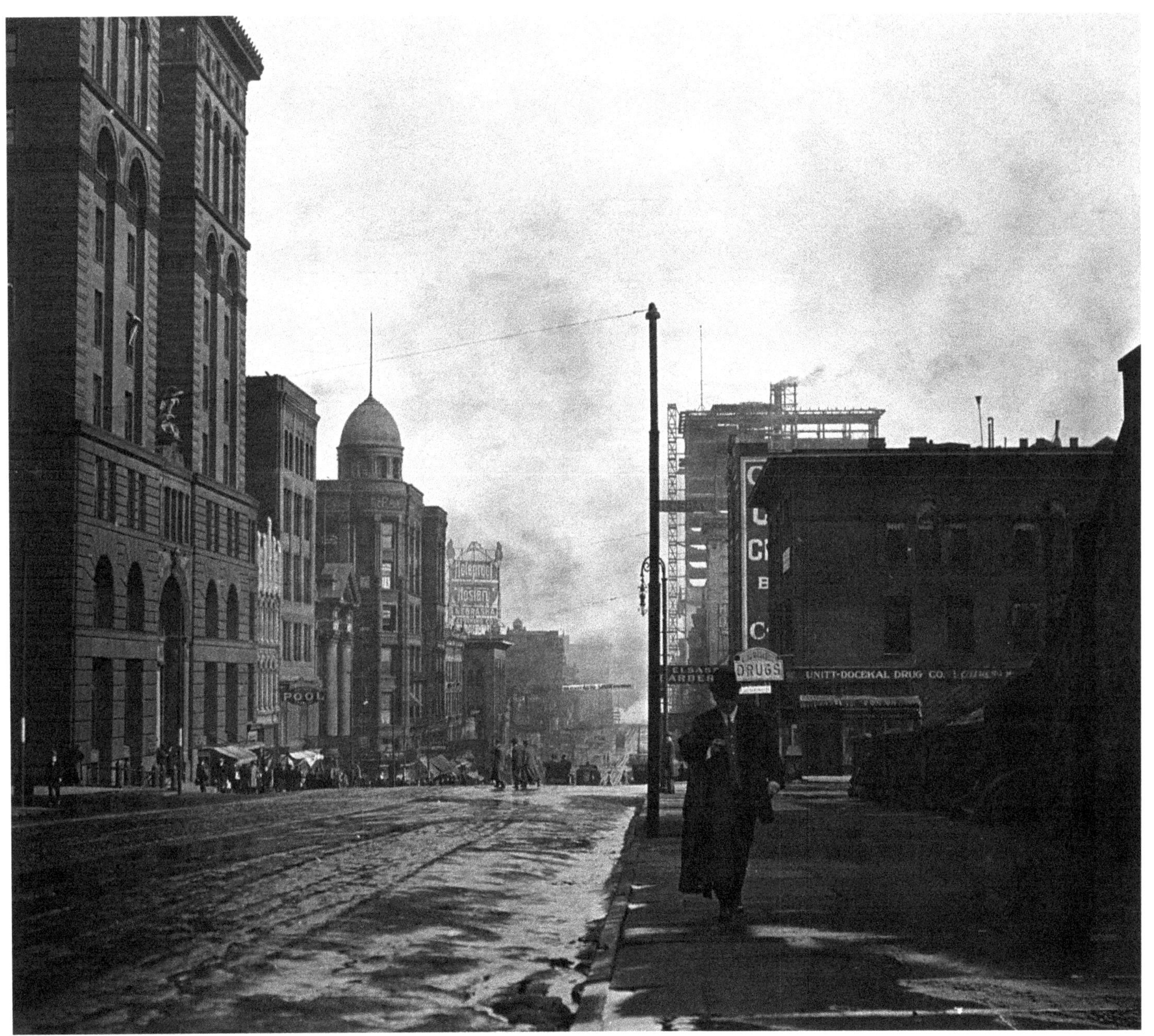

This view, taken about 1905 looking east down Farnam Street from the Douglas County Court House at 18th Street, shows the Omaha Building, a large office building, on the left. At left center is the Paxton Block on the northeast corner of 16th and Farnam streets.

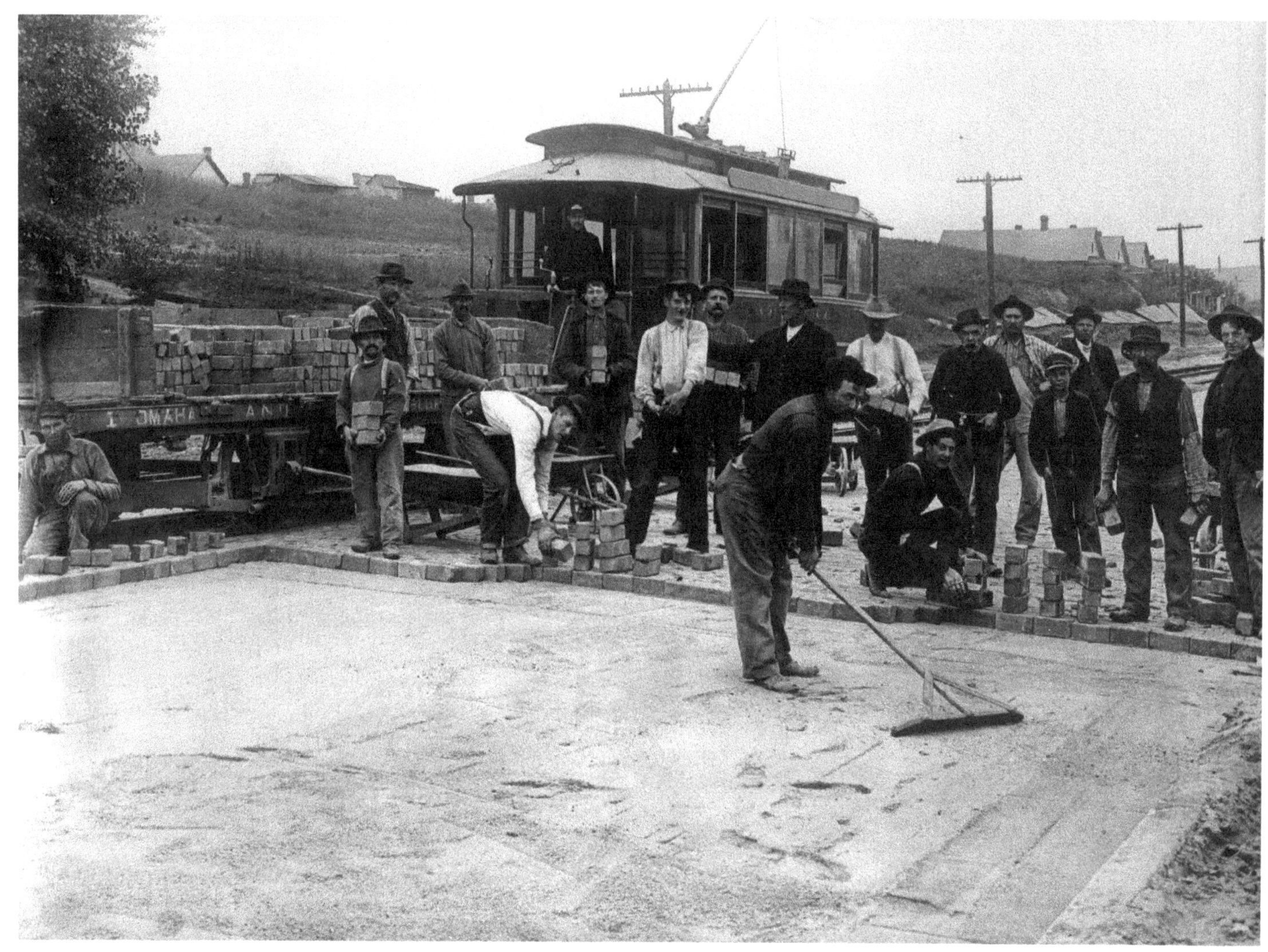

A crew of workers paving South 24th Street with bricks, approximately 1904. Note the street railway car, which was used to deliver workers to the site. Prior to 1890, many of Omaha's streets had no paving at all. When it rained, they became rivers of mud. The earliest form of paving was wooden blocks; however, they did not last long. Some of the early brick streets are still in use today.

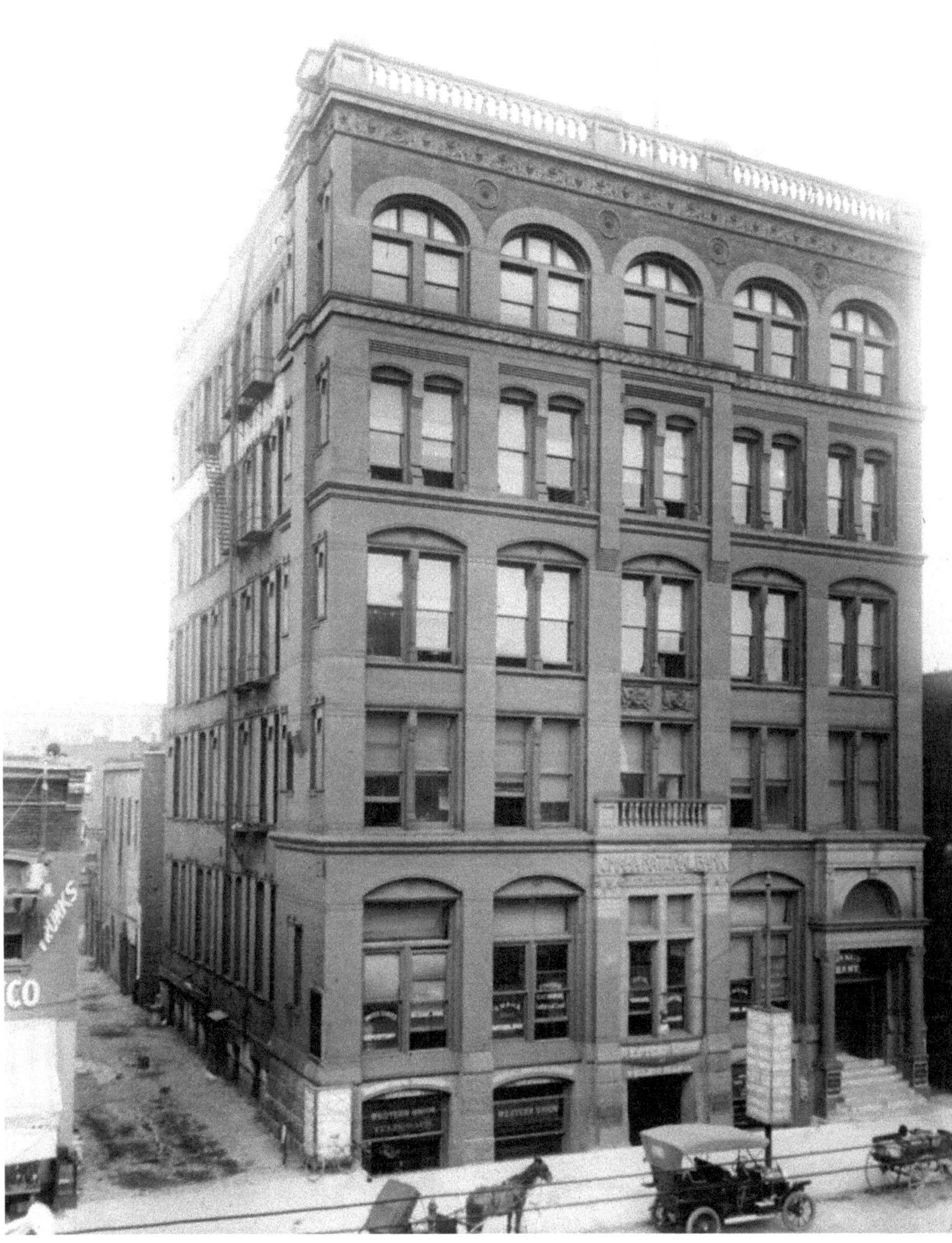

The Omaha National Bank at 208 South 13th Street, in 1909. This substantial, six-story structure was built in 1882. The bank, which opened for business in Omaha July 2, 1866, outgrew this location and shortly thereafter moved to the New York Life Building at 17th and Farnam streets.

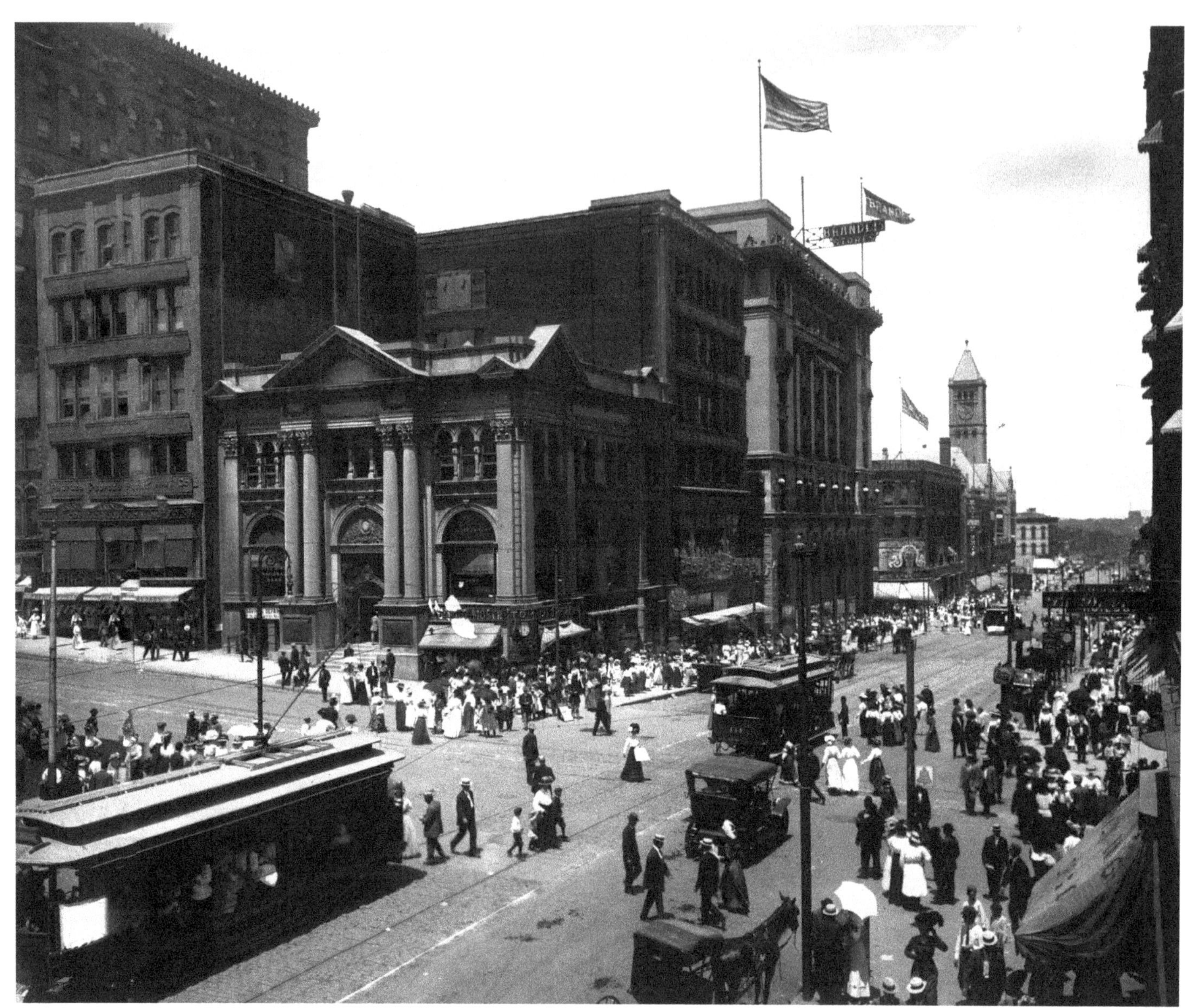

This view of downtown Omaha, July 13, 1909, shows the intersection of 16th and Farnam streets, in the heart of the main business district. The United States National Bank is in the center. To its right is People's Store, and beside it banners proclaim the recently completed store of J. L. Brandeis and Sons. The U.S. Post Office tower rises further down the street. At this time of transition, electric streetcars, gasoline-powered automobiles, and horse-drawn vehicles all travel the streets between crowded sidewalks.

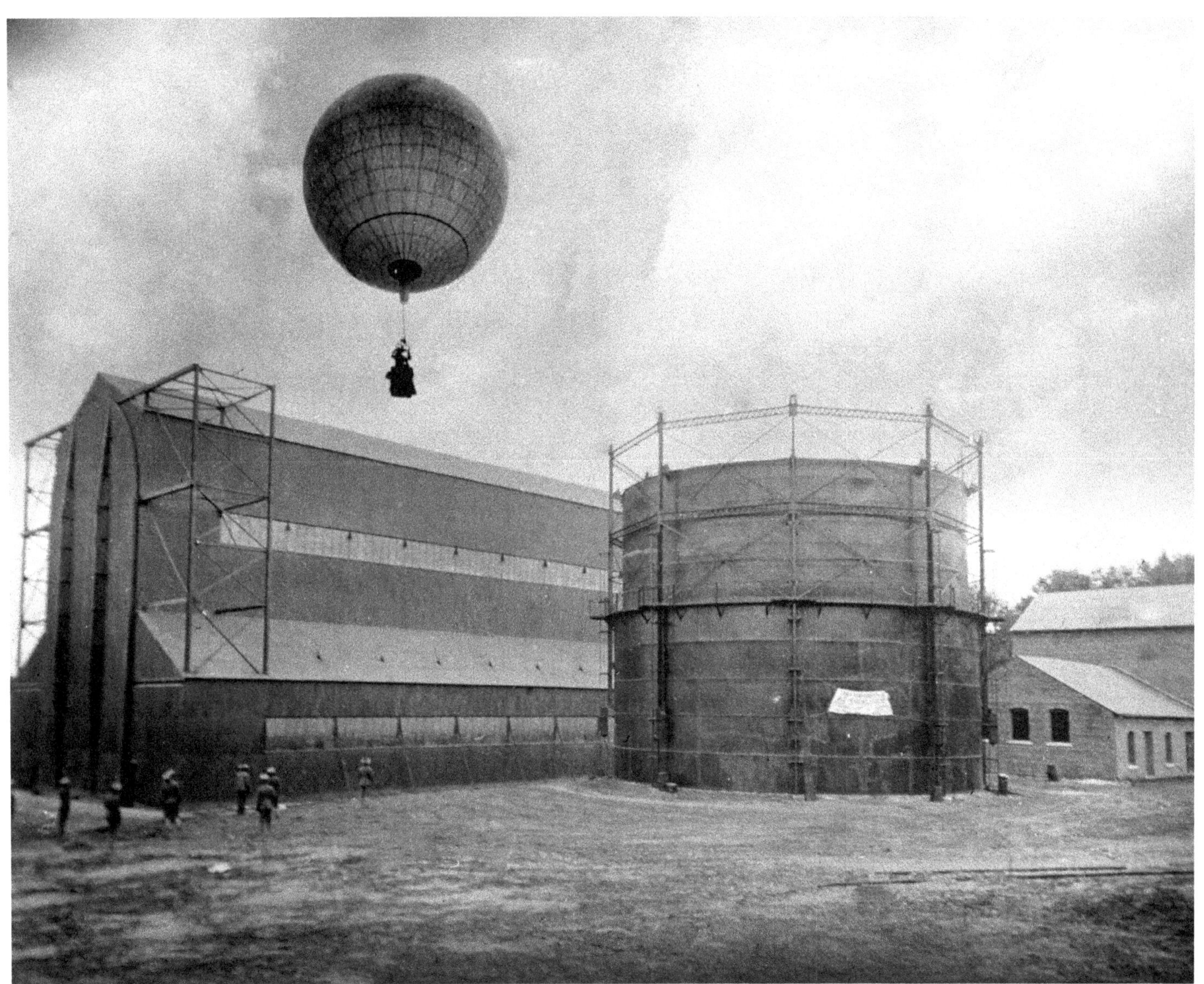

A photograph taken about 1910 of the large, steel hanger built at Fort Omaha, 30th and Fort streets, in 1907 for dirigible experiments. After the United States entered World War I, this facility was utilized by the U.S. Signal Corps to establish the Fort Omaha Balloon School. Eighteen hundred men received training there to become the "Eyes of the Army."

Elmwood Park on West Dodge Street was originally established when pioneer Lyman Richardson and others made a donation of 55 acres of land in 1890. The City of Omaha soon added additional property, and by 1895 the total expanded land area was 210 acres. Today, this is one of the most beautiful parks in Omaha. This image shows a couple driving a Velie automobile through it around 1910.

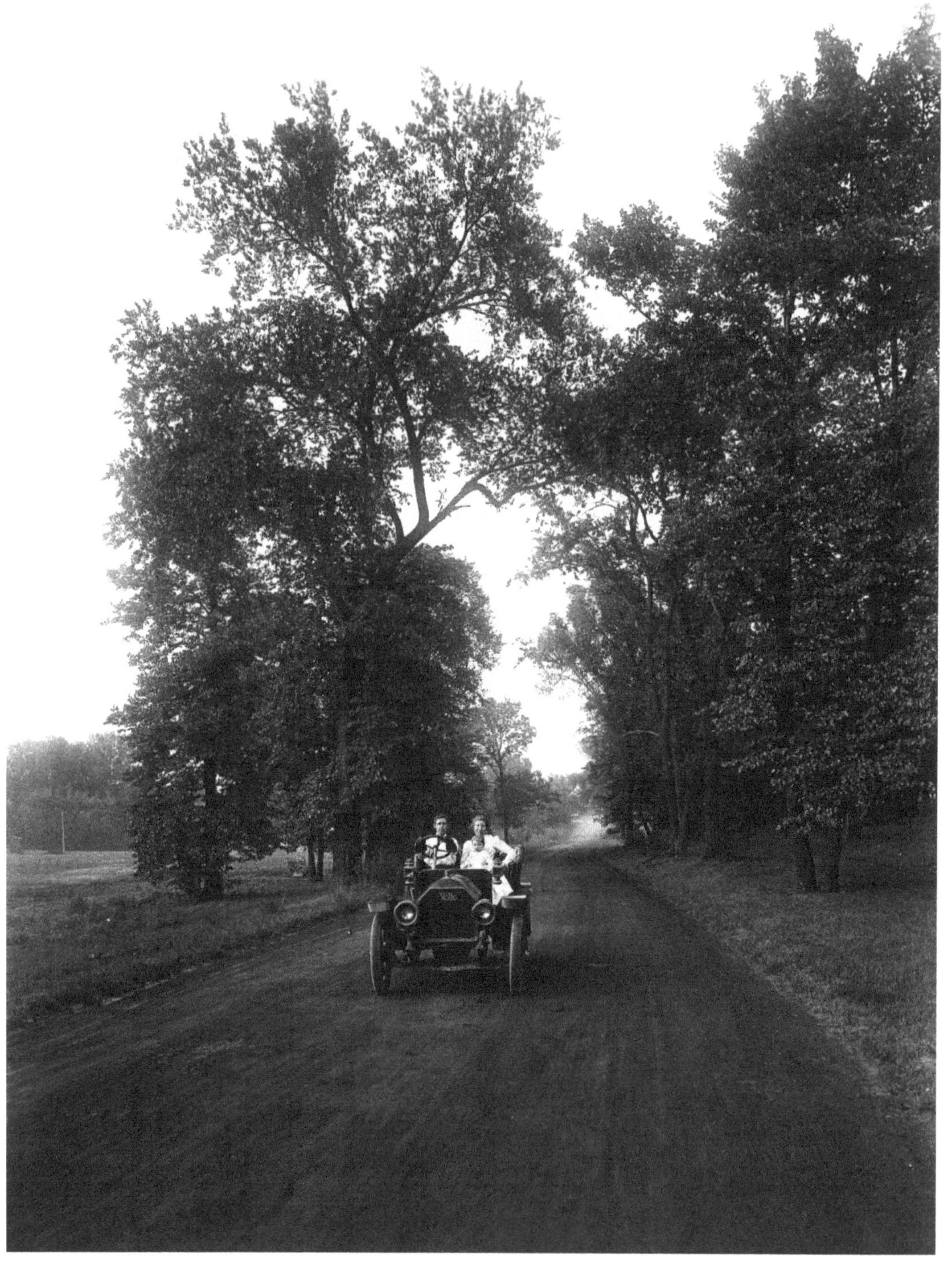

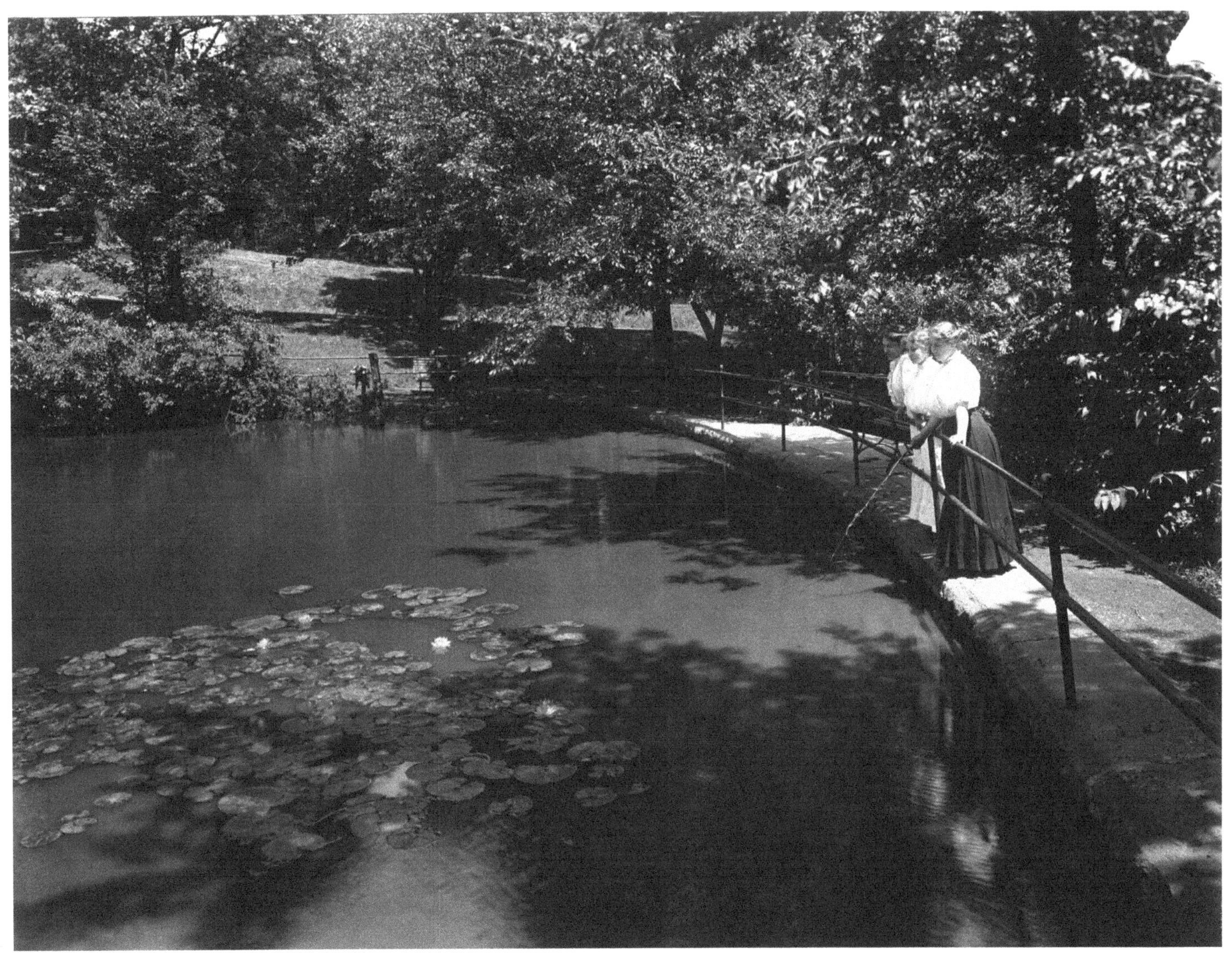

The lily pond in Riverview Park, 3625 South 10th Street, about 1910. Visiting one of Omaha's many parks was an enjoyable weekend activity for residents, and this park was especially popular, with its beautiful natural setting and many interesting landscape features.

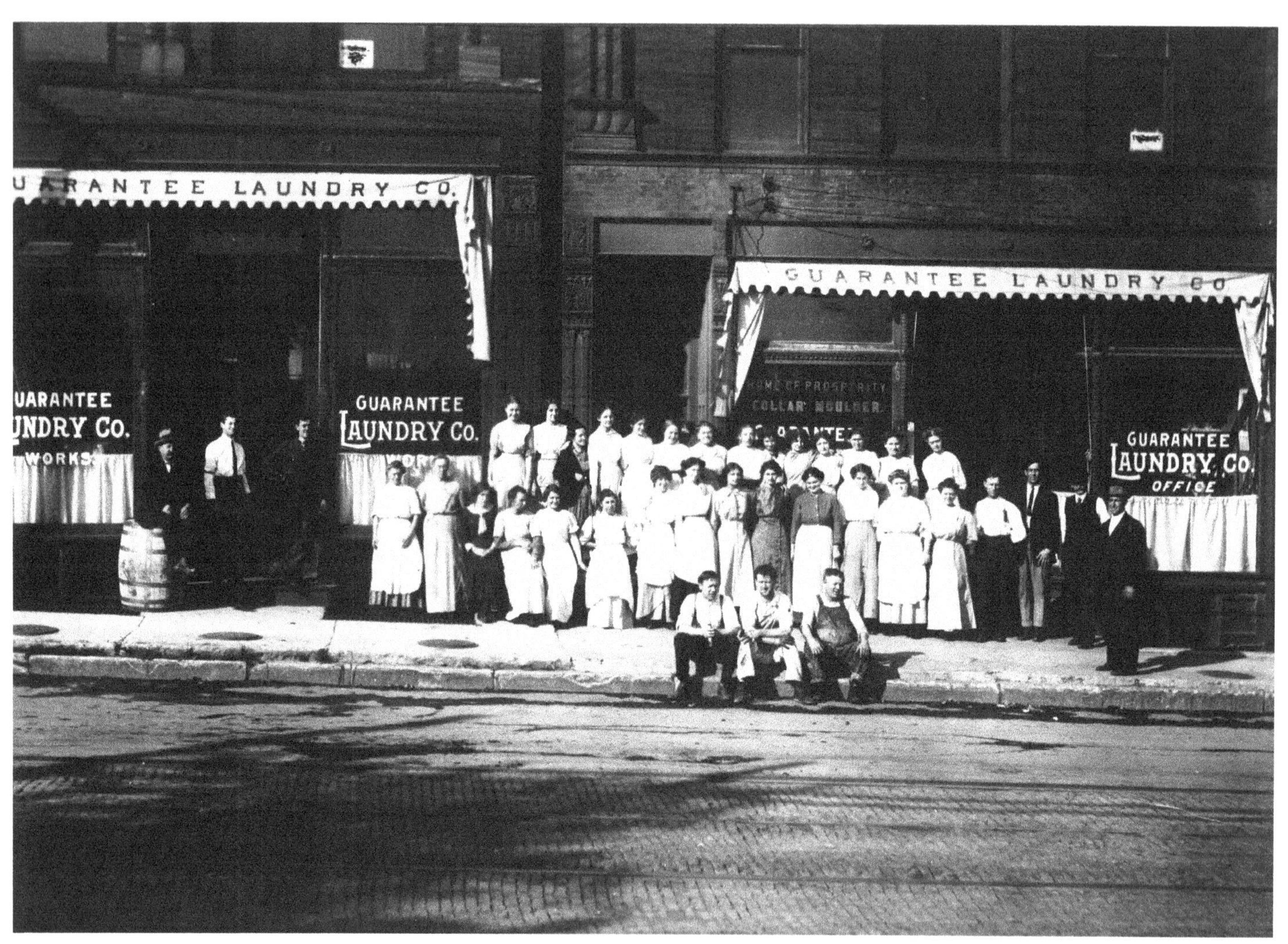

The Guarantee Laundry, 1468 South 16th Street, was owned and operated by Leonard C. Heine. Laundry workers have assembled for a group portrait.

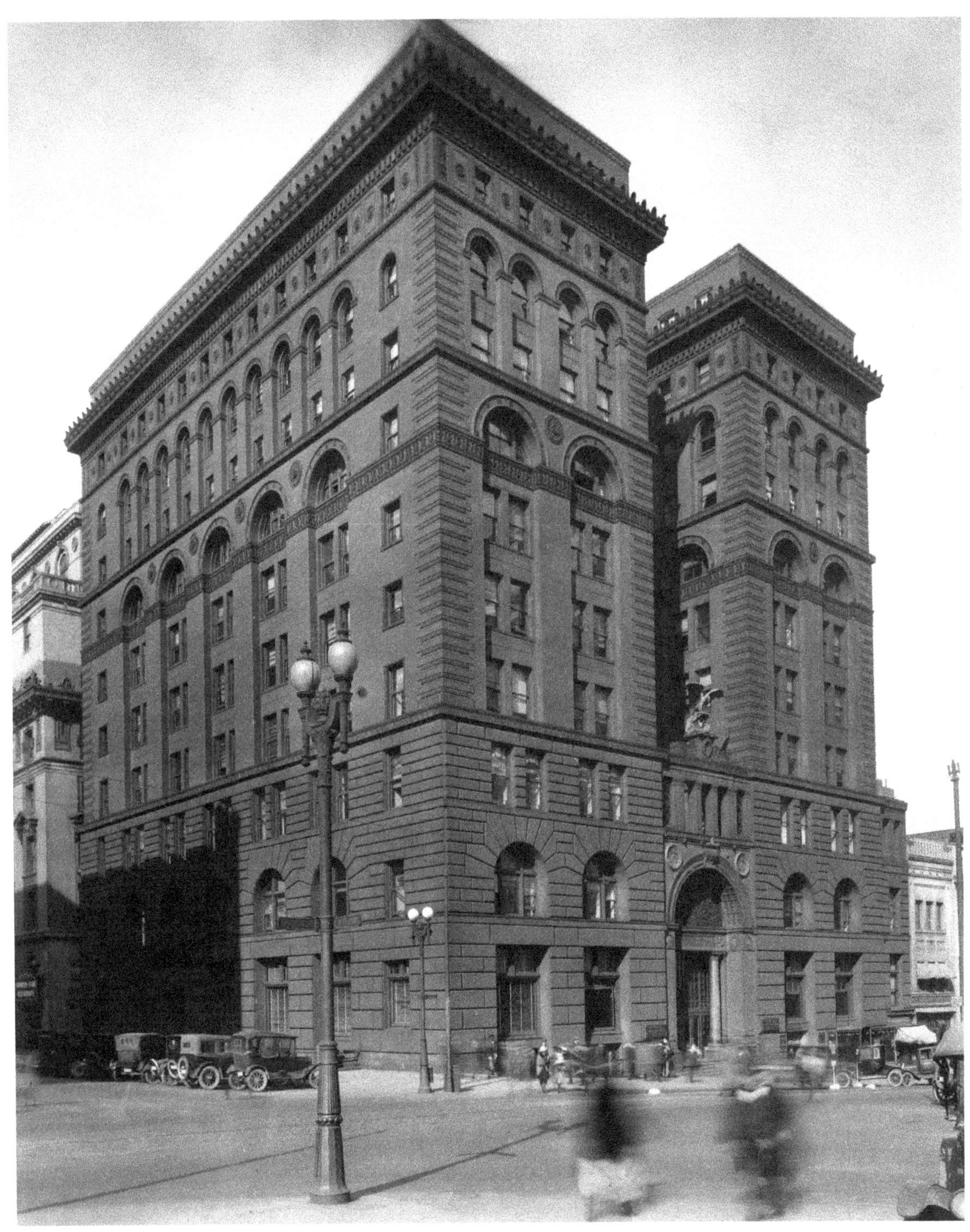

The New York Life Building at 17th and Farnam streets, as it appeared about 1910, soon after the Omaha National Bank had moved its offices there. Completed in 1889 at a cost of $750,000, this ten-story building was Omaha's first "skyscraper." It was designed by the prestigious New York City architectural firm of McKim, Meade and White. An eleventh floor was added in 1920. This structure today is one of the most important architectural and historic landmarks in the city.

Disaster struck in Omaha on Easter Sunday, March 23, 1913, at about 6:00 p.m. A tornado moved through the city from the southeast, traveling northwest. Approximately 185 people were killed. The ruins in this image had been the home of Judge W. W. Slabaugh at 4912 Underwood Avenue in Dundee.

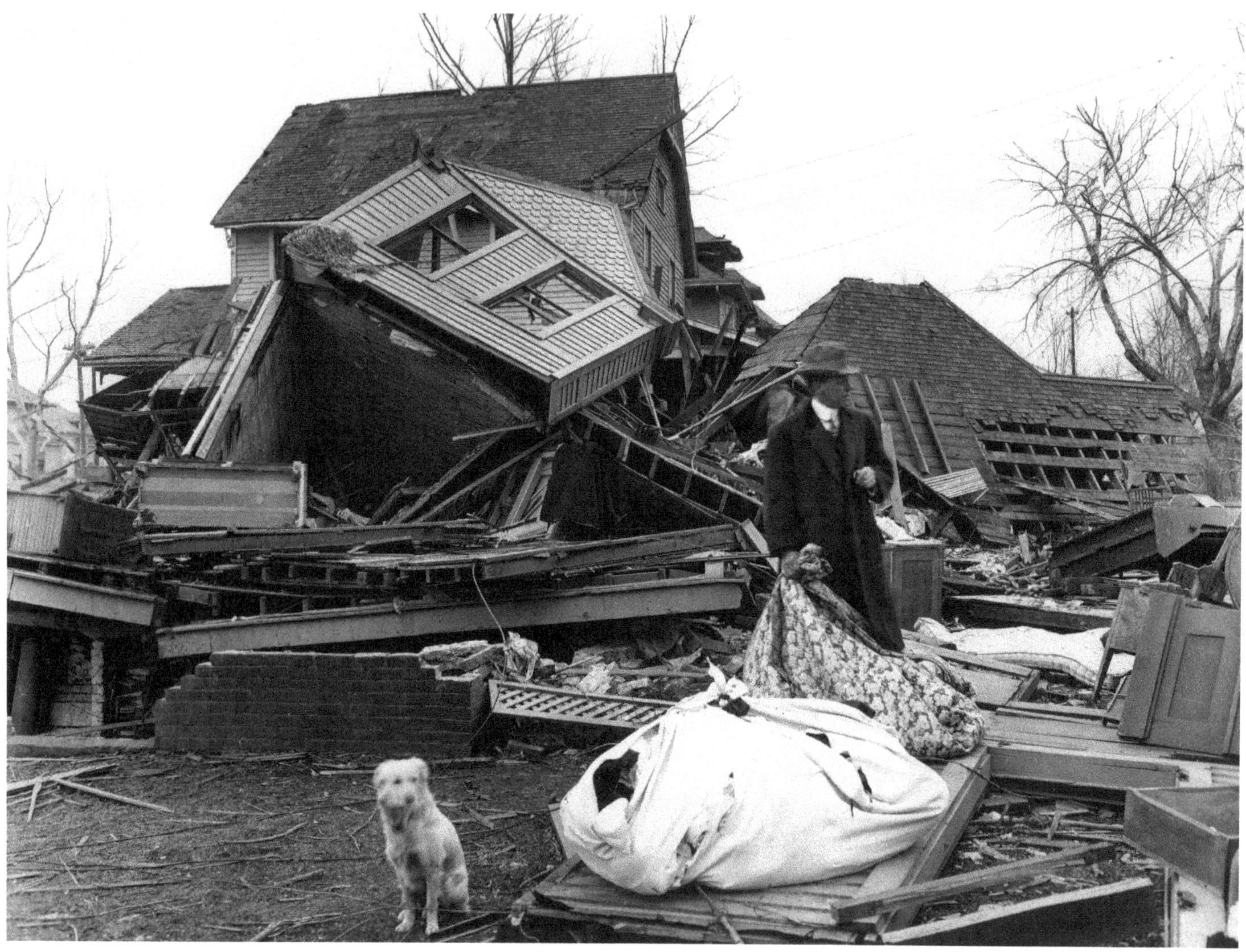

These workers' tenement houses, located in the vicinity of 6th and Pierce streets, were photographed about 1910. This was an area in which many recent immigrants lived who had come to Omaha to find work in the meatpacking houses.

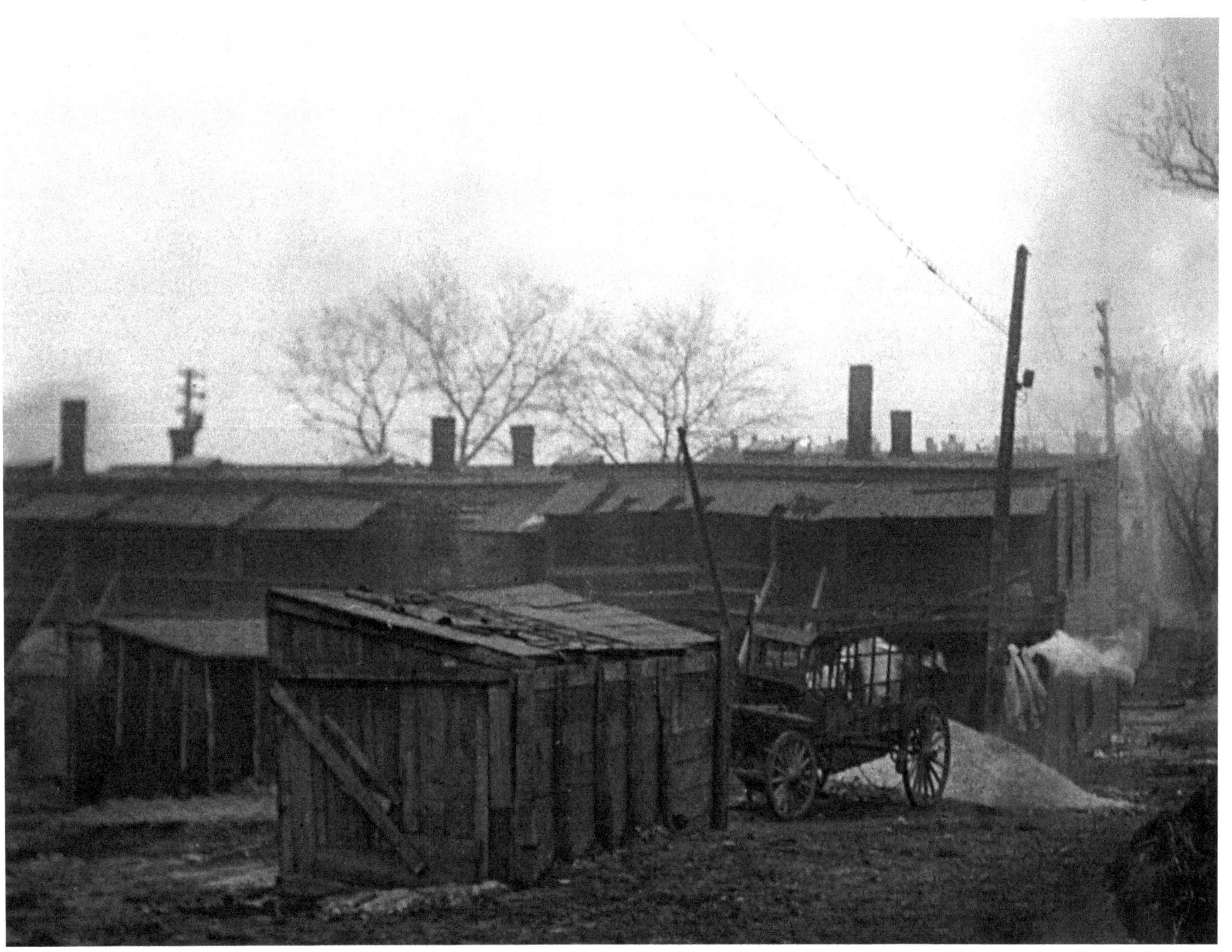

Following Spread: Livestock pens at the Union Stockyards Company in South Omaha about 1908, in the vicinity of 33rd and O streets. The Armour Packing Company appears near the top. In 1887, Philip D. Armour first became involved in the meatpacking business in Omaha. His reorganized company built their own large plant there in 1898. By the beginning of the twentieth century, Armour and Company was one of the four largest meat processors in Omaha.

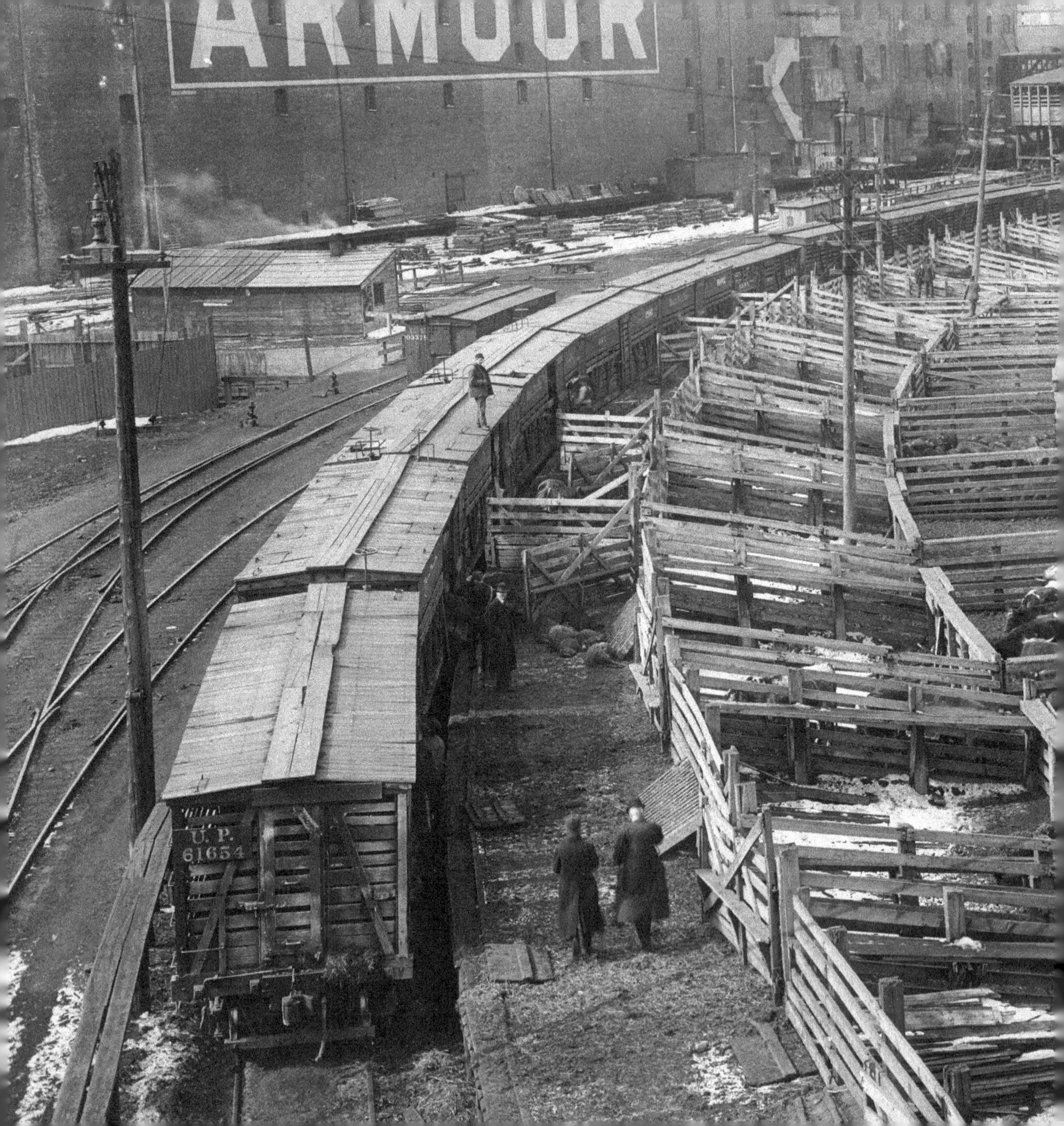
ARMOUR
U.P.
61654

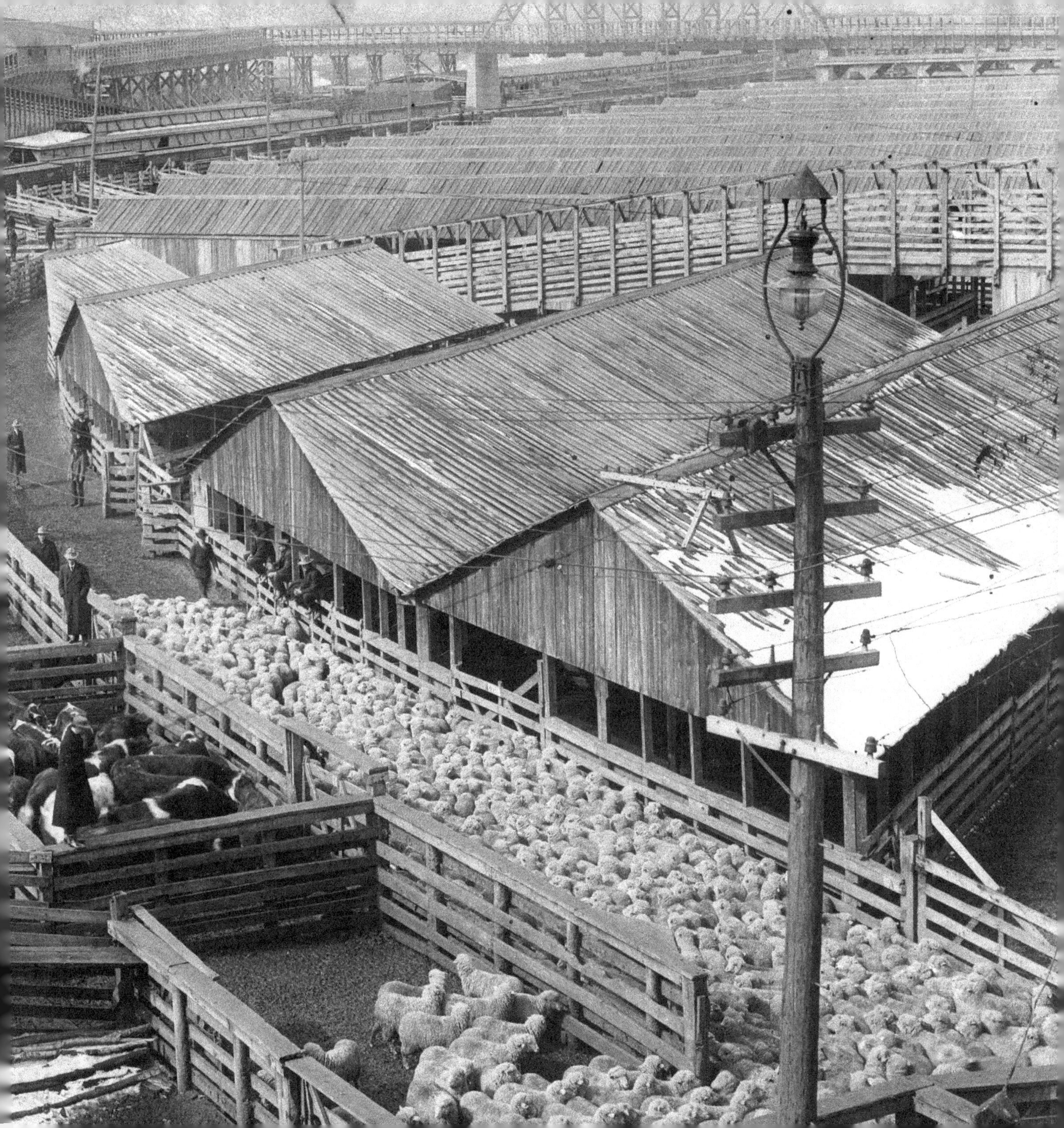

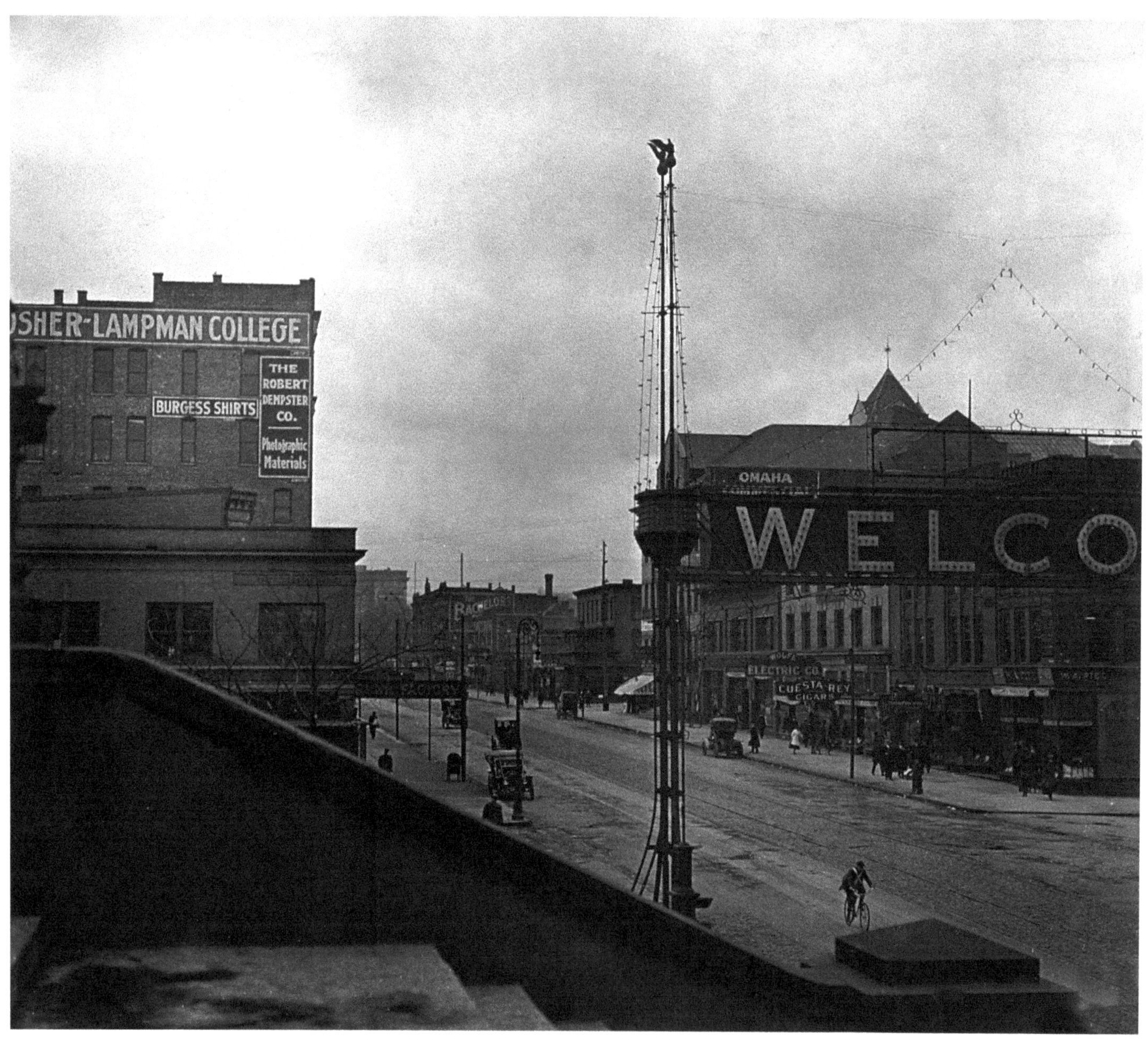

In this west-facing photo from about 1910, the steps of the Douglas County Court House are in the foreground, along with one section of the AK-SAR-BEN welcome arch which spanned Farnam at 18th Street. In the middle of the block, across from the business college, is the Wolfe Electric Company. Down the street, The Bachelor's was a saloon and billiard hall.

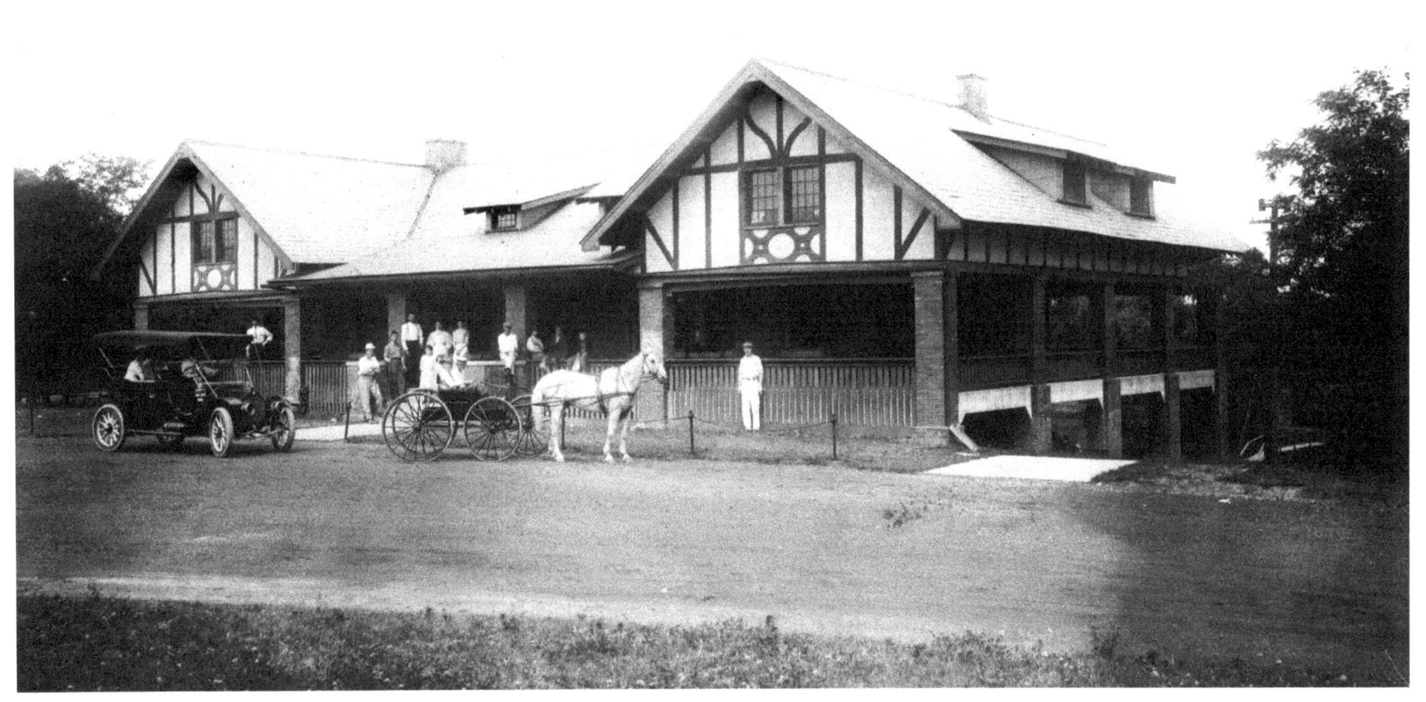

The pavilion at Miller Park, 2707 Redick Avenue, as it appeared about 1910. The seventy-eight acres of this park were obtained by the city in 1893. It later had a golf course, a fountain, beautiful walkways and gardens and was considered one of the finest parks in the city. It was named in honor of pioneer Dr. George L. Miller, who had served as the first president of the Omaha Board of Park Commissioners.

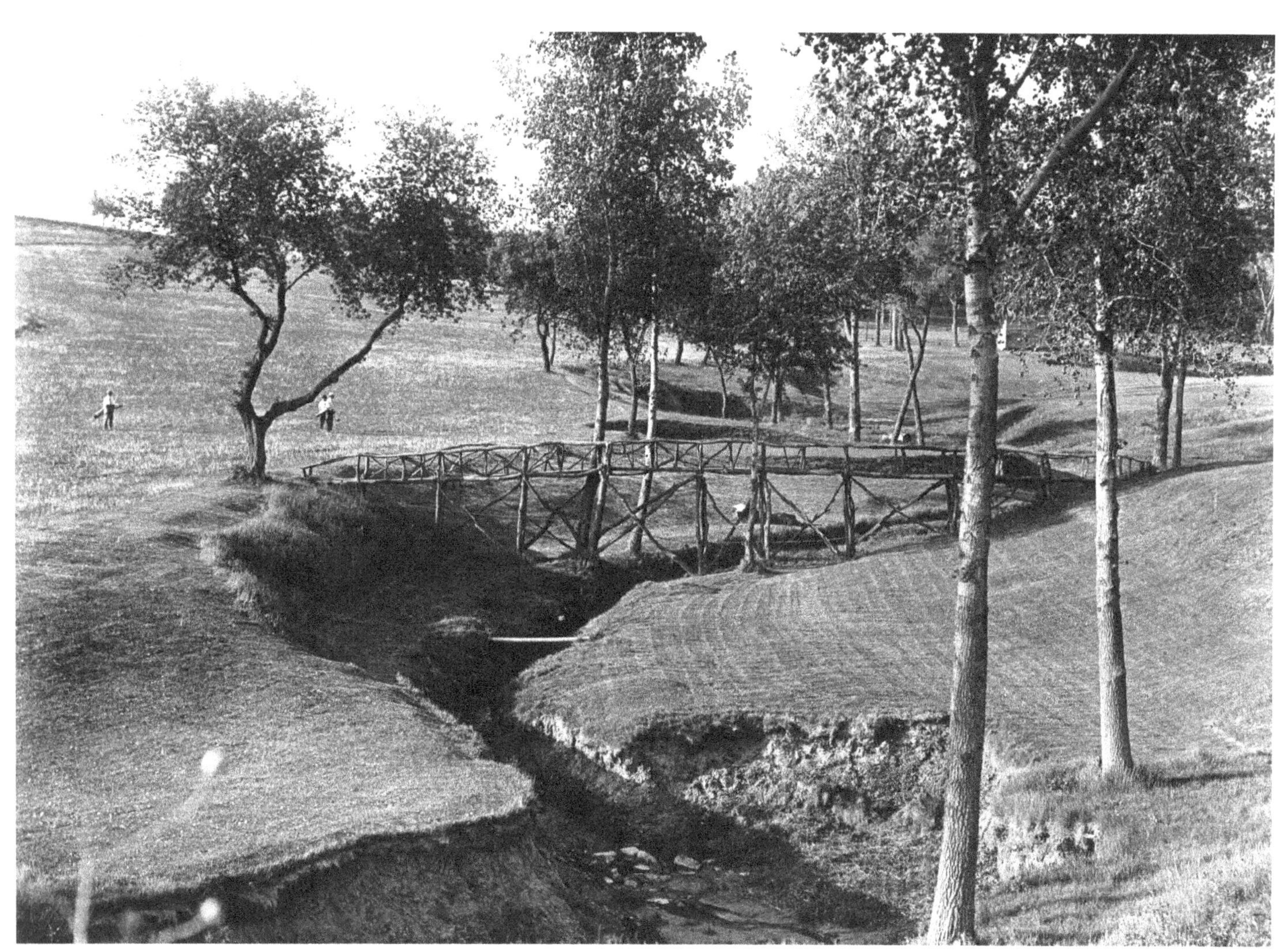

Elmwood Park, located west of Dodge Street (802 South 60th Street) opened its golf course in 1916. This has always been a popular municipal course due to its accessibility and convenient midtown location. By the 1960s, nearly 30,000 rounds of golf were played annually.

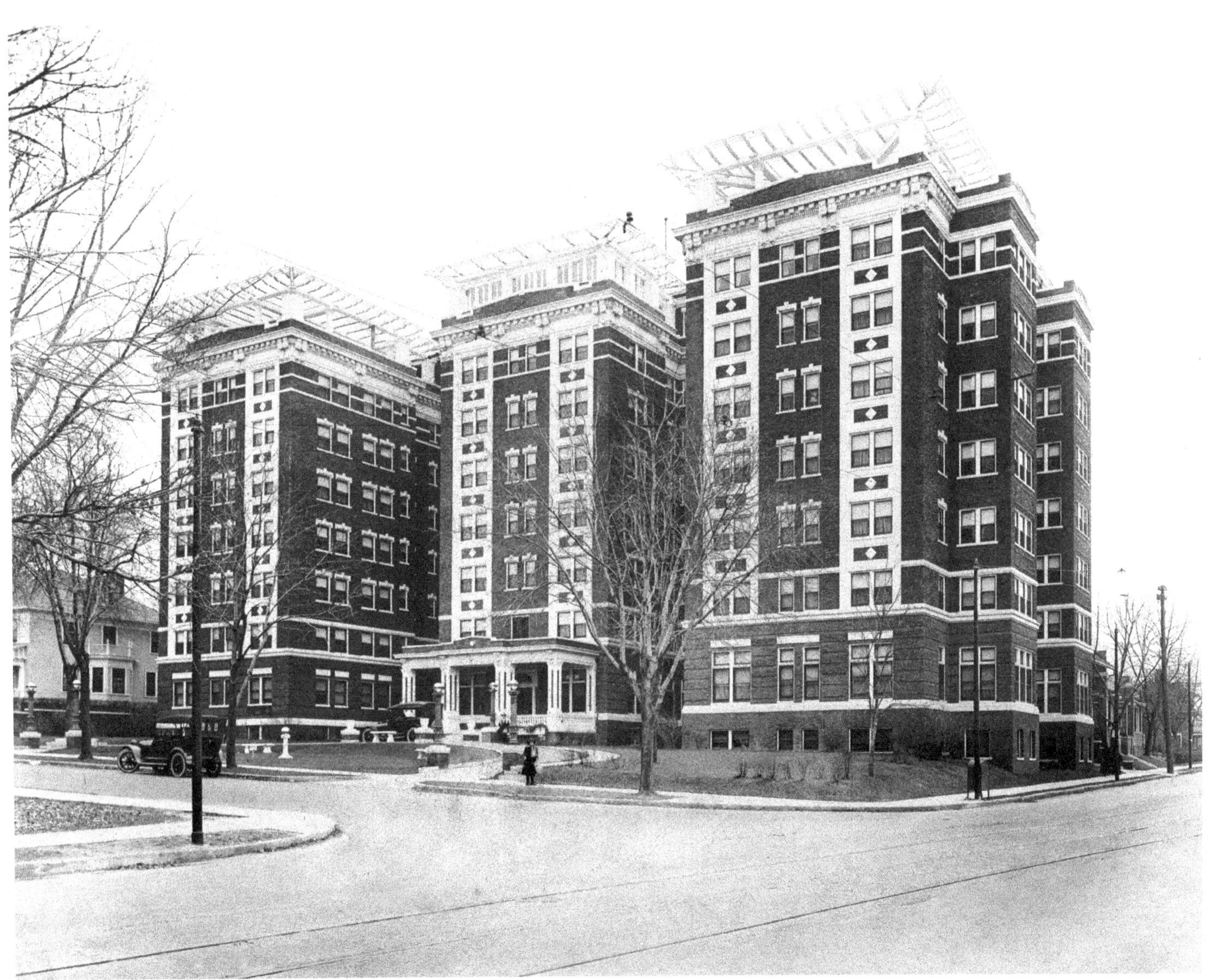

The Blackstone Hotel at 302 South 36th Street as it appeared shortly after it opened in 1916. One of the finest residential hotels in the city, it was built in the prosperous "Gold Coast" neighborhood, where many of the most prominent families in the city lived. It closed in 1976 and was later renovated for use as a commercial office building.

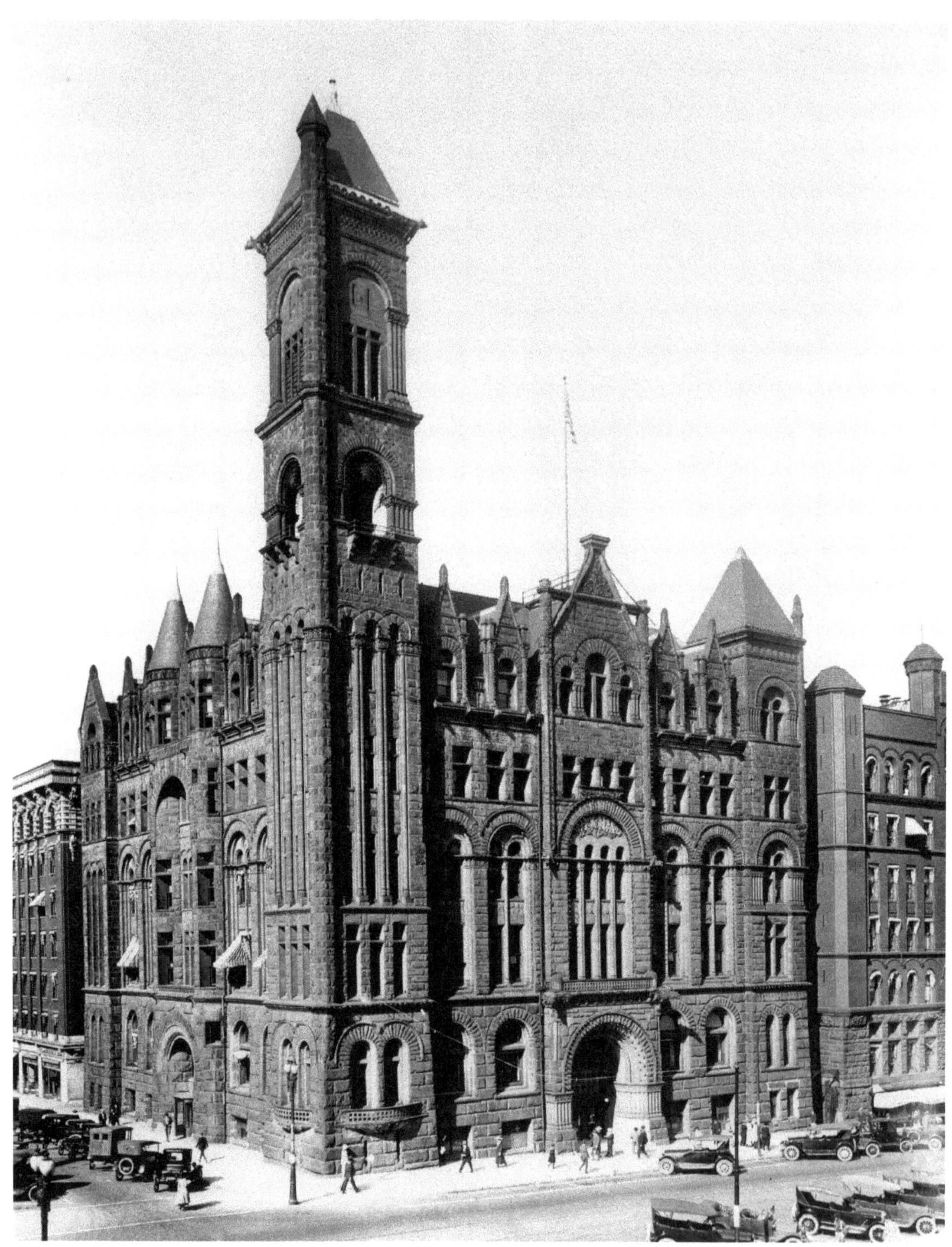

The ornate old city hall building on the corner of 18th and Farnam streets was designed by Omaha architect Charles F. Biendorf and completed in 1890 at a total cost of $550,000. A tower on the southeast corner rose to a height of nearly 200 feet. Construction flaws necessitated removal of the tower in 1919. Remodeled extensively in 1950, the building later became obsolete. The city sold the site in 1966, and in March of that year, the structure was torn down.

THE GATE CITY

(1921–1939)

The two decades between 1920 and 1940 brought profound changes to Omaha and to the entire country. After World War I, agricultural prices gradually declined, as did manufacturing. Many of the railroads experienced financial difficulties, but the meatpacking industry in South Omaha remained strong. In the 1920s, roughly fifty percent of the total population of Omaha was comprised of immigrants and their children. Omaha was known as the "Gate City"—a slogan adopted by the Omaha Board of Trade and later the Chamber of Commerce—because its geographic location positioned it to be the gateway to the West.

In 1920, Job's Daughters, a national Masonic Youth Organization, was founded in Omaha. The American Legion held its national convention in Omaha, October 5-9, 1925, drawing more than 50,000 Legionnaires, one of the largest gatherings in the city's history. Among them were President and Mrs. Calvin Coolidge. The President addressed the Convention on October 6.

In 1929, the Omaha Chamber of Commerce adopted the slogan "Onward Omaha" as a stated objective of the business community in its hope for continuing economic prosperity. However, within a short time, Omaha was suffering the Great Depression along with the rest of the country.

There were bright spots. In 1931, the beautiful Joslyn Memorial opened, a gift to the City of Omaha from philanthropist Mrs. Sarah Joslyn. Construction of the magnificent art museum and concert hall cost 3.5 million dollars. The University of Omaha, originally founded in 1908, became the public Municipal University of Omaha in 1931. In 1936, it purchased a site on West Dodge Street, where a new administration building was constructed. It was dedicated November 1938.

The economic situation remained bad throughout most of the 1930s. In April 1935, another serious strike by the streetcar company crippled the city. The governor had to declare a period of martial law before the strike was finally settled in June. It was only in the following years that the hopes of the business community began to be realized, and the city started to prosper again. By 1940, the population had increased only slightly, to about 225,000.

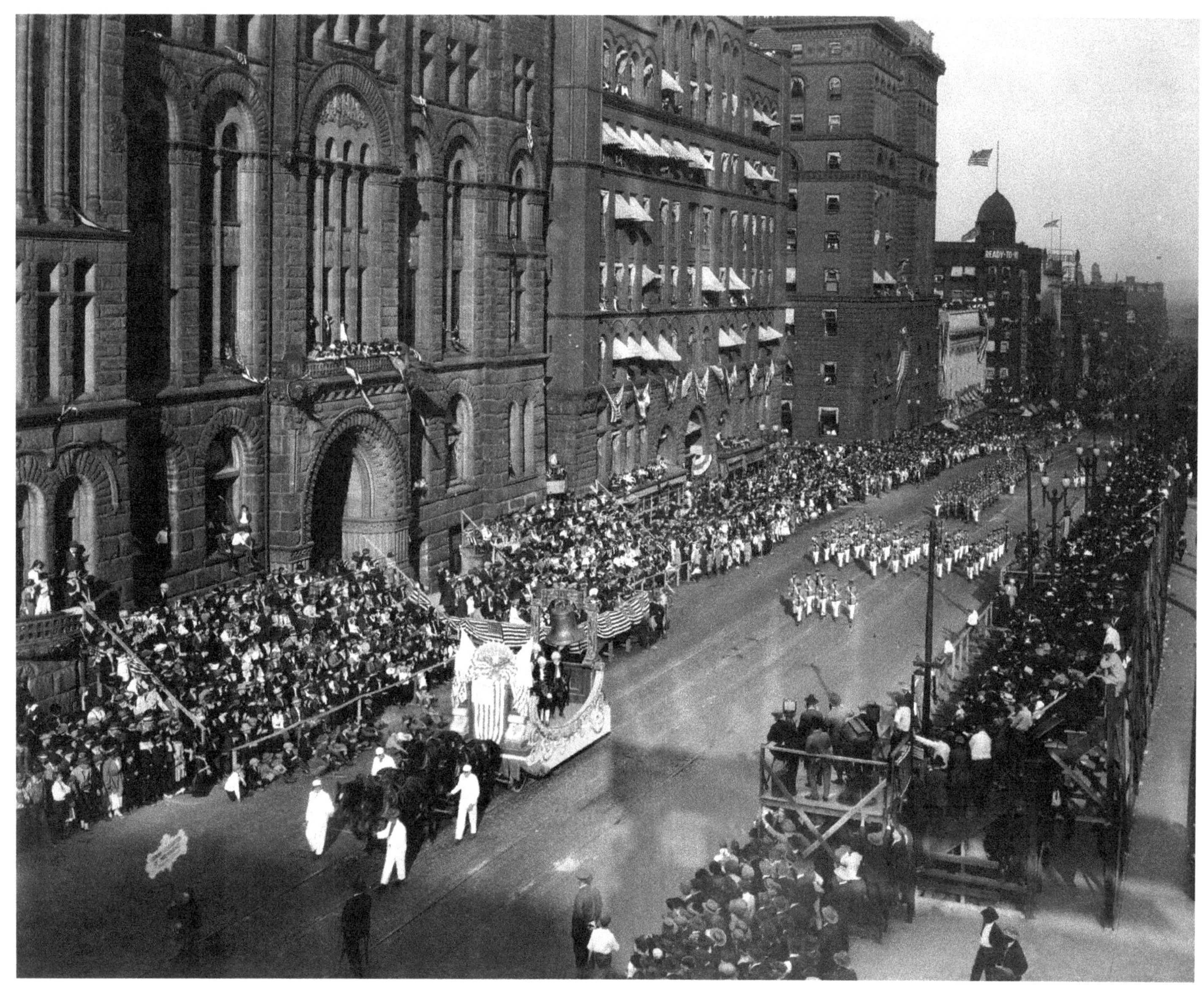

AK-SAR-BEN was an important community service organization founded in Omaha in 1895. Each year, it produced an elaborate parade, often using electrified floats. This parade on September 23, 1920, was photographed on Farnam Street between 16th and 18th streets.

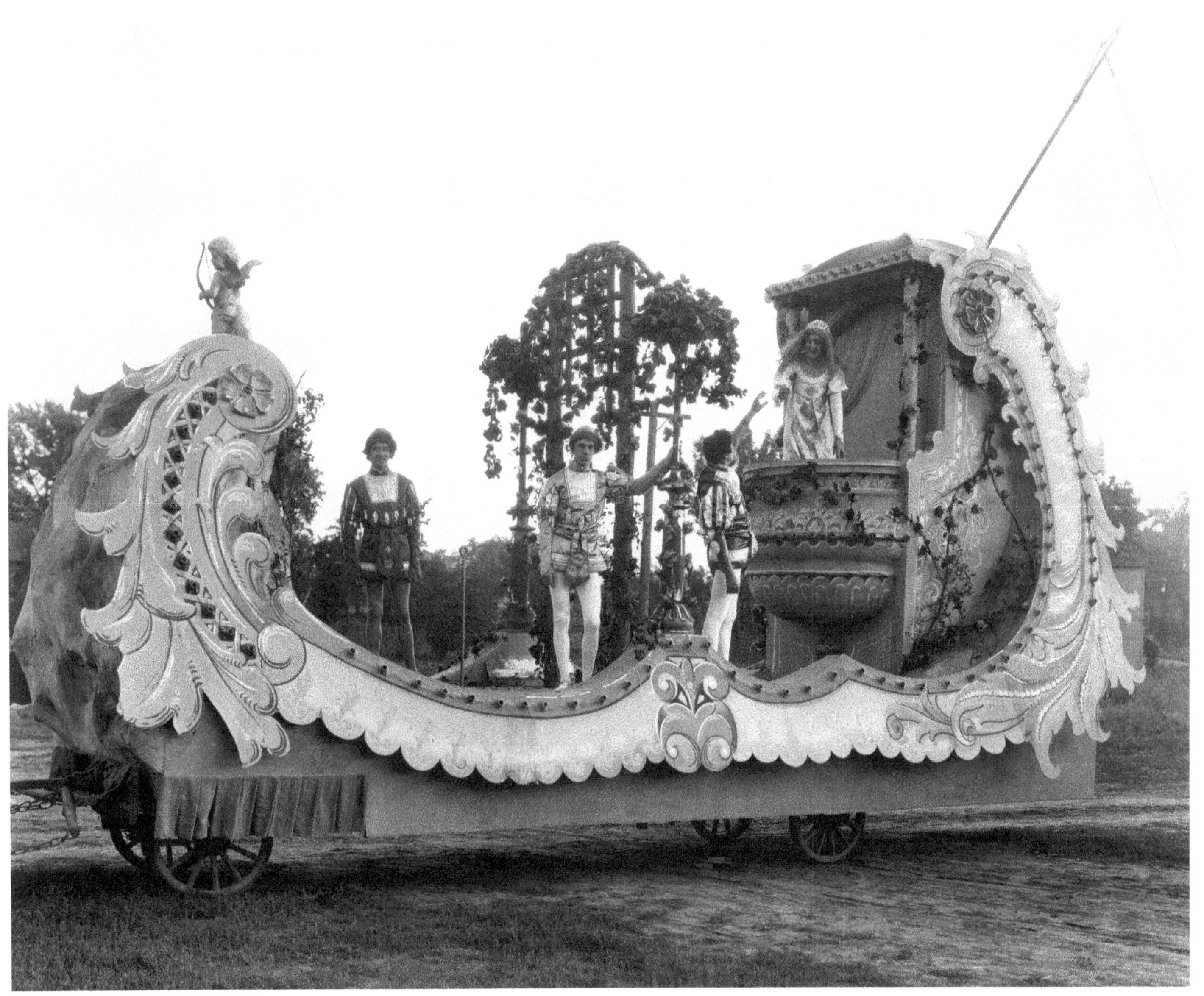

A major attraction every year was the "electrical parades" put on by the Knights of AK-SAR-BEN. This float, entitled "Romeo and Juliet," was part of the September 1920 parade, which had the theme "Famous Love Tales." Thousands of people lined the downtown streets to view the parades every fall.

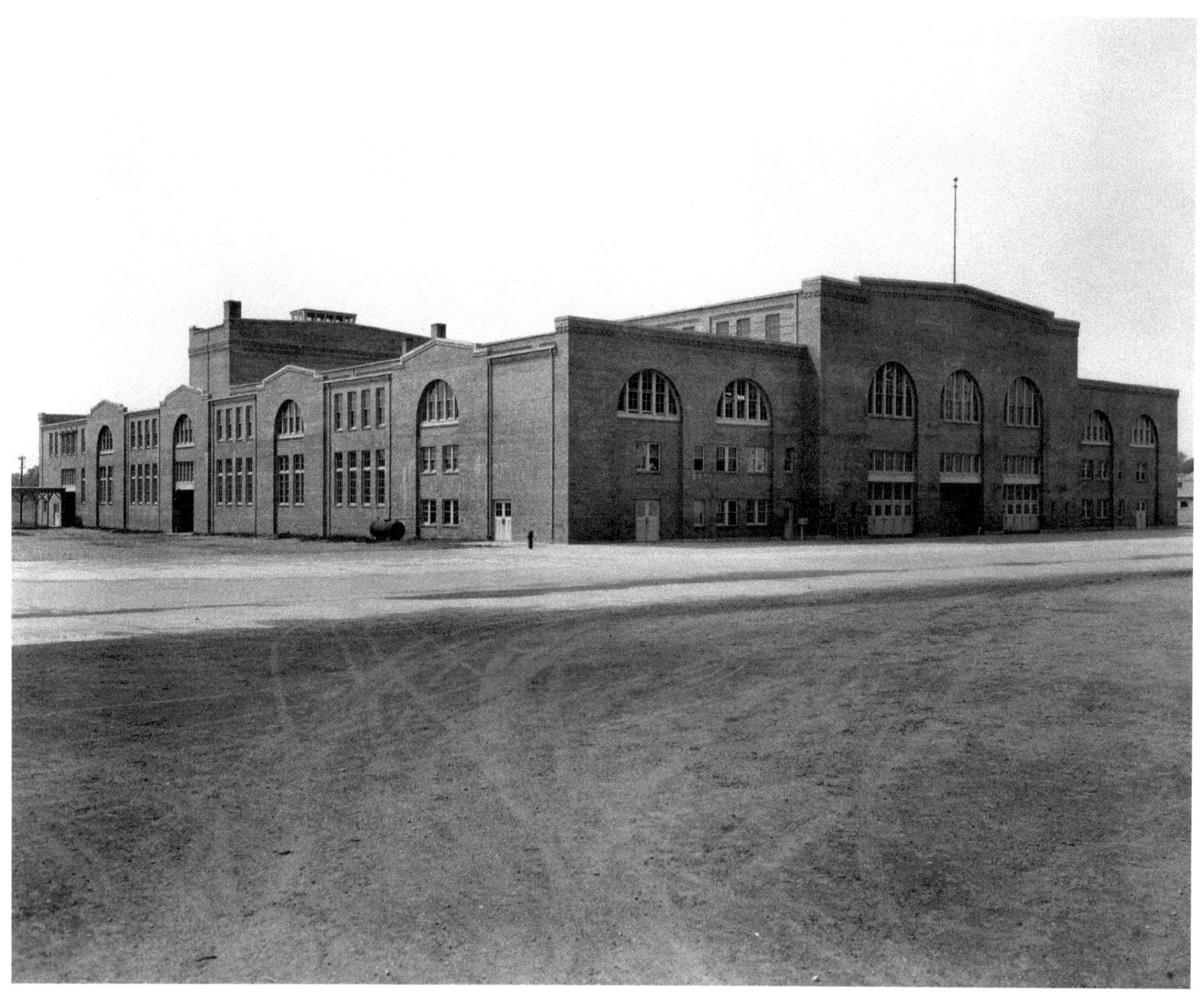

The $400,000 AK-SAR-BEN Coliseum as it appeared shortly after it was completed in 1928. It became the location of all the organization's functions for many years. Located at 64th and Center streets, it had a capacity of 7,200. The coliseum was torn down in 2005, after the property had been sold for redevelopment.

The Fontenelle Hotel, photographed in 1928 at the height of its popularity, was located at 1806 Douglas Street and opened with great celebration in 1915. Prominent architect Thomas R. Kimball designed it for the Douglas Hotel Company. For many years, the Fontenelle served as Omaha's premier hotel, hosting many important events. After closing in 1971, it was unoccupied for several years. When redevelopment plans were not forthcoming, it was torn down in 1983.

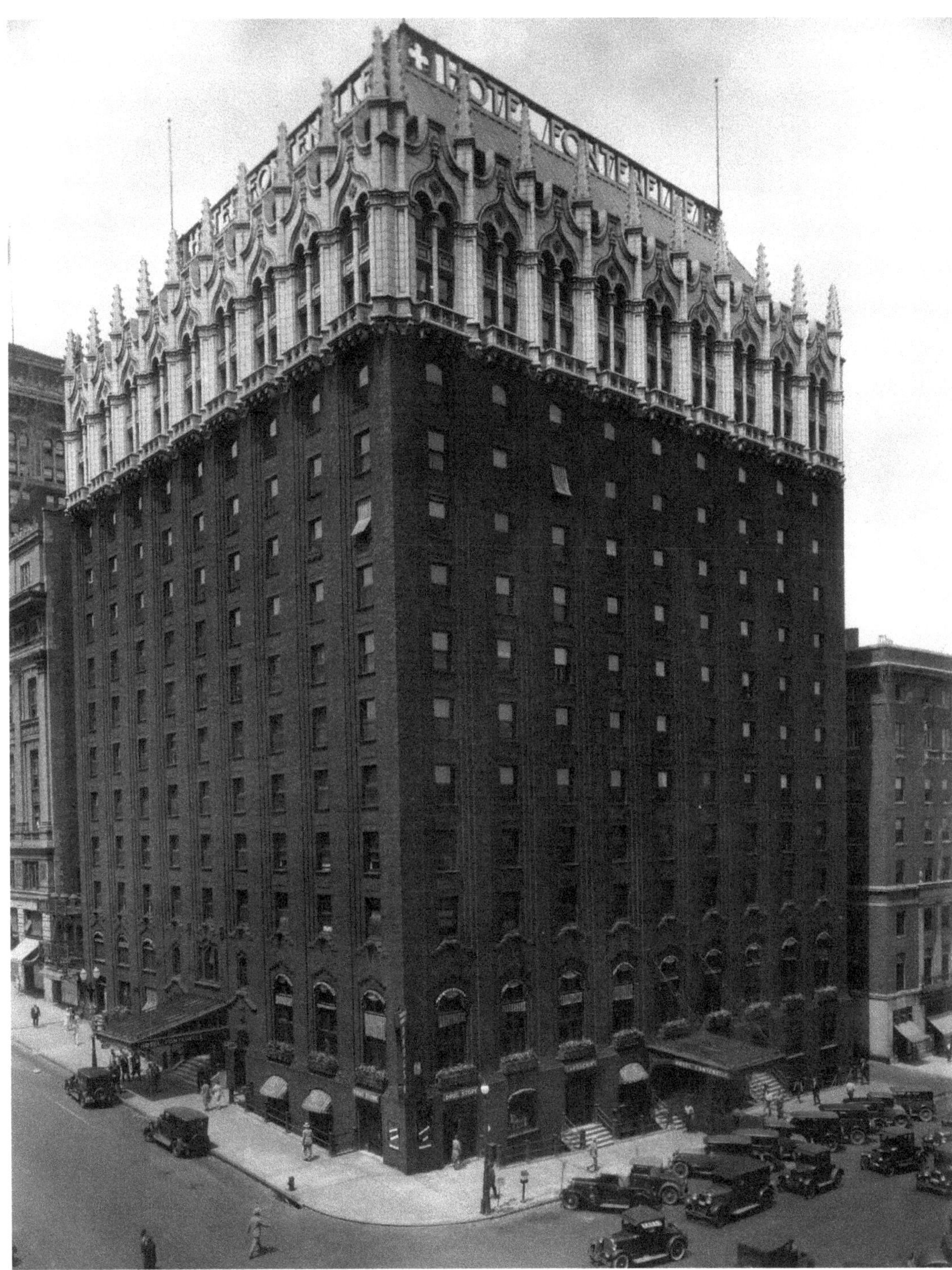

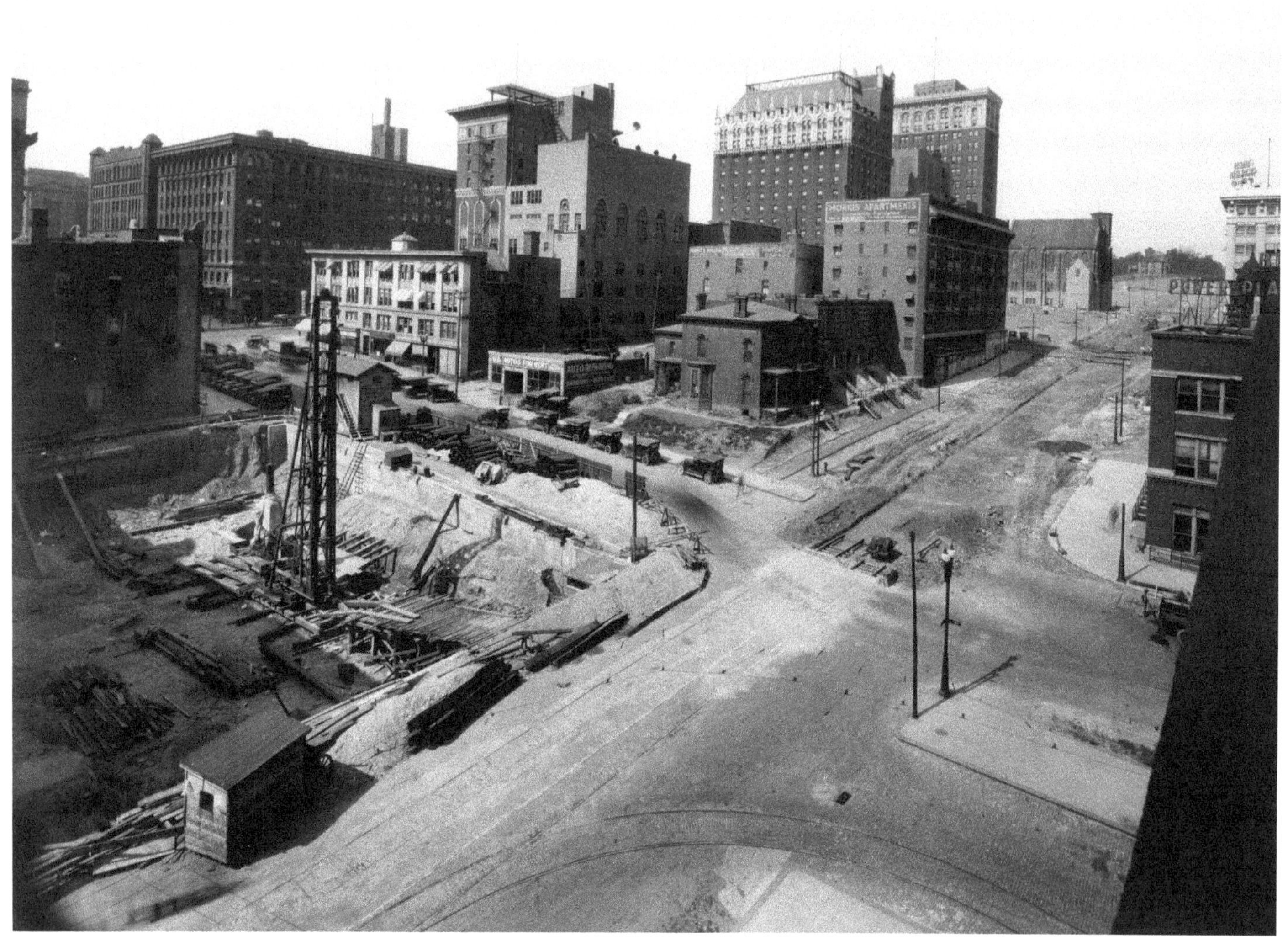

This picture, looking southwest on Dodge at 17th Street, was taken in the early 1920s during excavation for the Medical Arts Building. The building was finally completed in 1926 after being plagued by delays and financial difficulties. Containing seventeen floors, it included commercial space, medical offices and even a 500-seat auditorium. A gem of art deco architecture, it was the last major commission undertaken by noted Omaha architect Thomas R. Kimball. It was torn down in 1999.

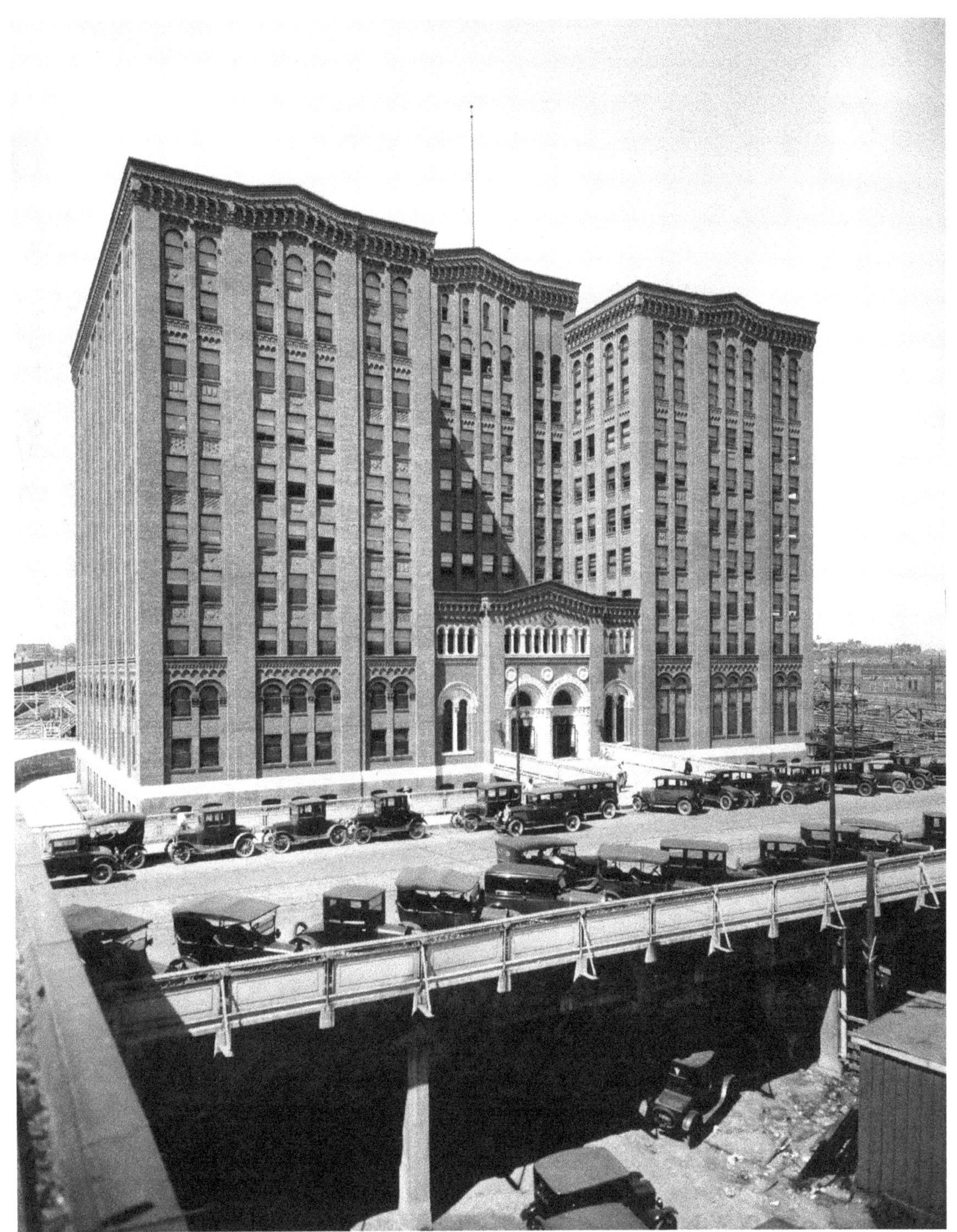

The newly completed Livestock Exchange Building at 2900 O Plaza in 1926. Designed by prominent Omaha architect George B. Prinz, this structure remains today the most distinctive landmark in South Omaha. Built by Peter Kiewit and Sons Construction Company at a cost of one million dollars, it was for many years a symbol of the national role played by Omaha in the livestock and meat-processing industry. Recently, it was redeveloped for commercial and residential usage.

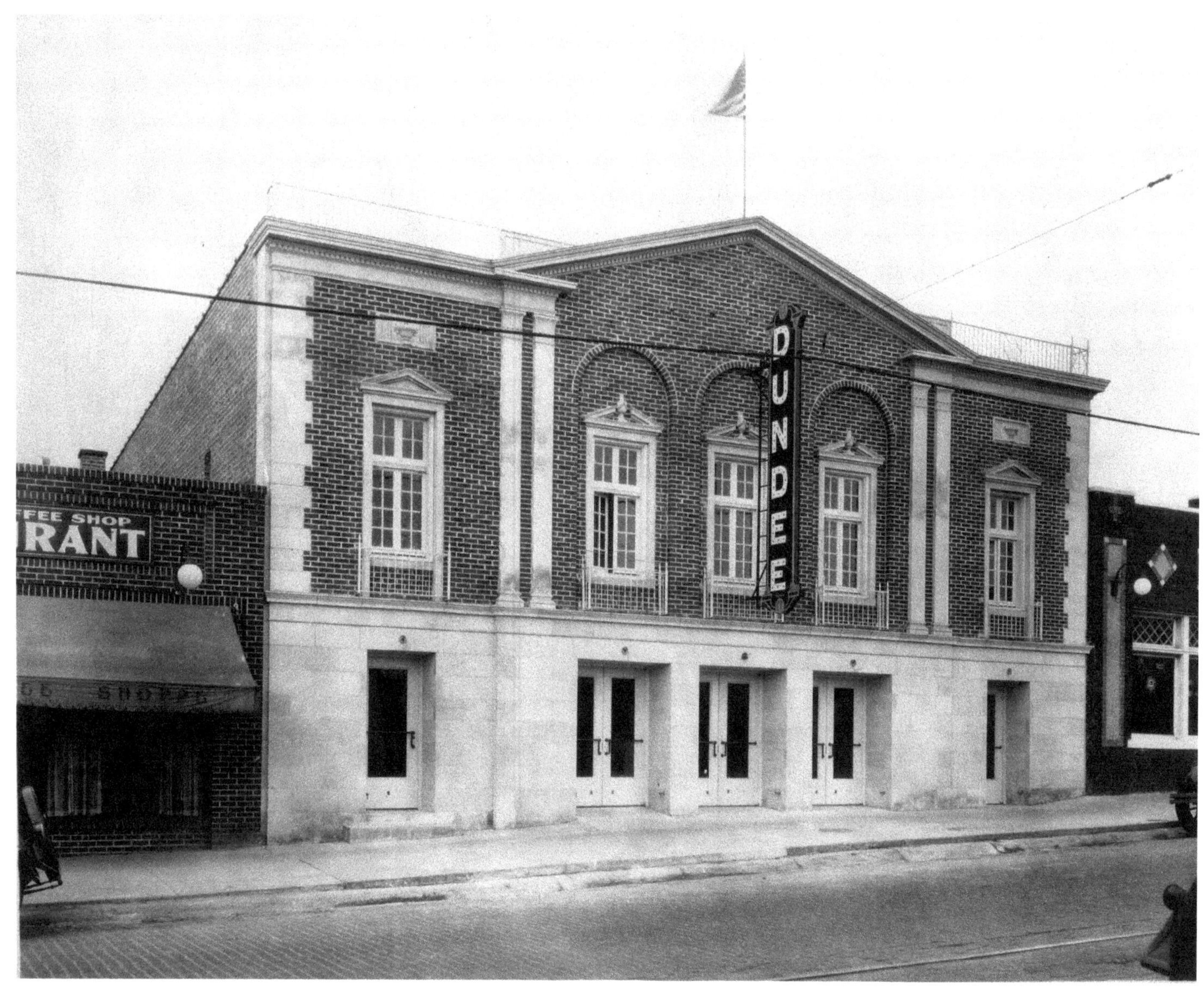

The Dundee Theater, 4952 Dodge Street, soon after it was built in 1925. Originally a stage theatre used for vaudeville and live performances, it was converted to a movie house in the 1930s. An important landmark in the Dundee area, it is considered to be the last neighborhood theatre still operating in Omaha.

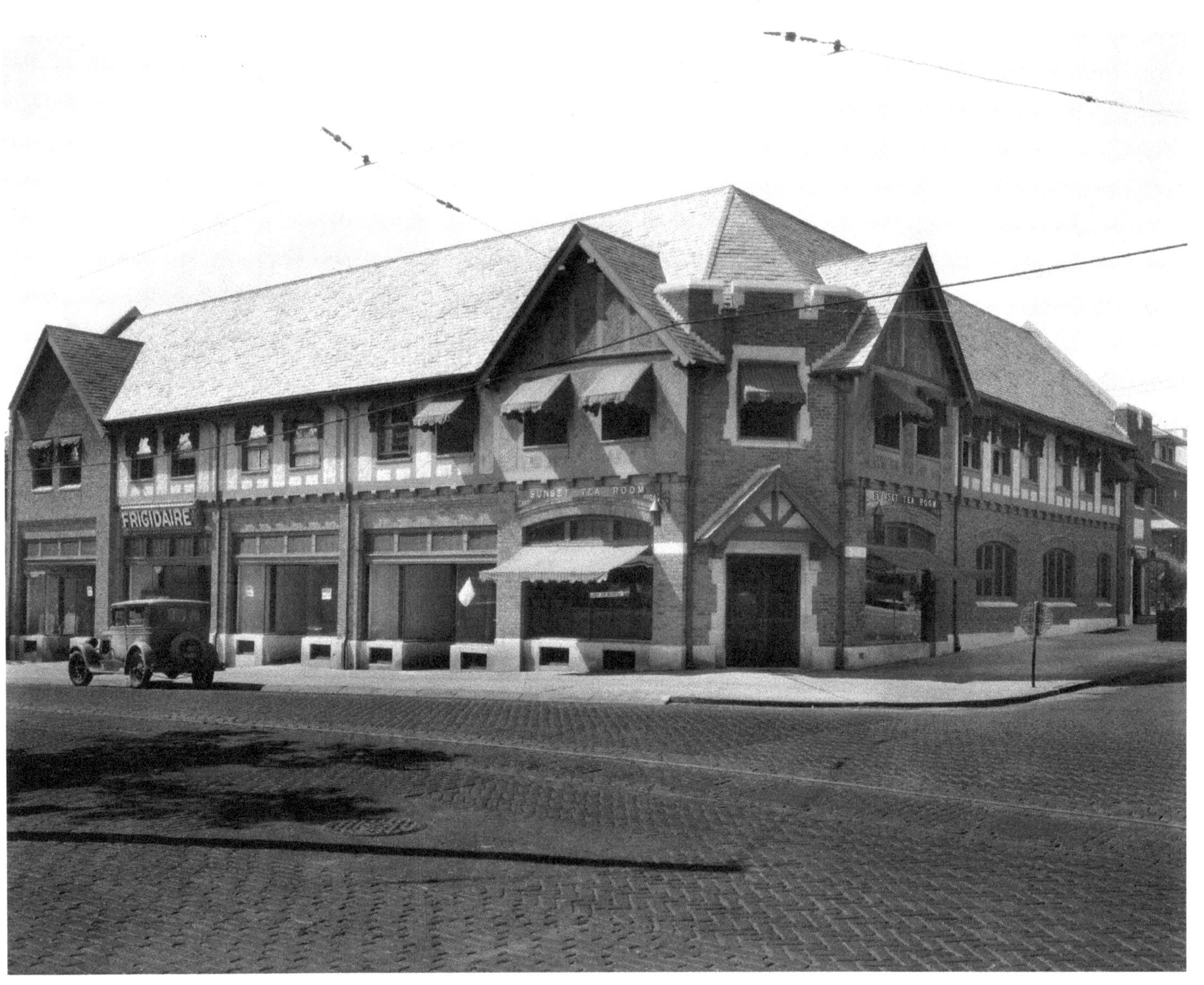

Located on the northwest corner of 49th and Dodge streets, this building was originally the Dundee Hotel. This picture made in July 1927 shows the Sunset Tea Room which occupied the ground floor. Through the years, the building has had many residential and commercial tenants, and is still in use today.

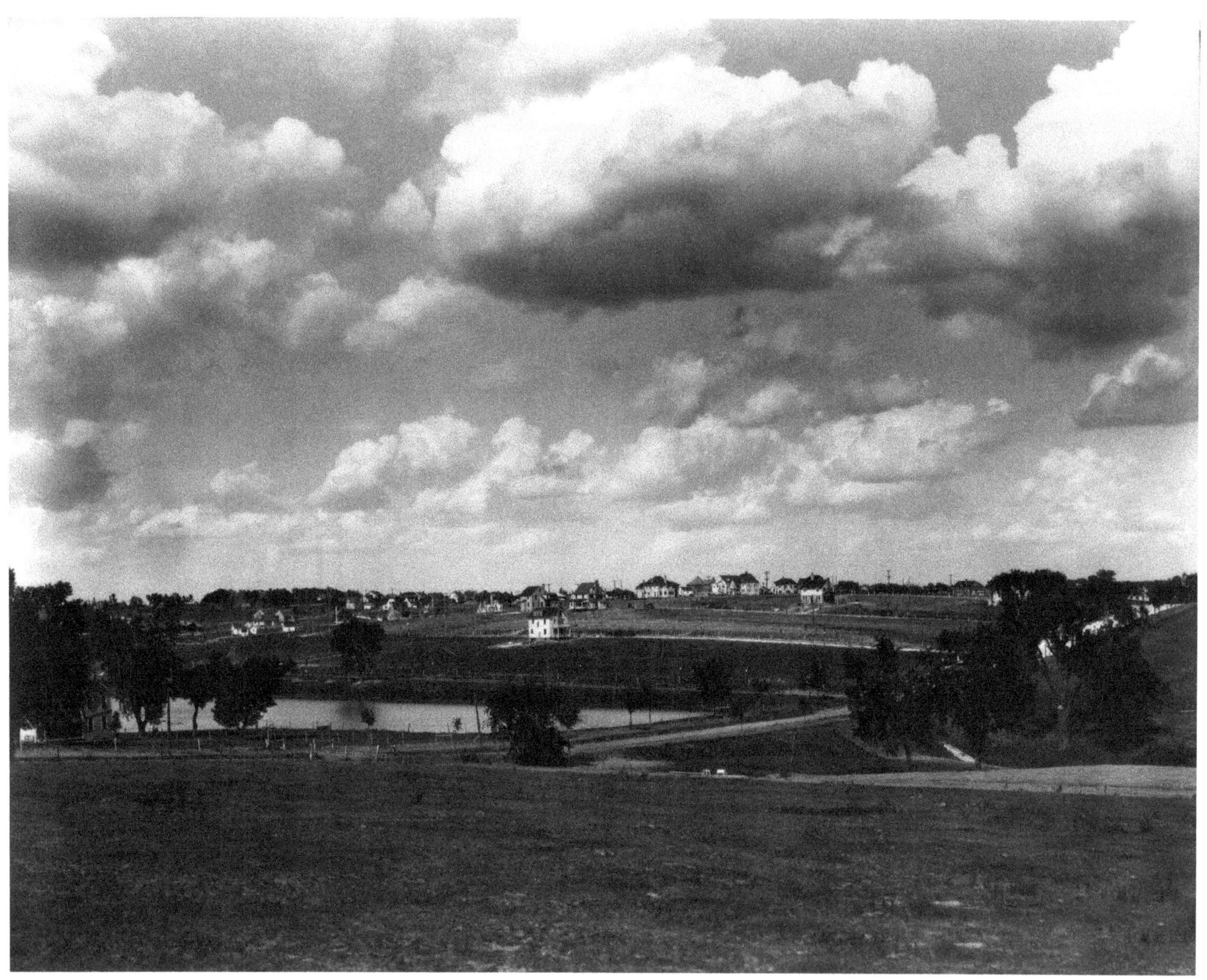

Looking slightly northwest around 52nd Street and Underwood Avenue in the Dundee neighborhood, this photograph was taken in June 1926. Lake George in the foreground—named for the George brothers who developed the area—was later filled in. Dundee was an affluent residential area, which at one time had been a separate town. It was annexed into the city of Omaha in 1915.

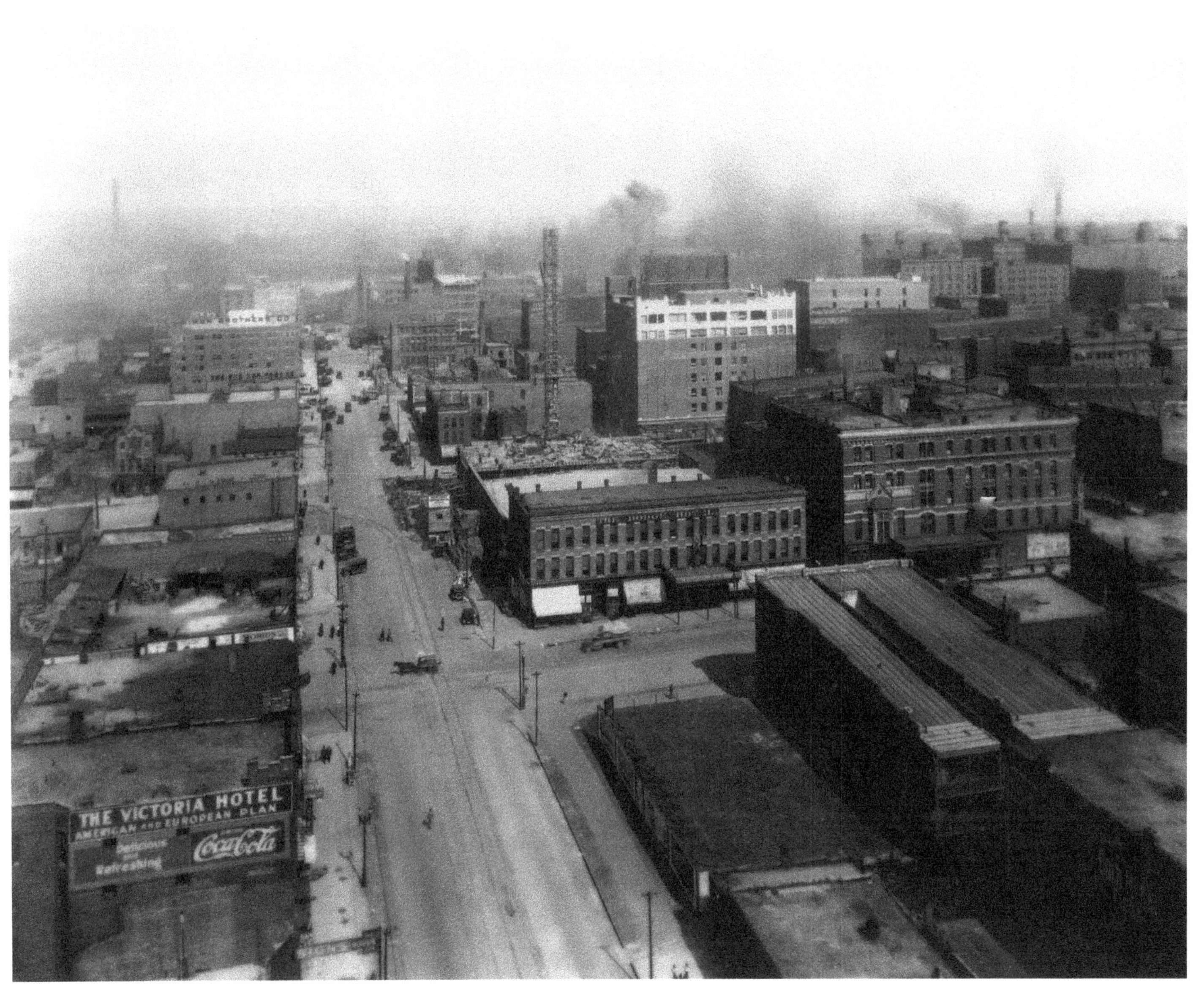

In the early 1920s, this picture was taken from the rooftop of the Union Pacific Railroad's headquarters building, looking east along Dodge from 14th Street. The Dodge Hotel is on the corner. The jobbing and warehouse district is visible at upper right.

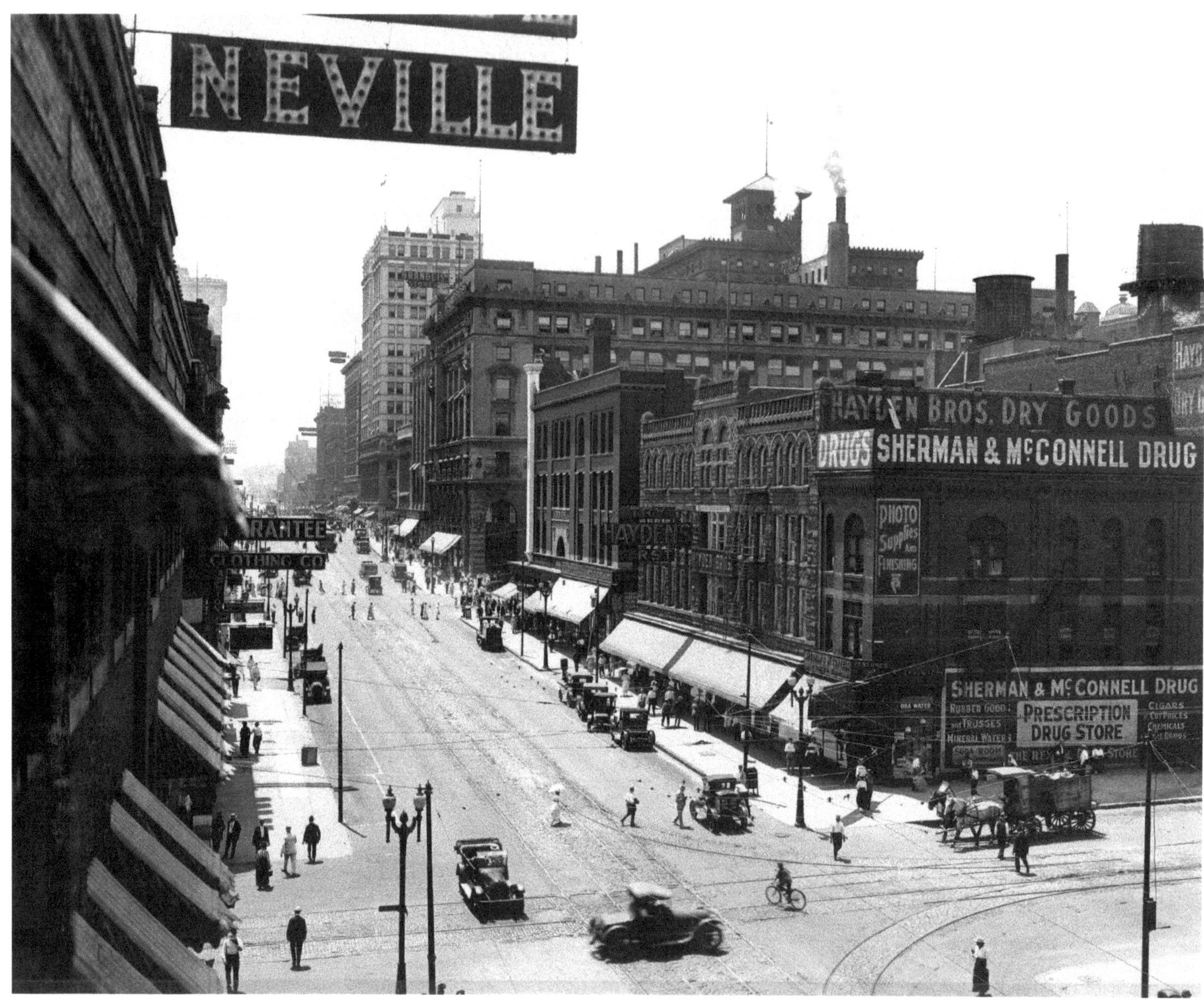

The downtown commercial district, south from 16th and Dodge streets in 1921. On the right side of the street, at the upper center, is the First National Bank building at 16th and Farnam. To its right, the tall, white building is J. L. Brandies and Sons department store at 16th and Douglas streets. Across Douglas is the Boston Store and beside it Hayden Brothers Department Store. In the left foreground is the Hotel Neville, 107 North 16th Street, which advertised itself as, "A modern home away from home in the heart of the business district."

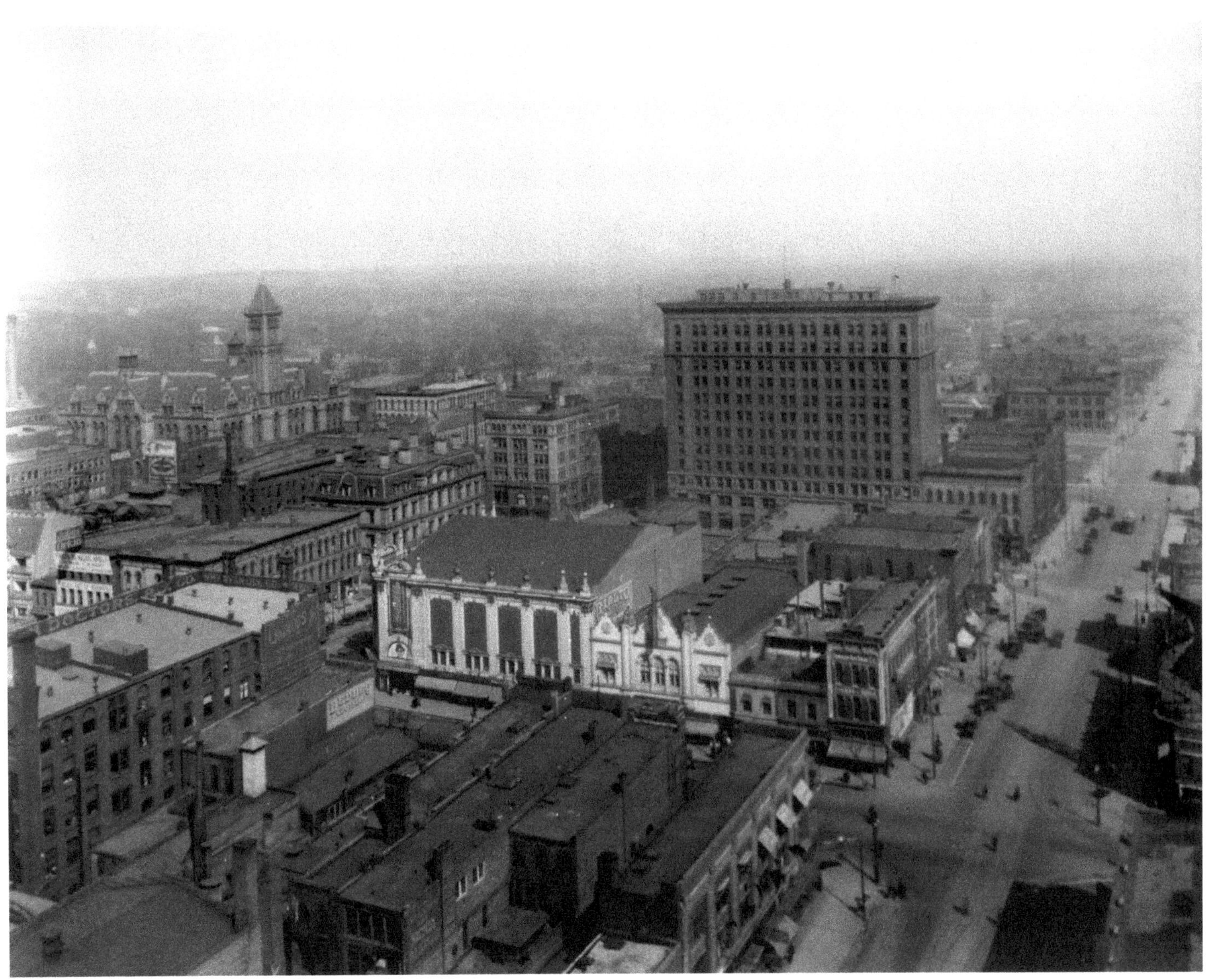

This picture was taken March 31, 1920, facing north-northwest from the top of the Woodmen of the World Building on the corner of 14th and Farnam, which was Omaha's tallest building at the time. The U.S. Post Office is to the upper left and at upper right is the large headquarters building of the Union Pacific Railroad at 15th and Dodge streets.

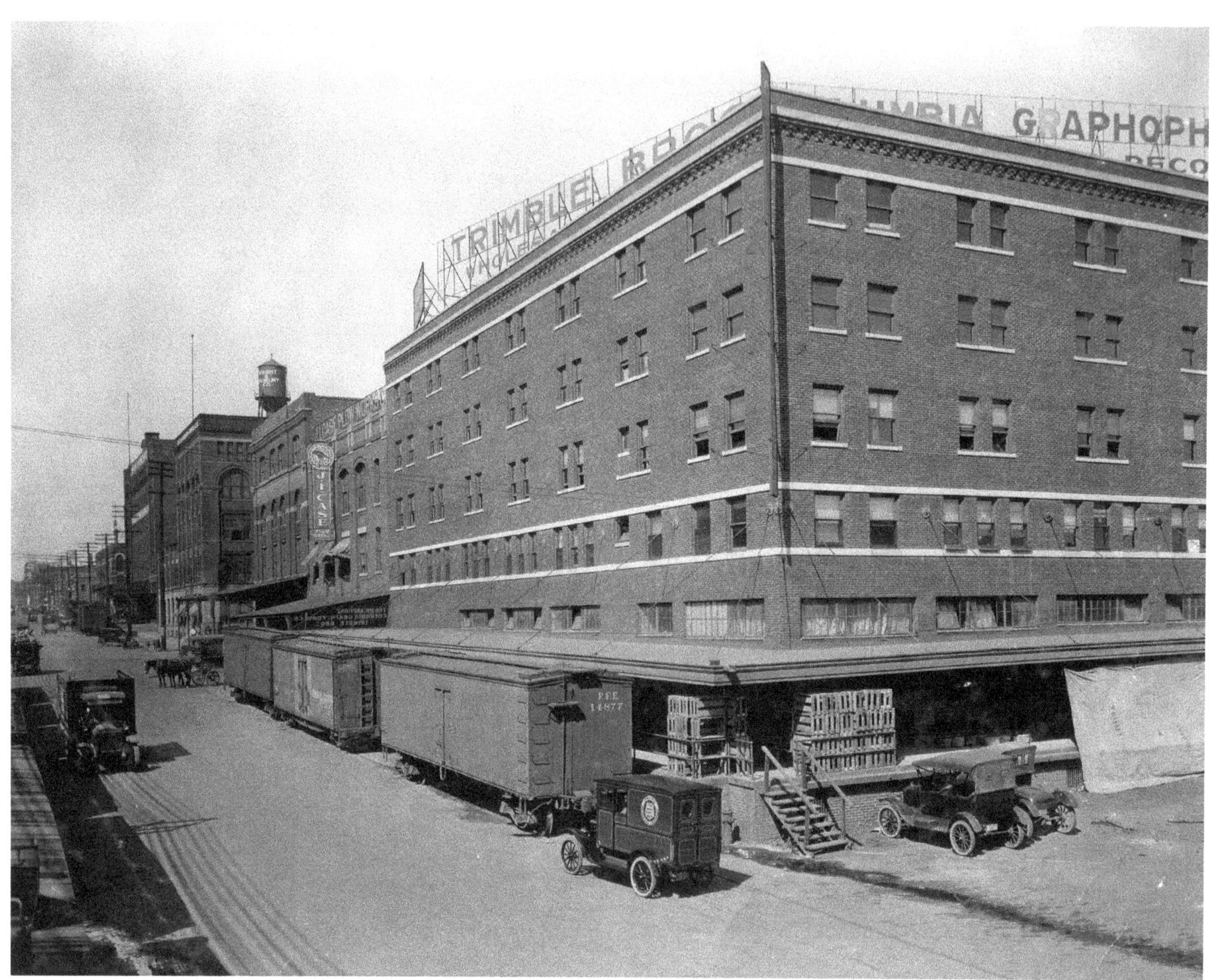

Howard Street west from 8th Street in the wholesale district or "Jobbers Canyon" as it was known, in 1921. The "canyon" was formed by the continual line of large warehouse buildings that housed manufactured goods. A truck from the Omaha Printing (and office supplies) Company is in the foreground, while the Jicase Plow Works Company and the water tower for Wright & Wilhelmy appear beyond the box cars. The warehouses were built to have direct access to the rail line. Several of the remaining warehouse buildings in this area have been redeveloped into residential properties.

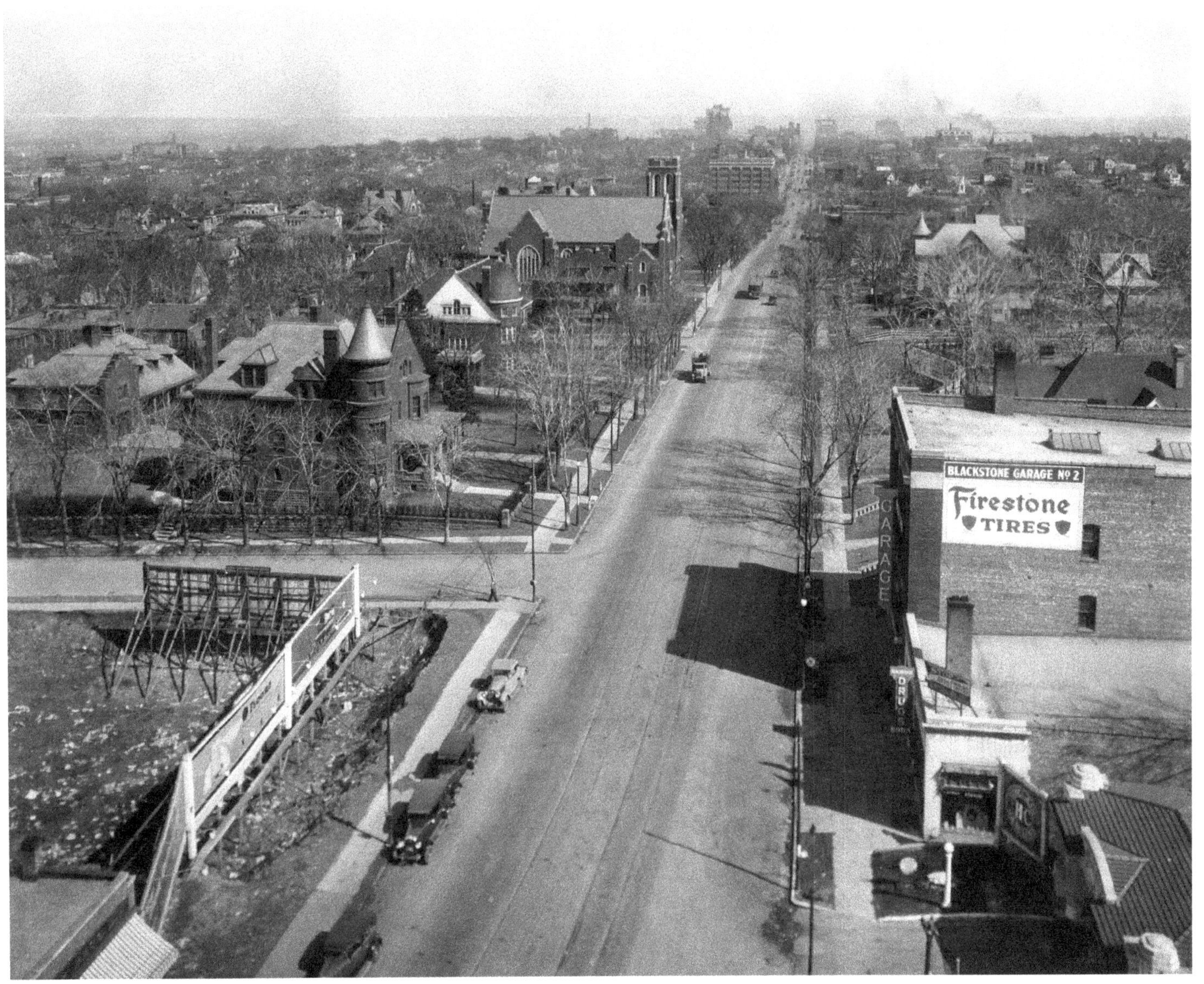

This picture was taken from the roof of the Blackstone Hotel, looking east on Farnam Street near 36th Street in 1921. Towards the top left of the picture is the First Presbyterian Church, built in 1917. Several of the large, elegant mansions of prosperous families in what was called the Gold Coast neighborhood can be seen as well. In the foreground, a lot is being redeveloped for commercial use.

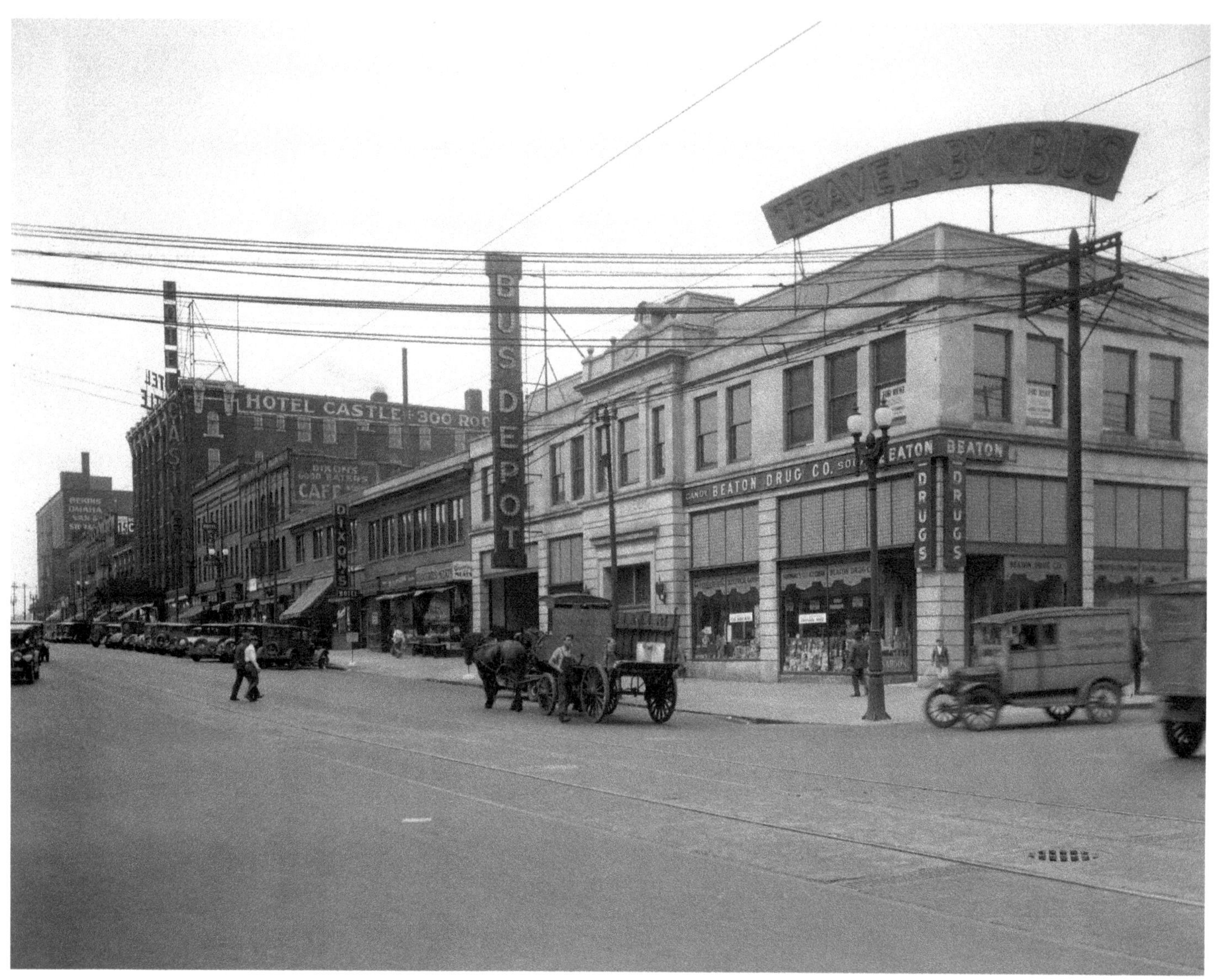

The west side of 16th Street at Jackson in May 1929. At left is the Castle Hotel. In the center foreground is the bus depot, with the Beaton Drug Company located in a corner of that structure. It is interesting to still see a horse-drawn delivery wagon at this late date.

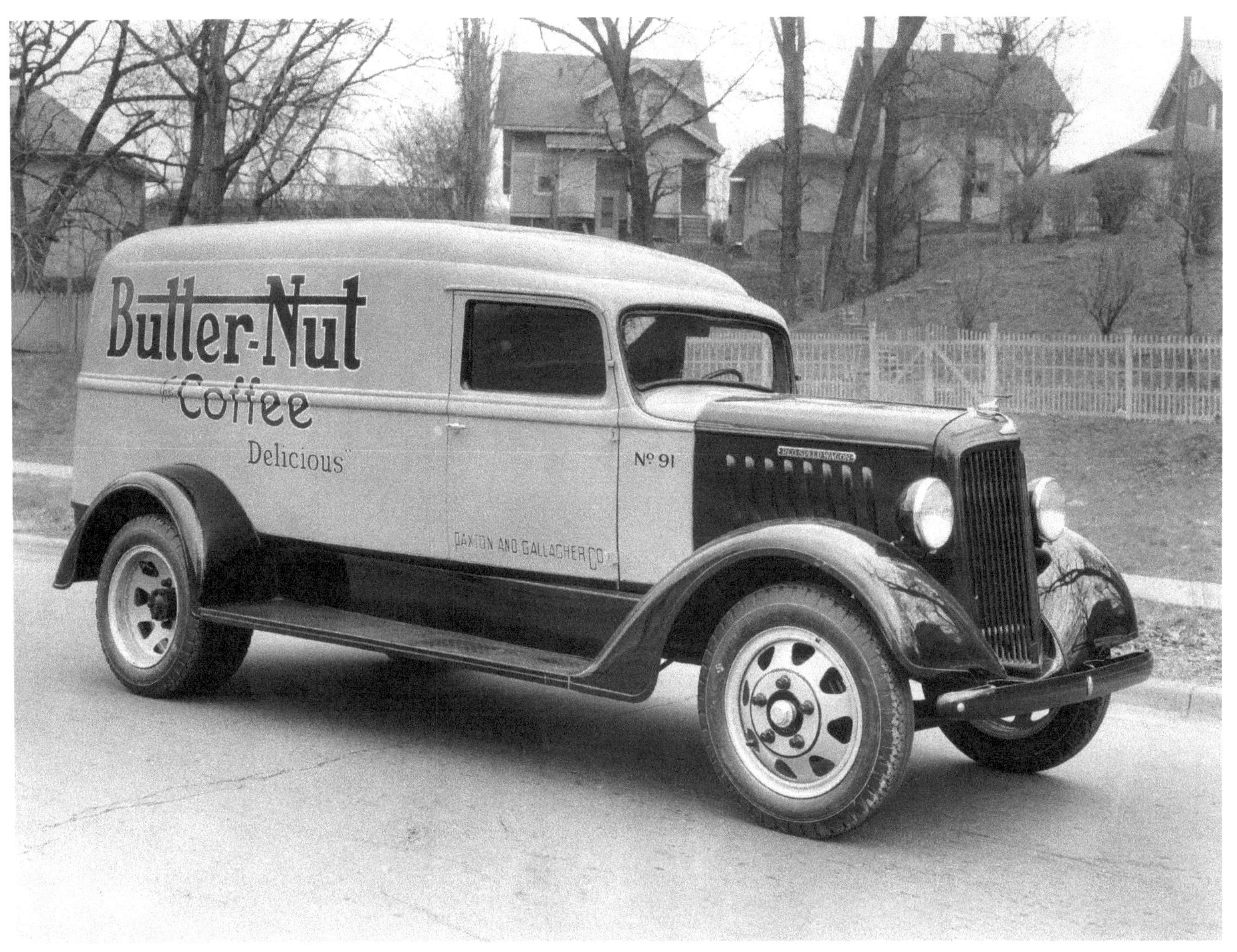

The Paxton and Gallagher Grocery Company was founded in Omaha in 1882. One of its most popular products was Butter-Nut Coffee, which was roasted and packaged here. This 1931 photograph shows one of the company's delivery trucks. The Paxton and Gallagher Company existed until 1958, when it was sold and absorbed into the Swanson Food Company.

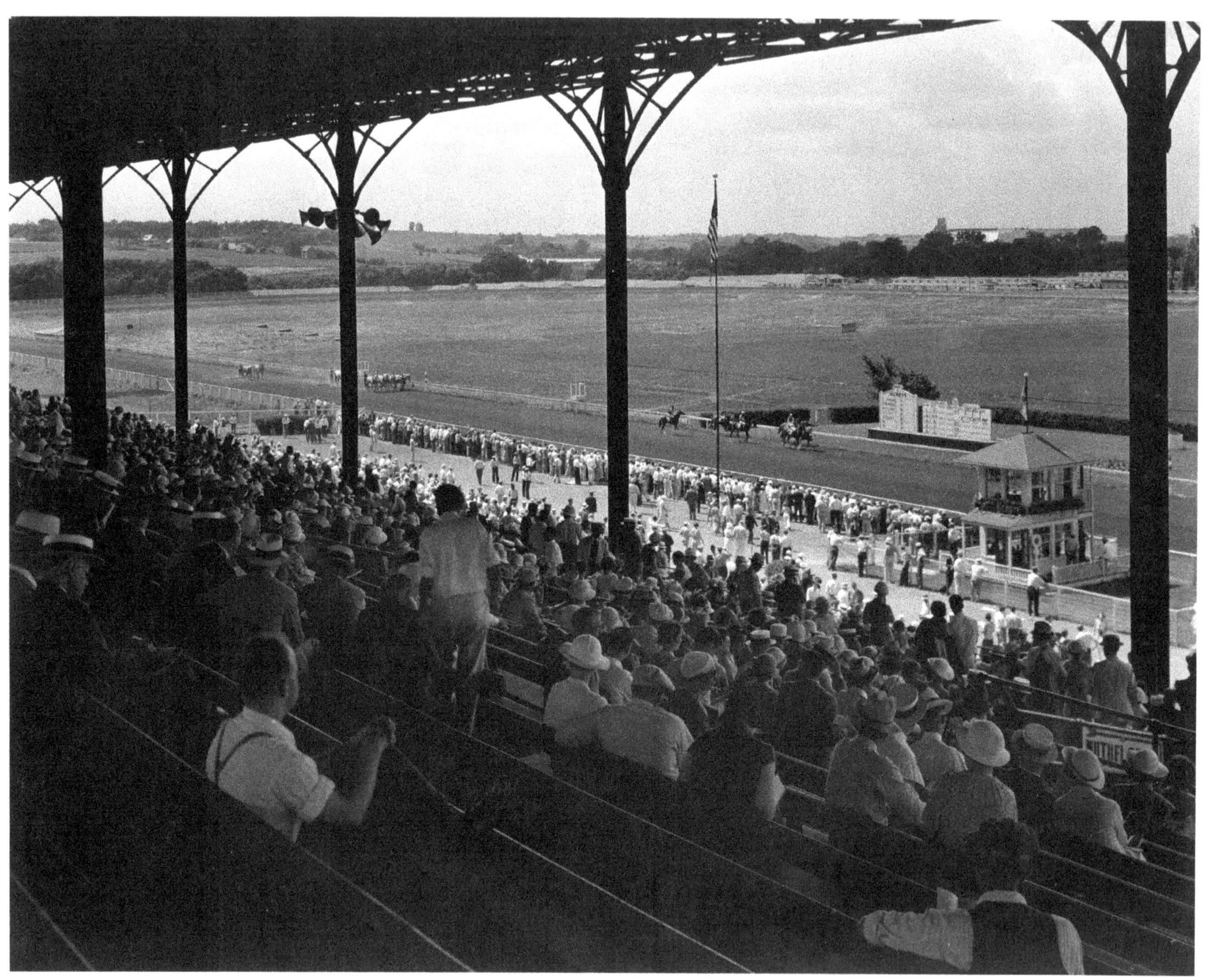

The AK-SAR-BEN racetrack and grandstand, as it appeared in 1935. On September 14, 1920, the racetrack was officially dedicated at the new property on west Center Street. In 1921, the large grandstand seen here was completed. It held more than 6,500 spectators. A complete horse-racing program was available, which included trotting, pacing, and running.

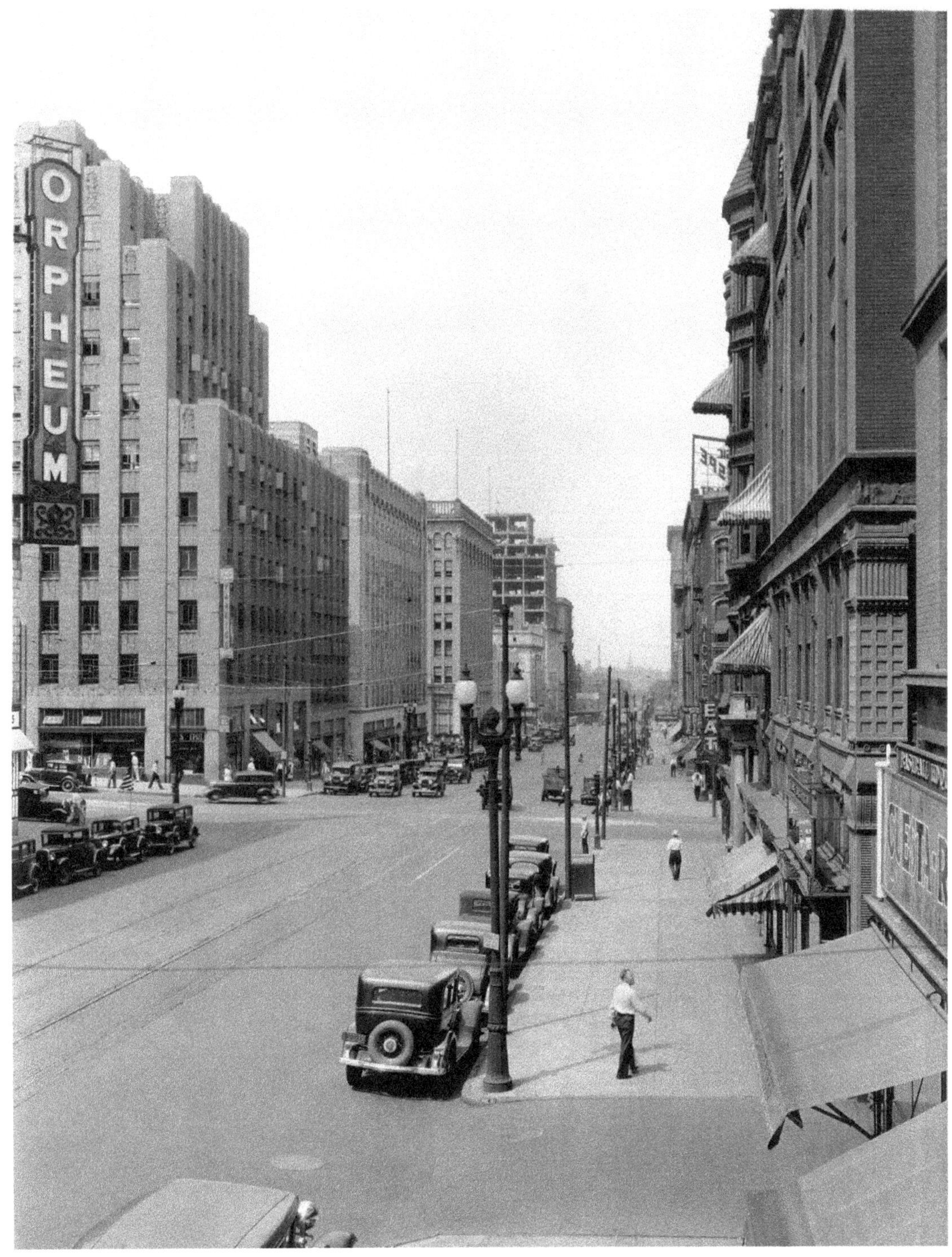

August 1933, facing north on 15th Street from the Carlton Hotel located on the corner of 15th and Howard streets. On the left is the sign at the back of the Orpheum Theatre. Beyond it is the Redick Tower at the northwest corner of 15th and Harney streets, and to the right of that, the Barker Building, southwest corner of 15th and Farnam streets.

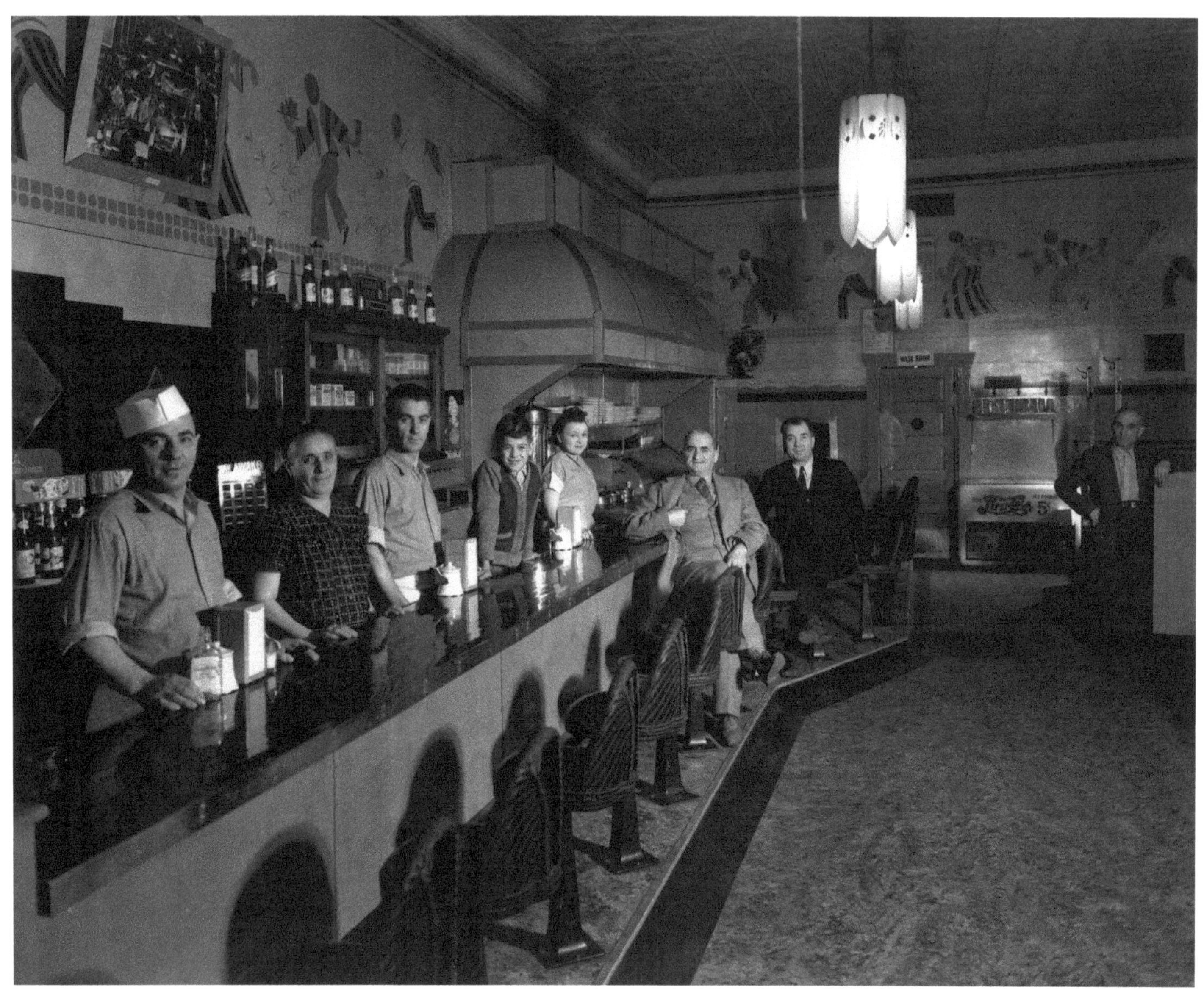

This is a November 1939 interior view of the bar and café owned by William Gaftas at 4940 South 26th Street. It is typical of the neighborhood gathering places which were popular at that time. This South Omaha establishment was frequented by livestock commission men.

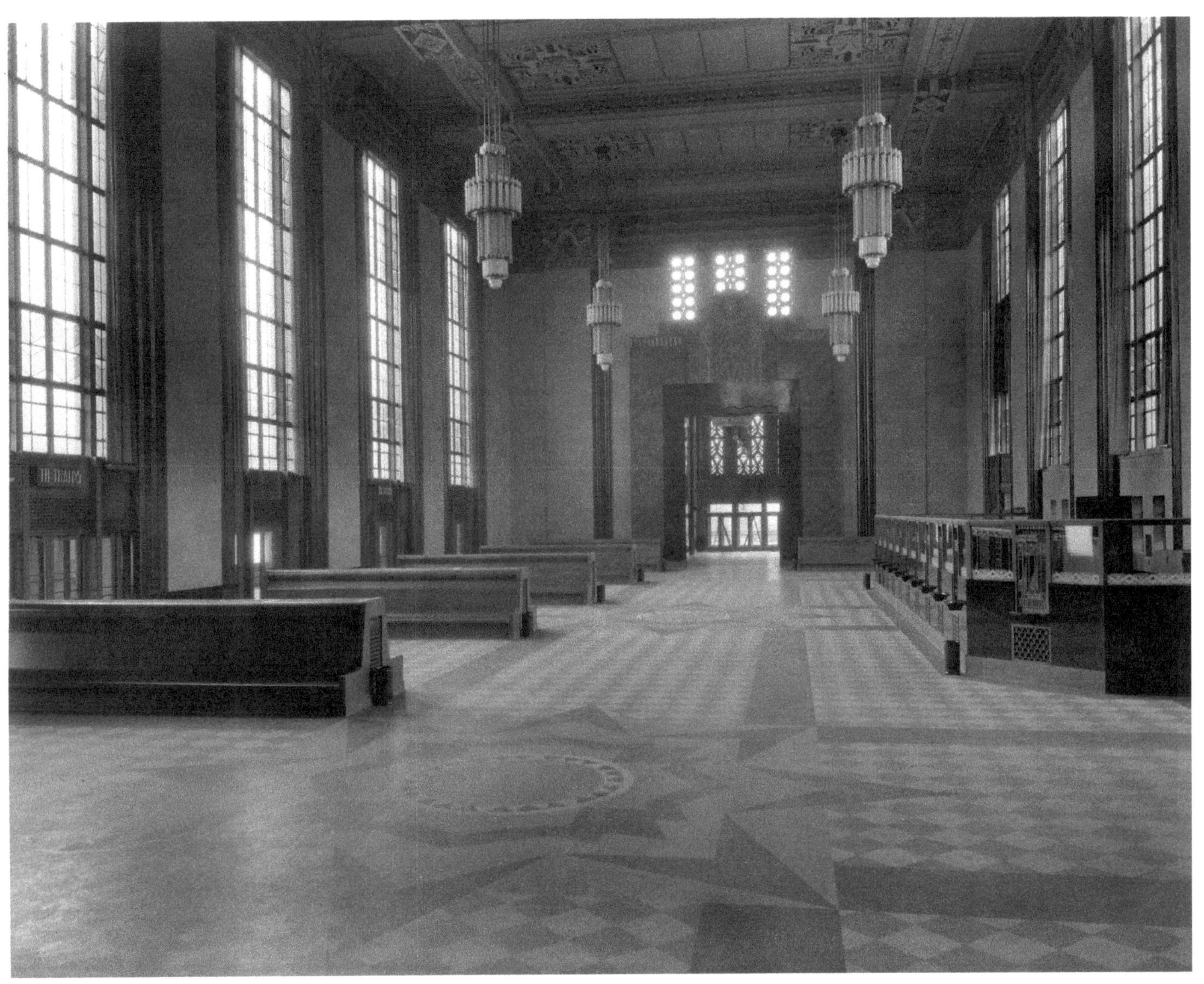

Interior of the imposing Main Waiting Room in Union Station, 10th and Mason streets. This view was taken at the time the station was completed in January 1931. This great hall was 72 feet wide and 160 feet long. The ceiling rose to a height of 60 feet. The station was closed in 1971, and after remaining empty for a time, became home to the Durham Western Heritage Museum, still housed there today.

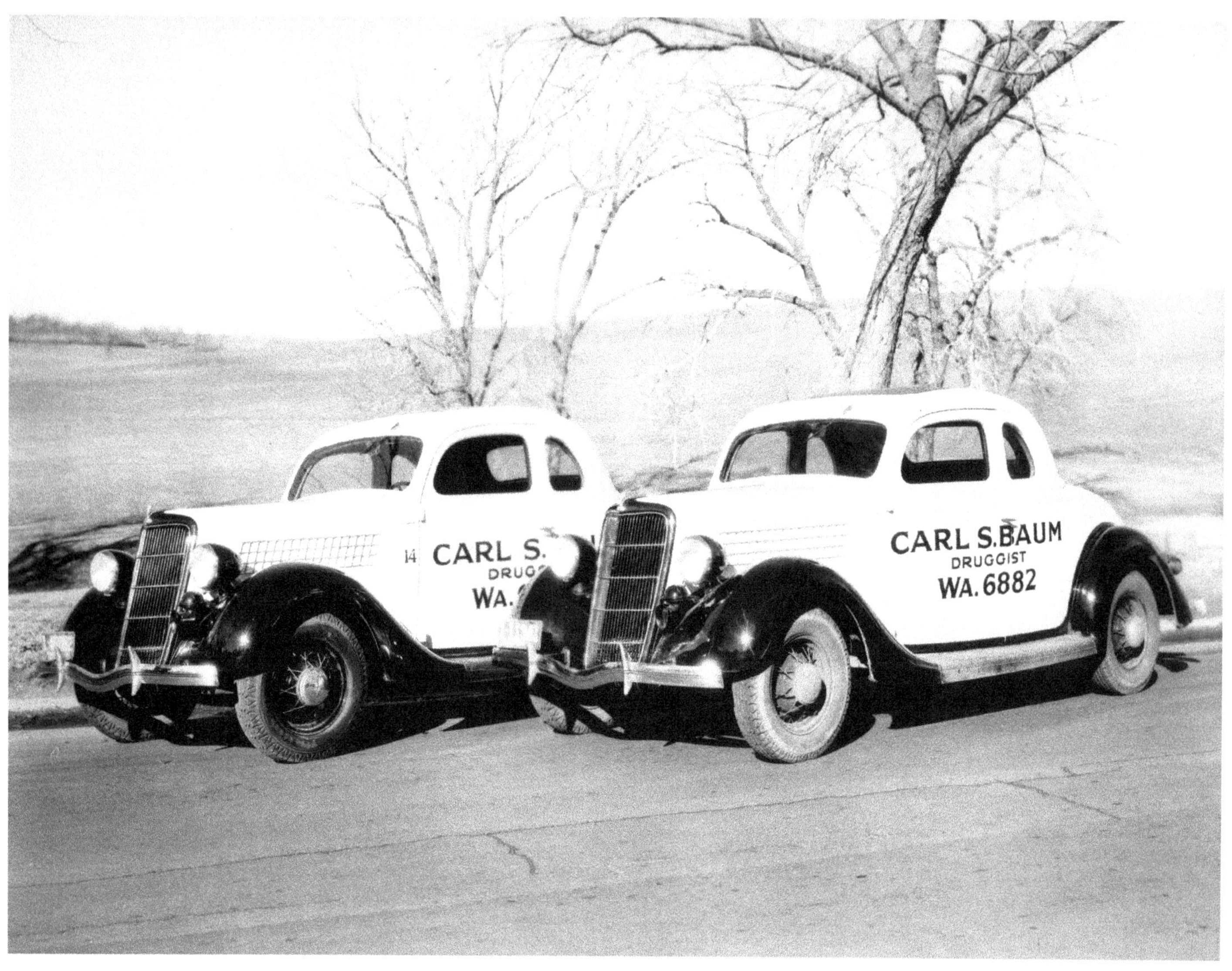

Two of the delivery cars for the Carl S. Baum Drug Company in 1935. This locally owned firm was located at 5001 Underwood Avenue in the Dundee neighborhood.

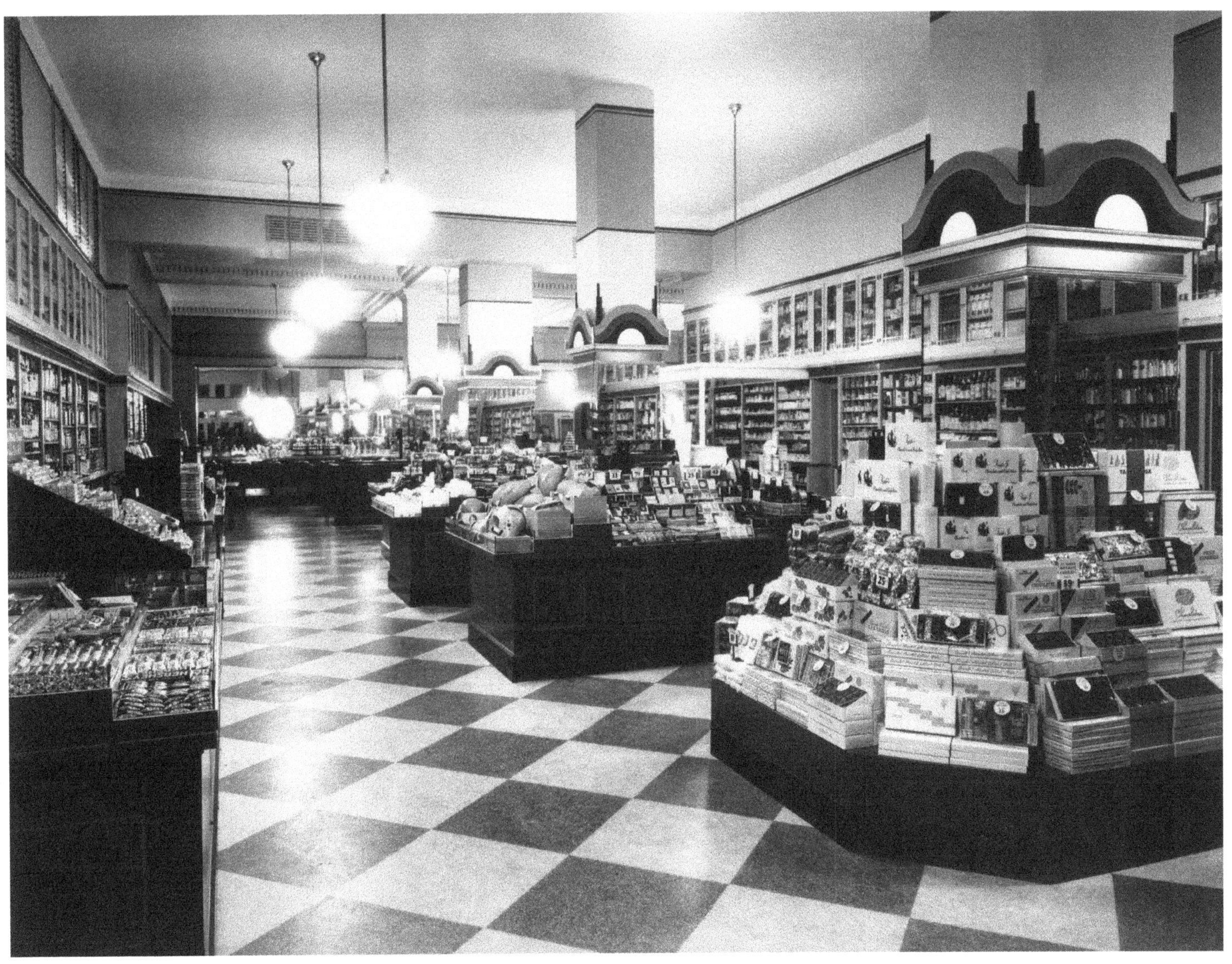

The interior of Walgreen's Drug Store at 1624 Harney Street, one of two locations in Omaha around 1935. The other was at 4902 Dodge Street. This company has continued to grow and prosper, with stores throughout Omaha today.

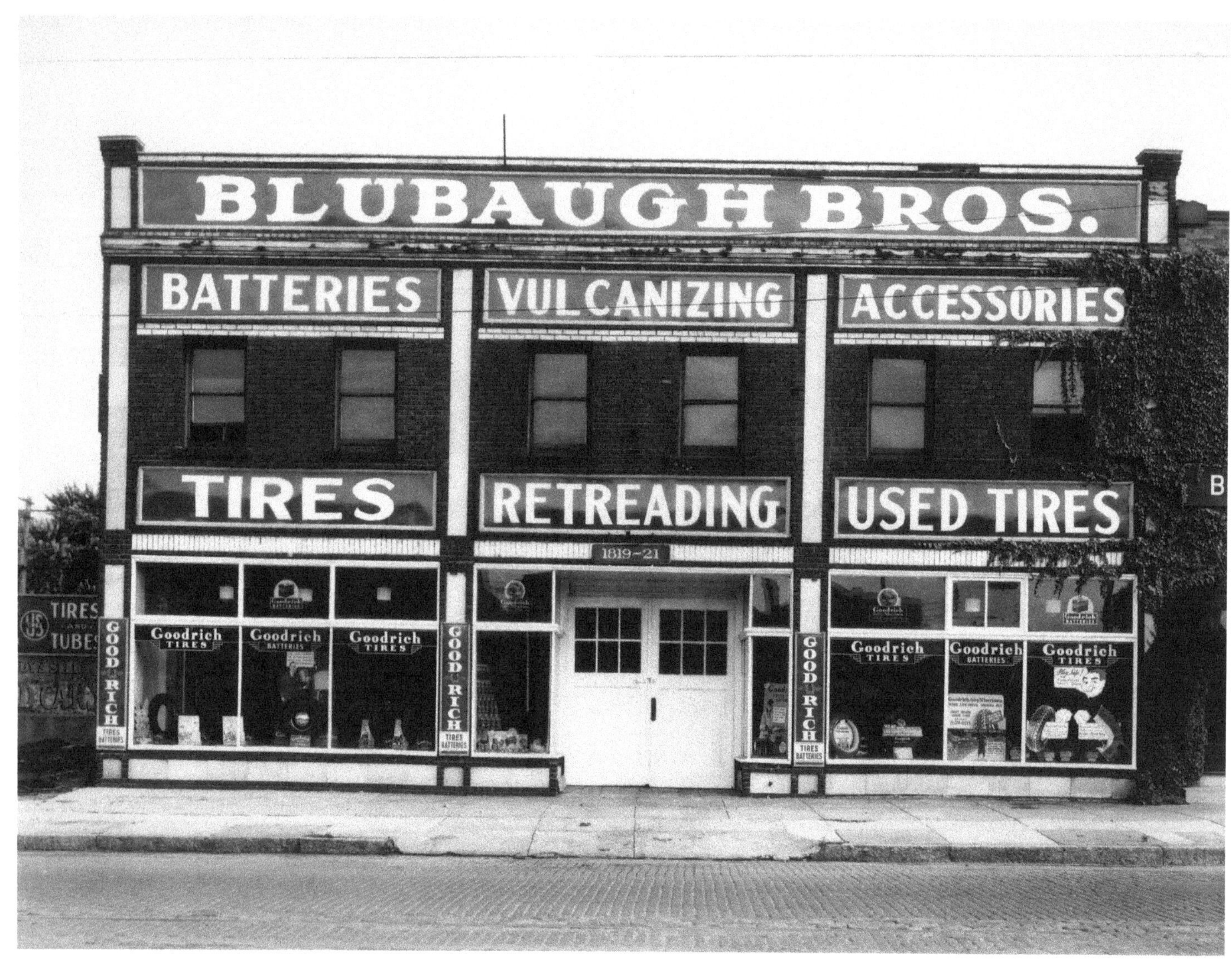

Brothers Charles D. and Clyde A. Blubaugh operated a full-service tire business at 1819–1821 Cuming Street, shown here in 1935.

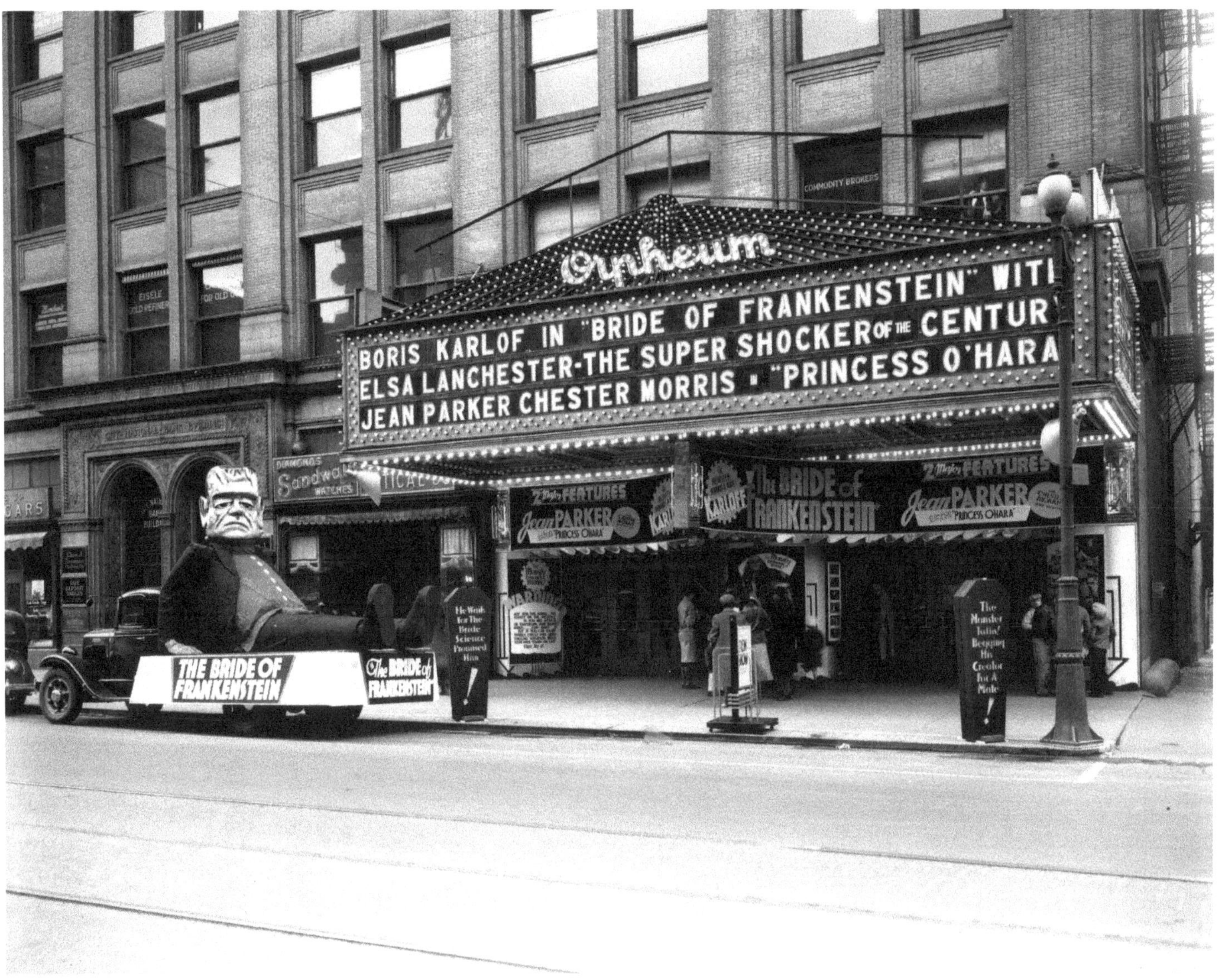

The main entrance of the Orpheum Theatre at 409 South 16th Street, when the 1935 *Bride of Frankenstein* movie was showing. On this site in 1895, John Creighton built the Creighton Theatre. In 1898, when it became a vaudeville house associated with the Orpheum Circuit, the name was changed to the Orpheum Theatre. This was closed on April 25, 1926, and the original building was torn down. A new theater was built, shown here.

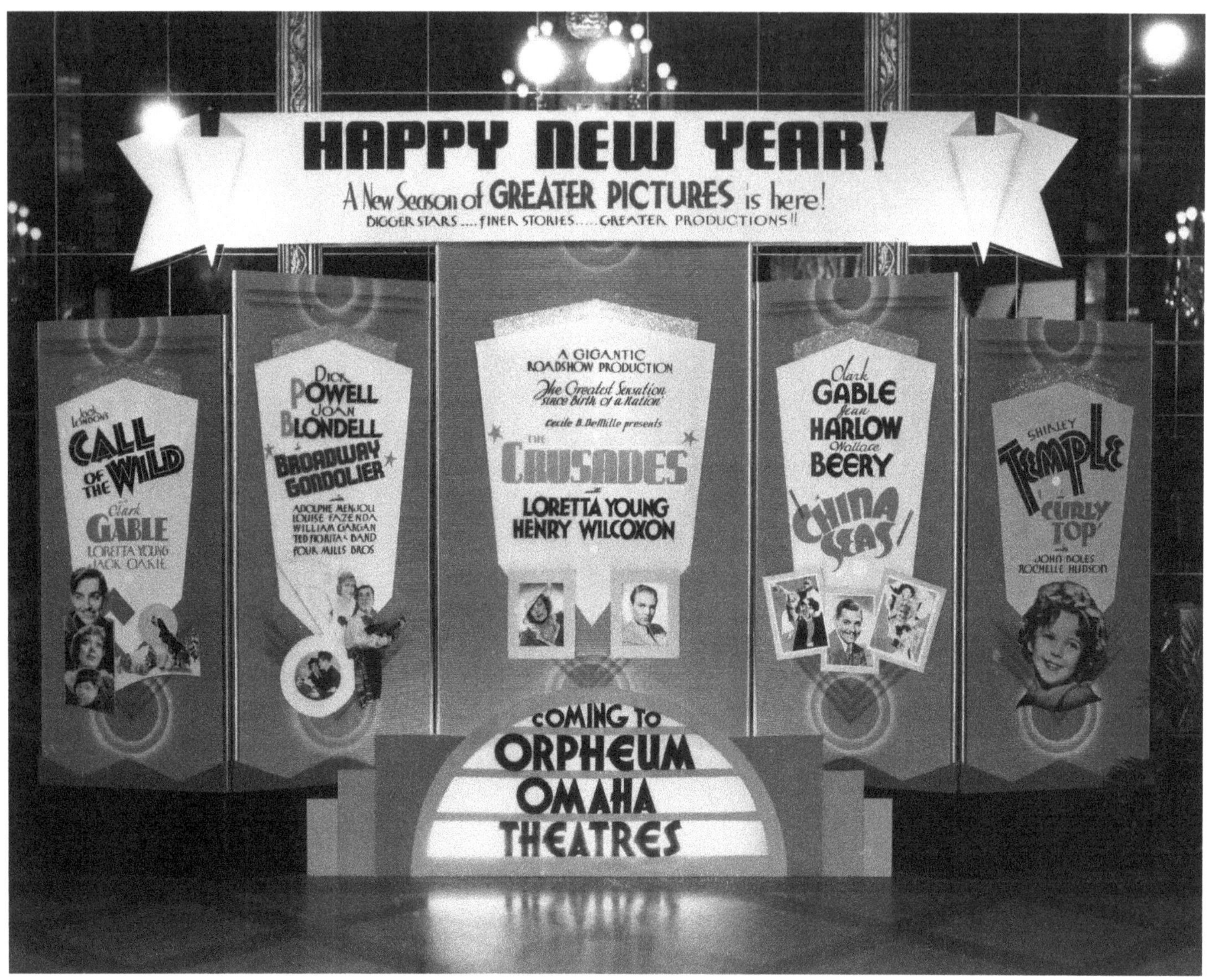

When the new Orpheum Theatre opened in 1927, it was truly magnificent. The main entrance had been changed from 15th Street to 16th, and the auditorium could seat 3,000. These are advertisements for attractions that were coming after New Year's Day 1934.

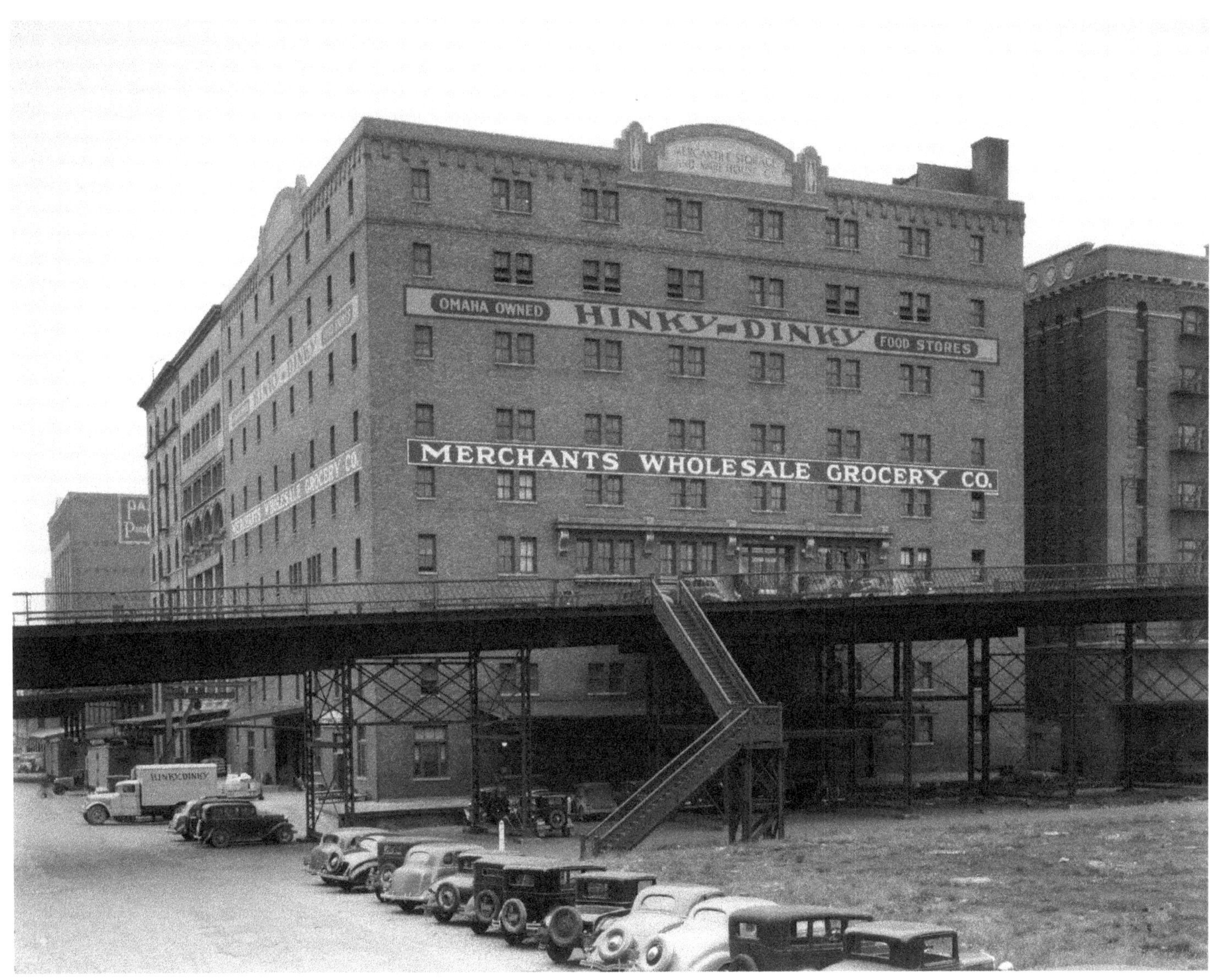

The Mercantile Storage and Warehouse Building at 711 South 11th Street, photographed in the 1930s. Constructed in two phases during 1919-20, it originally had six stories; three more were added in 1920. It was used as a wholesale warehouse for several large grocery companies. Completely renovated in 2001, it was readapted for residential use.

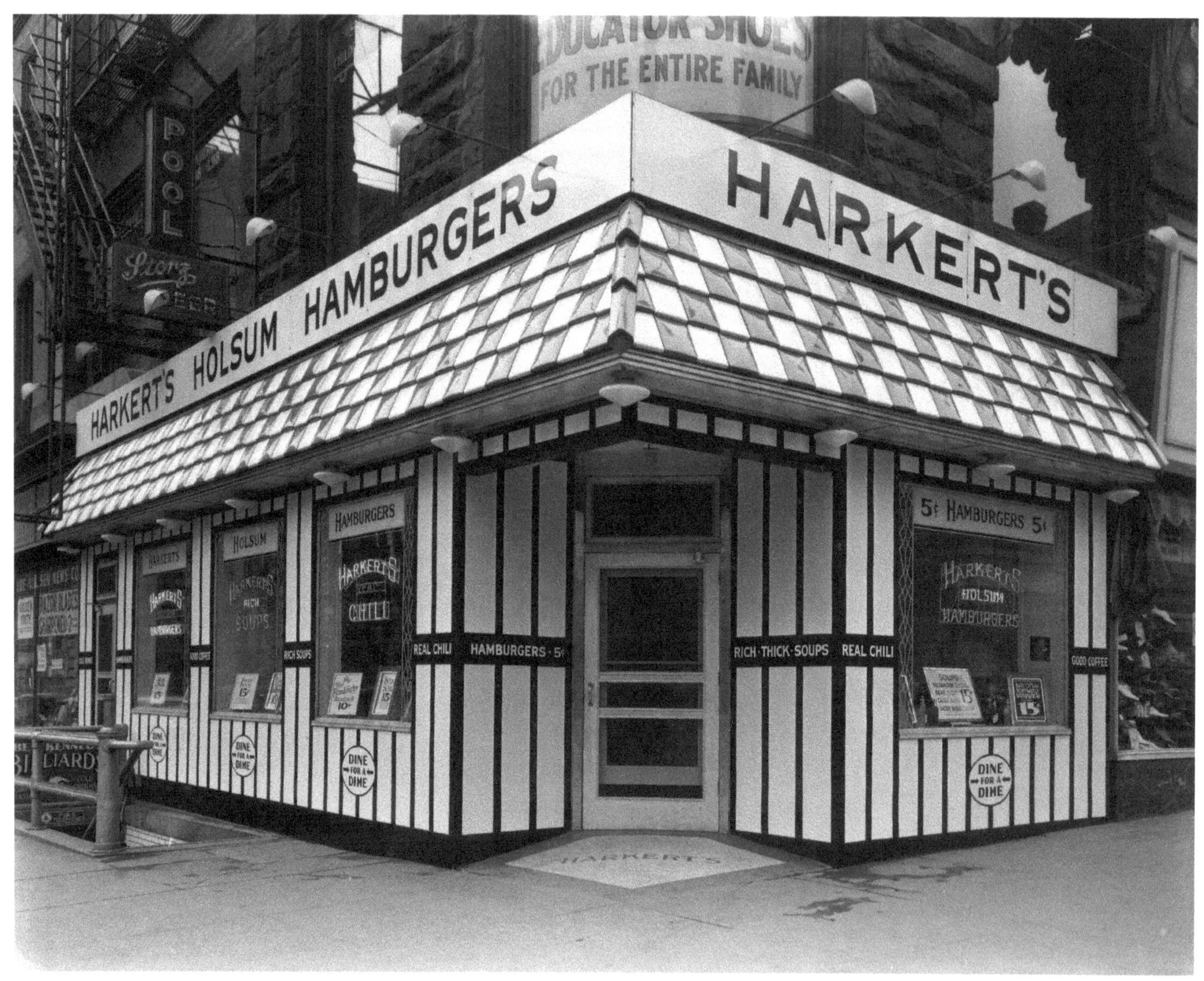

Harkert's Holsum Hamburgers at 16th and Dodge streets in 1935. Walter E. Harkert started his business in Omaha in 1925, selling sandwiches to people attending the American Legion National Convention. Later, he opened a series of small restaurants, eventually owning 21 locations. During the Depression, he offered a cup of coffee and a hamburger for 10 cents. He retired and sold his business in October 1967. The last of his restaurants, under new ownership, closed in February 1974.

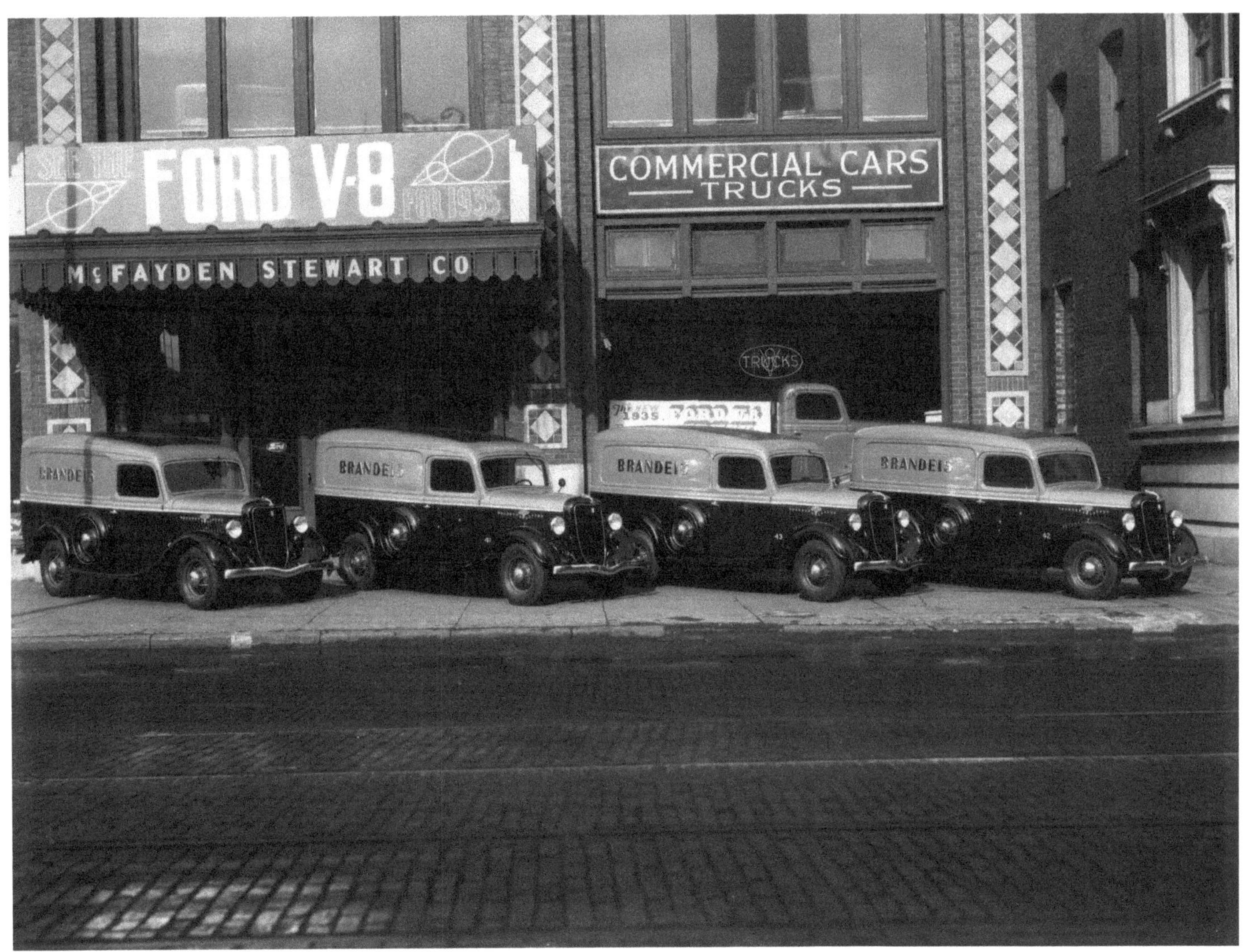

McFayden Stewart Company was an automobile and truck business at 1923 Harney Street. In this 1935 picture, a fleet of delivery trucks belonging to the J. L. Brandeis and Sons Department Store sit in front of the dealership. McFayden Stewart later became McFayden Ford and was in business in Omaha for many years.

The new Technical High School was built at 33rd and Cuming streets in 1923. At the time of its construction, it was considered one of the finest school buildings in the entire country. It cost 3.5 million dollars to build and had a capacity of more than 3,000 students. This 1934 picture shows the marching band.

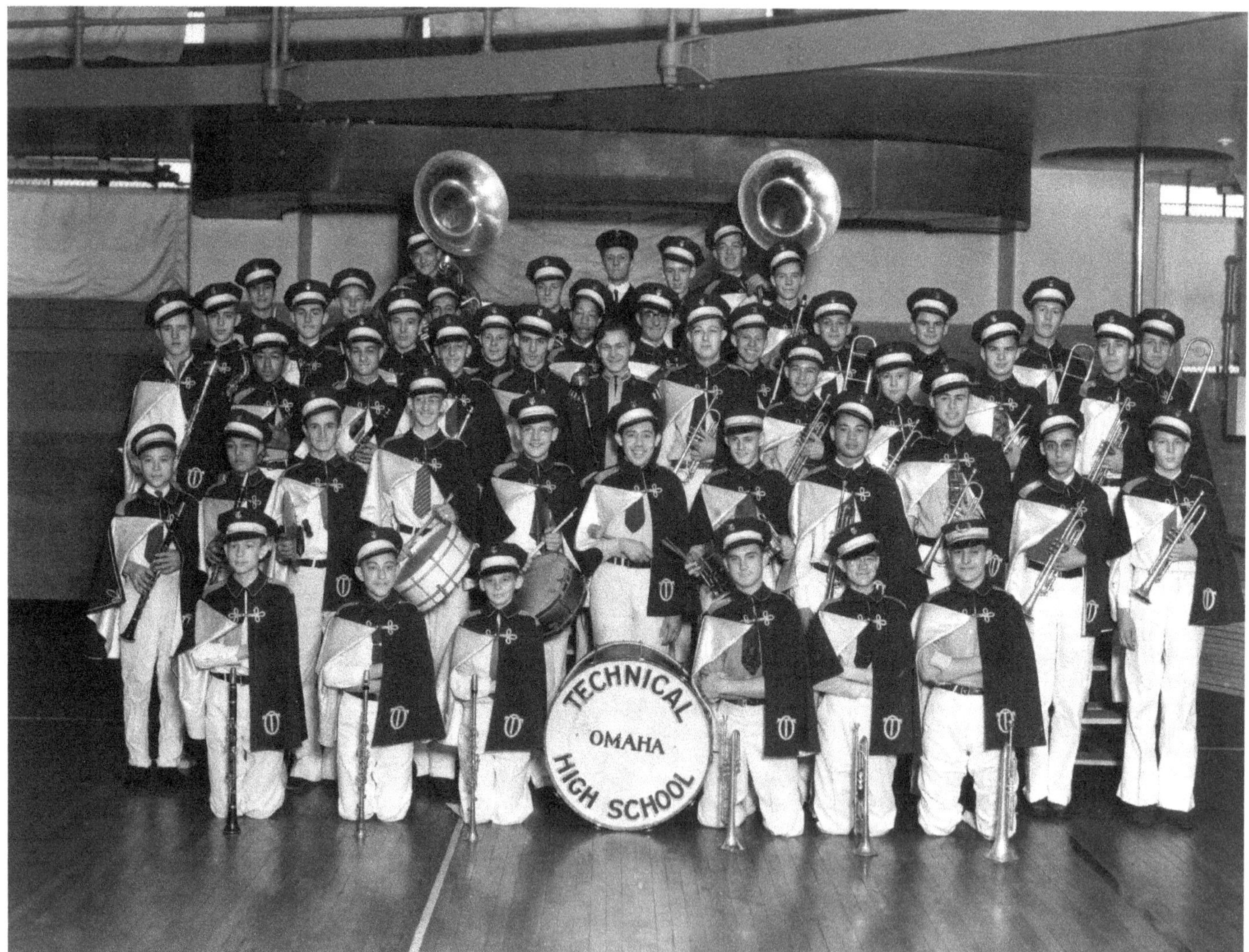

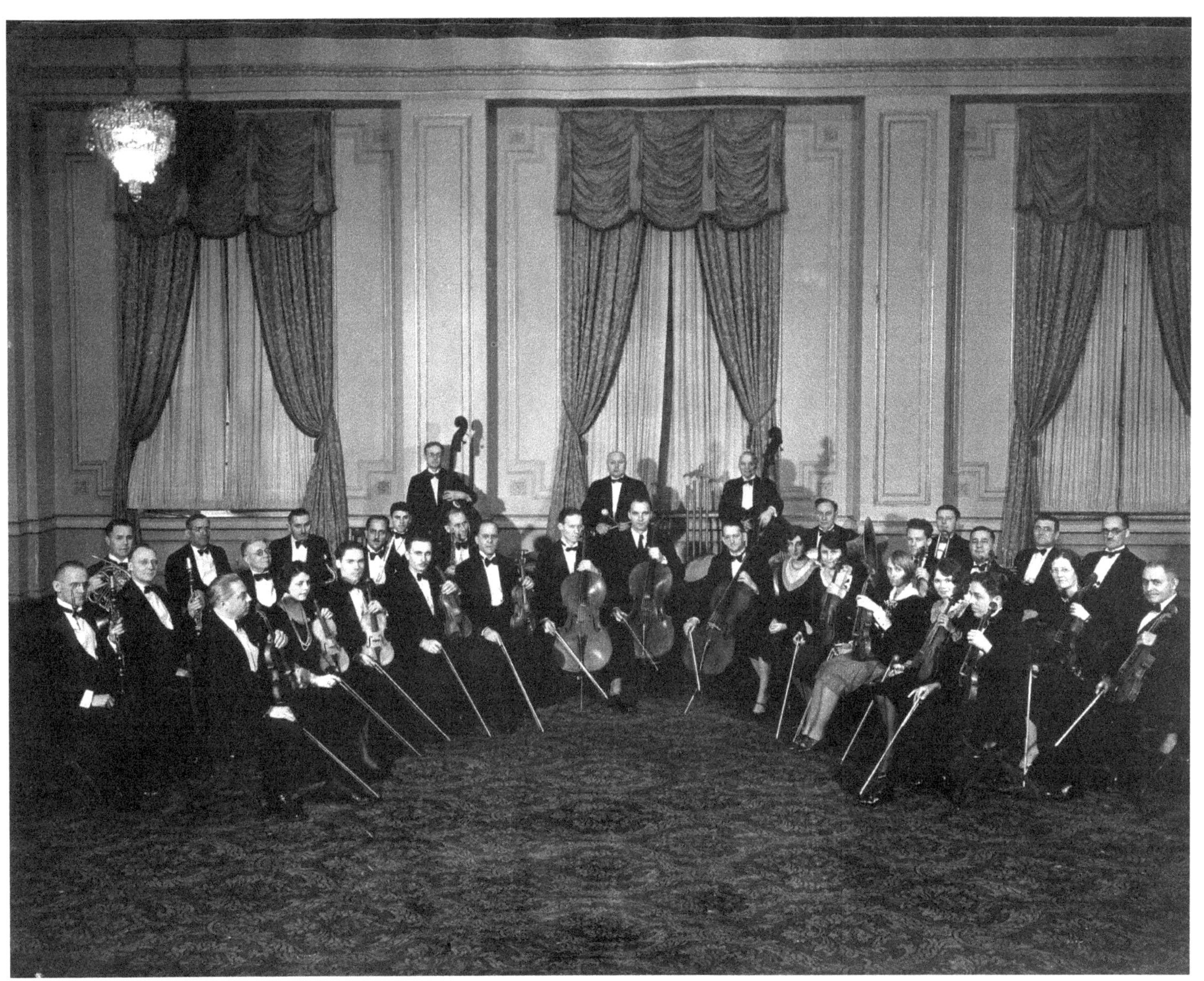

The Barnsdall Symphony Orchestra performing in Omaha in November 1930, sponsored by local radio station KOIL. This was the second radio station licensed in Omaha and began broadcasting on July 10, 1925. The "OIL" in the call letters "KOIL" indicated the fact that the station was owned by the Mona Motor Oil Company.

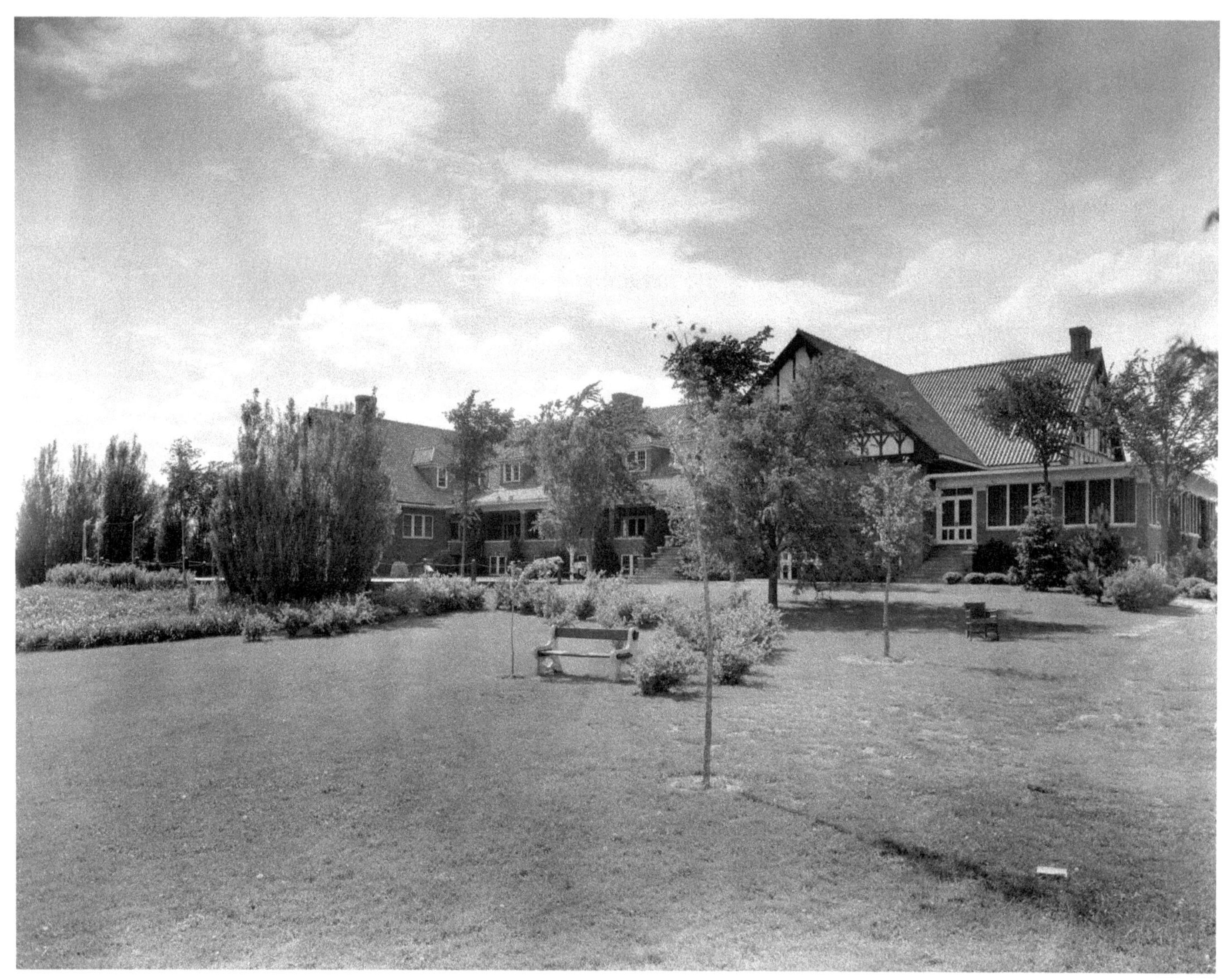

The clubhouse of the Happy Hollow Club at 1701 South 105th Street in June 1931. Originally founded in 1907, the club decided to relocate in 1922. A large tract of land in West Omaha was obtained, and local architect Harry Lawrie was commissioned to design an elegant and spacious clubhouse. A grand opening celebration on May 25, 1925, drew about 600 people. The Happy Hollow Club remains today one of Omaha's most outstanding features.

Reaching Toward the Future

(1940–1969)

As Omaha began to emerge from the devastation of the Great Depression, a new sense of optimism was felt in the community. New industry was coming into the area, and in 1940 the Army Air Corps selected Offutt Field just south of the city as the site for a new bomber plant, operated by the Glenn L. Martin Company. America was beginning to build its defenses in response to the war that had begun in Europe the previous year. This provided many jobs and helped to revitalize Omaha's economy. In 1948, three years after the war ended, the headquarters of the Strategic Air Command (SAC) was relocated there, and the field was renamed Offutt Air Force Base. Since 1992, this headquarters has been named STRATCOM.

For many years, the local economy had been dominated by the livestock and meatpacking industry. In 1956, the Omaha market surpassed Chicago to become the largest livestock market in the world. Omaha continued to be an important rail and transportation center.

Because of its central geographic location, Omaha became a convenient site for many businesses. Presently, there are five major Fortune 500 companies headquartered here: Berkshire-Hathaway, ConAgra Foods, Kiewit Corporation, Mutual of Omaha, and Union Pacific Corporation.

The Omaha Municipal Stadium opened in 1948 and provided a venue for professional baseball. It was renamed Rosenblatt Stadium in 1964, to honor former mayor Johnny Rosenblatt who helped bring professional baseball to Omaha. Today, the city is host every year to the NCAA Men's College World Series. On June 5, 1948, the World War II Memorial in Elmwood Park (Memorial Park) was dedicated, with President Harry S. Truman delivering the dedicatory address.

Omaha has continued to grow and prosper in the intervening decades, moving westward from the original settlement along the banks of the Missouri River. Neighborhood redevelopment and historic preservation, which began in the 1950s, have greatly improved the community. Omaha today enjoys all of the advantages of an urban environment. The representative photographic images presented in these chapters will hopefully give the reader a clear picture of the City of Omaha.

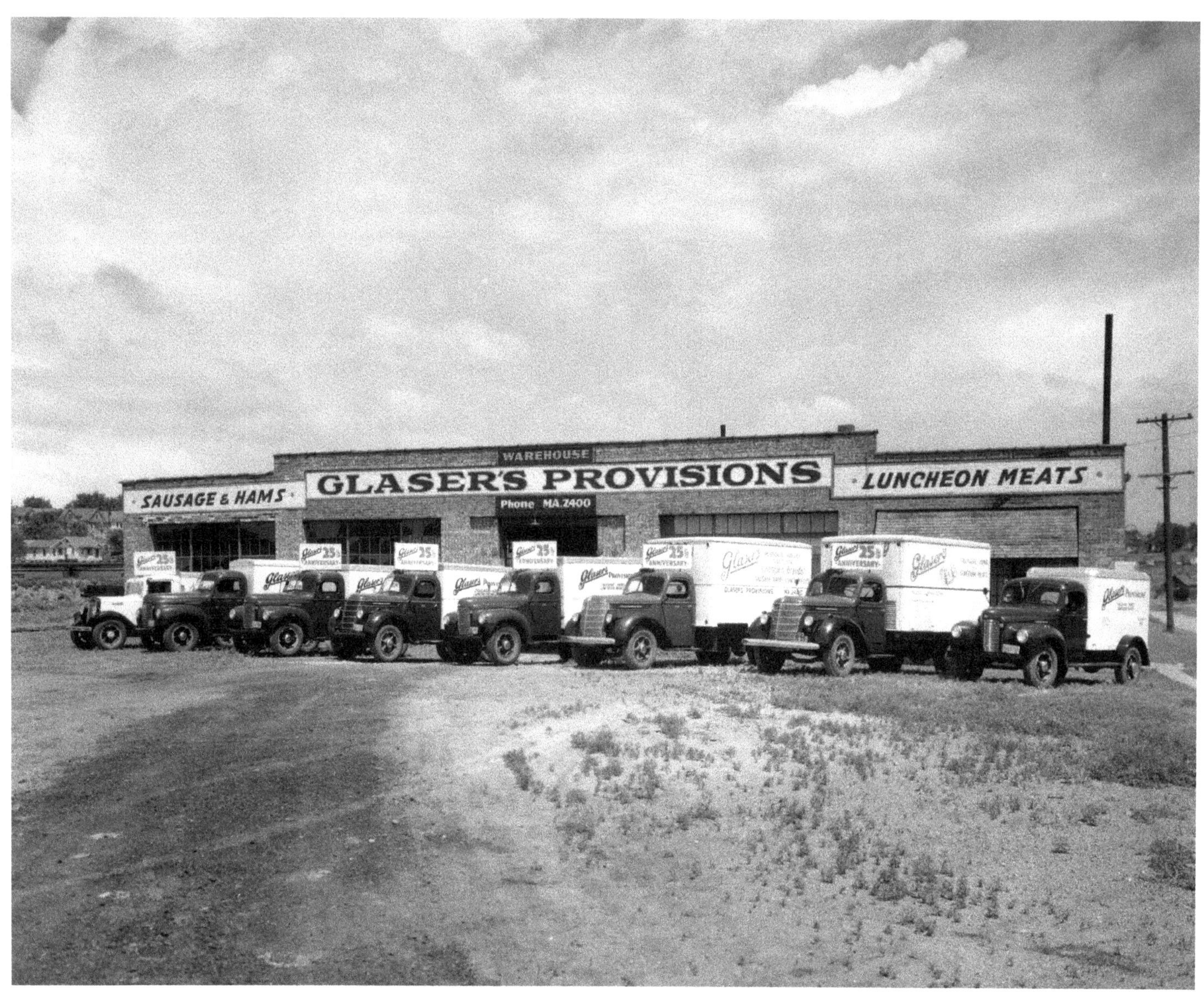

Glaser's Provisions, located at 5036 South 26th Street in South Omaha, was operated by Fred H. Glaser, who was engaged in the wholesale meat business. He supplied schools, hotels, and restaurants. His fleet of delivery trucks was photographed outside the business in June 1941.

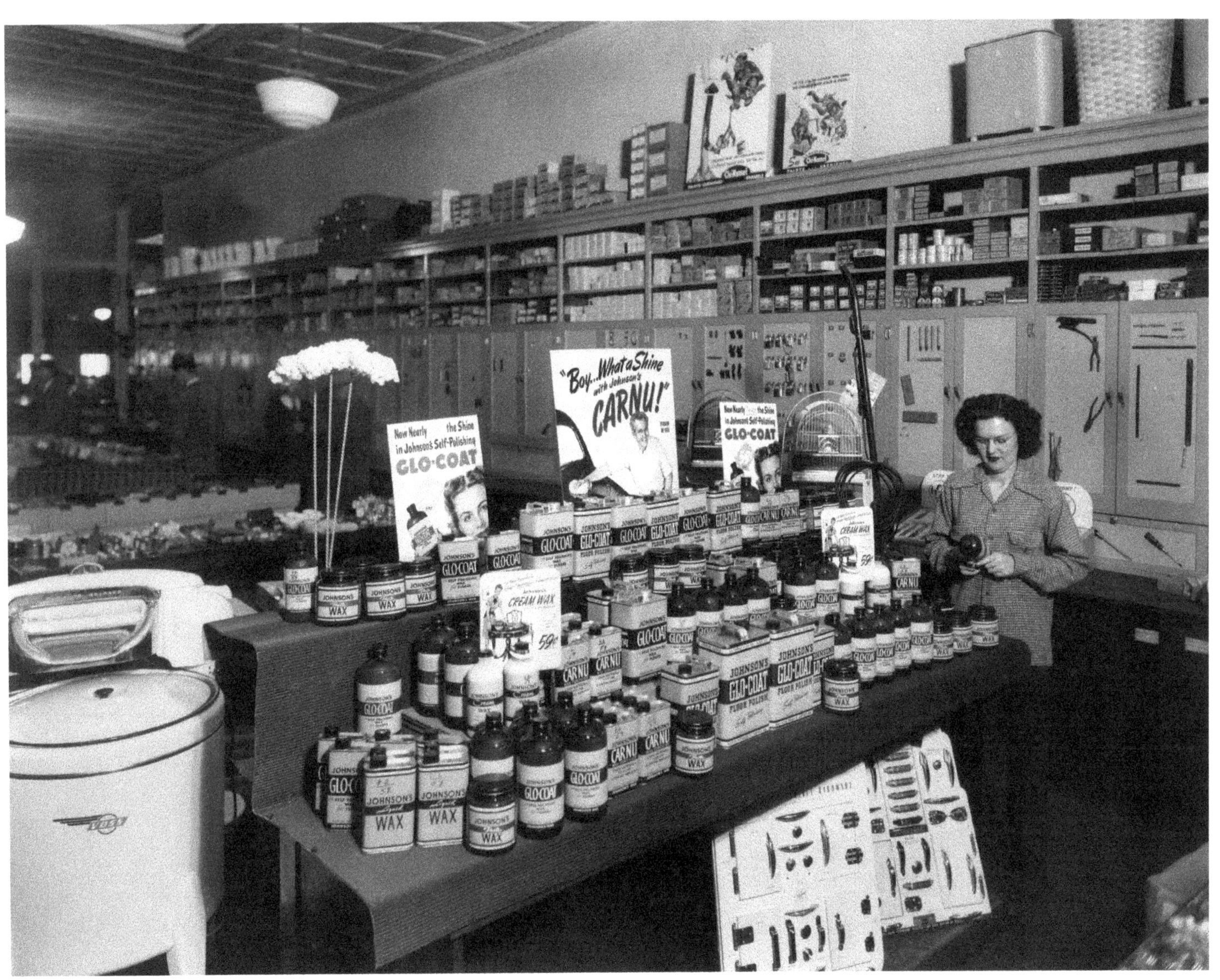

The Petersen and Michelsen Hardware Store, 4916 South 24th Street in South Omaha, carried a wide range of products and supplies. This interior view was taken in December 1947.

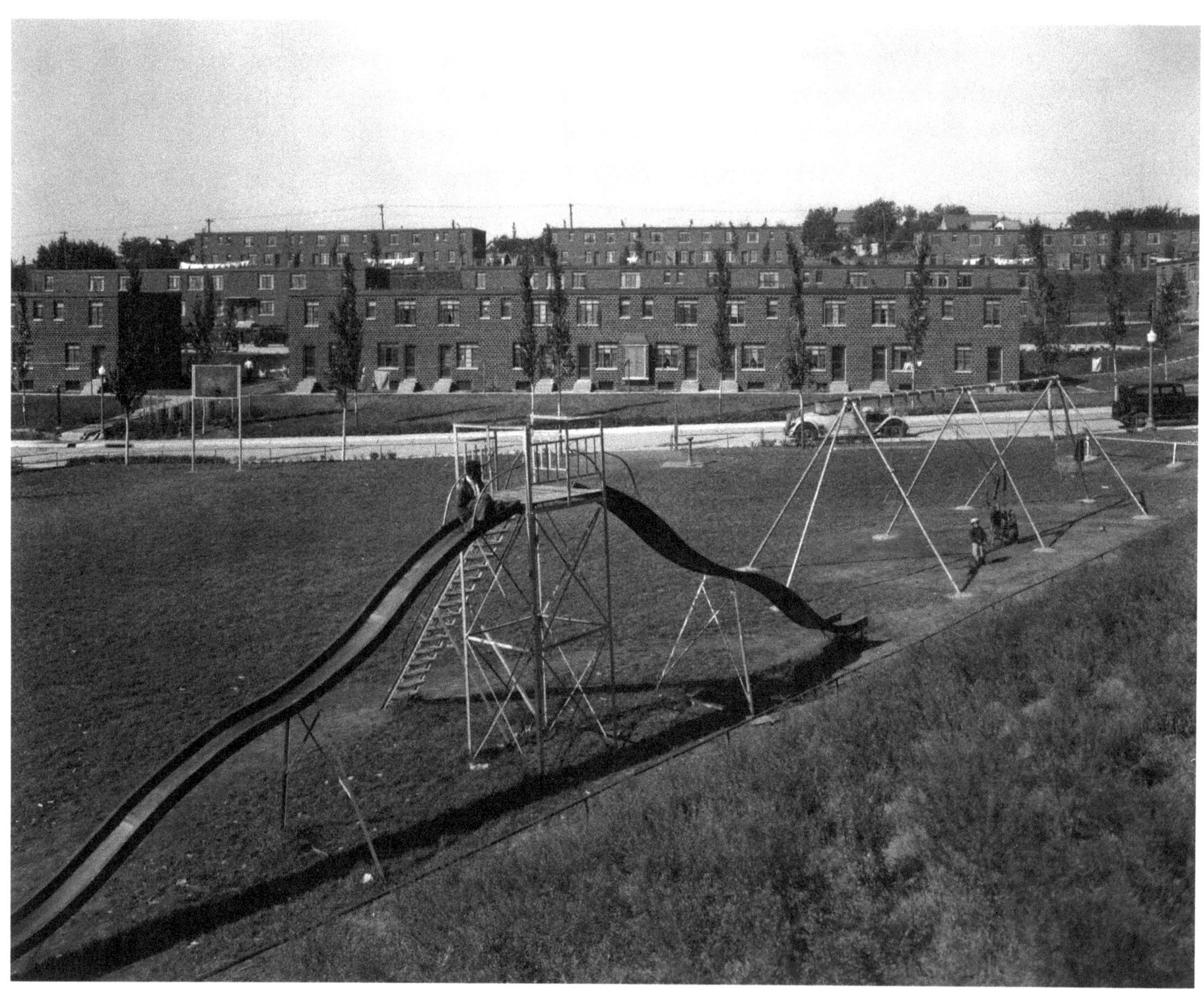

This picture of Southside Terrace Homes public housing, located between R and W streets, South 28th to South 30th, was taken in the early 1940s, soon after the project was built. The largest residential facility operated by the Omaha Housing Authority, it originally contained 522 units. After density reduction and improvement, it was redesigned to have 363 units.

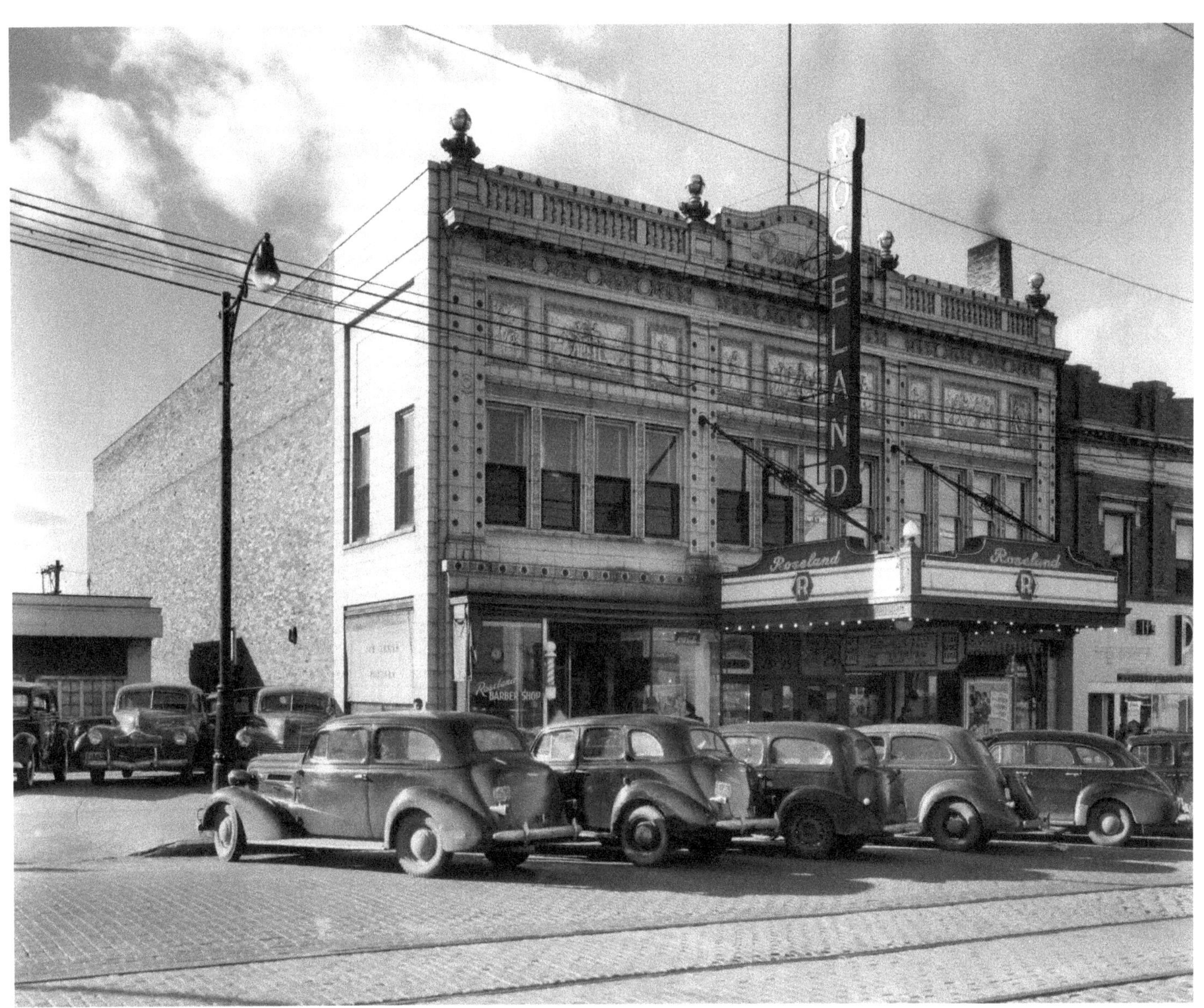

In November 1948, when this photo was taken, ladies' admission was free on Friday nights at the Roseland Theater, and men were urged to bring their girl, their mother, or their wife. Located at 4939 South 24th Street, in the heart of the South Omaha business district, it was originally built in 1922 by entrepreneur James W. Murphy and designed by South Omaha architect James T. Allen. It closed in 1950. A year later, Murphy converted the building into the Roseland Arcade and indoor shopping center. The Roseland Redevelopment Corporation later turned it into apartments.

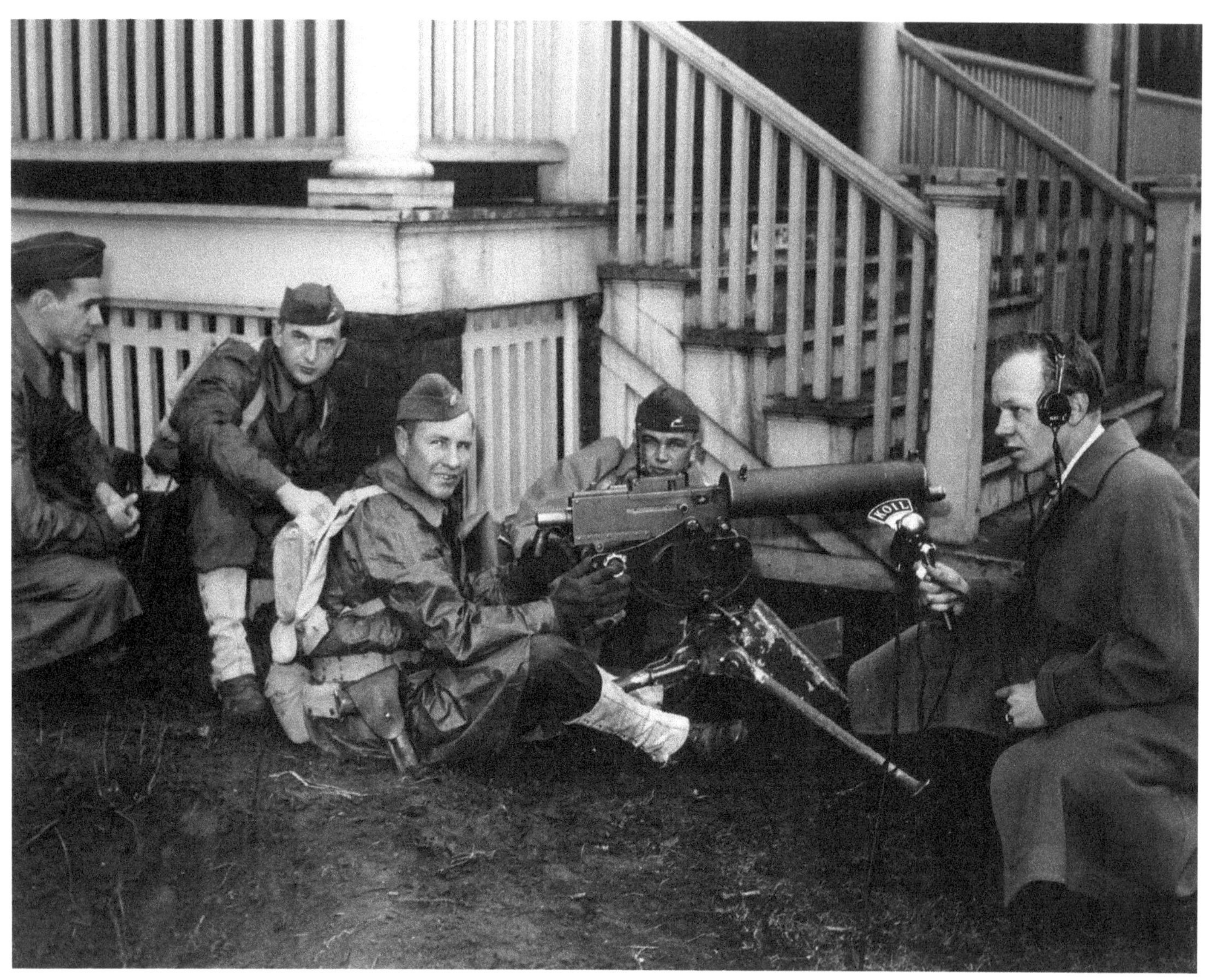

During a 1941 Army Day exercise at Fort Omaha, an announcer from Radio Station KOIL was photographed broadcasting live beside one of the barracks.

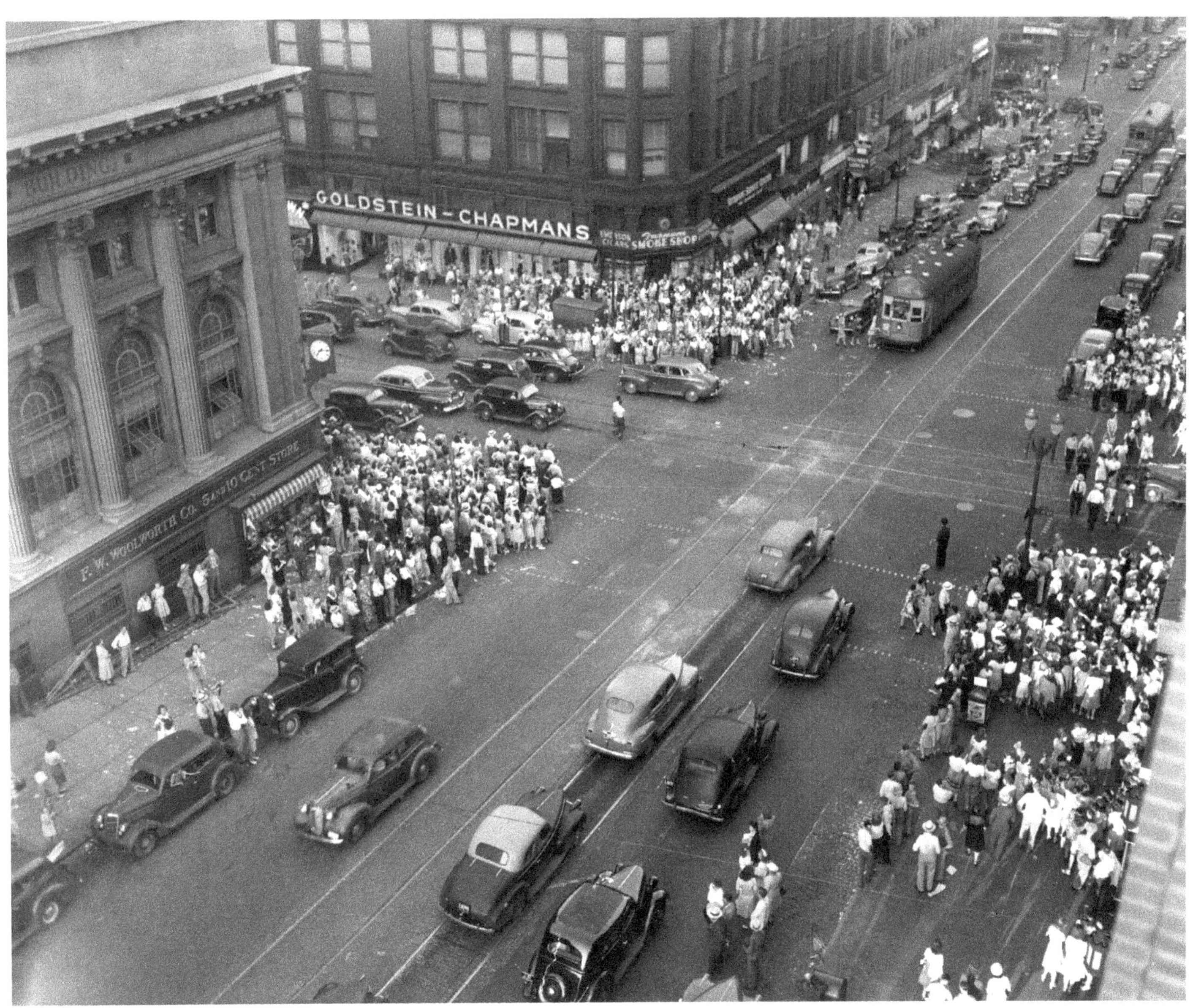

Omaha joined the rest of America in celebrating the end of World War II on V-J Day (Victory over Japan) in August 1945. This image shows the crowded corner of 16th and Farnam, littered with paper debris from the joyous celebrations. The United States National Bank building, with F. W. Woolworth on its ground floor, stands to the left, across 16th from Goldstein-Chapman's Department Store.

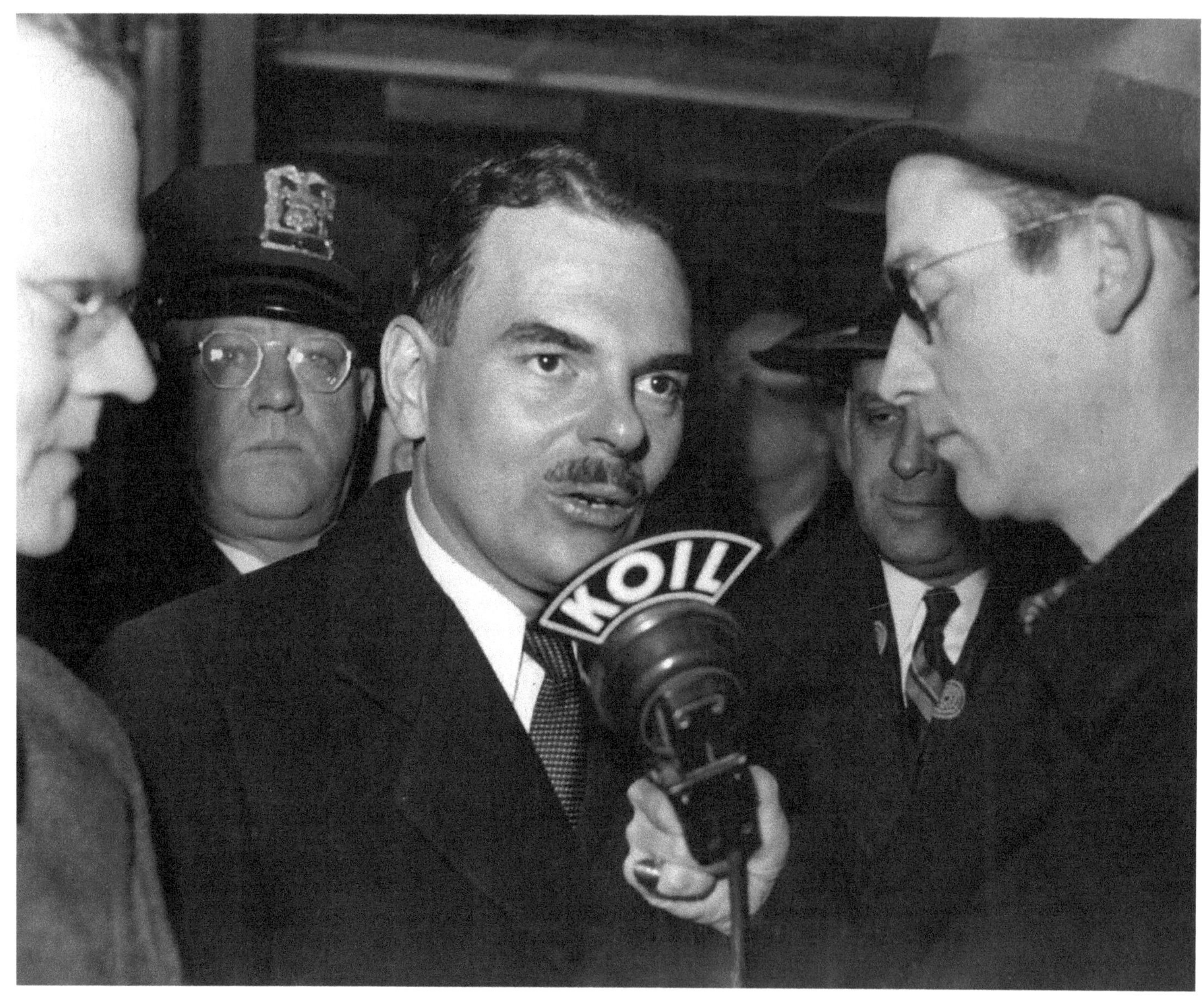

During the 1948 presidential campaign, Republican candidate Thomas Dewey of New York made a stop in Omaha. Here, he is being interviewed on live radio by Bud Thorpe from Radio Station KOIL.

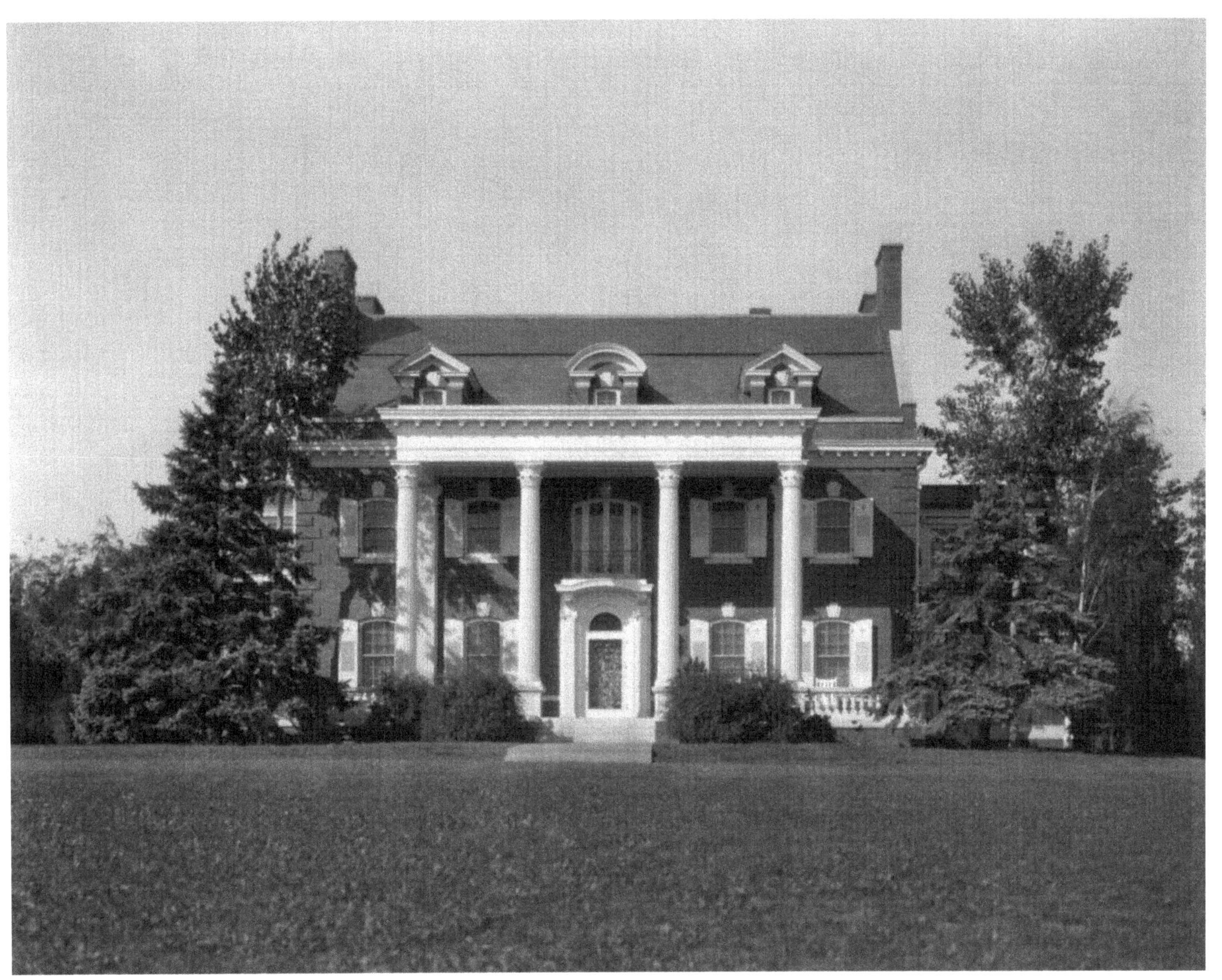

The elegant home of Rufus E. Lee, 6312 Dodge Street, pictured in 1942. Lee was a very prominent Omaha businessman, involved in real estate and investment. He headed the Rufus E. Lee Company and at one time was President of the Board of Directors of the Presbyterian Theological Seminary. In 1925, he purchased the City National Bank building. This home was later torn down and the site used for redevelopment.

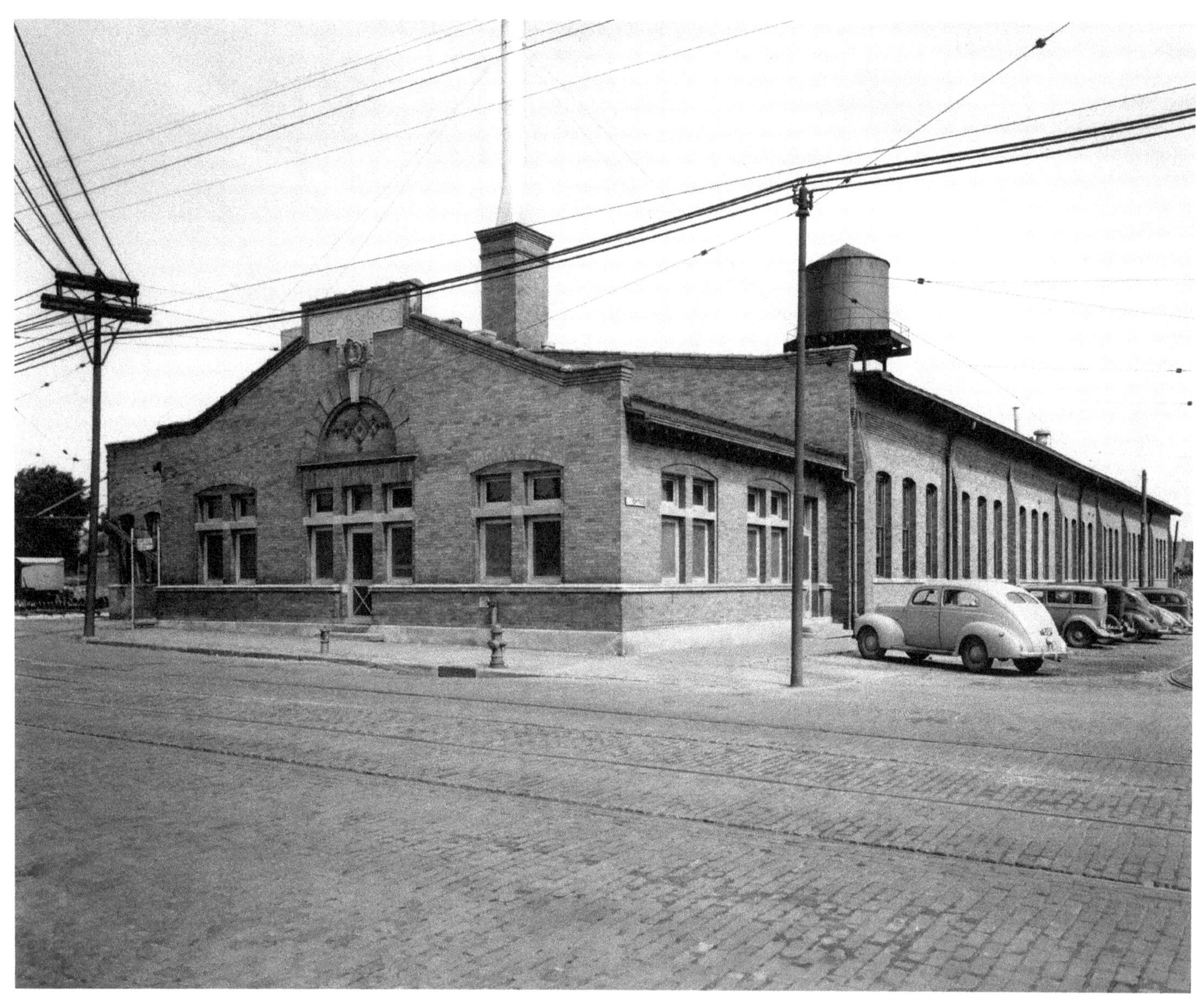

Constructed in 1905 as part of the shops for the Omaha and Council Bluffs Street Railway Company, this 120-foot-wide × 245-foot-long structure was one of two main buildings at 26th and Lake streets. When the shops were closed in 1953, part of this building was remodeled by the city to house their street and vehicle maintenance department. This image was taken around 1940.

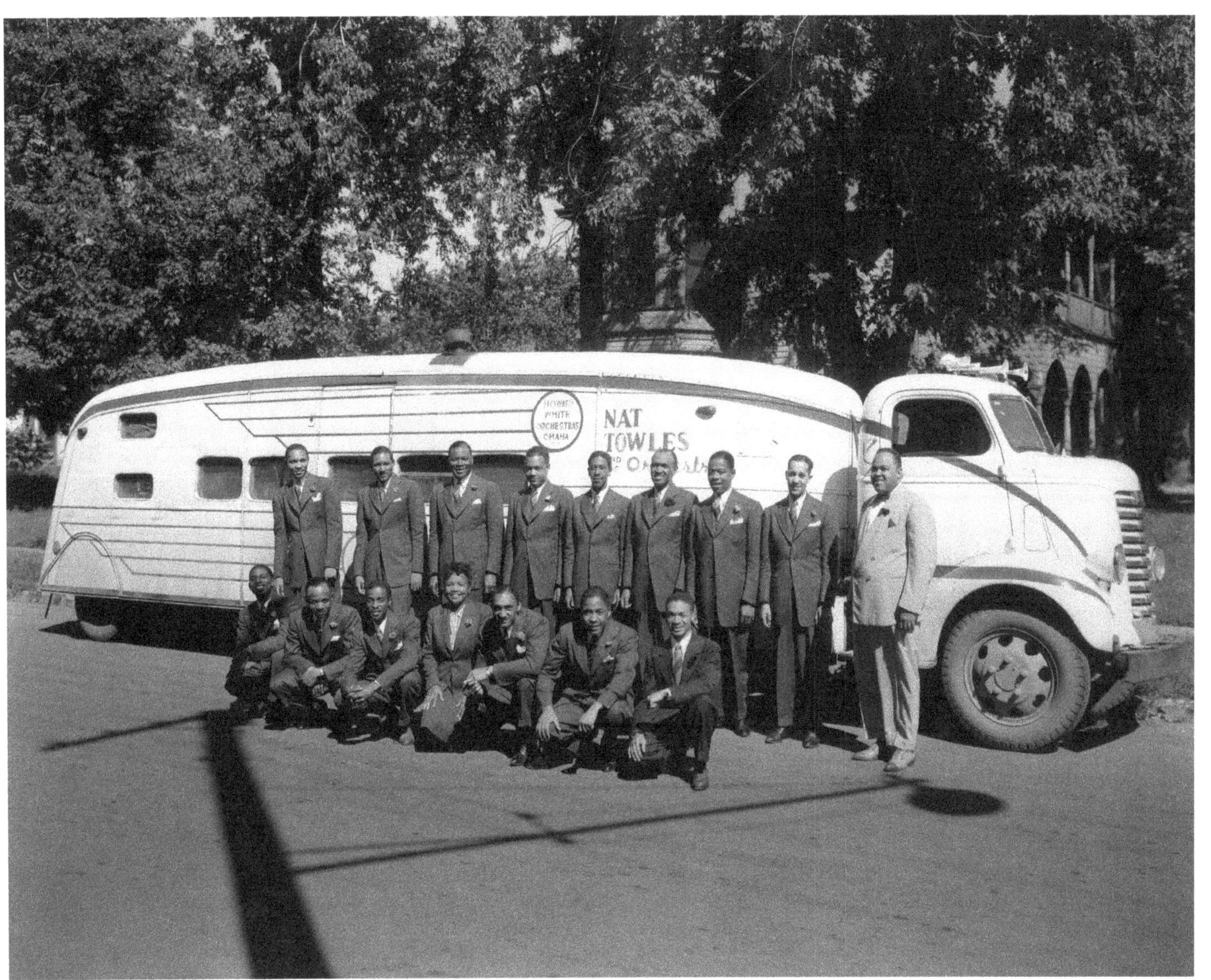

"Nat Towles Great Orchestra: 14 Southern Gentlemen," with their touring bus in September 1940. The son of New Orleans bassist Phil "Charlie" Towles, Nat was a significant influence on the development of jazz. Born in 1905, he formed his first band, the Creole Harmony Kings, in 1923. He established himself permanently in Omaha at the Dreamland Ballroom in 1936. He worked through the 1950s and retired to California.

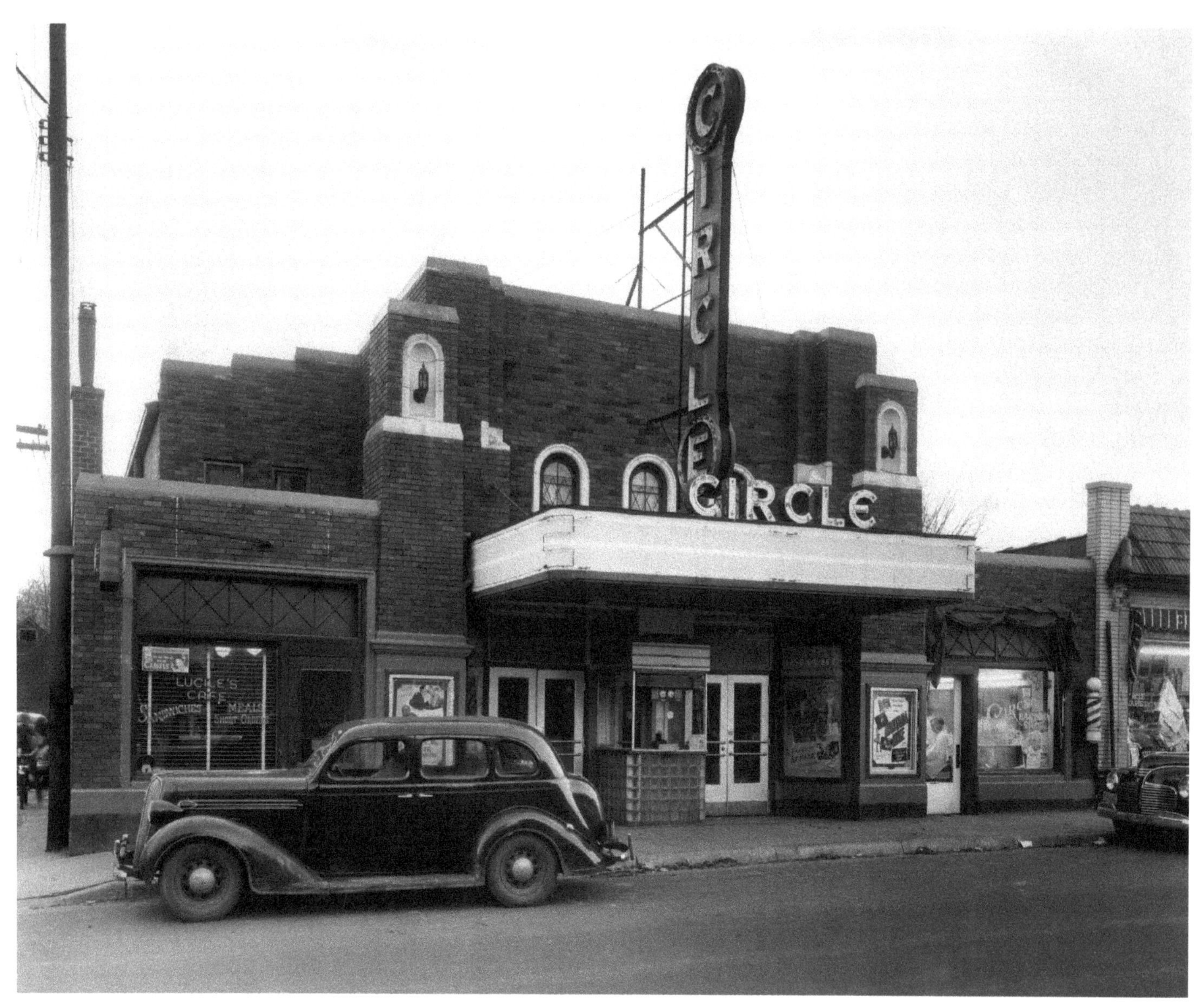

The Circle Theater, 524 North 33rd Street, was showing *A Foreign Affair* on November 6, 1948. This neighborhood movie house has experienced many changes. By the 1980s, it held a bet messenger service. Then, a local group attempted to purchase it and develop it into a local venue for live theater, but the attempt was not successful.

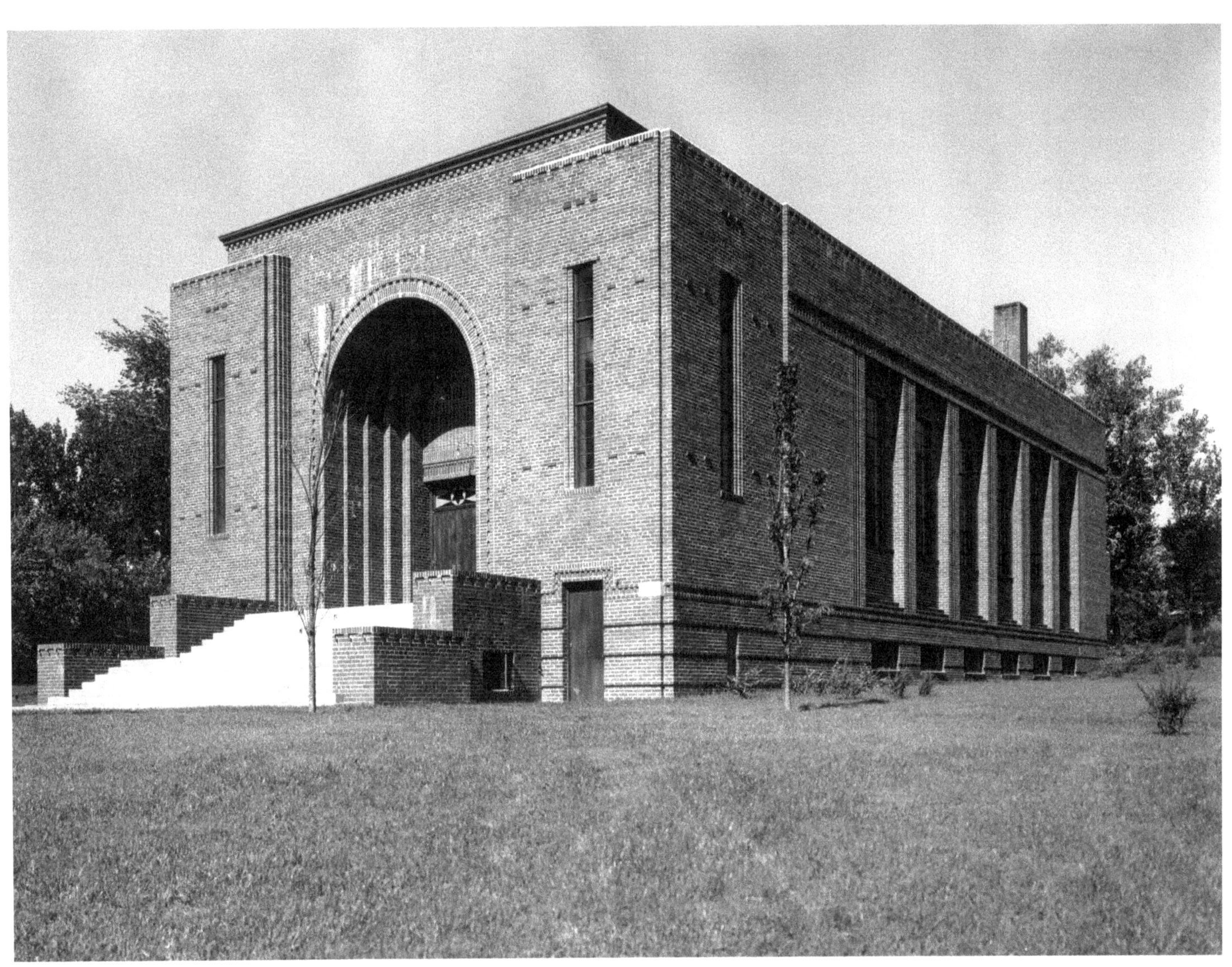

Beth El Synagogue, 210 South 49th Street, at the time of the building's dedication in 1941. Designed by noted Omaha architects John and Alan McDonald, it contained 30,000 square feet. In 1952, Noel Wallace designed an educational wing on the north side. The congregation relocated in 1988, and the building was sold to the Omaha Symphony in 1991. In 1996, a local architectural firm purchased the structure, and it serves as their offices today.

Benson Park at 70th and Military Avenue was established in 1931, after numerous attempts to provide a neighborhood park for that part of Omaha. Utilizing land from a former apple orchard, development took place in the 1930s with assistance from the WPA (Works Progress Administration). The pavilion pictured here in 1942 was constructed at that time.

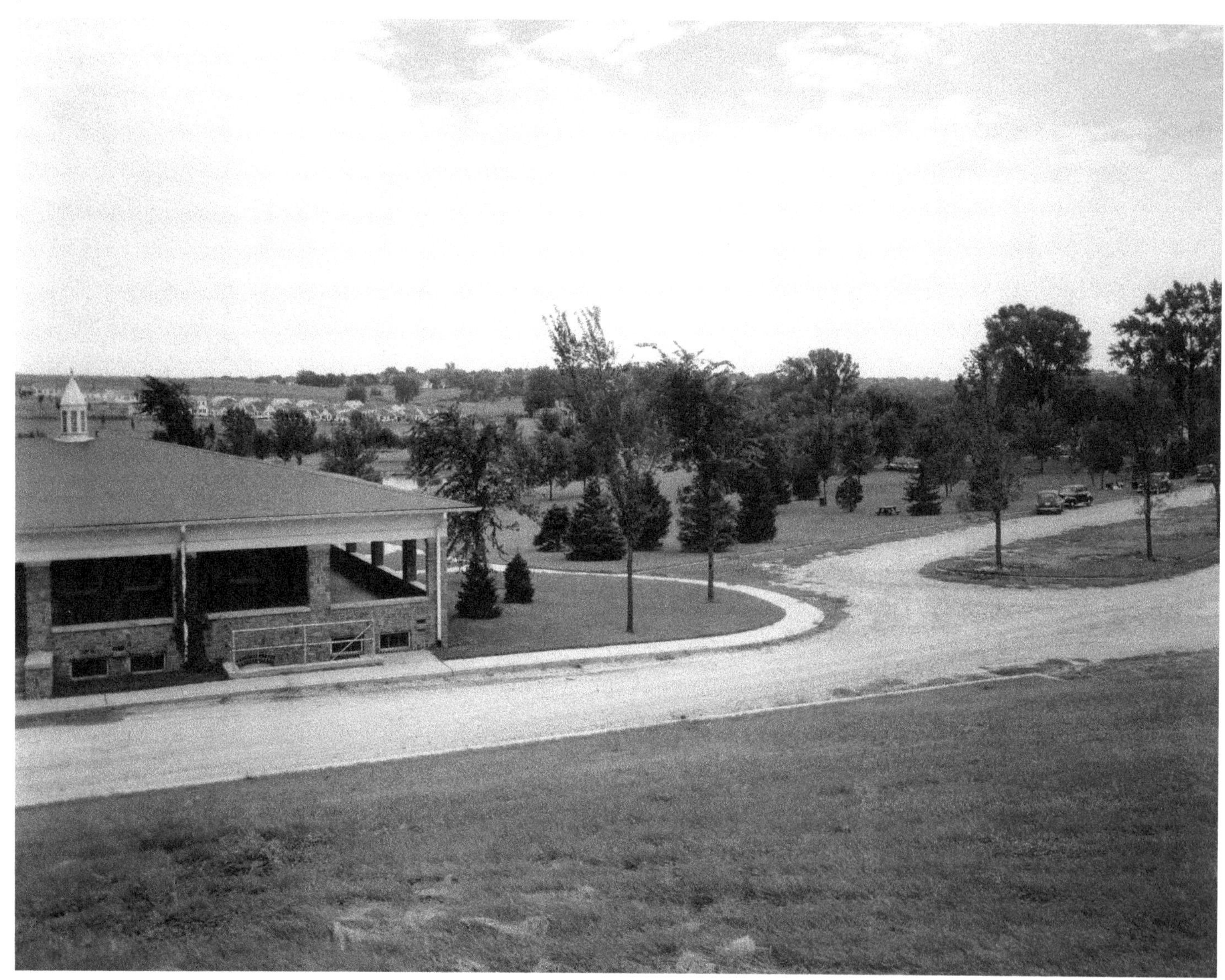

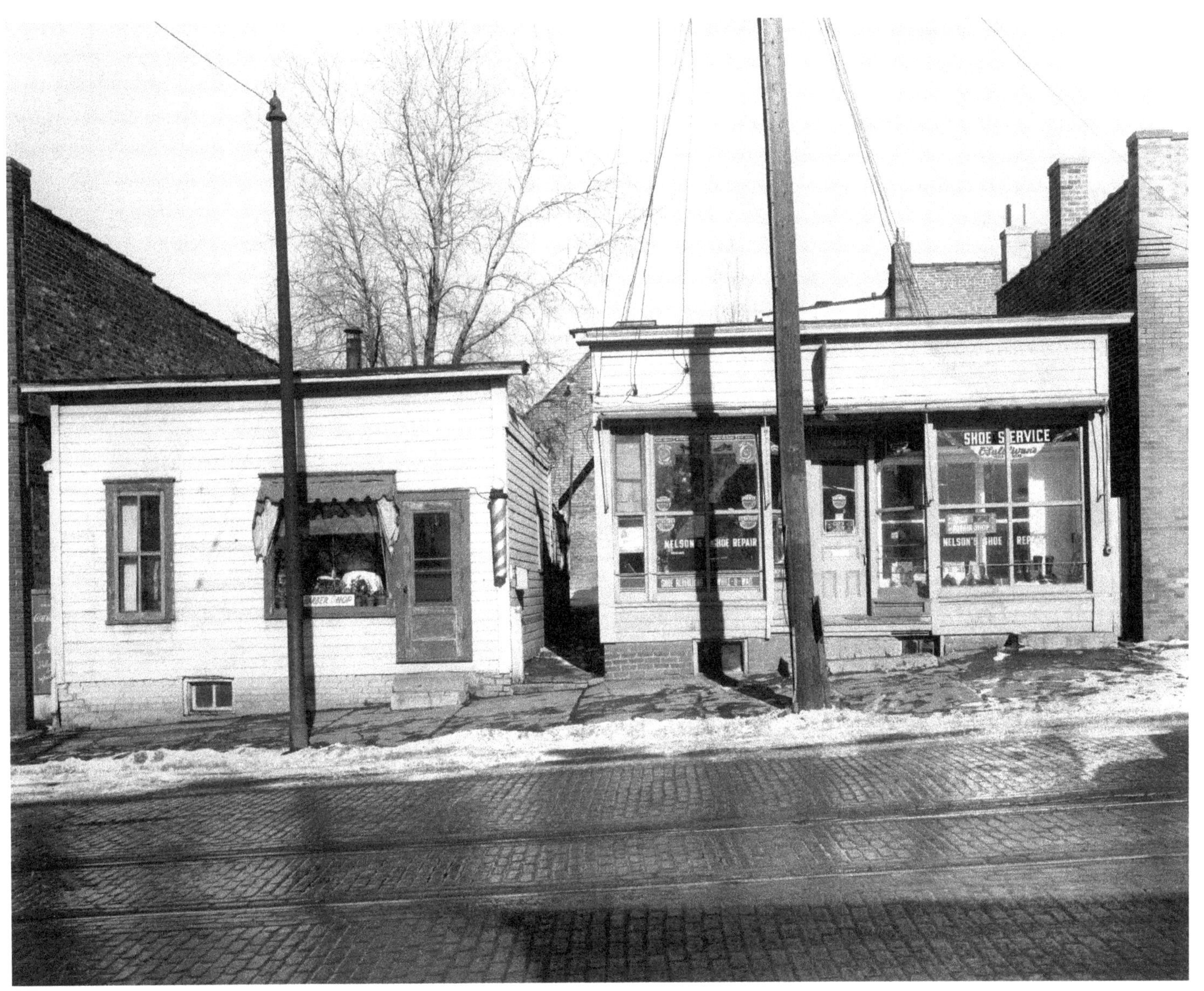

A neighborhood barber shop on the north side of Q Street at 24th, as it appeared in December 1948. To the right, Nelson's Shoe Repair offered "Shoe Rebuilding While-U-Wait."

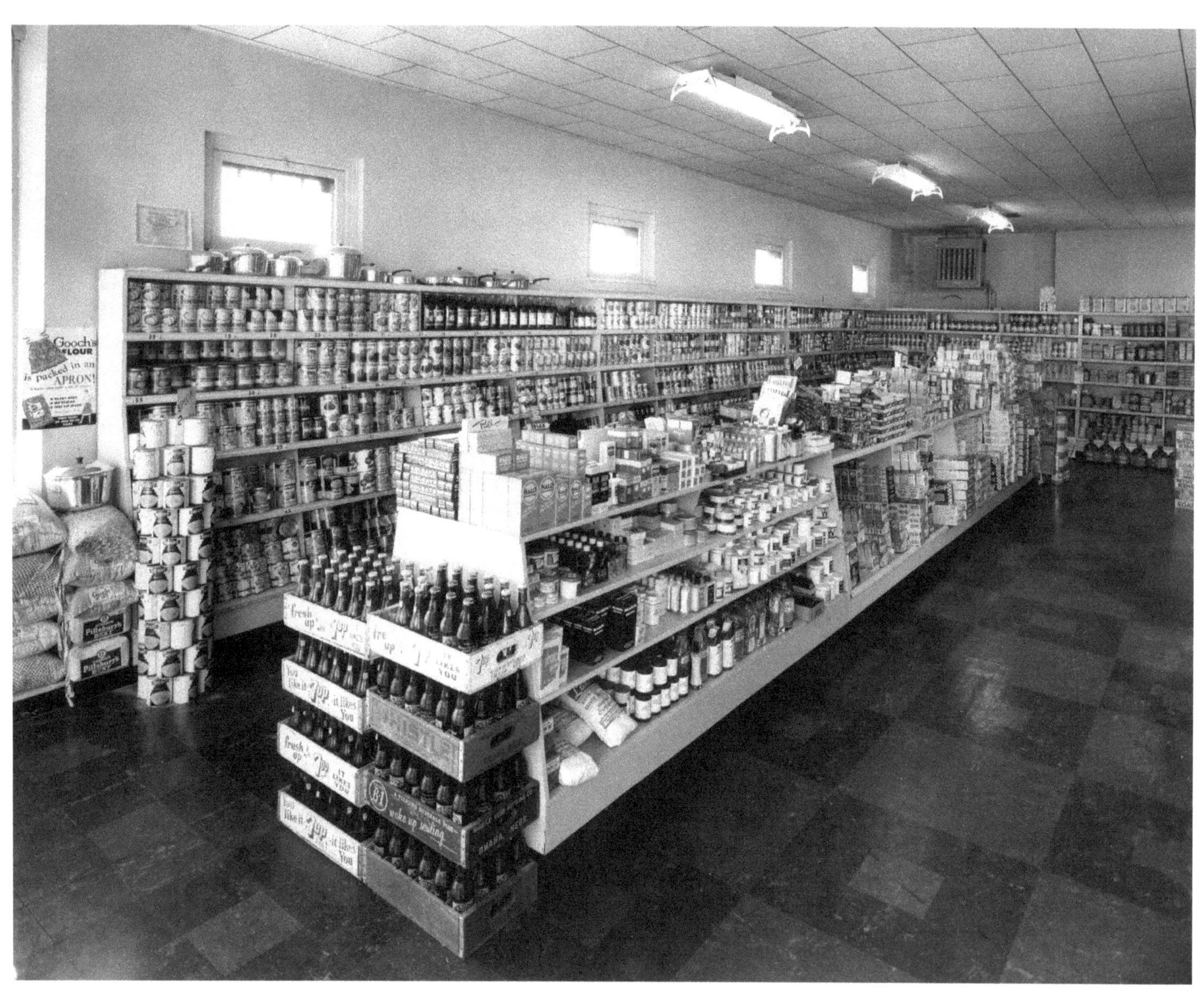

Bosanek Grocery Store at 5140 South 24th Street, operated by Frank E. Bosanek. This December 1948 photo shows a sign for Gooch's Flour "packed in an apron—ready made, no sewing, just rip seams." A wooden crate from Omaha's Whistle Vess Bottling Company, filled with bottles of root beer, says "Drink B-1. A pleasing beverage plus—wake up smiling."

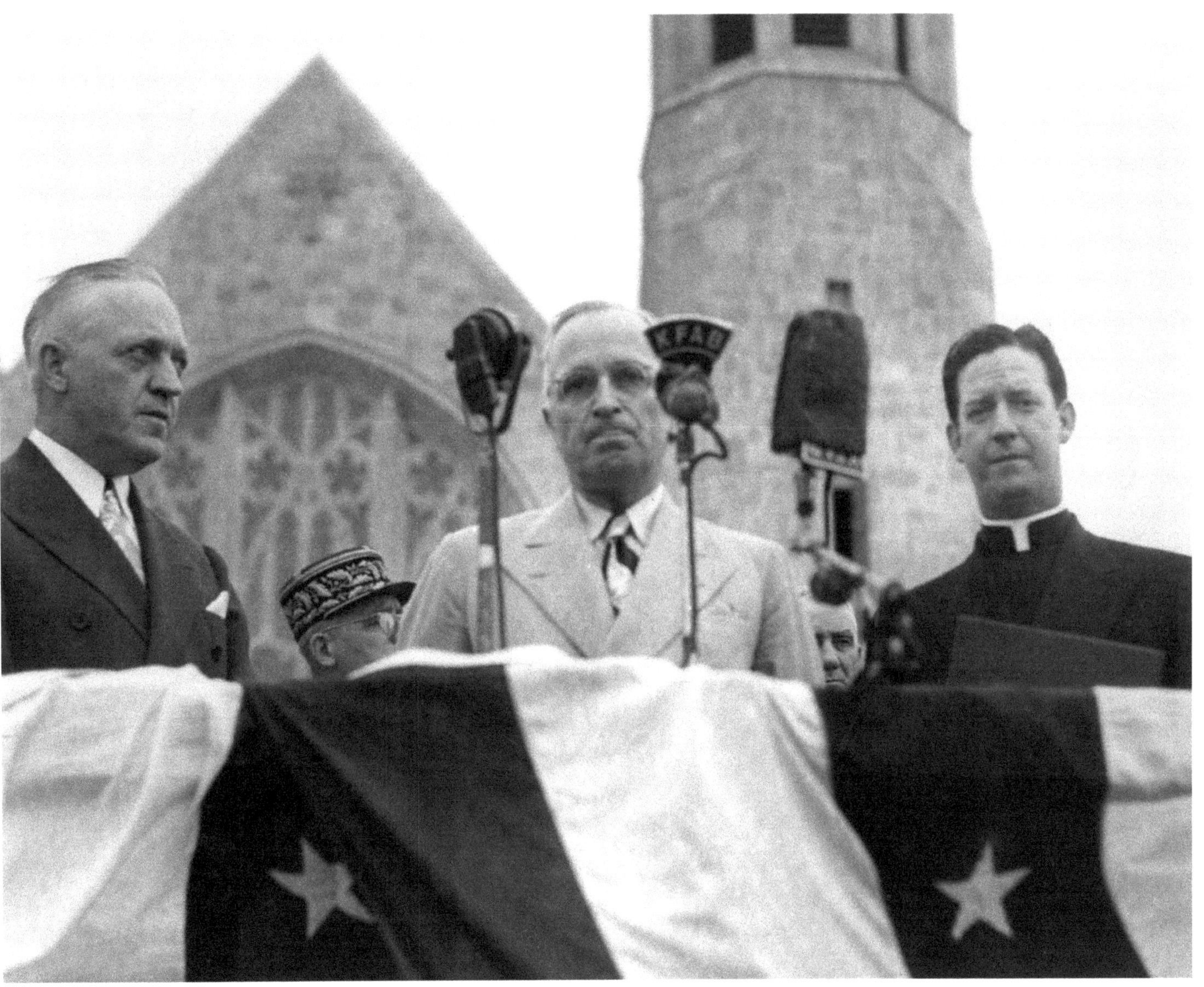

President Harry S. Truman visited Boys Town in June 1948, while in Omaha to dedicate the World War II Memorial. To his left is Monsignor Francis P. Schmidt, music director. Patrick Norton, general manager and nephew of Boys Town founder Edward J. Flanagan, is on his right. Father Flanagan had died the previous month in Germany; President Truman had asked him to go there for discussions on European children left homeless and orphaned by the war.

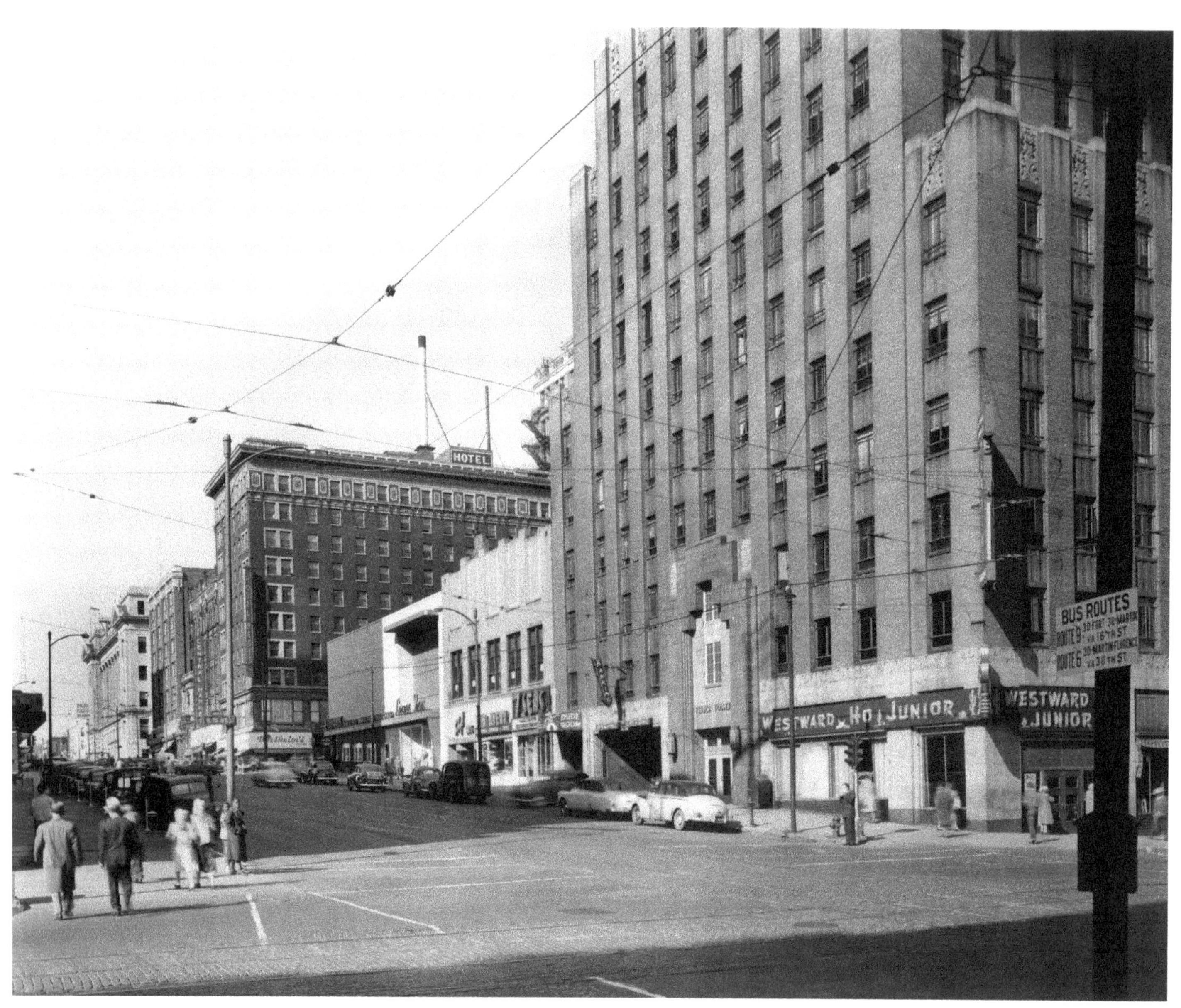

Harney Street, west from 15th in October 1951. The twelve-story, art deco Redick Tower office building at right, 1504 Harney Street, was built in 1930 at a cost of $453,000. To its left are a tavern and a sporting goods store. The large building further left is the Regis Hotel, 314 South 16th Street.

A city engineering project in August 1951, digging a trench in front of city hall at 18th and Farnam streets. The Douglas County Court House is south across the street and to the west , the Wellington and Keen hotels.

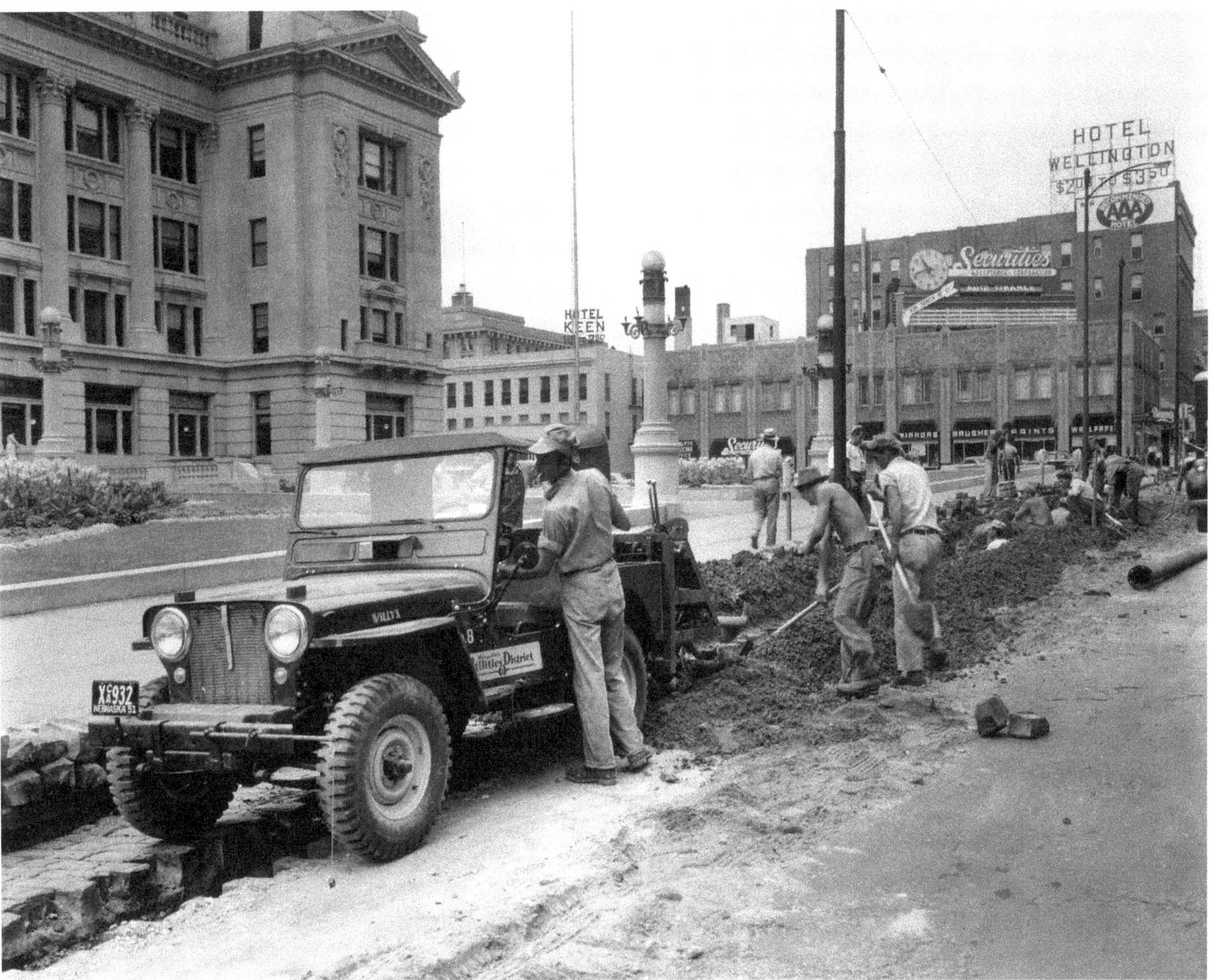

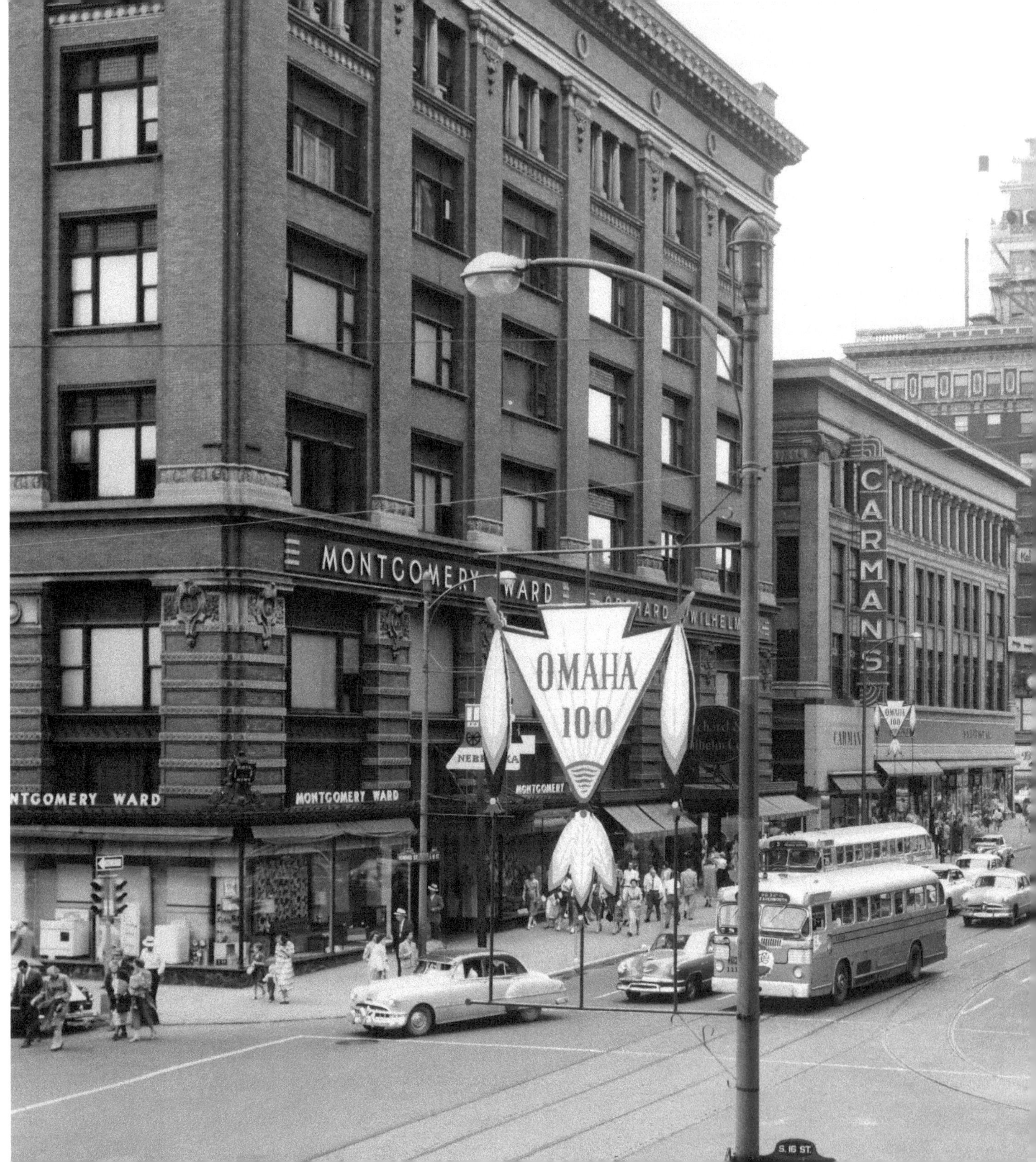
MONTGOMERY WARD
OMAHA
100
CARMANS
NTGOMERY WARD
MONTGOMERY WARD
MONTGOMERY
NEBRASKA
S. 16 ST.

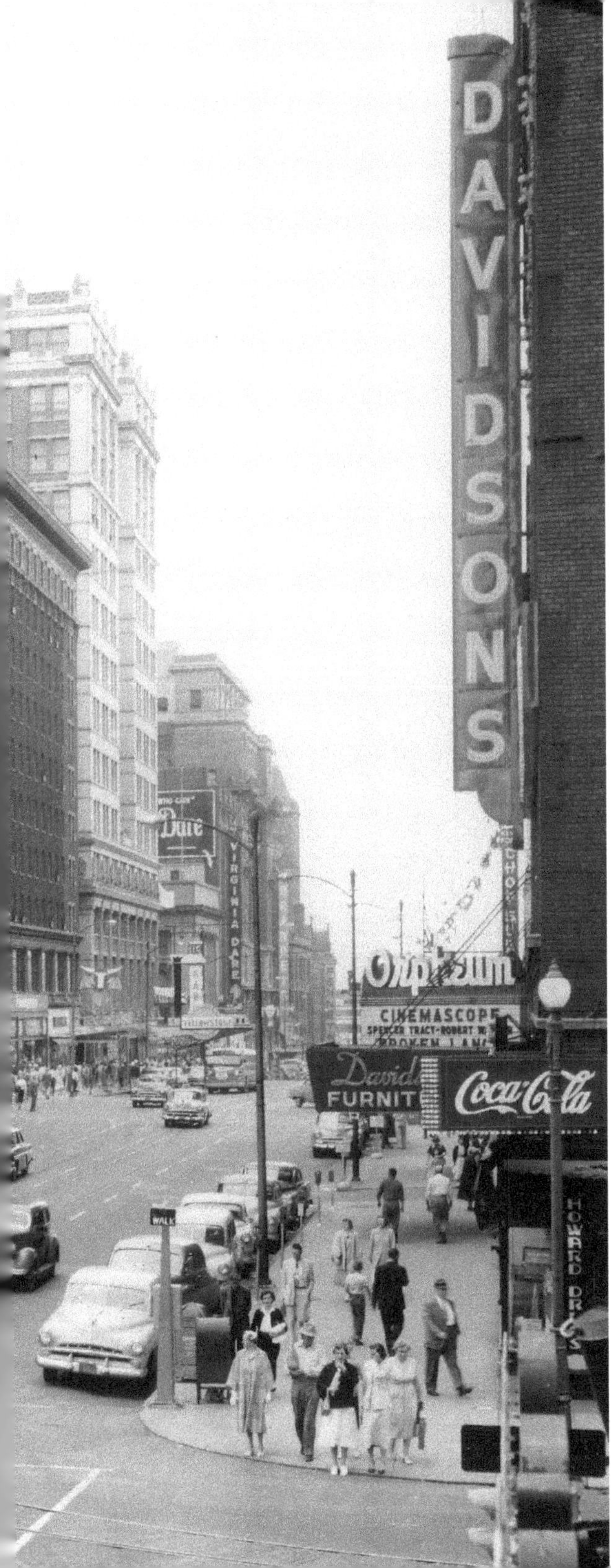

Looking north from the area of 16th and Harney streets, August 12, 1954. Beyond the Montgomery Ward Department Store is Carmen's. This was a women's clothing store operated by Reuben W. Natelson at 412 South 16th Street. Next to it is the Regis Hotel, followed by the First National Bank. Note the banners proclaiming Omaha's 100th Birthday, which was celebrated that year.

North on 15th toward Farnam Street, February 1956. On the left is the Barker Building, 306 South 15th Street, and beyond it the Kilpatrick Building at the southeast corner of 15th and Douglas. On the right side of 15th Street is the corner of the Nebraska Clothing Company and down the street, the headquarters of the Union Pacific Railroad.

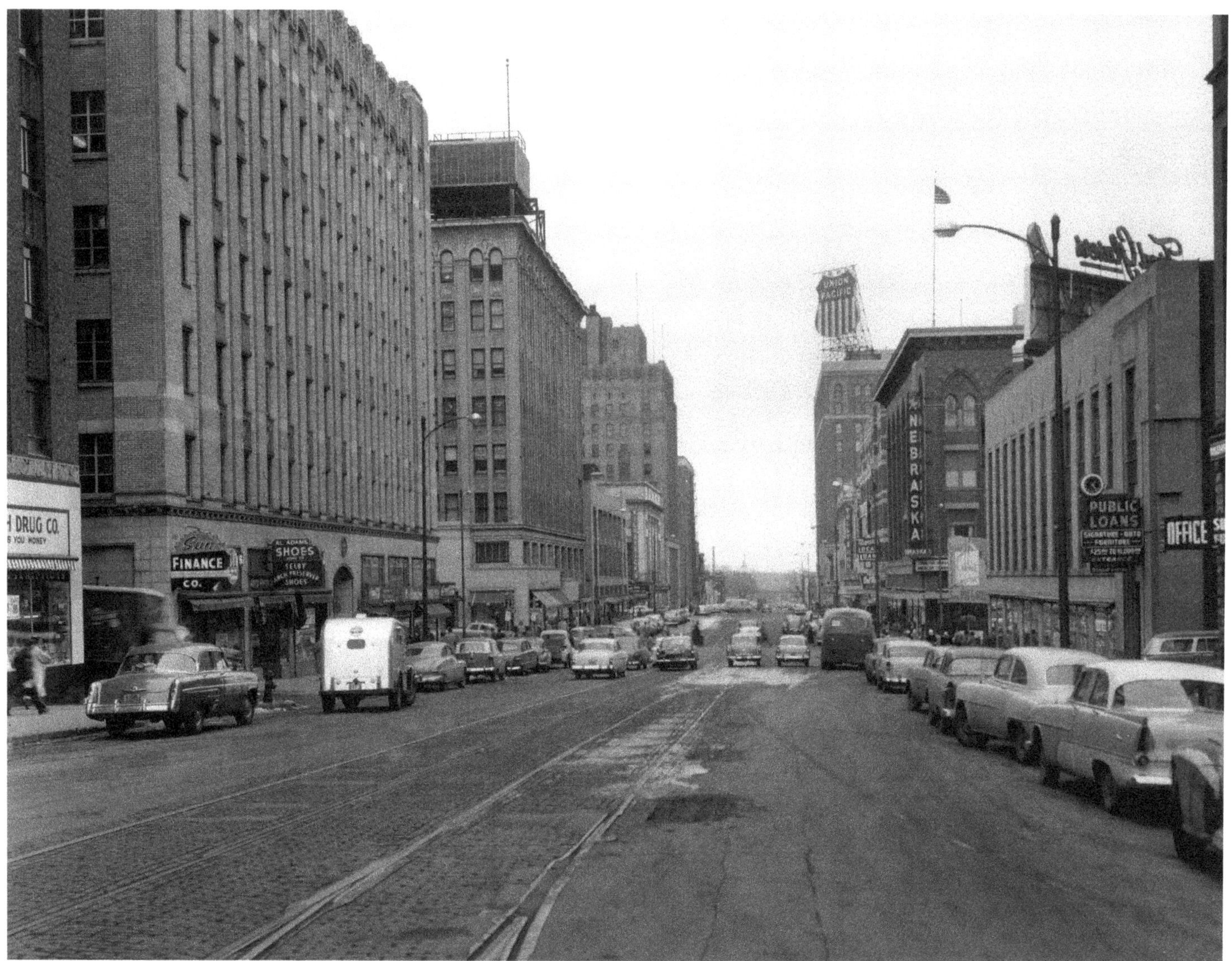

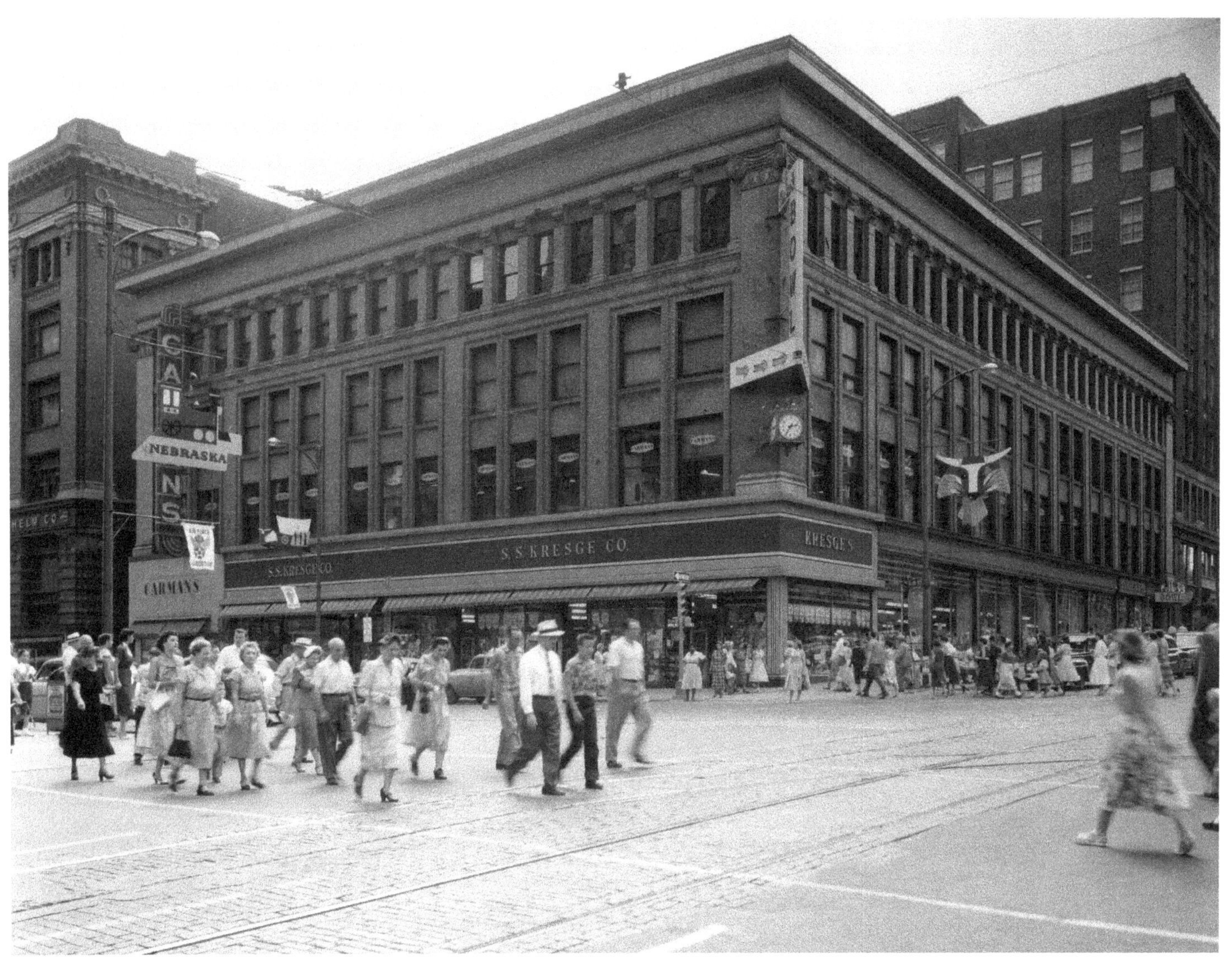

The sidewalks in front of the S. S. Kresge Company store at 402 South 16th Street were crowded on August 18, 1954.

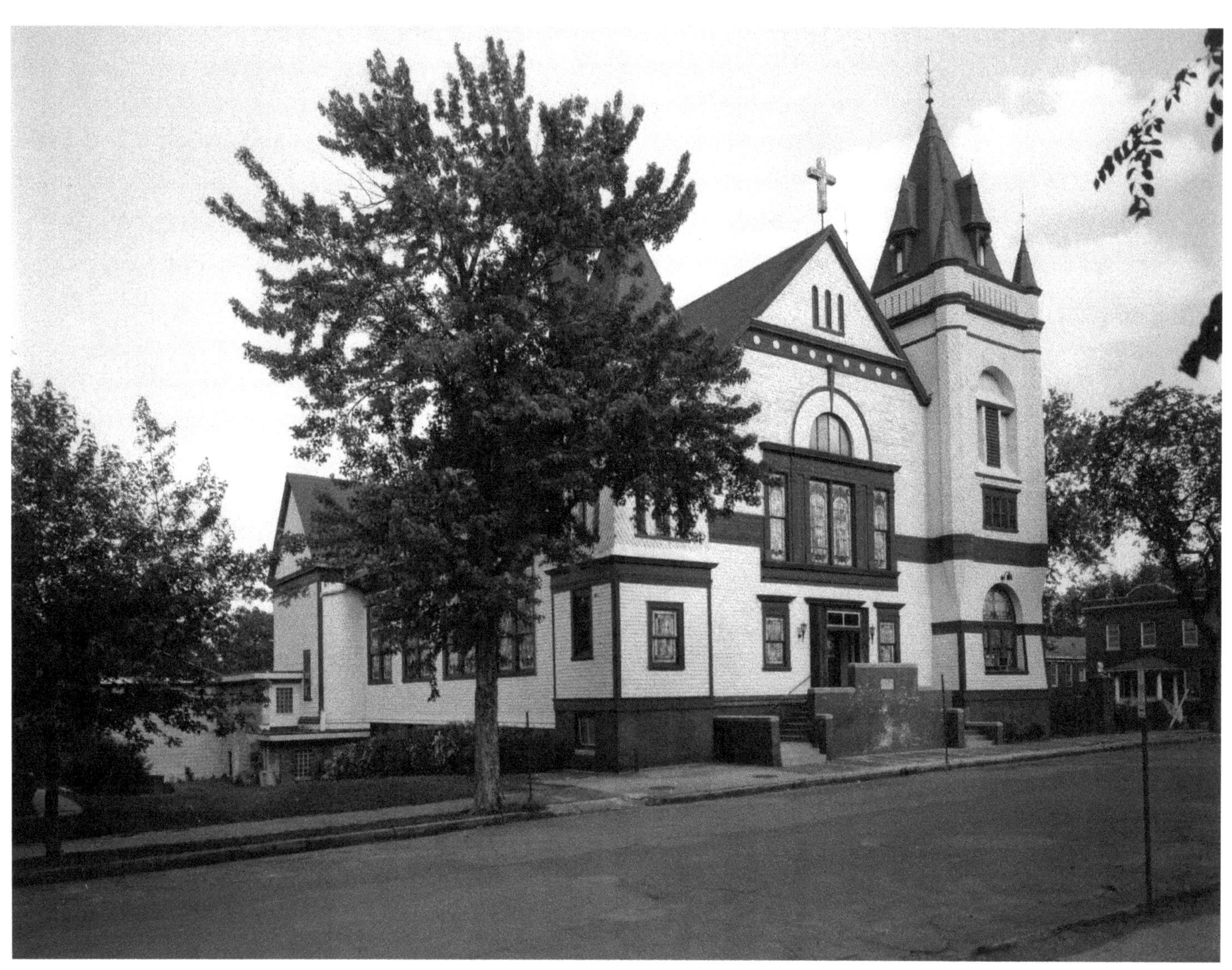

The second Hanscom Park Methodist Church building, constructed in the fall of 1892 at a cost of $20,000, was located at 1345 South 29th Street. The congregation later relocated to 4444 Frances Street, where they continue to meet today. This picture of the church was taken in June 1959.

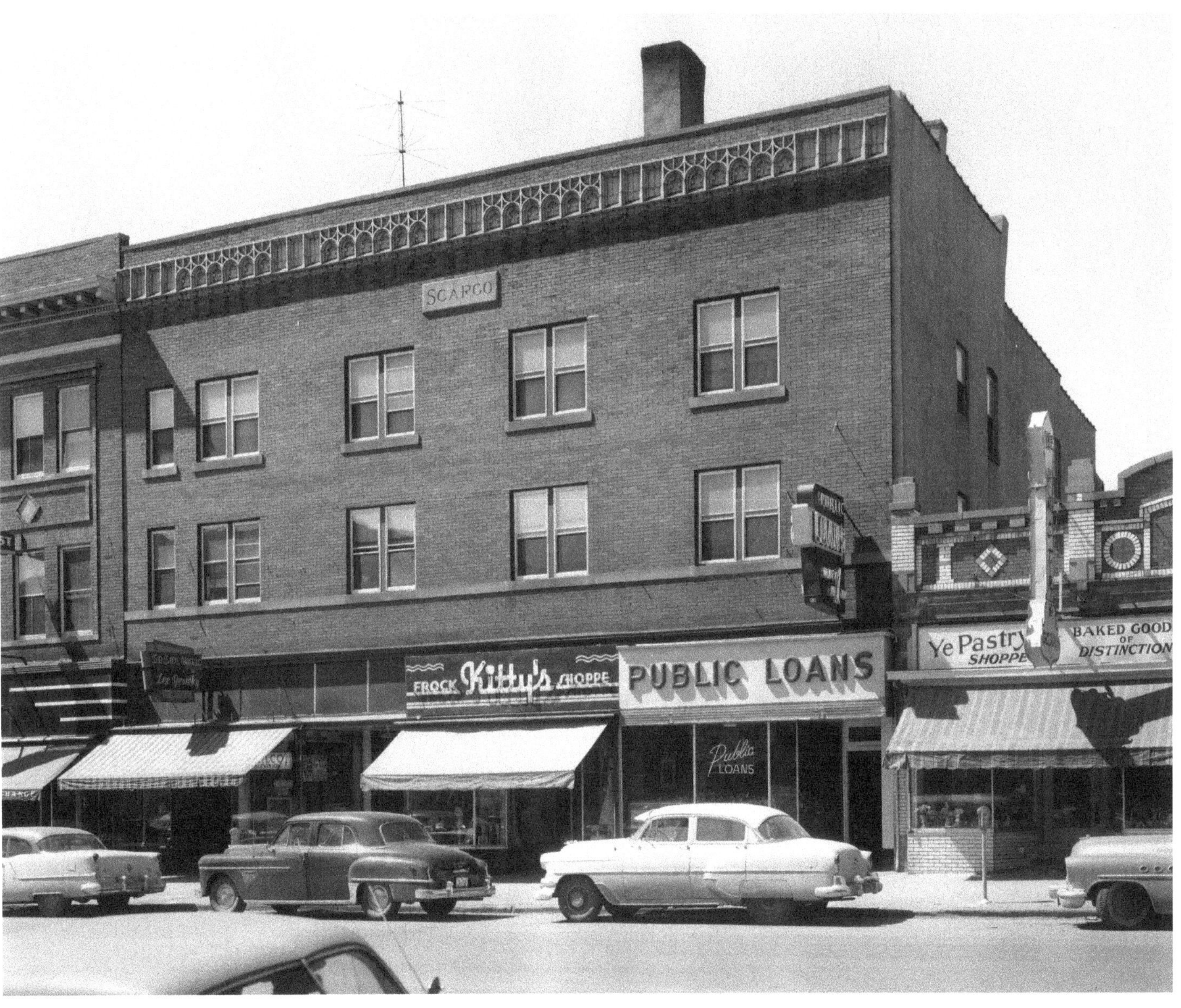

South Omaha was incorporated on October 16, 1886, and was a separate city until it was annexed into Omaha in 1915. A vibrant community with strong ethnic influences, it was the location of the Union Stockyards Company and the enormous meatpacking industry. Called the "Magic City," it experienced tremendous growth and prosperity. This September 1951 picture of the Scargo Building at 4718 South 24th Street shows the diversity of activity in the central business district of South Omaha.

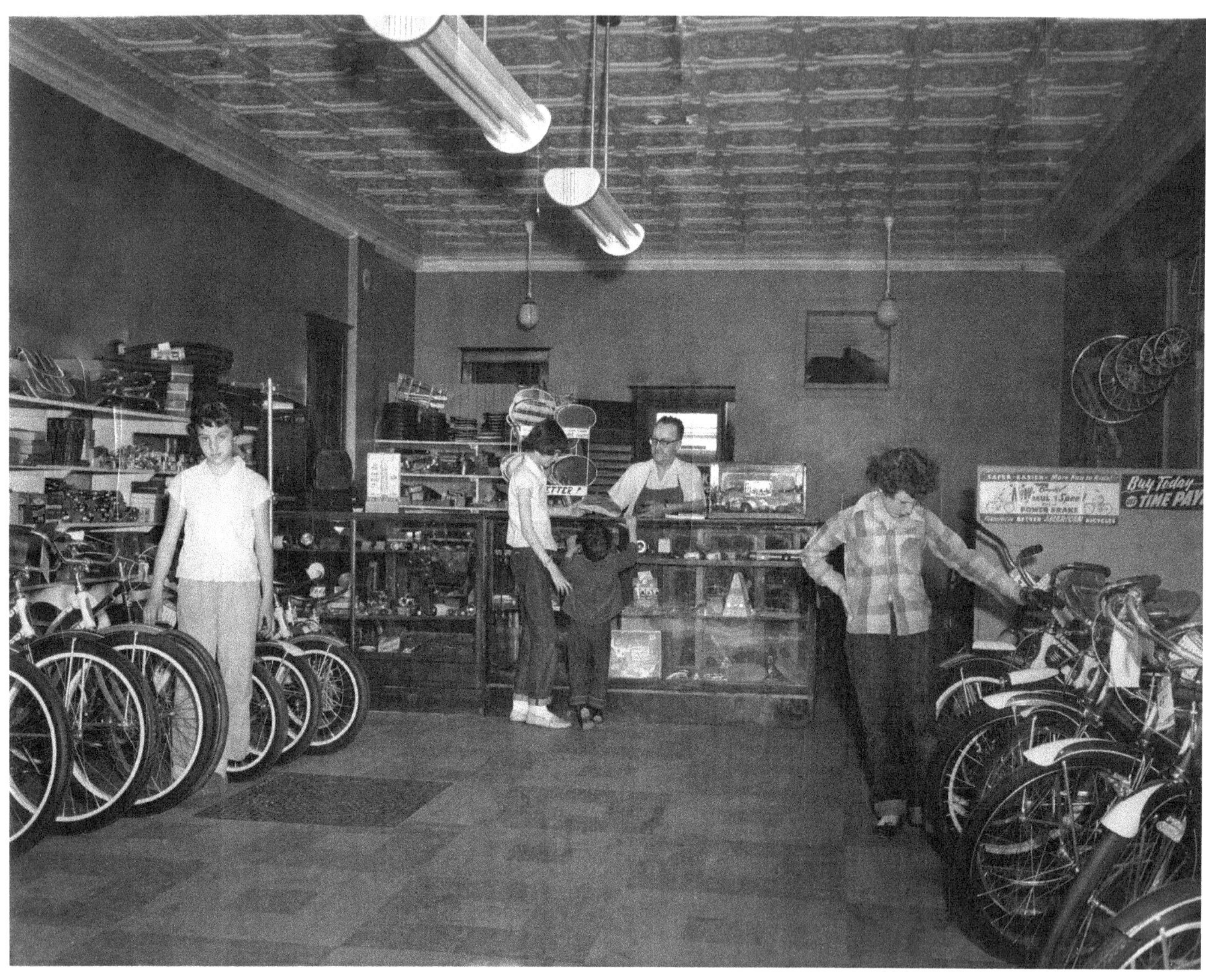

An interior view of Craddock's Bicycle Shop. This shop was located at 5901 North 30th Street, in the Minne Lusa neighborhood.

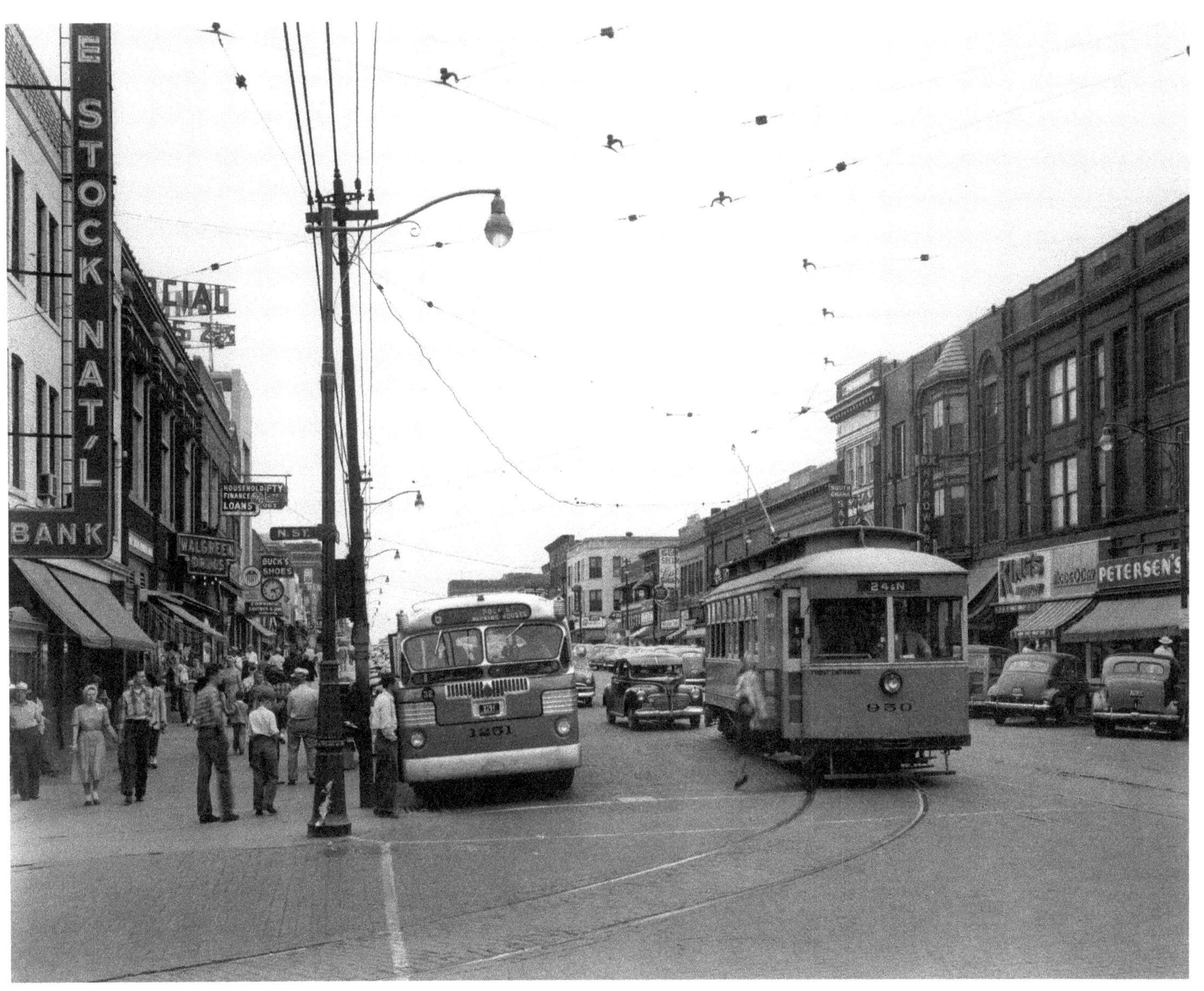

Automobiles, city buses, and an electric streetcar at the intersection of South 24th and N streets in South Omaha, September 1951. The bus line here carried workers to and from their jobs in the large packing houses. On the left is the Stockyards National Bank, in the heart of the commercial district.

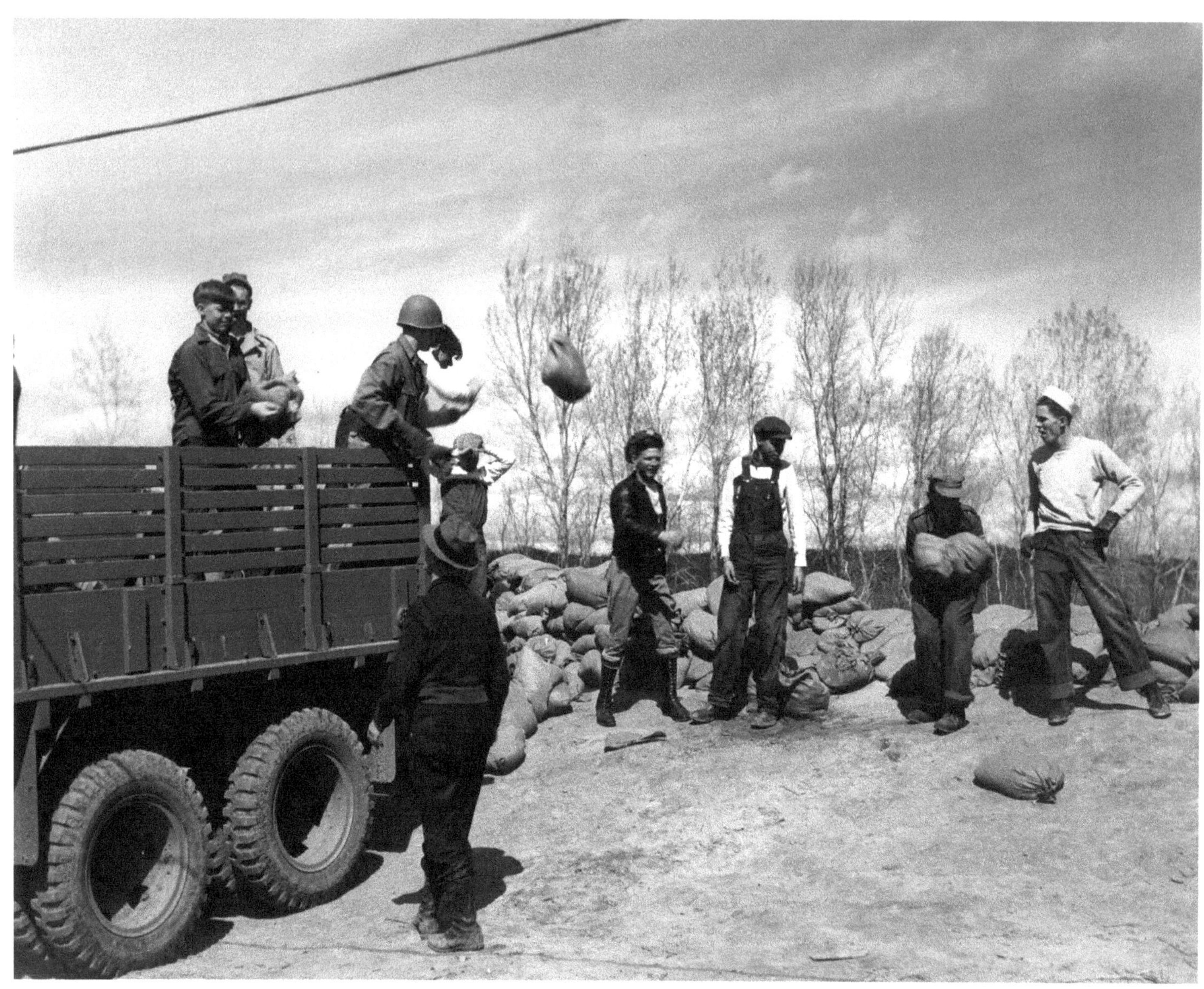

In April 1952, the Missouri River began to rise dangerously, causing stress on the levees at Omaha. The mayor declared an emergency. Thousands of community volunteers joined military units in an effort to reinforce the levees and raise them with sand bags. On April 17, the river crested in Omaha at 30.25 feet, the highest level ever recorded. Although there was widespread damage in the area, the reinforced levees held.

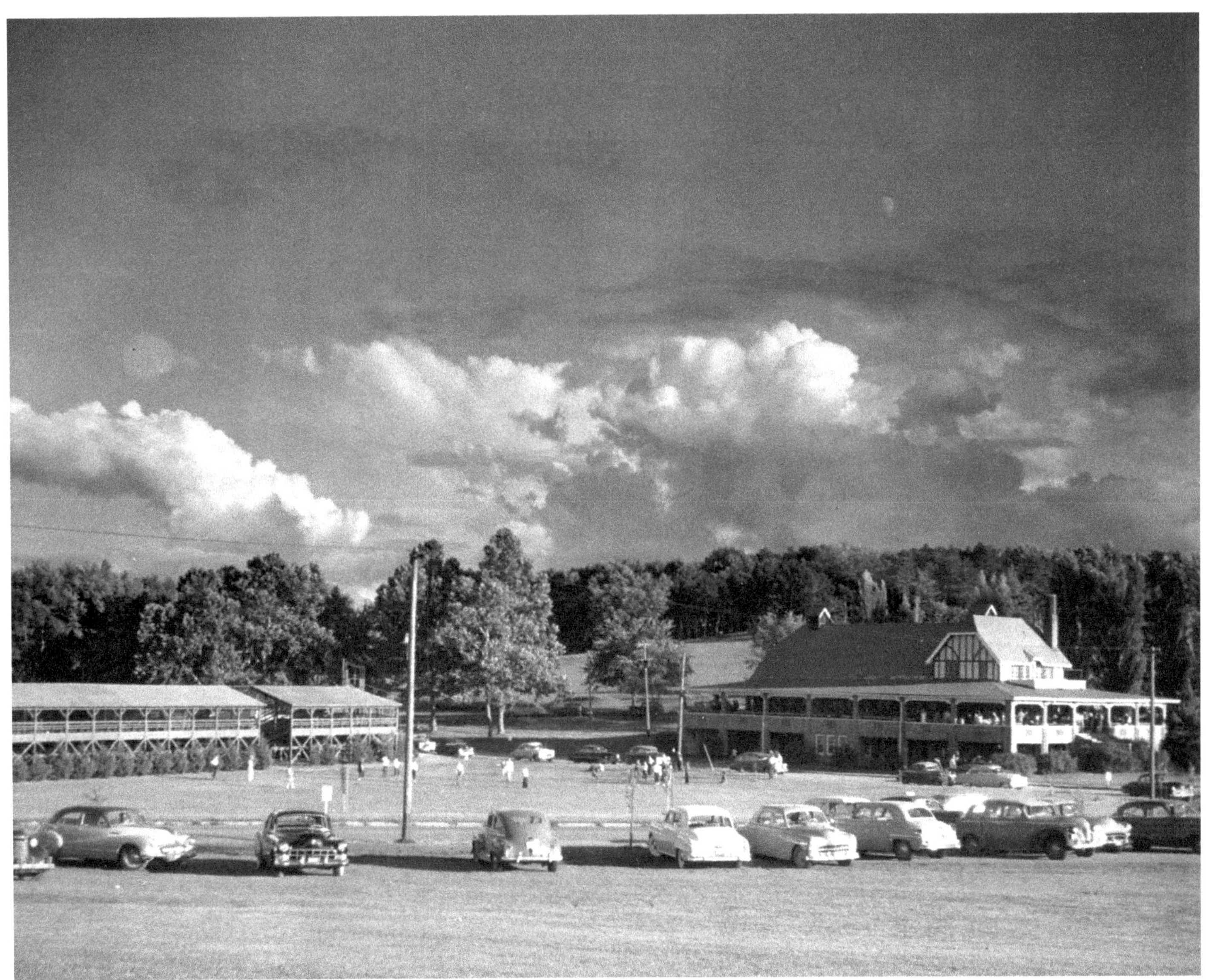

The pavilion and baseball grandstands at Fontenelle Park in the early 1950s, located from 42nd to 48th streets, between Ames Avenue and Pratt Street in North Omaha. The large pavilion, the city's largest, was designed by Omaha architect Leo A. Daly. It was built in 1927 at a cost of $60,000 and also served as a community center. The 110-acre park included a nine-hole golf course, a lagoon and a baseball diamond. The stands there could hold about 2,000 spectators.

At the time this aerial view of Omaha was taken in 1955, the population of the city had risen to well over 250,000. In the center is the rapidly developing downtown business district and above that, the Missouri River. Across the river is Council Bluffs, Iowa.

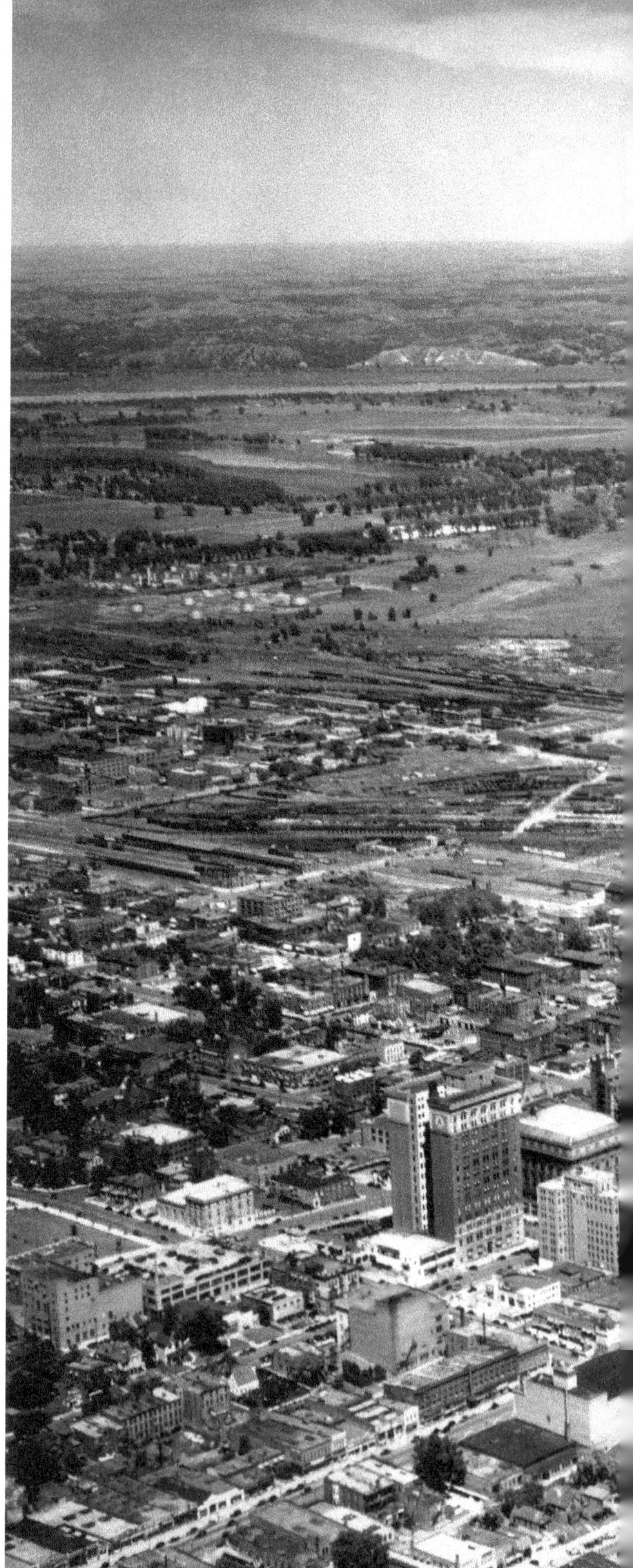

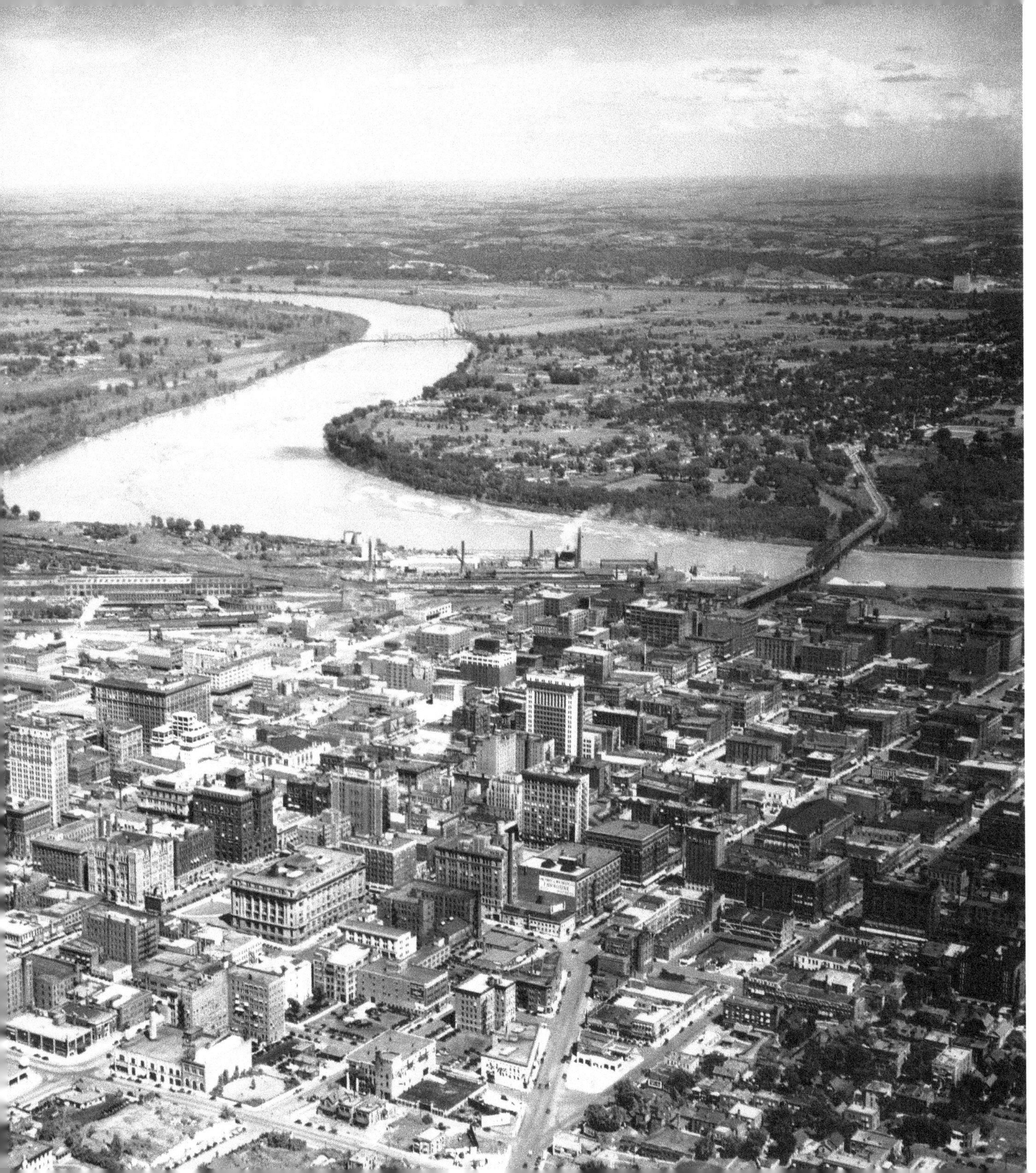

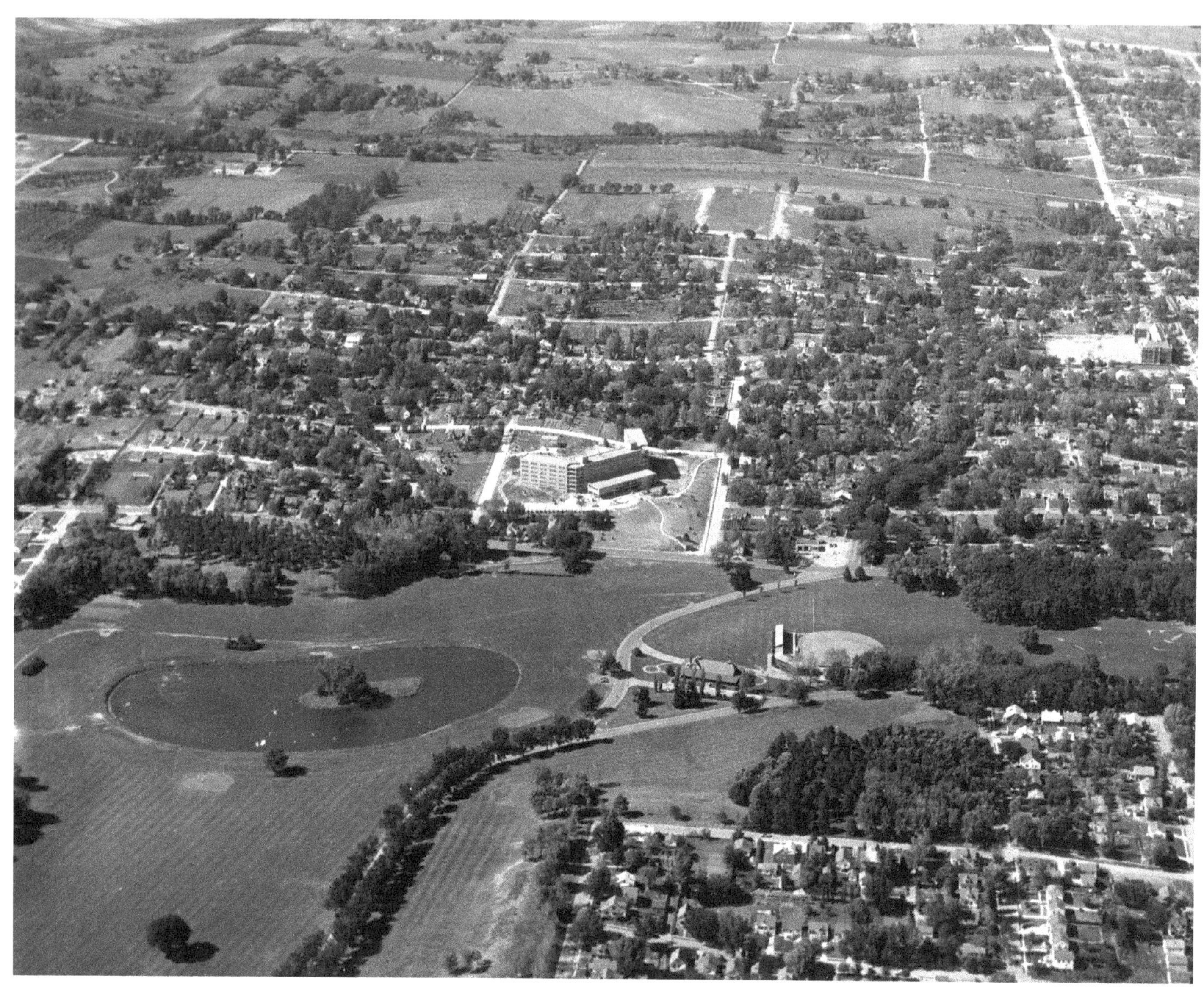

Aerial view of popular Fontenelle Park in the 1950s, looking north. Four tennis courts were installed in 1963. In the center of the photo is St. Vincent's Home for the Aging, located at 45th and Ames Avenue.

St. Catherine's Hospital at 8th Street and Forest Avenue in February 1966. The hospital first opened in 1910. On the left is the newer addition, built in 1948 at a cost of $800,000. Just to the right is the section built in 1925, and on its right, the section constructed in 1953. The hospital closed in 1972, and the facility became St. Catherine's Continuing Care Center.

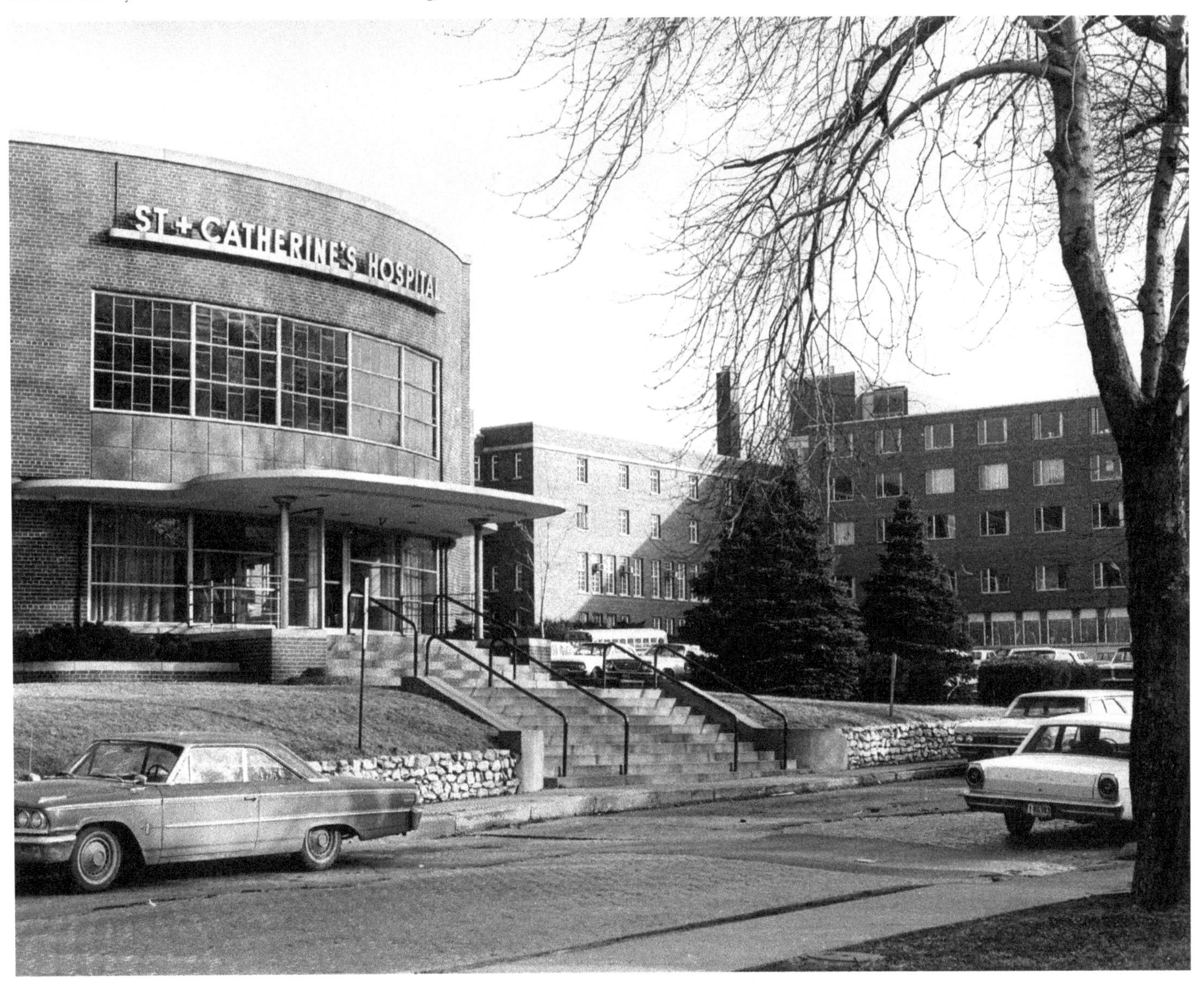

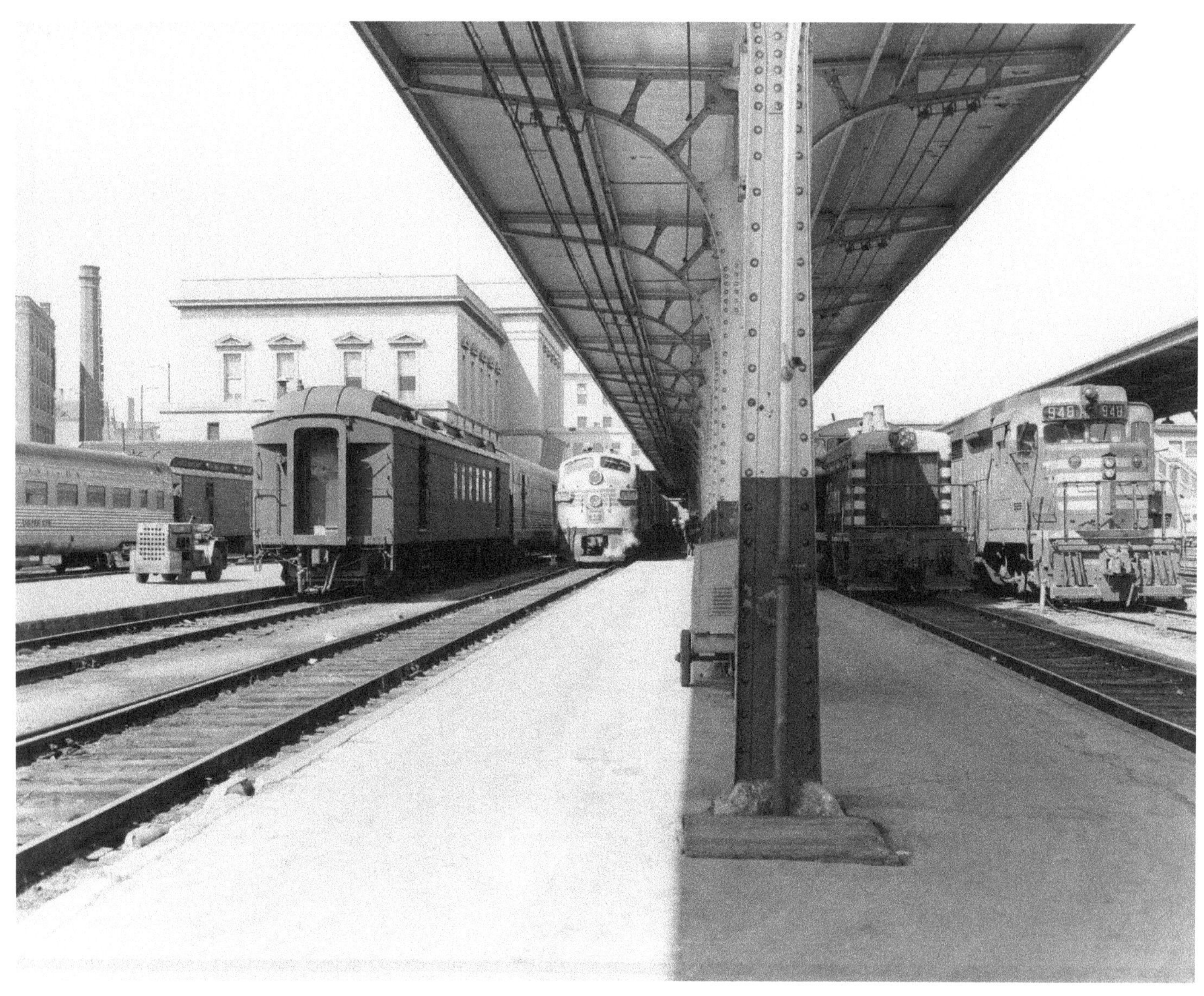

The main track lines and depot (upper left) of the Chicago, Burlington and Quincy Railroad (CB&Q). The depot was located at 925 South 10th Street and was originally opened in 1898. An extensive remodeling was undertaken in 1929-30, and additional work was done on the exterior in 1954. All train service ended there on February 1, 1974, and the building was vacant for many years. Now, as "The Burlington," it is being restored and redeveloped for commercial and residential space. This picture was taken in August 1968.

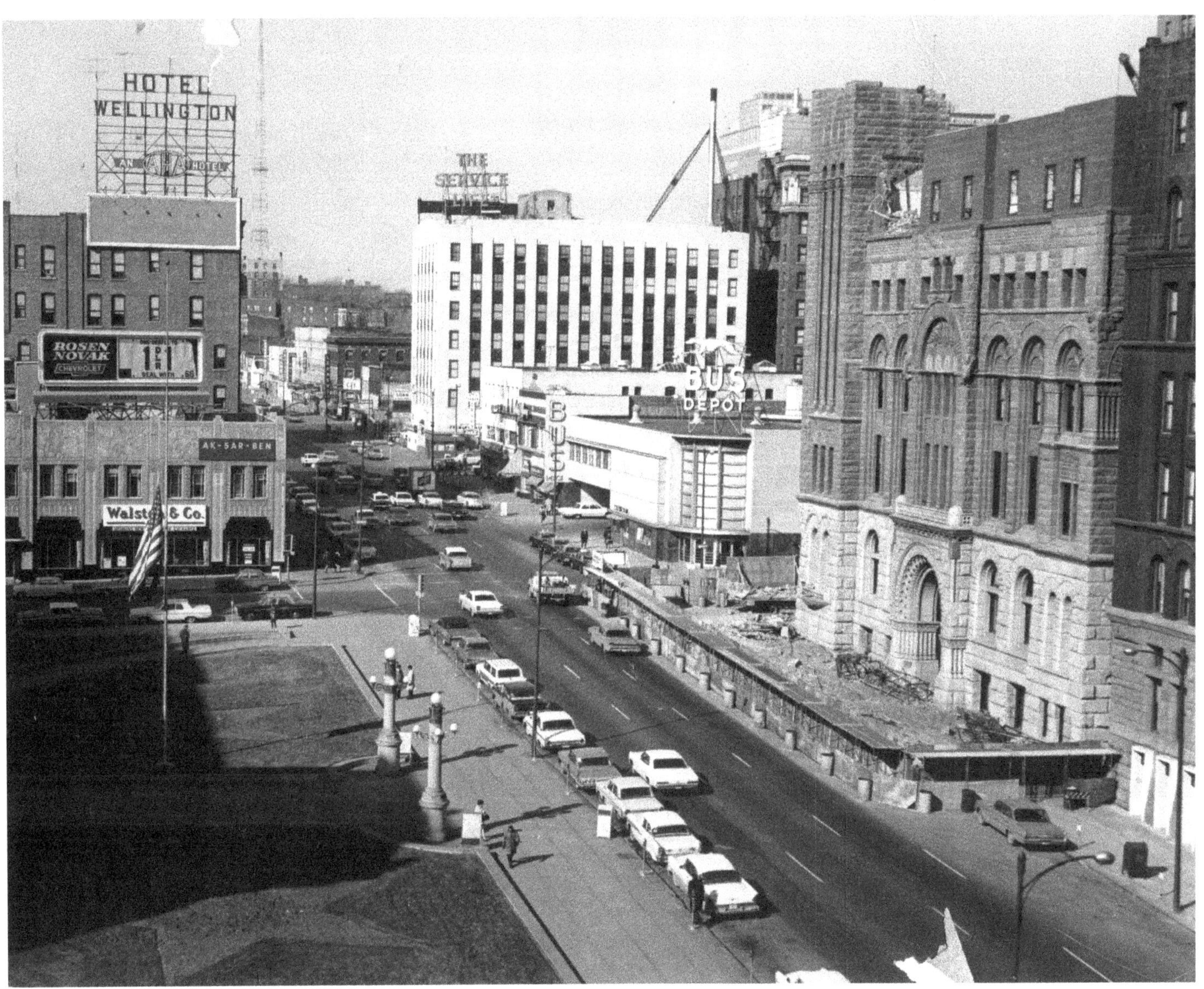

In February 1966, the old Omaha City Hall building at the corner of 18th and Farnam streets was demolished. It had been built in 1890 and was one of the most elegant structures in Omaha. The original cost was $550,000. The southwest corner of the building contained a 200-foot tower. This was partially taken down in 1919 when construction flaws appeared. The Public Safety Director officially classified the building as dangerous in 1962, and plans were made to replace it. The Woodmen Tower was built on the site.

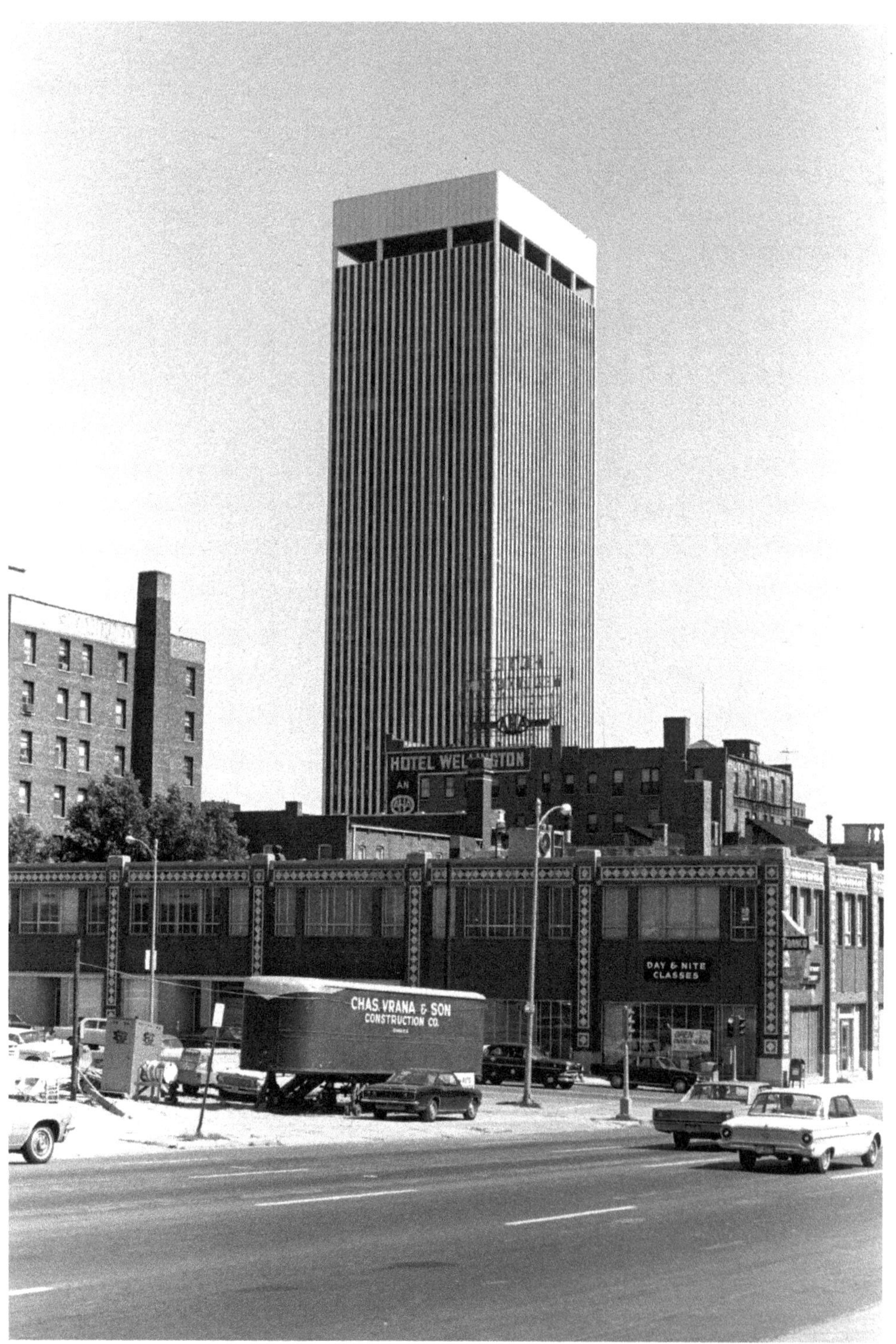

The new Woodmen Tower, 1700 Farnam Street, shown in September 1968. The headquarters of the Woodmen of the World fraternal insurance company was dedicated in 1969. This international organization had been founded in Omaha in 1890. This new structure became the "premier symbol" of the city, rising to a height of 30 stories (498 feet). Today, it continues to serve the Woodmen of the World and also provides office space for other tenants. It was designed by Omaha architect Leo A. Daly.

Notes on the Photographs

These notes, listed by page number, attempt to include all aspects known of the photographs. Each of the photographs is identified by the page number, photograph's title or description, photographer and collection, archive, and call or box number when applicable. Although every attempt was made to collect all available data, in some cases complete data was unavailable due to the age and condition of some of the photographs and records.

II **Birds-eye View of Omaha High School**
Omaha Public Library
alb002_005

VI **The Exposition Building and Grand Opera House**
Omaha Public Library
pho_487

X **Union Station at 10th and Mason**
From the Bostwick-Frohardt Collection, owned by KM3TV and on permanent loan to Durham Western Heritage Museum, Omaha, Nebraska
31-782

2 **Douglas Street**
From the Bostwick-Frohardt Collection, owned by KM3TV and on permanent loan to Durham Western Heritage Museum, Omaha, Nebraska
14-67

3 **The Pacific Street School**
Omaha Public Library
ster_016

4 **The Missouri River Transfer Company**
Omaha Public Library
alb002_005

6 **Caldwell Block**
Omaha Public Library
pho_050

7 **First Presbyterian Church**
Omaha Public Library
pho_018a

8 **Missouri River Bridge**
Omaha Public Library
alb002_013

10 **The Tremont House**
Omaha Public Library
pho_153b

11 **City Hotel**
Omaha Public Library
pho_150

12 **Druggist Julius A. Roeder's Business**
Omaha Public Library
pho_151

13 **Metz Brothers Beer Hall**
Omaha Public Library
pho_152

14 **Omaha to the Northwest**
Omaha Public Library
alb001_044

15 **Union Pacific Railroad Depot in 1882**
Omaha Public Library
ster_012

16 **Paxton Hotel**
Omaha Public Library
ster_001

17 **First Baptist Church**
Omaha Public Library
ster_005

18 **Kountze Memorial Lutheran Church**
Omaha Public Library
pho_018d

19 **Boyd's Opera House**
Omaha Public Library
ster_002

20 **Flood**
Omaha Public Library
1s_00204

22 **1424 Castelar Street**
Omaha Public Library
pho_019

23 **Creighton College**
Omaha Public Library
pho_025

24 **East on Douglas Street**
Omaha Public Library
pho_010c

25 **Young Men's Christian Association**
Omaha Public Library
pho_014c

26 **Merchants National Bank**
Omaha Public Library
pho_016c

27 **Lowering Q Street**
Omaha Public Library
pho_503

28 **United States National Bank**
Omaha Public Library
pho_016f

29 **First Congregational Church**
Omaha Public Library
pho_018f

30 **Territorial Capitol**
Omaha Public Library
alb001_049e

31 **Brownell Hall**
Omaha Public Library
pho_019a

32 **The Sheely Block**
Omaha Public Library
pho_030

33 **Omaha High School**
Omaha Public Library
pho_024

34 **The Douglas County Court House**
Omaha Public Library
pho_458

35 **President and Mrs. Benjamin Harrison Visiting Omaha**
Omaha Public Library
pho_402

36 **Bridge**
Omaha Public Library
pho_072

38 **Post Office**
Omaha Public Library
pho_477

39 **Millard Hotel**
Omaha Public Library
pho_027

40 **The Cudahy Packing Company**
Omaha Public Library
pho_033c

41 **Mercer Mansion**
Omaha Public Library
pho_038f

42 **Omaha Board of Trade Building**
Omaha Public Library
pho_014d

43 **Offices of Klopp, Bartlett and Company**
Omaha Public Library
pho_064

44 **Union Pacific Railroad Shops**
Omaha Public Library
pho_036

45 **Paxton and Vierling Iron Works**
Omaha Public Library
pho_035

46 **Joseph Hopkins Millard Residence**
Omaha Public Library
pho_038c

47 **Executive Officers of the Trans-Mississippi Exposition**
Omaha Public Library
pho_183

48 **Residences in the "Gold Coast"**
Omaha Public Library
1s_00049

49 **United States Post Office**
Omaha Public Library
pho_103

50 **Larson's Store**
Omaha Public Library
pho_200

51 **Woodman and Ritchie Company**
Omaha Public Library
pho_037

52 **Portable Bandstand**
Omaha Public Library
pho_418

53 **13th Street at Douglas**
Omaha Public Library
1s_00011

54 **Workers Excavating**
Omaha Public Library
pho_403

55 **Klopp, Bartlett and Company**
Omaha Public Library
pho_065

56 **Pavilion**
Omaha Public Library
pho_415

57 **Farnam Street**
Omaha Public Library
1s_00008

58 **Residence of Christian Hartman**
Omaha Public Library
pho_038b

59 **Central Elementary Students**
Omaha Public Library
pho_293

60 **Lake Nakoma**
Omaha Public Library
pho_410

61 **Farnam Street West from 13th Street**
Omaha Public Library
1s_00007

62 **Omaha Public Library Reference Room**
Omaha Public Library
1s_00029

64 **St. John's Collegiate Church**
Omaha Public Library
1s_00033

65 **Neighborhood Grocery Store**
Omaha Public Library
pho_404

66 **Farnam School**
Omaha Public Library
1s_00038

67 **Lowering the Falconer Residence**
Omaha Public Library
1s_00125

68 **Street-Lowering Project**
Omaha Public Library
1s_00130

69 **Street Regrading**
Omaha Public Library
1s_00138

70 **Fort Omaha**
Omaha Public Library
1s_00144

71 **Cavalry Maneuvers**
Omaha Public Library
1s_00147

72 **Government Building**
Omaha Public Library
TMI00041

73 **Mini Roller Coaster**
Omaha Public Library
TMI00355

74 **Agricultural Building, Entrance**
Omaha Public Library
TMI00001

75 **General Electric Exhibition**
Omaha Public Library
TMI00183

76 **North Midway**
Omaha Public Library
TMI00228

77 **Great Naval Fight Cyclorama**
Omaha Public Library
TMI00373

78 **Marine Band**
Omaha Public Library
TMI00125

79 **Blatz Beer Display**
Omaha Public Library
TMI00070

80 **Decorated Carriage**
Omaha Public Library
TMI00326

81 **Giant See-Saw**
Omaha Public Library
TMI00048

82 **American Wringer Company Exhibit**
Omaha Public Library
TMI00204

83 **Cafe—Streets of Cairo**
Omaha Public Library
TMI00095

84 **Streets of All Nations**
Omaha Public Library
TMI00290

85 **Chief of Guards and Staff**
Omaha Public Library
TMI00337

86 **Indian Congress Parade**
Omaha Public Library
TMI00313

87 **The Wigwam**
Omaha Public Library
TMI00137

88 **U.S. Life Saving Service**
Omaha Public Library
TMI00368

89 **Hagenback's Wild Animal Show**
Omaha Public Library
TMI00378

90 **Fleischmann & Company Booth**
Omaha Public Library
TMI00193

91 **Chiquita—The Living Doll**
Omaha Public Library
TMI00357

92 **Streets of All Nations**
Omaha Public Library
TMI00035

93 **Waitresses and Band**
Omaha Public Library
TMI00187

94 **Cotton Belt Route Display**
Omaha Public Library
TMI00037

95 **Fire on the Midway, June 3, 1898**
Omaha Public Library
TMI00039

96 **The William Wallace Residence**
Omaha Public Library
1s_00162

98 **Omaha High School Building**
Omaha Public Library
1s_00039

99 **Omaha High School Building—Study Room**
Omaha Public Library
1s_00229

100 **Omaha High School Building—Shop Class**
Omaha Public Library
1s_00228

101 **Second Courthouse**
Omaha Public Library
1s_00027

102 **South from 15th and Dodge Streets**
Omaha Public Library
1s_00016

103 **O Street Viaduct**
From the Bostwick-Frohardt Collection, owned by KM3TV and on permanent loan to Durham Western Heritage Museum, Omaha, Nebraska
25-A1

104 **Omaha National Bank**
Omaha Public Library
1s_00217

105 **Omaha National Bank**
Omaha Public Library
1s_00218

106 **Omaha National Bank**
Omaha Public Library
1s_00024

107 **Omaha Country Club**
Omaha Public Library
1s_00190

108 **The Pavilion at Elmwood Park**
Omaha Public Library
pho_432

109 **Paxton Block**
Omaha Public Library
pho_249

110 **Pavilion at Riverside Park**
Omaha Public Library
pho_451

111 **The Riverside Park Pavilion**
Omaha Public Library
pho_452

112 **Riverside Park about 1905**
Omaha Public Library
pho_476

113 **Looking East Down Farnam Street**
Omaha Public Library
1s_00012

114 **Paving South 24th Street**
From the Bostwick-Frohardt Collection, owned by KM3TV and on permanent loan to Durham Western Heritage Museum, Omaha, Nebraska
6153-664

115 **Omaha National Bank**
Omaha Public Library
1s_00215

116 **Downtown Omaha**
Omaha Public Library
pho_144

117 **Fort Omaha Balloon School**
Omaha Public Library
1s_00152

118 **Elmwood Park**
Omaha Public Library
pho_420

119 **Lily Pond in Riverview Park**
Omaha Public Library
pho_444

120 **The Guarantee Laundry**
Omaha Public Library
pho_297

121 **New York Life Building**
Omaha Public Library
pho_056

122 **1913 Tornado**
From the Bostwick-Frohardt Collection, owned by KM3TV and on permanent loan to Durham Western Heritage Museum, Omaha, Nebraska
397-12

123 **Workers' Tenement Houses**
Omaha Public Library
1s_00109

124 **Union Stockyards**
From the Bostwick-Frohardt Collection, owned by KM3TV and on permanent loan to Durham Western Heritage Museum, Omaha, Nebraska
25-11

126 **West on Farnam St.**
Omaha Public Library
1s_00015

127 **Miller Park**
Omaha Public Library
pho_467

128 **Elmwood Park**
Omaha Public Library
pho_431a

129 **Blackstone Hotel**
Omaha Public Library
pho_049

130 **Old City Hall**
From the Bostwick-Frohardt Collection, owned by KM3TV and on permanent loan to Durham Western Heritage Museum, Omaha, Nebraska
61-73

132 **AK-SAR-BEN Parade**
From the Bostwick-Frohardt Collection, owned by KM3TV and on permanent loan to Durham Western Heritage Museum, Omaha, Nebraska
771-102

133 **AK-SAR-BEN Float**
From the Bostwick-Frohardt Collection, owned by KM3TV and on permanent loan to Durham Western Heritage Museum, Omaha, Nebraska
771-80

134 **AK-SAR-BEN**
From the Bostwick-Frohardt Collection, owned by KM3TV and on permanent loan to Durham Western Heritage Museum, Omaha, Nebraska
771-380

135 **Fontenelle Hotel**
From the Bostwick-Frohardt Collection, owned by KM3TV and on permanent loan to Durham Western Heritage Museum, Omaha, Nebraska
506-348

136 **Excavation for the Medical Arts Building**
From the Bostwick-Frohardt Collection, owned by KM3TV and on permanent loan to Durham Western Heritage Museum, Omaha, Nebraska
1933-19

137 **Livestock Exchange Building**
From the Bostwick-Frohardt Collection, owned by KM3TV and on permanent loan to Durham Western Heritage Museum, Omaha, Nebraska
25-467

138 Dundee Theater, 4952 Dodge Street
From the Bostwick-Frohardt Collection, owned by KM3TV and on permanent loan to Durham Western Heritage Museum, Omaha, Nebraska
3325-1

139 Sunset Tea Room
From the Bostwick-Frohardt Collection, owned by KM3TV and on permanent loan to Durham Western Heritage Museum, Omaha, Nebraska
1996-14

140 Lake George
From the Bostwick-Frohardt Collection, owned by KM3TV and on permanent loan to Durham Western Heritage Museum, Omaha, Nebraska
15-320

141 Dodge Street East from 14th Street
From the Bostwick-Frohardt Collection, owned by KM3TV and on permanent loan to Durham Western Heritage Museum, Omaha, Nebraska
15-217

142 16th and Dodge Streets in 1921
From the Bostwick-Frohardt Collection, owned by KM3TV and on permanent loan to Durham Western Heritage Museum, Omaha, Nebraska
15-231

143 North-northwest from the Top of the Woodmen of the World Building
From the Bostwick-Frohardt Collection, owned by KM3TV and on permanent loan to Durham Western Heritage Museum, Omaha, Nebraska
15-213

144 Howard Street West from 8th Street
From the Bostwick-Frohardt Collection, owned by KM3TV and on permanent loan to Durham Western Heritage Museum, Omaha, Nebraska
61-22

145 East on Farnam Street from the Blackstone Hotel
From the Bostwick-Frohardt Collection, owned by KM3TV and on permanent loan to Durham Western Heritage Museum, Omaha, Nebraska
61-142

146 16th Street at Jackson
From the Bostwick-Frohardt Collection, owned by KM3TV and on permanent loan to Durham Western Heritage Museum, Omaha, Nebraska
60-225

147 Butter-Nut Coffee
From the Bostwick-Frohardt Collection, owned by KM3TV and on permanent loan to Durham Western Heritage Museum, Omaha, Nebraska
426-135

148 Racetrack
From the Bostwick-Frohardt Collection, owned by KM3TV and on permanent loan to Durham Western Heritage Museum, Omaha, Nebraska
771-393

149 North on 15th Street from the Carlton Hotel
From the Bostwick-Frohardt Collection, owned by KM3TV and on permanent loan to Durham Western Heritage Museum, Omaha, Nebraska
3496-20

150 Bar and Café
From the Bostwick-Frohardt Collection, owned by KM3TV and on permanent loan to Durham Western Heritage Museum, Omaha, Nebraska
5881-1

151 Union Station
From the Bostwick-Frohardt Collection, owned by KM3TV and on permanent loan to Durham Western Heritage Museum, Omaha, Nebraska
31-764

152 Baum Drug Co. Cars
From the Wentworth Collection. Owned by Durham Western Heritage Museum, Omaha, Nebraska
WW335-1

153 Walgreen's Drug Store
From the Wentworth Collection. Owned by Durham Western Heritage Museum, Omaha, Nebraska
WW361-1.04

154 Tire Store
From the Wentworth Collection. Owned by Durham Western Heritage Museum, Omaha, Nebraska
WW328-1

155 Orpheum Theatre
From the Wentworth Collection. Owned by Durham Western Heritage Museum, Omaha, Nebraska
WW104-16.01

156 Orpheum Theatre Posters
From the Wentworth Collection. Owned by Durham Western Heritage Museum, Omaha, Nebraska
WW86-21.01

157 Warehouse Building at 711 South 11th Street
From the Wentworth Collection. Owned by Durham Western Heritage Museum, Omaha, Nebraska
WW85.1

158 Harkert's
From the Wentworth Collection. Owned by Durham Western Heritage Museum, Omaha, Nebraska
WW54-3.05

159 McFayden Stewart
From the Wentworth Collection. Owned by Durham Western Heritage Museum, Omaha, Nebraska
WW145-23

160 Technical High School
From the Wentworth Collection. Owned by Durham Western Heritage Museum, Omaha, Nebraska
WW5T-47

161 Barnsdall Symphony Orchestra
From the Bostwick-Frohardt Collection, owned by KM3TV and on permanent loan to Durham Western Heritage Museum, Omaha, Nebraska
3622-139

162 Happy Hollow Club
From the Bostwick-Frohardt Collection, owned by KM3TV and on permanent loan to Durham Western Heritage Museum, Omaha, Nebraska
47-104

164 Glaser's Provisions
From the Bostwick-Frohardt Collection, owned by KM3TV and on permanent loan to Durham Western Heritage Museum, Omaha, Nebraska
5600-30

165 Petersen and Michelsen Hardware Store
From the Bostwick-Frohardt Collection, owned by KM3TV and on permanent loan to Durham Western Heritage Museum, Omaha, Nebraska
3452-23

166 Southside Terrace Homes Public Housing
From the Bostwick-Frohardt Collection, owned by KM3TV and on permanent loan to Durham Western Heritage Museum, Omaha, Nebraska
5859-12

167 Roseland Theater
From the Bostwick-Frohardt Collection, owned by KM3TV and on permanent loan to Durham Western Heritage Museum, Omaha, Nebraska
6369-1

168 Army Day at Fort Omaha
From the Bostwick-Frohardt Collection, owned by KM3TV and on permanent loan to Durham Western Heritage Museum, Omaha, Nebraska
3622-247

169 V-J Day
From the Bostwick-Frohardt Collection, owned by KM3TV and on permanent loan to Durham Western Heritage Museum, Omaha, Nebraska
4820-40

170 Candidate Thomas Dewey Interview on KOIL
From the Bostwick-Frohardt Collection, owned by KM3TV and on permanent loan to Durham Western Heritage Museum, Omaha, Nebraska
3622-252

171 Rufus E. Lee Residence
From the Bostwick-Frohardt Collection, owned by KM3TV and on permanent loan to Durham Western Heritage Museum, Omaha, Nebraska
2984-200

172 Omaha and Council Bluffs Street Railway Company
From the Bostwick-Frohardt Collection, owned by KM3TV and on permanent loan to Durham Western Heritage Museum, Omaha, Nebraska
2984-200

173 Nat Towles Great Orchestra
From the Bostwick-Frohardt Collection, owned by KM3TV and on permanent loan to Durham Western Heritage Museum, Omaha, Nebraska
5645-7

174 Circle Theater
From the Bostwick-Frohardt Collection, owned by KM3TV and on permanent loan to Durham Western Heritage Museum, Omaha, Nebraska
6369-5

175 Beth El Synagogue
From the Bostwick-Frohardt Collection, owned by KM3TV and on permanent loan to Durham Western Heritage Museum, Omaha, Nebraska
24H-12

176 Benson Park
From the Bostwick-Frohardt Collection, owned by KM3TV and on permanent loan to Durham Western Heritage Museum, Omaha, Nebraska
7-724

177 Barber Shop on the North Side of Q Street
From the Bostwick-Frohardt Collection, owned by KM3TV and on permanent loan to Durham Western Heritage Museum, Omaha, Nebraska
6372-3

178 Bosanek Grocery Store
From the Bostwick-Frohardt Collection, owned by KM3TV and on permanent loan to Durham Western Heritage Museum, Omaha, Nebraska
6372-5

179 President Harry S. Truman at Boys Town
From the Bostwick-Frohardt Collection, owned by KM3TV and on permanent loan to Durham Western Heritage Museum, Omaha, Nebraska
4820-53.02

180 Harney Street
From the Bostwick-Frohardt Collection, owned by KM3TV and on permanent loan to Durham Western Heritage Museum, Omaha, Nebraska
6387-5

181 Engineering Project
From the Bostwick-Frohardt Collection, owned by KM3TV and on permanent loan to Durham Western Heritage Museum, Omaha, Nebraska
6340-29

182 North from 16th and Harney
From the Bostwick-Frohardt Collection, owned by KM3TV and on permanent loan to Durham Western Heritage Museum, Omaha, Nebraska
358-261

184 North on 15th Toward Farnam Street
From the Bostwick-Frohardt Collection, owned by KM3TV and on permanent loan to Durham Western Heritage Museum, Omaha, Nebraska
6496-7

185 S. S. Kresge Company Store
From the Bostwick-Frohardt Collection, owned by KM3TV and on permanent loan to Durham Western Heritage Museum, Omaha, Nebraska
358-263

186 Hanscom Park Methodist Church Building
From the Bostwick-Frohardt Collection, owned by KM3TV and on permanent loan to Durham Western Heritage Museum, Omaha, Nebraska
5333-7

187 Scargo Building
From the Bostwick-Frohardt Collection, owned by KM3TV and on permanent loan to Durham Western Heritage Museum, Omaha, Nebraska
3496-36

188 Craddock's Bicycle Shop
From the Bostwick-Frohardt Collection, owned by KM3TV and on permanent loan to Durham Western Heritage Museum, Omaha, Nebraska
61-264

189 South 24th and N Streets
From the Bostwick-Frohardt Collection, owned by KM3TV and on permanent loan to Durham Western Heritage Museum, Omaha, Nebraska
6153-799

190 Missouri River Flood
From the Bostwick-Frohardt Collection, owned by KM3TV and on permanent loan to Durham Western Heritage Museum, Omaha, Nebraska
4820-52

191 Fontenelle Park
From the Bostwick-Frohardt Collection, owned by KM3TV and on permanent loan to Durham Western Heritage Museum, Omaha, Nebraska
7-895

192 Aerial Shot of Downtown 1955
From the Bostwick-Frohardt Collection, owned by KM3TV and on permanent loan to Durham Western Heritage Museum, Omaha, Nebraska
4937-2

194 Aerial of Fontenelle Park
From the Bostwick-Frohardt Collection, owned by KM3TV and on permanent loan to Durham Western Heritage Museum, Omaha, Nebraska
7-894

195 St. Catherine's Hospital
Durham Western Heritage Museum
7004-5

196 Chicago, Burlington and Quincy Railroad
Durham Western Heritage Museum
7011-47

197 Razing of Old City Hall
Durham Western Heritage Museum
7008-4.01

198 New Woodmen Tower
Durham Western Heritage Museum
7003-29

HISTORIC PHOTOS OF OMAHA

From its beginnings as a frontier military post on the Missouri River, through its years as a transportation and meatpacking center, to its present role as a home to Fortune 500 companies, Omaha has always been a city of opportunity, growth, and change.

Historic Photos of Omaha captures this journey through still photography selected from the finest archives. In these pages are unique visual records of the city's history, presented in hundreds of historic photographs.

From the muddy streets of a cattle town to the bustling thoroughfares of a modern metropolis, these images tell a story of transportation and commerce, of churches and schools, of wars and disasters. Photographs of the great Trans-Mississippi and International Exposition and Indian Congress of 1898, Boys Town, city parks, neighborhoods, and the downtown of bygone eras are all here, preserved in striking black and white images that capture historic events and everyday life of a unique and vibrant city in the heart of America.

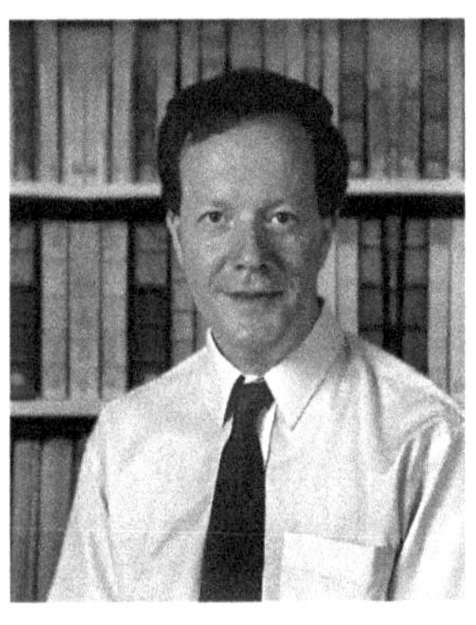

Jeffrey Spencer has long been associated with numerous historical and community organizations in the greater Omaha area. A graduate of the University of Nebraska, he has lectured and written extensively on many local history topics. He has served as a Trustee of the Nebraska State Historical Society; President of the Trans-Mississippi Exposition Historical Association; Executive Director of the Historic General Dodge House Museum in Council Bluffs, Iowa; Director of the Library/Archives Center of the Douglas County Historical Society; and Executive Director of Landmarks Incorporated, an organization involved with neighborhood redevelopment and historic preservation in Omaha.

In addition to these positions, he has served on the boards of several Omaha community service organizations and continues to assist many local groups involved with the arts and with philanthropic endeavors.

In 2004, he authored "Building for the Ages: Omaha's Historic Landmarks," detailing the history of the built environment in Omaha. He is called upon frequently to discuss and interpret the diverse history of Omaha.

An avid art collector, he also travels extensively in Southeast Asia providing assistance for the development of English Language programs in the Kingdom of Thailand.

WWW.TURNERPUBLISHING.COM

www.ingramcontent.com/pod-product-compliance
Lightning Source LLC
LaVergne TN
LVHW060605110826
845154LV00003B/42

* 9 7 8 1 6 8 3 3 6 9 7 5 2 *